# GOETHE
*as Woman*

# GOETHE
## *as Woman*

### THE UNDOING OF LITERATURE

*Benjamin Bennett*

WAYNE STATE UNIVERSITY PRESS   DETROIT

Kritik: German Literary Theory and Cultural Studies
Liliane Weissberg, Editor

*A complete listing of the books in this series can be found
at the back of this volume.*

Copyright © 2001 by Wayne State University Press,
Detroit, Michigan 48201. All rights are reserved.
No part of this book may be reproduced without formal permission.
Manufactured in the United States of America.
05 04 03 02 01     5 4 3 2 1

Library of Congress Cataloging-in-Publication Data
Bennett, Benjamin, 1939–
Goethe as woman : the undoing of literature / Benjamin Bennett.
p. cm.—(Kritik)
Includes bibliographical references and index.
ISBN 0-8143-2948-9 (alk. paper)
1. Goethe, Johann Wolfgang von, 1749–1832—Knowledge—Literature.
2. Goethe, Johann Wolfgang von, 1749–1832—Aesthetics.
3. Literature—History and criticism—Theory, etc. 4. Feminism
and literature. 5. Women and literature. 6. Gender
identity in literature. I. Title. II. Kritik (Detroit, Mich.)
PT2190 . A1 B46 2001
831'.6—dc21          00-012506

*In memory of*

HARRY KARP

*who was intelligent enough to be puzzled,*
*and determined enough to be killed by it.*

# Contents

# Acknowledgments

I am grateful, above all, to my colleagues and students at the University of Virginia, and also, particularly, to my wife, for providing the atmosphere of debate and support in which I wrote this book; and I am grateful to the University as an institution for providing the necessary free time, plus excellent working conditions and equipment. Special thanks, for helping at various stages with the physical preparation of the manuscript, are due to Gamin Bartle and Erin McGlothlin. I am also greatly indebted to the Wayne State University Press, its editors and consultants, and especially to the series editor, Liliane Weissberg, for their very swift and efficient handling of the project, and for their extremely useful criticism.

Some of the material in this book was developed from the following published essays:

"Goethe's Egmont as a Politician." *Eighteenth-Century Studies* 10 (1977): 351–66. © American Society for Eighteenth-Century Studies. Used by permission of the Johns Hopkins University Press.

"Goethe's *Werther:* Double Perspective and the Game of Life." *German Quarterly* 53 (1980): 64–81.

"Prometheus and Saturn: The Three Versions of *Götz von Berlichingen.*" *German Quarterly* 58 (1985): 335–47.

"Werther and Montaigne: The Romantic Renaissance." *Goethe Yearbook* 3 (1986): 1–20.

"Bridge: Against Nothing." In *Nietzsche and the Feminine,* ed. Peter J. Burgard, 289–315. Charlottesville: University Press of Virginia, 1994. Reprinted with permission of the University Press of Virginia.

I am grateful to the copyright holders for permission to use this material.

# Abbreviations

*Am*     Luce Irigaray. *Amante marine: De Friedrich Nietzsche.* Paris, 1980.

*JG*     *Der junge Goethe.* Ed. Hanna Fischer-Lamberg. 6 vols. Berlin, 1963–1974.

*KSA*     Friedrich Nietzsche. *Sämtliche Werke: Kritische Studienausgabe in 15 Bänden.* Ed. Giorgio Colli and Mazzino Montinari. Munich and Berlin, 1980.

M&R     Goethe's "Maximen und Reflexionen" in Hecker's standard numbering.

MM     Michel de Montaigne. *Oeuvres complètes.* Ed. Albert Thibaudet and Maurice Rat, Bibliothèque de la Pléiade. Paris, 1962.

*NT*     Goethe. *Die natürliche Tochter,* plus line numbers, from WA, vol. 10.

*P*     Heinrich von Kleist. *Penthesilea.* Ed. Roland Reuß. Basel, Frankfurt am Main, 1992. Vol. I/5 of Kleist, *Sämtliche Werke,* Brandenburger Ausgabe, plus line numbers.

*SA*     *Schillers Sämtliche Werke: Säkular-Ausgabe.* 16 vols. Stuttgart and Berlin, 1904–.

SE     *The Standard Edition of the Complete Psychological Works of Sigmund Freud.* Ed. James Strachey. 24 vols. London, 1953–74.

*SWB*     Heinrich von Kleist. *Sämtliche Werke und Briefe.* Ed. Helmut Sembdner. 2 vols. 4th ed. München, 1965.

WA     Goethe's *Werke,* Weimarer Ausgabe. 143 vols. Weimar, 1887–1918.

*Wvw*     Goethe. *Die Wahlverwandtschaften,* by page from WA, vol. 20.

# Introduction

"Literature," etymologically considered, is a thoroughly unsuitable word for the aesthetically restricted sense in which it is used nowadays to name (among other things) academic disciplines. It acquires this sense, moreover, only very late in history—most of us would say in the eighteenth century, where Batteux, for example, associates it with belles lettres. And most of us would probably also say, with Peter Widdowson, that although the specific concept had earlier been absent, "the *thing* is recognisable in all cultural periods."[1]

My first main point in this book is that Goethe would not agree with that last statement. In chapter 7 I argue that "literature," in Goethe's view, in the sense that it might take the form of a nation's "classical" literature, is in truth a gross *violation* of the "thing" that it claims as its historical lineage (going back, say, to Homer). A more accurate name for the "literature" of modern nation-states, suggests Goethe, is "literary sansculottism." The task of the writer who is truly interested in the tradition that this inevitably nationalistic movement usurps, therefore, is what I call "the undoing of literature."

My second main point is that Goethe is by no means alone in this sense of the general situation of literature. I contend that the undoing of literature—or as I also call it, the literary resistance (or guerrilla warfare) against literature—continues as a significant factor in European culture since the eighteenth century, and continues, interestingly, to be marked by the sign of "Goethe." We will of course not expect to find this resistance proclaimed (except by a kind of co-optive hypocrisy) in literature itself, as it presents itself to modern national publics. But we can detect it, I suggest, by way of the idea of the revolutionary, in Nietzsche's unexpected compatibility with certain feminist thinking, and in a kind of ghostly Goethean presence (marked strongly feminine) in psychoanalysis.

## Goethe and "Goethe"

The material of this book therefore embraces two separate narratives, which I name Goethe and "Goethe." The first is the story of the man Goethe in his struggling with fundamental questions about the profession of literature, questions that in fact prevent him from acknowledging to himself his prime commitment to that profession until he is well into his forties, despite his possessing by then a widespread reputation as Germany's leading poet. The second is ultimately the whole story of European literature, at least since the Renaissance, but especially the last part of that story, the shifting of literature into an adversarial position not only with respect to civilization in general, but with respect even to any institutionalized version of itself.

These two stories cannot be disentangled from one another. The first, the story of the actual author Goethe, cannot be told without reference to the emergence, in European literature, of the idea of the aesthetic, by which, for present purposes, I mean the idea that a literary text does not arrive at its own proper existence except in the process of being read, and that the process of reading, in turn, brings into play a substantial continuity between the signified of the text and the inner life of the reader. From early on, Goethe is profoundly suspicious of this view of literature, which he regards not as an instance of the conscious self-development of human freedom—this being, in effect, the position later adopted by Kant and Schiller—but as an open invitation to political co-option of the individual, in a coming age that Götz von Berlichingen already characterizes as an age of fundamental "deceit" or "treachery." Hence, for young Goethe, the attraction of pre-aesthetic literature—not only Shakespeare but also, I will point out, Montaigne—and hence his attraction to the idea of re-creating the pre-aesthetic, thus undoing literature, in his own time, an idea that turns out to be an impossible dream. For the aesthetic is not just a modifiable property of texts or of writing; it is ingrained in the whole of literary culture. It cannot be overturned or avoided, but can only be resisted, in a movement that becomes inevitably an esoteric literary resistance against literature itself.

Not until well into the 1790s does Goethe seem to have fully worked out the implications, and the thorough hopelessness, of this situation. But even as early as *Werther,* he begins to form a notion of *gender difference* as the site, possibly, of a maximally public challenge to the aesthetic bias of literary culture. This notion is then developed in *Iphigenie auf Tauris* and in the work on *Faust*— not to mention less prominent works like *Stella,* where a man functions as the medium of exchange in an erotic relation between women. But still, the literary *use* of gender difference, in any reasonable sense of this word, cannot produce the leverage against literature, the anti-aesthetic move, that Goethe requires, for such use inevitably only subjects gender difference itself to the rules of that aesthetic culture by which literature, after all, is defined. (Kleist's exploitation of the nonliterary aspect of drama founders, for Goethe, on the presupposition of a specific type of theater that cannot be textually willed or imagined into existence.) One must, rather, *be,* or in some manner become, a woman; one must assert in literature the excluded or disqualified position of a woman—in a sense that I will try to clarify in discussing *Die natürliche Tochter* and *Die*

*Wahlverwandtschaften.*
From here on, although the two stories are still intertwined, precedence is taken by the larger story of a significant disrupting current in the past two centuries of literary history. Goethe himself, at a clearly identifiable point in his career, recognizes that there is *no conceivable solution* to the problem of reading, the problem of an aesthetically conceived literature, or at least no solution that can be asserted, or even fruitfully hinted at, by an author via a text. An effective resistance against the aesthetic and its political consequences, if it is possible at all, must be situated in a strictly *intertextual* area (literally, between texts), out of the range of any hermeneutic (text-interpretive) procedures by which it might be co-opted. And my contention is that in the course of recent literary history, Goethe's textual body, so to speak, undergoes after the fact (belatedly, *nachträglich*) a development that now forms—together with later texts, especially from psychoanalysis and its feminist turn—the marking out of an area where literature might perhaps make a stand against the aesthetic version of itself after all. It is this curious historical afterlife that I call "Goethe."

## The Course of the Argument

Part I is concerned mainly with Goethe's early work, and with his developing grasp of the problem of reading, the problem of the reader's co-optedness in relation to a literature whose aesthetic conception of itself appears, delusively, to offer emancipation and a form of empowerment. In chapter 1, a pre-aesthetic idea of freedom—represented, both for Goethe and for us, by Montaigne's thinking—produces a neat parallel and contrast with the aesthetic idea of the reader's freedom in *Werther.* And in chapter 2, the interpretation of *Werther* is developed further until it arrives—by way of the suggestion that literary reading has become a model for life itself—at what I contend is Goethe's growing conviction of the wrongness of literature. Chapter 3 argues that even the apparent circumvention of strictly literary categories by the use of nonliterary aspects of the theater, in *Egmont,* only brings us back to the problem of the wrongness of literature from another angle, as a dramatizing of the reader's situation. And the whole problem-complex is recapitulated in chapter 4, beginning well before *Werther* with the original *Geschichte Gottfriedens von Berlichingen,* and then following the *Götz* material beyond *Egmont* into the developing *Faust* project. Here the relation between the reader's co-optedness *by* literature and the political co-optedness *of* aesthetic literature is discussed. Aesthetic literature is seen, from Goethe's point of view, as being corrupt at a level that must poison the activity and effectiveness of even a potentially Shakespearean genius.

This is, I hope, an unusual but not untenable interpretation of Goethe's early writing. But in the argument as a whole, as I have indicated, interpretation itself is an issue; and in part II, accordingly, a different type of procedure is developed.

Chapter 5 turns yet once more to *Werther*, showing that it is possible to read the novel as an attempt to use gender difference as a lever to pry open the aesthetic conception of literature. A sufficiently radical sense of gender difference perhaps invalidates altogether the more or less unitary idea of humanity that is implied by any staging of "the" reader. The argument here, moreover, begins to detach itself from the sphere of hermeneutics by requiring the interworking of features of the text with realities whose strictly untextualized quality is insisted upon, especially Lotte's body (whatever that might be for a reader) and her relation to the real Lotte Buff-Kestner. But the project of exploiting the untextualizable in order to produce a historically definitive anti-aesthetic move, in the very midst of an aesthetically conditioned public, turns out to be futile. Chapter 7 argues that in the mid-1790s, Goethe acknowledges this futility once and for all—because, among other things, the crucial untextualized elements in the procedure can only operate historically by becoming in some sense textualized after all. Especially the essay "Literarischer Sansculottismus" shows that from now on, although the problem of reading, the problem of the wrongness of aesthetic literature, remains a burning one, Goethe has given up the dream of solving that problem as a writer. The problem in fact cannot be solved and will persist indefinitely into the future; the most that can be hoped for is that a certain underground resistance will also persist, a kind of guerrilla warfare, conducted by what Goethe calls cryptically an "invisible school" of thinkers resolutely unseduced by the classic-manufacturing industry that literature becomes in the modern nation-state.

This, I think, is the point at which it begins to make sense to speak of "Goethe" in referring to literature's internal self-resistance. It is the point at which Goethe himself (without quotation marks) does two things: commits himself finally to the profession of literature as his main work, and withdraws from any personal authorial attempt to deal directly with the most deep-seated problem of that profession. Neither the problem itself—the problem of the wrongness of aesthetic literature—nor one's responsibility in relation to it can simply be dismissed, but Goethe seems now to understand that while the responsibility remains his, the actual work of discharging it belongs at the historically shifted site I have called "Goethe." A sense of the problems created by this situation arises, for example, from the study of Goethe's and Schiller's dilettantism project, and especially from *Die natürliche Tochter*, where the question of gender is recoupled with the problem of the aesthetic on a level one step further on from *Werther*.

Then, in chapter 9, the structure of this "Goethe" is recognized as involving, in a privileged way, the texts of Freud, of psychoanalysis in general, and of psychoanalytically informed feminism in their tension with the somewhat longer tradition of texts that tries to pin Goethe down as a national classic. The crucial point here has to do with the question of the existence of a text, and with the possibility of writing in such a way that alongside the actual text, a nonexistent, hence hermeneutically inaccessible text emerges, which opens onto the strictly intertextual domain that we are primarily interested in. *Die natürliche Tochter* is again important here, as is the tendency of the historical Goethe to find himself surrounded by texts of thoroughly ambiguous authorship. But the concluding—and I claim conclusive—argument, in chapter 10, concerns *Die Wahlverwandtschaften,* in which Goethe manages to operate as it were posthumously with respect to himself, manages himself, as Goethe (not merely as "author" or "narrator"), to occupy the rarefied extratextual atmosphere of "Goethe," and to speak there with the voice—shared absolutely with his character Ottilie—of Goethe as woman.

## Deviations

Two chapters deal primarily with figures other than Goethe. Chapter 6, which discusses Heinrich von Kleist's play *Penthesilea,* performs two tasks that I think are indispensable in the argument as a whole. First, it provides a clear historical context for my interpretations of early Goethe, a context that supports the association of a resistance against aesthetic literature with an attentiveness to questions of gender. I could have described this context more broadly; I will, in the future, certainly supplement this book with essays on Lessing, on Karsch, on La Roche and Wieland. But a summarizing chapter would not have had the intensity of focus necessary to get at the ideas that count here. One text had to be chosen, and my reason for choosing *Penthesilea* has to do with the second main task performed by chapter 6: that it in a sense *completes* the first part of the argument on Goethe, that it shows exactly the kind of project Goethe himself would have had to undertake if he had not, in the mid-1790s, somehow come to terms with the perfect futility of anti-aesthetic writing. The direction of Goethe's later development is not easy to follow; his work becomes cryptic, esoteric. But with respect to the main questions that concern us, Kleist's play at least shows clearly the path from which Goethe deviated.

The second deviating chapter, chapter 8, deals with Nietzsche and is equally indispensable, for it confronts the question of whether my final argument on "Goethe" is *possible*—whether it is possible, without slipping into the relatively trivial idea of reception-history, to expound the elusive notion of a kind of authorial afterlife that supports the anti-aesthetic, thus somehow untextualizable self-adversarial tendency within literature. In Goethe's case this question has to be deferred; the possibility of the argument has to be taken on faith, until most of the argument is actually there. In Nietzsche's case, however, an argument having practically the same structure as the argument on

"Goethe" can be made—convincingly, I think—in a relatively small compass. The Nietzsche chapter thus provides a *scale model* of the book's whole argument, hence a demonstration of its possibility. As a scale model, moreover, and as a historical bridge, it plays an important part in supporting the crucial arguments that involve Freud in chapter 9 and Kristeva in chapter 10.

Finally, chapter 8 also lends the occasion for introducing and developing the concept of the revolutionary. For Goethe, the task of undoing literature presents itself mainly in the form of a resistance to the aesthetic. By the time we get to Nietzsche, the situation appears more desperate, to the point of requiring revolution; and exactly the same type of revolutionary need characterizes a certain segment of recent feminist thought. Thus, between Goethe's cultural situation and that of revolutionary feminism a definite analogy obtains, which is a main component of the notion of "Goethe as woman."

## Gender Matters

Despite its title, this book could have been constructed so as to avoid questions of gender almost completely. The main argument, after all, concerns the problem of modern national "literature," which means literature in the aesthetic sense, and this problem does not *logically* involve gender issues, nor, in the broad context of the growth of modern European nation-states, does it *historically* involve such issues. The connection with gender arises entirely from the manner in which Goethe—perhaps also his contemporary Germany, if we can take Kleist as representative—happens to view and develop the problem of literature; it arises, that is, more or less *by accident,* and perhaps, in large measure, even owes its persistence in the nineteenth and twentieth centuries (in relation to Nietzsche, for example) to a persistence of that accident in the broader historical "Goethe."

In any case, while gender issues do eventually form a pattern here, which I call "Goethe as woman," they enter the picture only separately, on an ad hoc basis. And I think, therefore, that it would be both futile and misleading to attempt an overall theoretical justification of this aspect of the argument. This is not to say that I wish to avoid responsibility for the theoretical implications of what I write. I think it will be found, for example, that the idea of the irreducible constructedness of gender operates as a presupposition throughout, that the argument never loses contact with the understanding (in Judith Butler's formulation) that "gender identity . . . is performatively constituted in the very 'expressions' that are said to be its results."[2] But in most instances, the question of exactly *how* gender is constructed has no special bearing on the relation with the problem of literature. And in these instances I have bracketed any theoretical questions of gender in order to maintain a relatively clear focus.

## Terms

It may attract notice that in referring to "the reader," where one commonly expects "he or she," the text below often has only "he." This practice has to do in each case with an either textually or historically *implied* gendering of the reader, and is connected to the specifics of the argument in ways that can be followed without difficulty.

And finally, there is no way to avoid slippage in the use of the term "literature," since there has never been a special term, other than "literature" itself, for whatever it is in literature that aims at resistance or revolution or undoing. In Goethe, in fact, the role of that special term may often be filled by "world literature"—as distinguished from national literature. But this concept, for Goethe as for us, has a rather narrow range of suggestions. I will simply use "literature" and let the slippage happen, trusting that it will be clear from context in all cases which aspect of the term is in focus. Such slippage, in any event, the turning of literature against itself, mirrors a real complexity in the argument.

# PART I

# Man and the Problem of Reading

$$\approx 1 \approx$$

# Werther and Montaigne:
# Reading in the Aesthetic Sense

According to *Dichtung und Wahrheit,* Montaigne was one of Goethe's "friends" as early as 1771.[1] I will argue accordingly that the idea of the human condition, and of its ethical consequences, that is developed in *Die Leiden des jungen Werthers* is in fact practically identical to the idea that emerges from several of the major *Essais,* especially "Du repentir" and "De l'experience." I will not attempt to treat all the possible parallels between *Werther* and Montaigne. (One might wonder, for example, if Goethe knows the discussion of suicide in "Coustume de l'isle de Cea.") My aim is to mark Goethe's historical situation— his distance from Montaigne, or more generally, from the Renaissance idea of freedom—in strictly *technical* terms.[2] What is at issue is not meaning itself (which I claim is close to being the same in the two texts anyway) so much as the mechanism of meaning production. *Werther* means what it means only by way of a dramatization of the reader, only insofar as the reader adopts a certain specific role with respect to both the text and the fiction. And this communicative procedure involves a number of inherently questionable assumptions about the act of reading, assumptions (I will argue later) that have the effect, among other things, of gendering that act. It is in anticipation of this point that I speak of "man" and the problem of reading.

## What Is Man?

There is more than merely a hint of Montaigne in the question by which the main theme of *Werther* is established: "O was ist der Mensch, daß er über sich klagen darf!" (p. 5, 4 May). "What is man, that he is permitted to complain about himself?" This question has two distinct meanings. First, it expresses a certain pragmatic humility—what right has a man to complain about himself, if it is really himself he is complaining about?—and in this meaning it echoes a main point of the essay "Du repentir":

23

There are some impetuous, prompt and sudden sins: let us leave them aside. But as for these other sins so many times repeated, planned, and premeditated, constitutional sins, or even professional or vocational sins, I cannot imagine that they can be implanted so long in one and the same heart, without the reason and conscience of their possessor constantly willing and intending it to be so. And the repentance which he claims comes to him at a certain prescribed moment is a little hard for me to imagine and conceive.[3]

A person's constitutional faults, says Montaigne, cannot in honesty be taken as the object of repentance, and the applicability of this idea to Werther is clear. Despite his early protestations—"ich will mich bessern, will nicht mehr ein bißchen Übel, das uns das Schicksal vorlegt, wiederkäuen" (p. 5), "I will improve, I'll stop chewing over the bit of evil fate presents me with"— Werther in the end not only must accept his constitutional "hypochondria,"[4] but actually defends it on quasi-theological grounds in the letters of 15 and 30 November 1772.

However, Werther's question, "O was ist der Mensch, daß er über sich klagen darf," is also a theoretical question rich in implications: What is this creature, man, that is permitted to be dissatisfied with itself? How is it possible to be a single entity, yet at the same time stand over against oneself as one's own accuser? And the question in this meaning expresses not humility but pride, the recognition of man's unique status among created things, his *freedom*. If all our faculties were the direct expressions of a single level of existence, like the faculties of a horse or an angel, then obviously we could never be dissatisfied with ourselves; but neither would we be that creature to whom God says in Pico's *Oration,* "We have made you neither heavenly nor earthly, neither mortal nor immortal, so that, with free choice and as a mark of honor, you, as it were the shaper and maker of your own self, might present yourself in whatever form you please."[5] If our nature did not include the possibility of existing on completely different levels, if we did not therefore possess a capacity for radical self-dissatisfaction, then *change* (or self-alteration) would be impossible for us, and the idea of a free existence would be meaningless. Therefore Montaigne, even in arguing against repentance, must still distinguish two acceptable forms of self-dissatisfaction, one more superficial than ordinary repentance—"le regretter"—and one more profound: "It [repentance] must grasp me by the vitals and afflict them as deeply and as completely as God sees into me" (MM, 791). Therefore the essay "Du repentir" must be prefaced by a vivid evocation of the mutability of all things, including one's own self. Our recognition that the text cannot honestly claim to be more than a "record of various changeable occurrences [*accidens*], and of irresolute and, when it so befalls, contradictory ideas" (MM, 782) has the effect of *relativizing* statements like, "I customarily do wholeheartedly whatever I do, and go my way all in one piece" (MM, 790). Such claims of self-unity on Montaigne's part are themselves ultimately only "accidents" of the text's development; they have to be relativized, for if a man is *absolutely* "of one piece," then he is also incapable of free action.

The idea of freedom does not occur explicitly in the essay "Du repentir," at least not in anything like Pico's radical formulation, but the idea of man's protean mutability includes freedom as an implication.[6] And in "De l'experience" Montaigne in fact argues that we should deliberately exercise our mutability: "A young man should violate his own rules to arouse his vigor and keep it from growing moldy and lax. And there is no way of life so stupid and feeble [*sot et . . . debile*] as that which is conducted by rules and discipline" (MM, 1061). Satisfaction with oneself tends to degenerate into a doctrinaire incapacity for change or activity, whereupon even virtue becomes a kind of vice: "it is always a vice to mortgage oneself" (MM, 1079). Self-contentment and consistency are therefore nothing to be especially proud of, which I suppose is what is meant by the idea of a conscience that is satisfied with itself "not as with the conscience of an angel or a horse, but as with the conscience of a man" (MM, 784).

In "Du repentir," then, we have an ironic hovering in the tension produced by the understanding that a capacity for self-dissatisfaction, while always potentially the source of grave internal disorder, is also a precondition of free activity. In *Werther* the hovering fails, the intellectual poles are forced into direct conflict. Werther talks in an early letter of being entirely at peace in the bosom of nature, but concludes as follows:

> mein Freund! wenn's dann um meine Augen dämmert, und die Welt um mich her und der Himmel ganz in meiner Seele ruhn wie die Gestalt einer Geliebten; dann sehne ich mich oft und denke: ach könntest du das wieder ausdrücken, könntest du dem Papiere das einhauchen, was so voll, so warm in dir lebt, daß es würde der Spiegel deiner Seele, wie deine Seele ist der Spiegel des unendlichen Gottes!—Mein Freund—Aber ich gehe darüber zu Grunde, ich erliege unter der Gewalt der Herrlichkeit dieser Erscheinungen. (p. 8, 10 May)

> [My friend! when my eyes are bathed in fading light, and the world around me and the heavens repose wholly in my soul like the figure of a beloved, then comes a yearning: oh if only you could express that, if you could take what thus lives in you so full and warm and breathe it into your drawing paper, that it become the mirror of your soul, as your soul is the mirror of infinite God!—My friend—but I am crushed by this thought, I succumb to the power and glory of these visions.]

At this stage in the novel Werther's goal is to regain his personal equilibrium. But in the very process of actually becoming satisfied with his situation, of finding the world in a state of balance and repose in his soul, he becomes dissatisfied with his satisfaction and longs for more. And this perverse self-torment is related to his conscious rejection of bourgeois normality ("die gelassenen Herren" [p. 18, 26 May]), of that complacent, conventional state of mind which supposedly resists the free expression of Promethean genius and so denies human existence the realization of its full potential. What in Montaigne is a fruitful ironic tension becomes, in Werther, a process of practically deliberate self-destruction, fueled by the Faustian proposition that satisfaction is a form of unworthy servility and must be avoided: "Wie ich beharre bin ich Knecht" (*Faust*, l. 1710).

If self-contentment is both desired and feared by Werther, then the same is true of freedom. Werther not only desires for himself the active freedom of artistic creativity, but is also disturbed by the way others waste their freedom.

> Es ist ein einförmiges Ding um das Menschengeschlecht. Die meisten verar-beiten den größten Theil der Zeit, um zu leben, und das Bißchen, das ihnen von Freiheit übrig bleibt, ängstigt sie so, daß sie alle Mittel aufsuchen, um es los zu werden. O Bestimmung des Menschen! (pp. 11–12, 17 May)

> [Things are pretty much the same for all mankind. Most people spend the bulk of their time working in order to live, and the little bit of freedom left over worries them so that they do whatever they can to get rid of it. Oh human destiny!]

And yet exactly this fear of freedom is present in Werther himself. Freedom awakens fear because it entails a sense of our own malleability and so exposes us to an awareness of *change* that Werther experiences as intensely as Montaigne: "Kannst du sagen: *Das ist!* da alles vorüber geht? . . . Himmel und Erde und ihre webenden Kräfte um mich her: Ich sehe nichts, als ein ewig verschlingendes, ewig wiederkäuendes Ungeheuer" (pp. 75–76, 18 Aug.). "Can you say: *That is!* given that everything passes away? Heaven and earth and their network of forces around me: I see nothing but an eternally voracious, eternally cud-chewing monster." Only that person who either has no intellectual freedom to begin with ("manchmal wünschte ich ein Tagelöhner zu sein" [p. 77, 22 Aug.]) or else divests himself of at least the feeling of freedom (as Werther imagines Albert does, whom he sees "über die Ohren in Acten begraben" [p. 77]), only that person whose whole existence is determined by externals, remains exempt from the anxiety that freedom produces. Accordingly, within four days of his letter on nature as ceaseless change, Werther begins to think seriously of sacrificing his freedom by tying himself down to a job; and it is perhaps also no accident that Werther's "fable of the horse that grew impatient with its freedom and accepted saddle and bridle" (p. 77) reminds us of the discomfort of "le cheval eschappé" (MM, 34) in Montaigne's "De l'oisiveté." Werther's inner conflict, again, is closely related, as an exaggeration, to the tension in Montaigne between self-contentment and freedom.

But Werther is not merely an individual case of abnormal psychology. On the contrary, his difficulties arise from the excessive insistence upon certain *valid general perceptions* concerning the human condition. "O was ist der Mensch, daß er über sich klagen darf!" What is the use of human freedom if we retain it only at the price of endless self-discontent and the terror of mutability? Werther's clear awareness of his plight only drives him further into despair, for the source of his difficulties is not any error, but an excessive intensity and exactitude of awareness. His hypochondria has in common with Montaigne's idea of repentance that reason, far from "effacing" it, actually "engenders" it (MM, 784). Reason, given the premises with which Werther's intensity of vision forces it to operate, inevitably produces the conclusion that human freedom is truly useful only by making us capable of suicide, that a person's consciousness of being free is one with the sweet feeling "daß er diesen Kerker verlassen kann, wann er will" (p. 16, 22 May), "that he can leave this dungeon whenever he wishes."

Reason and knowledge, the indispensable preconditions of human freedom, thus become for Werther the vehicle of a progressive self-enslavement; and this process is mirrored over and over on a small scale in the text. Werther complains about the people in court society, people among whom he is supposedly immersing himself in therapeutic activity: "Manchmal möcht' ich sie auf den Knieen bitten, nicht so rasend in ihre eigenen Eingeweide zu wüthen" (p. 99, 8 Feb.). "Sometimes I want to beg them on bended knee not to root so furiously in their own entrails." But he himself, in that he insists on seeing society in this light, in that he refuses to overlook its faults, is doing exactly what he is railing against, as it were rooting mercilessly in his own entrails, and he is doing it in the very act of railing against it.

## Morality and Reason

The contradictoriness of Werther's inner state is not only potentially present in Montaigne, but to an extent actually present, except that Montaigne appears to take it more lightly: "So, all in all, I do indeed contradict myself now and then; but truth, as Demades said, I never contradict" (MM, 782).[7] We must not take this statement too lightly; there are real logical contradictions in the essay "Du repentir," and the relation between contradiction and "vérité" is an indispensable part of the text's meaning. We read, for example, that "There is no one who, if he listens to himself, does not discover in himself a pattern all his own, a ruling pattern [*forme maistresse*], which struggles against education and against the tempest of the passions that oppose it" (MM, 789)—which, incidentally, reminds us of Goethe's later idea of "Daimon." And there is simply no way to reconcile this statement with the autobiographer's earlier admission, "I cannot keep my subject still. It goes along befuddled and staggering, with a natural drunkenness. . . . If my mind could gain a firm footing, I would not make essays, I would make decisions; but it is always in apprenticeship and on trial" (MM, 782). The one statement says that every man can form a unified idea of himself; the other says that Montaigne in particular finds it impossible to achieve such an idea.[8] Moreover, given what Montaigne says about the identity between himself and his work, this logical difficulty must reflect a constitutional difficulty in the speaker, or as we may infer further, in "l'humaine condition" (MM, 782) as a whole.

In order to understand this difficulty, we must deal with the suggestion that truth includes contradictions, which means that in "Du repentir," as earlier in the "Apologie de Raimond Sebond," Montaigne is concerned with the idea of the limits of thought. Rational thought, while indispensable to human existence, is by no means an unqualified benefit, being a source of such evils as "peché, maladie, irresolution, trouble, desespoir" (MM, 437); there are inherent pretensions in reason that quickly become morbid when not restrained, and repentance, as the attempt to apply to ourselves rational standards that (by our own avowal, in that we repent) do not belong to our actual condition, is a prime instance of such morbidity. Repentance for things truly wrong with us is rational but not reasonable, for by setting us over against ourselves it confuses us and aggravates our internal disorder; it is a kind of rooting in our own entrails, or as Montaigne puts it more mildly, "Repentance is nothing but a disavowal of our will and an opposition to our fancies, which leads us about in all directions [*qui nous pourmene à tout sens*]" (MM, 785–86). But it does not follow that we ought to renounce all judgment on ourselves. On the contrary, "Those of us especially who live a private life that is on display only to ourselves must have a pattern established within us by which to test our actions, and, according to this pattern, now pat ourselves on the back, now punish ourselves" (MM, 785). The renunciation of self-judgment merely commits us to anarchy; what we must do is *limit* our judgment and content ourselves with the state of being "neither an angel nor Cato" (MM, 791). Otherwise judgment itself becomes a worse fault than those it condemns, which is clearly what happens in the case of Werther, whose judgment about the human condition is not wrong, but is dangerously unrestrained.

Here, however, is the difficulty: on what basis shall we judge how to limit our judgment? It is this difficulty that produces the logical contradictions in "Du repentir." At the beginning of the essay it is made clear that we have no stable point of view from which to verify our idea of ourselves, which means that the "forme maistresse" our experience supposedly reveals to us is bound to be conditioned by the way we happen to view ourselves at any given moment. Nor do long life and the accumulated evidence of our memories enable us to achieve true self-knowledge; Montaigne makes a point of mentioning not only the weakness of his own memory—"que je meritoy que la memoire me secourut mieux" (MM, 783, also 940, 1051)—but also the typical degeneration of the mental faculties with age. The simple fact of the matter, in other words, is that even if there is such a thing as a "forme maistresse" in us, our idea of this form must remain totally unreliable. Montaigne practically says as much when (in a different context) he speaks of "des parties secrettes aux objects qu'on manie et indivinables, signamment en la nature des hommes, des conditions muettes, sans montre, inconnues par fois du possesseur mesme" (MM, 792), "secret parts in the matters we handle which cannot be guessed, especially in human nature—mute factors that do not show, sometimes unknown to their possessor himself."

But the trouble with this truth—that we can never form an accurate idea of our own character—is that it is *useless:* if we try to draw conclusions from it, it becomes a source of endless negation "qui nous pourmene à tout sens." Just as reason becomes unreasonable, so truth becomes senseless when carried to excess; as we hear elsewhere: "la verité mesme n'a pas ce privilege d'estre employée à toute heure et en toute sorte: son usage, tout noble qu'il est, a ses circonscriptions et limites" (MM, 1055), "truth itself does not have the privilege to be used at any time and in any way; its use, noble as it is, has its circumscriptions and limits." That we can never achieve a true knowledge of ourselves does not alter our *need* for such knowledge. If we do not possess a relatively uncomplicated idea of our own character, then we cannot function in the world, except perhaps by committing ourselves pedantically to a set of abstract principles and so leading the life Montaigne calls "sot et . . . debile." Therefore the statement concerning our "forme maistresse," though it contradicts a manifest fact, is still a *true statement* in the sense that it opens for us the possibility of living effectively. Truth is determined not by fact, not by *what* we think, but by *how* we think; it has a moral component that limits it. It has more to do with the character of our *thinking,* as a responsible act, than with the consistency of our *thought,* as a system of propositions, which is why it is not necessarily incompatible with logical contradiction.

The basic difficulty remains, however, and the danger is unabated. If a morally justifiable idea of truth may contain logical contradictions, then there can never be any convincing logical structure in morality. Moreover, if we *know* that morality is illogical, that reason is inadequate as a guide to action—as Werther knows this when he rejects Wilhelm's "Entweder Oder" (p. 61, 8 Aug.), "Either Or," or in the conversation with Albert on suicide—then it becomes possible for us to believe in any moral doctrine, even the most perverse. It is this dangerous knowledge that produces what I will call Werther's morality of maximum suffering.

## The Problem of Freedom

The reason for Montaigne's insistence on limits to thought and judgment, and the goal for the sake of which he accepts the danger inherent in his argument, is *freedom,* the possibility of significant decision and action. Repentance is wrong because it is an act of judgment by which the faculty of judgment becomes enslaved to a helplessly confused idea of the self; and Montaigne says elsewhere of philosophy that "in excess, it enslaves our natural freedom and, by an importunate subtlety, diverts us from the clear and level road laid out for us by nature" (MM, 196). Nor is this "chemin" that nature lays out for us merely a path of least resistance; in "De l'experience" Montaigne returns to the same image: "Popular opinion is wrong: it is much easier to go along the sides [*les bouts*], where the outer edge serves as a limit and guide, than by the middle way [*la voye de milieu*], wide and open, and to go by art than by Nature; but it is also much less noble and less commendable" (MM, 1090). The broad path of nature, in which we remain by avoiding intellectual excess, is not the easiest path but the hardest, and Montaigne thus invokes the characteristic Renaissance paradox of nature and freedom. Our true nature, insofar as we conform to it, is not a haven of repose or contentment; it does not bind us in any way, but rather releases us into a noble but arduous freedom, a state of infinite responsibility for ourselves in which not even the principle of logical consistency guides the decisions we must make.

In relation to this doctrine of nature and freedom, Werther, who is fascinated by extremes in human experience—"les bouts" or "Gränzen" (p. 68, 12 Aug.)—is the perfect negative case in point, for he maneuvers himself into a self-enslavement such that even his rational awareness of it only enslaves him more fully. In the midst of his anguish he writes to Wilhelm: "Doch wozu das alles? warum behalt' ich nicht für mich, was mich ängstigt und kränkt? warum betrüb' ich noch dich? warum geb' ich dir immer Gelegenheit, mich zu bedauern und mich zu schelten? Sei's denn, auch das mag zu meinem Schicksal gehören!" (p. 116, 4 Sept.). "But why do I do all this? Why do I not keep to myself what worries and offends me? Why do I trouble you with it too? Why do I always offer you the opportunity to pity and scold me? That's the way it is, and may just be a part of my fate." This could almost be a bitter travesty of Montaigne. The notion of the "forme maistresse"—what Werther sees as his "Schicksal," the tendency to cause himself and others as much suffering as possible—no longer enables the individual to live actively and effectively, but has been perverted into a means of avoiding freedom and responsibility. It is no longer the result of an honest (if ultimately hopeless) striving for self-mastery, but has become an excuse for Werther's deliberately letting himself go, as he does in precisely those passages where he speaks of it: "wie ich so wissentlich in das alles Schritt vor Schritt hineingegangen bin!" (p. 62, 8 Aug., Evening), "how I have so knowingly walked into all of this, step by step." Not only the strained situation that costs him his diplomatic post, and not only the situation from which he is fleeing at the beginning of the novel, but also the whole central situation with Lotte is Werther's own more or less deliberate creation—in the last case, as a response to the warning he receives while on his way to meet Lotte for the first time, "Nehmen Sie sich in Acht . . . daß Sie sich nicht verlieben!" (p. 25, 16 June), "Be careful not to fall in love." Deliberate, but not in the sense that, say, artistic creation is deliberate; in the sense, rather, of a deliberate groping for "les bouts," for the absolute limits of human existence, by which he hopes to steady himself against the dizzying experience of freedom.

Moreover, as I have suggested, Werther shapes this "fate" of his on the basis of general perceptions about humanity. It is thus not merely a fanciful self-image, but rather a conscious moral doctrine which he later justifies philosophically, as a kind of *imitatio Christi (vel Socratis)*: "Was ist es anders als Menschenschicksal, sein Maß auszuleiden, seinen Becher auszutrinken?" (p. 130, 15 Nov.). "What is it but human fate, to suffer one's full measure, to drain one's goblet to the dregs?" If man's lot is to suffer; if, as Montaigne says (but without drawing the same conclusion), "il n'y a satisfaction çà bas que pour les ames, ou brutales ou divines" (MM, 966), "in this life there is no satisfaction for souls that are not either sub-human or divine"; if Christ himself cried, "Mein Gott! mein Gott! warum hast du mich verlassen?" (p. 131; Matt. 27:46, Mark 15:34): then has not each individual a moral *duty* to experience anguish as fully as possible, even if it means causing anguish in others? If the true character of existence is anguish, then surely any failure to embrace an opportunity for anguish shows not merely cowardice, but also intellectual dullness, the ignorant complacency of the typical bourgeois.

This perverse morality of Werther's, this morality of maximum suffering, even though it is clearly opposed to everything Montaigne teaches, still bears a very close intellectual relation to Montaigne. Not only is it related in general to the dangerous notion of moral illogicality, but in the structure of the novel it is also made to develop naturally from certain *specific* elements of Montaigne's thinking. Werther's defense of life's simple pleasures against the saturnine Herr Schmidt, for example—"Wenn wir immer ein offenes Herz hätten das Gute zu genießen . . ." (pp. 44–45, 1 July), "if we only had an open heart to enjoy what is good . . ."—agrees entirely with Montaigne in "De l'experience": "Xerxes was a fool, who, wrapped in all human pleasures, went and offered a reward to anyone who would find him others. But hardly less of a fool is the man who cuts off those that Nature has found for him" (MM, 1086). And in the same letter, Werther's evocation of the image of a deathbed attended by weeping friends reminds us strongly of the imagined deathbed scenes in "De la vanité" (though these are seen from the opposite point of view), so that his condemnation of ill-humor as a "Laster" (p. 46), "vice," seems clearly related to Montaigne's attack on the vicious tendency by which "We are not content that they [our friends] should be aware of our woes, unless they are also afflicted by them" (MM, 957).

Werther's opinions at this stage are thus sound and salutary; but as Lotte points out, they are also overstrained: "Und wie sie mich auf dem Wege schalt, über den zu warmen Antheil an allem, und daß ich darüber zu Grunde gehen würde! daß ich mich schonen sollte!" (p. 48). "And how she scolded me as we walked, about my over-warm feelings for everything, and that this would ruin me, that I should take it easier on myself." In fact, by the vehemence of his peroration in favor of maintaining a good mood, Werther has annoyed Herr Schmidt, saddened Friederike, and reduced himself to a state of lachrymose self-pity. In the very act of preaching he falls prey to the vice against which he preaches, and so inadvertently demonstrates the psychological precariousness of Montaigne's thinking. Simply by being too passionate in his defense of what are essentially Montaigne's precepts concerning the sensible conduct of life, Werther now finds himself in direct violation of those precepts; and it does not surprise us that only a month later, in the conversation with Albert on suicide, he has reversed himself and adopted Herr Schmidt's position on the incurability of certain anguished mental states. Eventually, by way of an entirely convincing psychological development, Werther arrives at a position diametrically opposed to Montaigne's when he asks, in effect, how can one claim to "lead the life of man in conformity with its natural condition" (MM, 787) if one has not explored the whole depth of suffering made possible by man's unique capacity for self-dissatisfaction, even at the price of senseless self-destruction and cruelty to others? Montaigne's ideas, by being implanted in Werther, are thus made to reveal their *own* potential self-conflict.

Montaigne himself, at least as an autobiographer, if not as a teacher, recognizes that his character contains a potential for extravagant Wertherian self-torment: "When I am in a bad way, I grow bent on misfortune; I abandon myself in despair, and let myself slip toward the precipice, and, as they say, throw the handle after the ax. I persist in growing worse, and think myself no longer worth my care: either entirely well or entirely ill" (MM, 924). Again, there is a danger, an inherent potential for despair, in the perceptions and ideas with which Montaigne operates; and *Werther* is the fictional realization of that potential.

## The Role of the Reader

Is *Werther* therefore an attempt to refute Montaigne, to reduce his thought to absurdity? This would conflict with young Goethe's professed admiration for Montaigne. But to understand exactly the relation between the French text and the German, and the function in this relation of a Renaissance idea of freedom, we must first understand exactly how Montaigne avoids Werther's despair.

"The value of the soul consists not in flying high, but in an orderly pace. Its greatness is exercised not in greatness [*grandeur*] but in mediocrity" (MM, 787), says Montaigne; and while the word "mediocrité" does not suggest here exactly what it would mean in a more modern text, it is still clearly opposed in meaning to "grandeur."[9] The statement thus contains a paradox, the resolution of which has to do with the vicious but strict logicality of Werther's fate. Considered as a structure of ideas, *Werther* shows that the effect of Montaigne's thinking is not to relieve the problems of human existence, but rather to intensify them, to reveal how difficult it is merely to *be* human. Greatness, in the sense of "To win through a breach, to conduct an embassy, to govern a people" (MM, 787),[10] is a relative matter, dependent for its existence on circumstances and opinions, but in its relativity not particularly problematic. A normal and orderly human life, on the other hand, if it can ever really be achieved at all, requires the utterly free, therefore absolute assertion of will in the face of an ever present abyss of despair, that abyss which Werther cannot resist experiencing, "like those who, from fear of the precipice, throw themselves over the edge" (MM, 333). Not only is there no reliable point of view from which we may know ourselves—and how shall we impose order or normality on something we do not know?—but it also appears in "Du repentir" that any order we do manage to create in life must contain inconsistencies, that we must accept our vices, for example, even though "There is no vice truly a vice which is not offensive, and which a sound judgment does not condemn" (MM, 784). If we wish to order our existence, therefore, we can do so only by restraining precisely that reason and judgment from which our conception of order must arise in the first place, and how shall we then decide how to apply this restraint? To live in this hopeless paradox, to face it and know it and somehow deal with it, is the only absolute achievement of the soul, an achievement that is rendered the more difficult by lacking all external attractions, since there can be no witness to it but oneself, and this witness is known to be unreliable. The logical inevitability of despair is thus overshadowed in Montaigne by a vision of *the heroic greatness of normal human life*—a vision, an idea, not a theory, since the "grandeur" of an orderly "mediocrité" resides precisely in the fact that no adequate theory is possible, that existence in "la voye de milieu," being strictly free, lacking all external guides, is in each particular case strictly *unprecedented,* thus inaccessible to general considerations.

Werther, then, is the direct representation of an abyss at the brink of which Montaigne constantly balances, and this abyss is present in every instant of every human life; there is never any compelling *reason* for not hurling ourselves over the edge like Werther, except perhaps the retention of our freedom, which freedom, however, is only the freedom to continue struggling endlessly and unillustriously with the insoluble problem of "l'humaine condition." Normal, orderly human life, when it occurs, is thus a kind of heroic triumph, and Montaigne is concerned to show us both its full difficulty and its full worthwhileness. Especially the essay "De l'experience" is a hymn to such heroism:

> Nostre grand et glorieux chef-d'oeuvre, c'est vivre à propos. . . . Il n'est rien si beau et legitime que de faire bien l'homme et deuëment, ny science si ardue

que de bien et naturellement sçavoir vivre cette vie; et de nos maladies la plus
sauvage, c'est mespriser nostre estre. (MM, 1088, 1091)

[Our great and glorious masterpiece is to live appropriately. . . . There is
nothing so beautiful and legitimate as to play the man well and properly,
nor any knowledge so arduous as knowing how to live this life well and
naturally; and the most barbarous of our maladies is to despise our being.]

A hymn, but an ironic hymn, mainly a treatise on the kidney stone, for
the heroism it refers to cannot be celebrated except indirectly, by example,
in words that *are* normal and orderly and unpretentious, like the resolutely
conventional praise of "ce grand et tout puissant donneur" (MM, 1094), "that
great and all-powerful Giver," who, in the common opinion, has made all things
ultimately good.

My point, however, is that the author of *Werther* understands Montaigne in exactly this spirit, and that precisely the heroism of normal human
life can also be said to constitute the novel's meaning—provided only that we
understand that "meaning" here involves a specific role for the reader, a role
that is practically spelled out in the verses that some early editions print as an
epigraph to Book 2:

Du beweinst, du liebst ihn, liebe Seele,
Rettest sein Gedächtniß von der Schmach;
Sieh, dir winkt sein Geist aus seiner Höle:
Sey ein Mann, und folge mir nicht nach. (p. 388)

[You weep for him, you love him, dear soul, and save his memory from shame.
See, his spirit calls to you from below: Be a man, and do not emulate me.]

Or we think of a much later passage where Goethe singles out for admiration, in Montaigne and others, the quality of "Behagen" (WA, pt. 2, 3:219),
"comfort, contentment." This concept is already prominent in *Werther*—
"Behaglichkeit" (p. 90, 20 Oct.) as an ideal, by contrast with Werther's own
"unbehagliche Ungeduld" (p. 77, 22 Aug.)—and around the time of the novel's
composition also occurs in the significant phrase "mit urkräftigem Behagen"
(*Urfaust*, l. 183). A kind of ease or comfort is thus associated by Goethe not
with weakness—which is what we might expect from Werther's opinion of the
average bourgeois—but rather with natural inner strength.

These ideas suggest an interpretation of *Werther* in the full spirit of
Montaigne. In reading the novel we are struck by the following points: first,
that Werther's fate, given his basic attitude, shows a strict logical inevitability
such that even his moments of rational perspective upon himself only increase

his helplessness; second, that this fate is the result not of a particular social situation, but of certain general perceptions concerning the human condition, that the social situations in which Werther finds himself are in fact more or less deliberately calculated by him to maximize his experience of what he recognizes as man's necessary and essential suffering; and third, that by understanding the book, we ourselves share Werther's perception concerning the inevitability of suffering, *while still not following his example in behavior.* Not only are Werther's comments on man's fate made available to us, but also, in Werther himself, we are given a vivid example of how the awareness of basic and undeniable human problems ("O was ist der Mensch, daß er über sich klagen darf!") initiates a process of utter personal degeneration. We know what Werther knows, we understand how his fate follows logically from his knowledge, we understand that no special external conditions are necessary to cause such a fate; we find ourselves, in other words, at the very brink of a Wertherian plunge, with no logical reason for resisting it. And yet, as detached readers, in spite of this dangerous mental situation, we continue to lead our own relatively normal lives; indeed, the form of the novel reminds us constantly of our normality by making us play the role of Wilhelm, the letters' original reader—since Wilhelm's responses must be supplied by *our* active imagination. *Werther* thus teaches us that our own existence—as represented, for the moment, by our condition as readers—is in truth the product of a constant struggle against despair, a repeated and entirely illogical act of will. Knowledge and logic are both on Werther's side; therefore it appears that we *must* be carrying out a free act of will or affirmation if we do not follow him.

The situation is made difficult for us by Werther's own negative attitude toward bourgeois normality. Is it really worthwhile to struggle endlessly for an orderly existence, if the result is merely to make us indistinguishable from the Philistines Werther despises? The decision with which *Werther* confronts us, between the hopeless struggle for self-mastery and a helpless plunge into self-destruction, is not even a decision that *must* be made. Most people in fact avoid it by living what passes for a normal life, but without ever thinking about it. The story of a man whose wife had had to embezzle her household money is an allegory of how the sheer miracle of orderly human life can be counterfeited by mere thickheadedness: "Aber ich habe selbst Leute gekannt, die des Propheten ewiges Ölkrüglein ohne Verwunderung in ihrem Hause angenommen hätten" (p. 53, 11 July). "I have even known people who would have accepted in their household without amazement the inexhaustible oil jar of the prophet." It is true that a normal existence based not upon a decision for order in the face of despair, but upon stupidity, is not what Montaigne means when he says, "C'est une vie exquise, celle qui se maintient en ordre jusques en son privé" (MM, 786), "an exquisite life, a life that keeps itself in order down to its most private level." But it is also true that there is no clear sign by which these two types of normality can be distinguished, which raises once again the question of whether it is really *worthwhile* to face the decision forced upon us by *Werther,* or whether, having faced it, we can reasonably decide otherwise than Werther does.

If we understand Goethe's novel, however; if we understand completely the consequences of the question, "What is man, that he is permitted to complain about himself?"; if we understand that self-dissatisfaction is a necessary condition of freedom, hence of life itself; and if we understand that this understanding is all that is needed in order to *be* Werther, since it both is and constantly compounds the self-dissatisfaction that it understands, since in order to retain its freedom, hence its very character *as* understanding, it must positively insist on an ever more complete dissatisfaction with itself, which leads ultimately to suicide: then we do, after all, necessarily face the decision between self-mastery and self-destruction. And yet, at the same time, we *are* simply readers, here and now; we are carrying out a normal and not obviously self-destructive human activity in a condition of relative comfort. Therefore, if we understand the novel (in the sense that understanding actually confronts us with the abyss), then it follows by a reasonably strict logic that our apparently passive situation as readers is in truth a radically active, strictly unprecedented *decision* in favor of human freedom with all its attendant paradoxes and difficulties. Thus a logical inference from the relation between the text and our attitude as readers is transformed into a discovery about our personal condition. This discovery, in an important sense, is the meaning of the novel; and that the decision we discover in ourselves is made as difficult as possible only contributes to its value, to our experience of the truth that normal human life *is* a matter of heroic decision.

Assuming, then, that the textual resonances between *Werther* and Montaigne, especially the essay on repentance, are significant; and assuming, on the basis of plentiful extrinsic evidence, that Goethe is here operating as a follower of Montaigne, not a negative parodist, that he is attempting to come to grips, in the same spirit as Montaigne, with the same problematic sense of the human condition: it follows that the meaning of *Werther* simply does not arise, does not exist, except in the strictly private situation of the reader. It is not a meaning that can be derived from the novel's fiction, either by sympathetic identification or by rational allegorizing. It is not a meaning that can be captured in any conceivable exegetic formulation. It is not, strictly speaking, a meaning of the book *Werther* at all, but rather a meaning of the implied drama of reading that book, in which the role of the reader, again, is, first, to understand Werther's understanding of the human condition, and to recognize that in a strong sense, this understanding alone makes him practically indistinguishable from Werther as a person; and second, at the same time, simply to *be* a relatively detached and comfortable reader.

## "Negative Romanticism" and Montaigne

It seems to me, moreover, that a conclusion of this type (of course not always involving Montaigne) is possible for many other works in Morse Peckham's category of "negative Romanticism."[11] Given the quality of literature as a socially and historically established practice, it is hard to understand the literary use of nihilism or despair *except* as a way to confront the reader with a decision by which his own normal existence is revealed as a constantly self-creating work of art, an act of unceasing formative resolve on the brink of an ever present and potent abyss of emptiness. Hence, especially, the relation between Byronic or Wertherian Romanticism and the Romanticism, say, of a Wordsworth or an Eichendorff. The spirit of *Werther* is not basically different from the spirit of the preface to the *Lyrical Ballads:* poetic illumination of the universally human, an appreciation of the normal or non-extravagant as in itself laudable, not merely the rough foundation above which our real intellectual achievements must tower. The difference is that in "negative Romanticism" this illumination is accomplished by facing us not with an image of the truth itself but with a vision of the tempting abyss that makes the truth necessary. Nor is this point contradicted by the "editor's introduction" to *Werther,* where the reader is addressed as "du gute Seele, die du eben den Drang fühlst wie er" (p. 3), "you good soul, who feel the same impulse as he." Identification with Werther is clearly required of us. If we do not ourselves carry out in detail the suicidal reasoning that produces Werther's tragic vision of man, if we do not ourselves confront the abyss, then the underlying truth, that normal human existence is an act of heroic will, cannot actually characterize our situation.

The Luciferian sympathy in Byron's *Cain,* like the more or less deliberately nihilistic tendency we sense as the subterranean stream that feeds Werther's reflections,[12] or like the avalanche of cosmic upheavals which is the Fall in Blake, serves the communicative purpose of revealing to the reader an abyss inherent in his own existence, toward which not his passionate nature so much as precisely his free reason inclines him, an abyss at the brink of which he must always live and can maintain himself only by a constant affirmative and creative self-discipline, not discipline in the sense of anything like dogma or system, which are aspects of the abyss itself, but a discipline like that which is expressed, for example, in "Tintern Abbey," a discipline that must refrain from taking itself as such, so that it may include and allow for its inconsistencies, may speak in the same breath of "The dreary intercourse of daily life" and of "Our cheerful faith, that all which we behold / Is full of blessings," a self-discipline like that of Socrates, which is admired not only by Montaigne and by Goethe, but also, for instance, by Hölderlin: "Denn schwer ist zu tragen / Das Unglück, aber schwerer das Glück" ("Der Rhein," ll. 204–5), "For unhappiness is hard to bear, but happiness harder." These words, which could be a motto for *Werther* or *Cain,* express the same truth that is expressed in the question about man from *The Prelude,* "Why is this glorious creature to be found / One only in ten thousand?" (13.87–88): the truth that normal human life, in unchanging conformity with man's natural condition, is not simply given but must be achieved, as the rarest and worthiest accomplishment of the soul.

The crucial idea implicit in these considerations, however, is the idea of freedom, something very like the Renaissance idea of human freedom in its most radical form, as in Pico: freedom not only to do what we will but to *be* what we will. This idea is logically implied by the idea of normal human existence as an achievement of rare discipline, the idea, therefore, that there is no given generic nature to which we automatically conform and upon which we may build, the idea that even our normal existence is a strictly unprecedented act, that but for our continuing activity and decisiveness there is nothing but the abyss. When Montaigne, especially in "Sebond," attacks human self-exaltation, he is attempting not to refute this idea of freedom, but rather to rescue on a practical level what otherwise threatens to evaporate in the ether of earlier Renaissance theorizing. Philosophy in its excess enslaves us, and even a radical philosophy of freedom, when developed as theory, robs us of the actual use of our freedom by confining and anticipating us in its conceptual system.[13] Montaigne's aim, therefore, is "mesnager sa volonté" (MM, 980), "to use his will with care," which is no more a denial of freedom than is the characteristically Romantic affirmation of that state "when a man is capable of being in uncertainties, mysteries, doubts, without any irritable reaching after fact and reason." Keats, in this letter, is as it were playing the Montaigne to Coleridge's over-theoretical Ficino.[14]

Using Montaigne as a key figure, one could perhaps in fact sketch a large historical relation between the Romantic period and the Renaissance in terms of the tension between freedom and theory, a relation having to do with Romantic resistance to the Enlightenment idea of human self-perfectibility. This idea is a development of Renaissance thinking on the freedom and dignity of man, but theoretically hypertrophied to a point where the consequence of enslavement can no longer be denied. And Romantic resistance to it is of course carried out not on the plane of theory itself, but by way of the inexplicit, by implication. When Shelley, in the *Defence of Poetry,* says that poetry "reproduces the common Universe of which we are portions and percipients, and . . . purges from our inward sight the film of familiarity which obscures from us the wonder of our being," I think we ought to be reminded of the passage in "Du repentir" where Montaigne affirms his allegiance "to the common and authorized beliefs" (MM, 784); for in that passage, given the unostentatious but firm unrepentance from which it arises, Montaigne manages to transform common opinion into an object of free choice, thus revealing the hidden strength and activeness of what we otherwise feel merely as the dull round of the everyday. In Shelley and Montaigne, the paradox of absolute freedom and binding duty is present in every bit as radical a form as in Ficino and Pico on one hand, Kant and Fichte on the other. But no attempt is made at a systematic resolution; the paradox persists as an unresolved tension in the textual and conceptual weave. It is implied, for example, in Romantic thought, by the very idea of an arbitrary creative imagination as the source of poetry, since the imagination that does not somehow firmly bind itself to the common or conventional is an imagination that cannot communicate and so violates its own free nature by remaining trapped amid "the dull vapours of the little world of self." Precisely the idea of imagination as the presence in the individual of a virtually omnipotent creative divinity thus brings with it an apparently contradictory idea of the binding "forms of human nature, as existing in the mind of the creator, which is itself the image of all other minds." Again Shelley reminds us of Montaigne: "chaque homme porte la forme entiere de l'humaine condition" (MM, 782), "each man bears the entire form of human nature."

## The Place of Meaning

I do not want to make too much of the relation between Montaigne and Romantic poetic thought. My point is that the similarities in *substance*—the problem of freedom, the idea of human life as an unprecedented affirmative act, the resistance to theoretical closure—are sufficient to lend strong interpretive significance to differences in the mechanism of *meaning production*. How and where is meaning generated? The notion of "inexplicit" meaning is of course highly problematic in itself. But in cases where we cannot avoid this notion—in the case, for instance, of a concept, like freedom, that resists the very idea of adequate formulation—it is clear that we must find the production of meaning in some form of drama, where meaning is enacted cryptically as a role or interplay of roles. And it is here that a fundamental difference opens between Montaigne and his Romantic textual relatives, especially *Werther*.

Let us look again at the essay "Du repentir," at the passage by which its tone is set:

> Excusons icy ce que je dy souvent, que je me repens rarement et que ma conscience se contente de soy, non comme de la conscience d'un ange ou d'un cheval, mais comme de la conscience d'un homme, adjoustant tousjours ce refrein, non un refrein de ceremonie, mais de naifve et essentielle submission: que je parle enquerant et ignorant, me rapportant de la resolution, purement et simplement, aux creances communes et legitimes. (MM, 784)

> [Let me here excuse what I often say, that I rarely repent, and that my conscience is content with itself—not as the conscience of an angel or a horse, but as the conscience of a man; always adding this refrain, not perfunctorily but in sincere and complete submission: that I speak as an ignorant inquirer, leaving the decision purely and simply to the common and authorized beliefs.]

The important point in these words is not what is said but how it is said, the way in which submission to common standards and opinions is here transformed into an expressive personal gesture, an act of self-assertion. The speaker manages to say that he accepts "common and authorized beliefs," but without saying that they are *his* beliefs, and without specifying exactly where a final "decision" about his questioning might take place, or how it might affect his thought or his life. He opposes the concept "man" to the concepts "angel" and "horse," in a manner that by logic ought to narrow it down, setting upper and lower limits, but in fact only catapults that concept into the realm of the utterly nonspecific, where it might conceivably *give* meaning, but without *having* meaning. And above all, *the very existence of the text* conflicts with the speaker's assertion that his conscience (or consciousness) "is content with itself." Considered as a symptom—symptoms, revealing psychological symptoms especially, being after all a frequent object of Montaigne's comments—this text, like all texts, reflects a disorder that needs to be dealt with, a consciousness that is precisely *not* "content with itself." To return to the argument above, then, the speaker of these words is the sort of person "negative Romanticism" would make of us, a person whose faulty self-judgment, whose adamant normality, whose very submission to authority, is a manifestation of his inveterate activeness, his inconsistency, his arbitrariness, his freedom.

But whereas in *Werther,* and in other similarly "negative" texts, this meaning, this unresolvably paradoxical sense of the human condition, arises only from the achievement of the reader's role, in Montaigne the only role that appears to make any difference is that of the speaker or author. Montaigne himself is constantly onstage, and the idea of freedom is not represented except by *his* freedom, which at once both engages and defies us by way of the unashamed inconsistency of the discourse. The role of the reader is characterized by freedom only in the sense of being entirely undefined. We can be whatever we want to be in relation to this text, provided only, I suppose, that we are human, and that we do *not* pretend to identify with the author—since in the case of this man who says so much about himself that we cannot view him except in terms of information still waiting to be supplied, identification is clearly out of the question.

The new development in *Werther,* then—or in that novel's historical time—is the operation, in producing meaning, of a positive and definite role for the reader. What is required of the reader of *Werther* may not seem like much: that he understand, and that he observe the detachment that goes normally with being a reader. But these requirements are not imposed on the reader of Montaigne. We do not need to understand Montaigne in detail in order to find ourselves in the presence of his enactment of human freedom; in fact, we do not need to be there at all, as readers or otherwise, for him to carry out his role in his text. And this difference, in turn, between two texts that in other respects are so clearly related, can be understood historically as a reflection of the eighteenth-century development of the idea of the "aesthetic," the idea that the defining quality of art (especially literature) is found not in the work itself but in the reader's or recipient's response to the work, the idea that it makes more sense to approach the study of art by studying our sense of the beautiful than vice versa.[15]

But the aesthetic view of literature, especially in relation to the idea of freedom, brings with it certain problems. For the assignment of a role to the reader is unavoidably a co-optive move. Merely by understanding *Werther*, and yet also maintaining a normal readerly detachment, we are asked to believe that we have bought into quite a specific view of the human condition. (The text, so to speak, "forms" us, by contrast with Montaigne's text, which begins, "Les autres forment l'homme; je le recite" [MM, 782], "Others form man; I describe him.") The problem, in this case, may not seem particularly serious; it is, after all, a liberating view of our condition that we buy into. But how truly liberating can that view be if our supposedly free act of buying into it is co-opted as a role in the text's own extended structure? In any case, I will argue that even in *Werther*, this is a problem that Goethe cannot shake off, and that it becomes ever more of a problem for him as his career develops, a problem touching eventually the very nature of literature, and requiring of him an entirely radical revaluation of the notions of text and meaning.

$$\approx 2 \approx$$

# *Werther:* Double Perspective
# and the Game of Life

Anticipation of the reader's role is actually built into the text of *Werther* in much greater detail than we have yet seen; and this quality of the text is markedly more developed in the second version than it had been in the first. In fact, the role of the reader in *Werther* includes not only the tension between identification (by way of understanding) and readerly detachment, but also a detailed theoretical reflection on the process of reading itself and its relation to the text. We think of the sorcerer's apprentice. Once the aesthetic mechanism of meaning production, involving a specific role for the reader, has been established, there is no way to exclude the tension between freedom and its theory, hence the problem of co-option, from the sphere of meaning itself, whereupon that problem is reproduced and compounded by its quality, precisely, as theory.

## The Editor and the Real World

Why does Goethe introduce the "editor's" narrative at the end of *Werther*? Or at least, why does he develop it in the particular way he does? A third-person account of Werther's death is perhaps unavoidable, but does it have to involve such an abrupt change of narrative mode? Could the device of a diary, for example, not have transmitted much of the information in the novel's last pages?

The one genuinely enlightening answer to this question that I know of is suggested by Eric Blackall, who argues that the significance of the narrator's intrusion resides precisely in its failure to show Werther to us objectively, and in our awareness of this failure. In both versions of the novel, Blackall points out, even after the editor intervenes, the perspective from which the whole fiction is seen is still essentially Werther's. Documents composed by Werther are still a major portion and source of the text; the impossibility of an objective view is prominent as a theme; and most important, the editor relates a number of

43

facts that, at the very least, it is unlikely he could have learned from living witnesses. Especially Werther's solitary broodings while on his way to pick up Lotte, on the day the peasant boy is apprehended for murder, are something only Werther or an omniscient narrator could know of; but even in the first version, where the peasant boy is missing, far too many details of the Ossian scene are given, including some it is unreasonable to imagine as having been supplied by Lotte. The "editor," then, is not convincing as a person; he is obviously a device for manipulating our perspective. And Blackall suggests that precisely the transparency of this device creates for us a significant double perspective: "we remain with Werther's point of view and yet see it *as a point of view,* not as absolute."[1] The significance of the change from letters to narrative is that it does not effectively alter our point of view, yet compels (or at least encourages) critical reflection concerning the point of view we still occupy.

Blackall's argument can be developed if we begin by inquiring into the external aspect of the fiction. Is the novel really only a "soliloquy"? Werther, after all, writes about things that happen. Are we meant to regard these things merely as symbols of his inner state? Should we not attempt, for ourselves, to form an accurate idea of the people and personal relationships that make up his world? One of the most important additions in the 1787 version is the letter introducing the subplot of the peasant boy, where Werther resolves not to try to get a direct look at the object of the boy's love: "Es ist besser, ich sehe sie durch die Augen ihres Liebhabers; vielleicht erscheint sie mir vor meinen eigenen Augen nicht so, wie sie jetzt vor mir steht, und warum soll ich mir das schöne Bild verderben?" (p. 23, 30 May). "It is better that I see her through the eyes of her lover; in my own sight she would perhaps not appear as she now stands before me, and why should I spoil that lovely image for myself?" The significance of this passage becomes clear when we recall that these are the last words before Lotte's entrance upon the scene. We are thus warned that we will receive a distorted image of Lotte, and so are challenged to form a clearer picture of what she is really like. In the same letter, Werther stresses the inability of language to convey an exact sense of the way things are; again, we are reminded that we must seek somehow behind the language, to form an idea of Werther's actual world. Nor does this invitation to look at the world as a world, not merely as the symbol of an anguish, emerge only in the second version of the novel. Precisely Werther's obvious failure to perceive with any sort of objective clarity, in both versions, tantalizes us, challenges us to do better; and the challenge has of course been accepted often enough by commentators.[2]

The fictional object that most attracts our attention, however, is Lotte. Not only are we challenged to ask what sort of person she really is, and why she is so attached to Werther, but we are given quite sufficient evidence for a dispassionate answer to this question. Undoubtedly Lotte is a capable, energetic, and relatively level-headed young woman; but she is also an entirely ordinary young woman, despite Werther's enthusiasm about her intellect (*Geist*) and artistic sensitivity. She has read *The Vicar of Wakefield* and Klopstock's "Frühlingsfeier" well enough to know vaguely what they are about—although even here, I fail to see how "domestic life" characterizes Goldsmith's focus better than "fortune and disaster" (p. 29, 16 June). But where the occasion, the thunderstorm, appears to call for a quotation from Klopstock—where she could have recited the magnificent line, "Und der geschmetterte Wald dampft"— the best Lotte can manage is to pronounce the poet's not very euphonious surname. Whereupon Werther bursts into tears, borne along, presumably, on a sympathetic wave of knowledge and feeling. We, however, have cause to doubt whether his heart and Lotte's really beat in time with each other here, for he has already expressed strongly his need to *escape* from books and learning and poetry, except Homer (p. 10, 13 May; p. 13, 17 May). Indeed, he experiences the very idea of art as a temptation that spoils his pleasure in nature; he can feel "das Wehen des Allliebenden," "the breath of the all-loving," but the recollection of his art—"if only you could express that"—transforms his joy into despair: "I am crushed by this thought, I succumb to the power and glory of these visions" (p. 8, 10 May). And Goethe makes this yet clearer in the second version, where, in the same letter that challenges us to think objectively about Lotte, Werther complains, "muß es denn immer gebosselt sein, wenn wir Theil an einer Naturerscheinung nehmen sollen?" (p. 21, 30 May), "does it always have to be tarted up for us to sympathize with something in nature?" Precisely what he complains of is what Lotte then does; her reaction to an impressive natural phenomenon, quite literally, is "mit einem gestempelten Kunstworte drein [stolpern]" (p. 112, 11 June), "to blunder in with a fashionable artistic term," as Werther says later of the prince whose guest he is. On the face of it, Lotte's response to the thunderstorm is affected. Surely Shakespeare is as important to us as Klopstock was to that generation of Germans, but do we immediately think of Lear when it thunders? Does *The Winter's Tale* spring to mind when I am pursued by a bear? There is nothing extraordinary about Lotte's mind or character; or at least we have no evidence that there is. She is perfectly content to gossip callously about others' troubles (pp. 125–26, 26 Oct.); and Werther himself later accuses her of Philistinism when she offers a pat (but not at all implausible) psychological explanation of his behavior (p. 157).

Lotte has artistic and cultural pretensions, which it seems are not fully justified; and we may at least suspect that she is a habitual breaker of hearts—we think of the mad boy and of the warning Werther receives against falling in love with her. On this basis we can form a clear idea of her history and situation, and of the reason she is attracted to Werther. Her family had moved to the country only after her mother's death; she had been brought up in the city, or as we may assume, in a more exciting social and cultural atmosphere. She is therefore accustomed to thinking of social and especially cultural pursuits—in that age of intellectual ladies' clubs and literary annuals "for ladies of education"—as the proper occupation for young womanhood. This is why she clings to Werther; he is not only an admirer, a flattering entourage of one, but also her lifeline to a fuller world, her personal minister of culture, whose Greek and sketching are "zwei Meteore" (p. 13, 17 May) in her nonintellectual and socially uneventful surroundings. Toward the end of the first book, in the midst of Werther's intensifying passion, we are struck by one peculiarly quiet image: "ich sitze oft auf den Obstbäumen in Lottens Baumstück mit dem Obstbrecher, der langen Stange, und hole die Birnen aus dem Gipfel. Sie steht unten und nimmt sie ab, wenn ich sie ihr herunter lasse" (pp. 78–79, 28 Aug.). "I often sit up in the trees in Lotte's orchard, with a fruit-picker on its long pole, and pick pears from the highest branches. She stands below and takes them when I reach them down to her." Werther's function in Lotte's universe, that is, is to perch aloft and secure for her an otherwise unattainable intellectual amusement and nourishment.

Werther attempts to impose upon Lotte and himself—hence also upon his reader (Wilhelm) and the novel's reader (us)—a vague idea of natural personal excellences in Lotte that justify his passion. Lotte, in turn, has certain personal needs that prompt her to buy into the relationship, but in the posture (however hypocritical or deluded) of imposing a needful limit to its passionate component. The tensions that follow inevitably are the main action of the novel. What is important, however, is to recognize that the double perspective Blackall speaks of is present not only at the end of the novel, but throughout, as an integral part of the structure. We are strictly limited to Werther's point of view, since we have only his letters before us; yet precisely the form of the letter, in its limited narrative authority, leaves us room to form a relatively objective idea of how things are. Blackall's perception—that despite the switch to a narrator at the end, our point of view with respect to the novel's fiction does not change—is thus rather more deeply applicable than it at first appears. Even the definite doubleness created by the editor's intrusion is not something new, but represents an aspect of our relation to the text which, surprisingly, does not change, despite the radical change in mode of presentation.

Why, however, does Goethe create that double perspective in the first place? Merely to show the disharmony between subjective and objective reality, between "Innenwelt" and "Außenwelt," as they are called in much *Werther* criticism?

## The Ego and the Whole

Let us turn for a moment to another work of young Goethe that is relevant here, the enthusiastic address on Shakespeare. Shakespeare, especially Hamlet, hovering "zwischen Sein und Nichtsein" (p. 130, 15 Nov.), "between being and not being," is a constant presence in the background of *Werther,* and the image of the "Raritäten Kasten" from the Shakespeare speech (WA, 37:133)[3] also occurs to Werther in looking at court life (p. 96, 20 Jan.). But more important for understanding the novel is Goethe's remark that Shakespeare's plays "drehen sich alle um den geheimen Punckt ⸗: den noch kein Philosoph gesehen und bestimmt hat:⸗ in dem das Eigenthümliche unsres Ich's, die prätendirte Freyheit unsres Willens, mit dem nothwendigen Gang des Ganzen zusammenstösst," "turn on the secret point (which no philosopher has yet seen and determined) where the characteristic quality of our ego, the pretended freedom of our will, collides with the necessary operation of the whole." Is it merely a question here of the conflict between "Innenwelt" and "Außenwelt," between the way we see things and the way they really are? If so, why does Goethe call the point of collision "secret"? I act in accordance with my own view of things, and my intention is thwarted because my view of things had been subjectively limited; what is "secret" or mysterious or philosophically unfathomable about this?

We must recognize that "das Eigenthümliche unsres Ich's" stands in apposition to "die prätendirte Freyheit unsres Willens"; the uniqueness of our ego *is* our sense or belief that we are free; the ego, in other words, is here defined as a *point of view*, or a manner of viewing, by which things appear provisional, malleable, translucent, symbolic, subject to our arbitrary choice and responsive to our feelings. And the "nothwendiger Gang des ganzen," correspondingly, refers not to some specific idea of fate but rather to the point of view, or manner of viewing, by which all things appear indissolubly related through the laws of cause and effect; it refers to our sense of the world-whole as firmly organized by the principle of sufficient reason, by the category of causality.

The "ego" and the "necessary progress of the whole" are points of view or manners of viewing, and it is significant that just this duality of points of view figures prominently in Werther's development. On his early outing with Lotte to the parsonage with the walnut trees, he argues against the idea that ill-humor is a natural disease that must run its inevitable course; we must learn to assert our freedom, our ego, for "no one knows the extent of his powers till he has tried them" (p. 45, 1 July). But then Albert arrives, Werther's manner of viewing things changes, and in the conversation on suicide he defends exactly the opposite position, that emotional anguish can, after all, have the quality of an irreversible pathological process that must end in death (pp. 68–99, 12 Aug.). Or we think of his two opposed ways of looking at nature: as a mirror to his soul, a source of strength and exaltation (this the ego-attitude); and on the other hand, as a "lacquered miniature" (p. 128, 3 Nov.), or indeed as a pitiless "monster" (p. 76, 18 Aug.). We think of Homer and Ossian, of the endlessly resourceful Odysseus as opposed to the utterly resourceless resignation imagined by Macpherson.

In any case, we cannot make sense of the passage from the Shakespeare speech except by understanding the "ego" and the "whole" as points of view. If

we take the "necessary progress of the whole" to refer to an objective orderliness
in history that collides with our confused perception of our own situation, then
we cannot account for the approving assertion, in the same paragraph, that
"[Shakespeares] Plane sind, nach dem gemeinen Styl zu reden, keine Plane,"
"Shakespeare's plots are, in the common way of talking, no plots at all"; surely
a strict logical tightness of plot, even if not exactly in the sense of "rules,"
would be needed to symbolize the inevitability of the "whole" of history.[4]
What Goethe emphasizes, however, is the natural authenticity of Shakespeare's
characters, and what he means by authentic humanness is indicated in his very
first sentence: "Mir kommt vor, das sey die edelste von unsern Empfindungen,
die Hoffnung, auch dann zu bleiben, wenn das Schicksaal uns zur allgemeinen
Nonexistenz zurückgeführt zu haben scheint." "It seems to me that the noblest
of our feelings is the hope of continuing to exist even when fate appears to have
conducted us back into general nonexistence." We are authentically human
when we experience at its greatest intensity the collision between our sense of
indomitable being—"Ich! Da ich mir alles binn," "I! who am everything to
myself," or as Werther insists, "Wir *sind* ja!" (p. 178)—and our recognition
"dass keiner sein Ziel erreicht," that we are helpless in the machine of the
world-whole. And the point at which this collision occurs is not in the world
but *in the self*, which is how it is "secret." Only our own character and courage
determine the depth to which we experience it as a collision, as can be seen
by the negative example of those who live in the "Elysium, des sogenanndten
guten Geschmacks, wo sie . . . halb sind, halb nicht sind . . . nicht müde genug
zu ruhen und doch zu faul . . . um tähtig zu seyn," "the Elysium of so-called
good taste, where they halfway are, and halfway are not, not tired enough to
rest and yet too lazy to be active."

    The secret point at which the two forces named in the Shakespeare
piece and represented in the novel collide is thus *the happening of human self-
consciousness;* for the forces are two points of view that each individual occupies
with respect to himself. In the speech, however, self-consciousness is seen as a
distinction, a measure of our nobility, whereas in *Werther* it appears primarily
as a problem. At this point we return to the crucial question of chapter 1: "O
was ist der Mensch, daß er über sich klagen darf!" (p. 5, 4 May). What is this
creature who, with respect to his own being, occupies two distinct points of
view, which clash as accuser and accused? How can I still *be* that person with
whose conduct, in a broader view of things, I am dissatisfied?

    That the two points of view exist is undeniable: that we feel, desire,
and act, thus have pretensions to freedom of the will, while on the other hand
we also observe these motions critically, tracing their causes, calculating their
effects, recognizing their ultimate futility. But the relation with the Shakespeare
speech brings to light a further aspect of Werther's question, namely: where is
the *one* secret point at which these two halves of us meet and are revealed as

expressions of the one entity which I after all am? Or as Werther asks more than once, "What *is* man?" We can, in any case, now see the connection between the early Shakespeare address and the passage in *Wilhelm Meisters Lehrjahre,* Book 3 (WA, 21:310), where Shakespeare's figures are compared to clocks with glass cases, their inner workings visible. The secret point *within* us, at which our apparently multiple being is fully (if self-contradictorily) realized, is what Shakespeare, in Goethe's view, uncovers.

The existence of two points of view with respect to ourselves is the crux of Werther's situation; his oscillations between an ego-oriented and a causality-oriented point of view are not merely superficial symptoms of his disorder. He himself, in his letter on the concepts of "Here" and "There"—which is written in a relatively good mood—explains the basic human difficulty as one of point of view (p. 39, 21 June). And what else is his desire for death, if not a desire for self-unity, for the supersedure of consciousness, of that division between points of view that disrupts our inner life? The secret point at which we are a single, cohesive, indestructible entity, where the question "What is man?" is answered, is constantly the object of his yearning and is associated by him with death, the elimination of conscious self-division, the return to oneness. Even with regard to speculative theology, there is something in him that resists the doctrine of the Son of God as an unworthy self-division in the deity (p. 130, 15 Nov.; p. 138, 30 Nov.); he yearns for the Father alone.

All this is already present in the first version of *Werther;* but again, Goethe's revision throws it into sharper relief. There is a very significant letter which, in the rearrangement of the material, is placed as the last letter before the entrance of the editor; it concludes with these words (which are also present but differently situated in the 1774 version):

> Was ist der Mensch, der gepriesene Halbgott! [Practically a quotation from *Hamlet* (II.ii.304–24).] Ermangeln ihm nicht eben da die Kräfte, wo er sie am nöthigsten braucht? Und wenn er in Freude sich aufschwingt, oder im Leiden versinkt, wird er nicht in beiden eben da aufgehalten, eben da zu dem stumpfen kalten Bewußtsein wieder zurückgebracht, da er sich in der Fülle des Unendlichen zu verlieren sehnte? (p. 140, 6 Dec.)

> [What is man, that celebrated demigod! Do his powers not fail him just where he needs them most? And when he swings himself aloft in joy, or sinks in sorrow, is he not impeded in both just there, not just there brought back to his dull cold consciousness, where he had yearned to lose himself in the abundance of the infinite?]

Consciousness is the enemy: that second, unshakably objective point of view by which our sense of freedom and power, our submergence in *one* feeling, *one* mode of being, our sense of ourselves as an indivisible surge of energy or sensitivity, is repeatedly thwarted. This passage of course also raises, at a conspicuous point in the work's structure, a more specific question: how does Werther actually manage to commit suicide? If consciousness always interrupts our passionate feelings and actions, how does he actually achieve a "losing of himself" in the infinite? Why do his "powers" not fail him at the last minute? Does the concentrated decisiveness presupposed by suicide, the most irrevocable of acts, not perhaps constitute Werther's *overcoming* of his tormented doubleness?

We will come back to that question, but let us first recapitulate. The double perspective discussed by Blackall characterizes not only the second version of the novel, and not only the concluding third-person section; it characterizes the stance we find ourselves adopting with respect to the work as a whole in both versions. Moreover, not only we, in the process of reading, are subject to a double perspective, but Werther is as well, in enacting his destiny. This parallel produces complications and paradoxes. If Werther's anguish is constituted mainly by the conscious separation he repeatedly experiences from his own self, then *our* detached perspective upon his situation, by analogy, becomes a kind of sympathy with him, just as our sympathy must in turn necessarily involve a certain distance—as does our sympathy with any character in fiction. Goethe, in *Werther,* is thus operating with a rather extensive complex of relationships between the fictional psychology of his character and the presumed actual psychology of his reader, a complex that requires us to develop further the idea of the role of the reader that was established in chapter 1.

## The Reflecting Reader

"Double perspective" is the fundamental structural principle of *Werther,* reflected homothetically on the levels of content, form, and anticipated psychology of the reader. This is not particularly surprising, for the novel as a genre tends more or less naturally to employ multiple points of view; but Goethe's exploitation of the genre's possibilities is remarkably intense and consistent. For instance: because it consists mainly of Werther's own letters, the text gives the impression of being a single extended act of self-assertion on Werther's part, a manifestation of "pretended freedom," of the ego's point of view as a willing ego. But on the other hand, most of the letters are written to a man who disagrees on important issues. That these are letters, therefore, and not, for example, a diary, obliges Werther to explain, justify, or excuse himself repeatedly, to view his initiatives as belonging to a causally and morally ordered world-whole. Thus the mere device of the epistolary novel, as Goethe uses it, produces yet again that central double perspective.

But this recalls our original question. If the epistolary form is so appropriate, why does Goethe abandon it earlier than he absolutely needs to? and why does he abandon it in favor of an omniscient narrator, a conventional literary device which, by contrast with the subtlety of implication that precedes it, is wholly transparent as a device? This question can be answered very simply. The point at which the epistolary form gives way to third-person narration, in an important sense, *is* "the secret point," the "Punckt . . . in dem das Eigenthümliche unsres Ich's, die prätendirte Freyheit unsres Willens, mit dem nothwendigen Gang des Ganzen zusammenstösst." The transparency of the literary device with which the novel concludes is calculated to draw our attention *to our situation as readers*. Goethe's concern for this aspect of his text is reflected in the care he takes to prepare the ground more thoroughly in the final version, by adding a number of specific references to the art of poetry (p. 21, 30 May; p. 118, 4 Sept.; p. 133, 26 Nov.), and by emphasizing in the third-person section the variousness of opinions concerning people's "Sinnesarten" (p. 141), "personal ways of thinking," which reminds us that we too, in judging the characters, are limited by our own more or less unconscious habits of thought and by those of the "editor." The abrupt change to a different narrative mode raises for us the question of where we stand as readers, and so provokes our critical reflection upon the doubleness of perspective that has characterized our readerly situation.

A conscious distance is thus interposed between ourselves now and ourselves as we had been (we must imagine) while reading the epistolary section. But in spite of this distance—herein lies the significance of Blackall's argument—our stance as readers, the double perspective we occupy, has not changed. We are wrenched away from ourselves, compelled to view our situation objectively as a part of a larger whole. And yet our situation is not changed; our perceptual relation to the fiction is as complex and difficult as ever, and is complicated in the same way it had been before. Thus the two points of view we occupy as we read not only are in tension with each other, but in a sense are actually made to "collide" at the point where the narrative mode changes, in that a persistent conscious distance for a moment collapses into no distance at all. Our receptivity to this event in the process of reading, moreover, has been cultivated carefully, for we have observed the same sort of thing happening over and over again to Werther: he becomes critically conscious of himself, yet his consciousness only deepens or aggravates the state of affairs it criticizes.

Or let us consider the situation of the reader via the categories of freedom and limitation, "Freiheit" and "Einschränkung," which represent an aspect of the point-of-view dichotomy defined in the Shakespeare speech, and are also a recurrent theme in Werther's brooding. In the main portion of the novel we experience Werther's point of view as a restriction; if our range of vision were not limited by his passions and prejudices, we would be able to see the whole fictional situation a good deal more distinctly. And by the same token, the process of inference by which we piece together at least some "facts of the case" must appear to us as the domain of our own free mental activity, our ego. But then the third-person narrator begins to tell us the facts of the case; and because of the obviousness of the device, and of the narrator's own prejudices— or in the first version, somewhat less clearly, because of the exaggerated and obviously futile legalistic fastidiousness that Goethe imitates from Kestner— we are also induced to *question* the facts now presented to us. Therefore, by analogy, we must question our own earlier inferences about "facts" as well. What had earlier seemed our freedom, as opposed to Werther's imprisoning self-deception, is now revealed as our own inevitable imprisonment within a preconceived idea of things. Like Werther, who twists everything into an excuse for dying; like the first version's narrator with his legalistic complacency, or the second version's, who snobbishly associates his own attitude with that of "people who are not of the common run" (p. 141); indeed, like the little children who insist that Werther always tell the same story in exactly the same words: we too, in reading and inferring and imagining, are merely insisting on a fictional world derived from our own habits of thought. And yet, we could not experience this transformation of our freedom into our limitedness if we were not *still* asserting our freedom, our independence, our critical detachment not only from Werther's point of view, but now from the narrator's as well, in the same way as before. Thus, as in the later sonnet "Natur und Kunst," the qualities of freedom and limitation, while remaining opposed, are made to imply one another, not as terms of a dialectical progression but as an absolute paradox, a "secret point," inaccessible to systematic philosophy, which has to do with the inexpressible oneness of what we truly are. It is in relation to this paradox, moreover, that other paradoxes in the text must now be understood: the paradox that our detachment from Werther is a kind of sympathy, and our sympathy a kind of distance; that in every aspect of the reading experience, including our critical reflection upon it, we thus undergo some form of identification with Werther; that even in paying attention to Werther, therefore, we are also paying attention to the question of what we are doing as readers; that *Werther,* in other words, is very much *a novel about reading.*[5]

## Werther's Freedom

If the paradox of freedom and limitation is intricately knotted with respect to the reader, the same is true with respect to Werther. And for Werther, as for the reader, the change to third-person narrative is a crucial point. That change, first of all, transforms Werther from a voice into an object. He is no longer the source of the text, but its subject matter; his own words are now merely evidence, no longer the whole substance of the presentation. He has become, by comparison with his earlier function, an insect upon a pin. The "epic preterite," whatever else it may be, is still a preterite and so imprisons him inside a presumably completed causal structure. But he is also thus removed, to an extent, from our field of vision, which raises the issue of what we do *not* know about him, his mystery, his ineffable personal center, his freedom. We can understand this by way of a question that Goethe was at pains to emphasize in his revision: how does Werther manage to carry out the extreme act of suicide, despite the interference of critical consciousness?

This question is not only answered by the editor, it is answered ad nauseam. Over and over we are shown how Werther's suicide gradually becomes inevitable, how his calm decision is gradually hammered into shape by inner conflicts, personal tensions, and external pressures. Nothing is omitted; the subtlest inner motions in the characters, the minutest details of their relations to each other and to themselves, are scrutinized. The trouble is that this impressive web of explanation—obviously—explains nothing whatever.

The pistol is freshly loaded, therefore presumably reliable; Werther, having sat down with his wine, takes up the weapon, places the muzzle carefully over his right eye, pulls the trigger—and misses. He does not actually miss, as he is tricked into doing in Nicolai's parody; he does manage to destroy himself. But he does a remarkably messy job of it, and it takes him a full twelve hours to expire. The extent to which Goethe reproduces the circumstances of Jerusalem's actual suicide is of no special significance here. Nor is the comparison with the hero's drawn-out dying in, say, *Hamlet* or *Miss Sara Sampson;* both Hamlet and Sara have unfinished business to take care of, whereas Werther does nothing but bleed and death-rattle. My point is that the image of useless disorder in Werther's twelve hours of dying conflicts with the idea of his deed as the plucking of a ripe fruit, as the effortless natural and logical result of sufficient causes. We are, rather, given the impression of an event that could have happened completely otherwise, the impression of an *un*necessary event, an event we must regard either as sheer accident (if Werther had missed by a bit more he would still be alive) or as an expression of uncaused freedom, a gratuitous or strictly arbitrary act.

This impression is prepared for in Werther's own utterances. At the beginning of his last letter to Lotte, he prides himself on his ability to discuss, "without Romantic overstraining," his supposed "decision" to die ("Es ist beschlossen, Lotte, ich will sterben" [p. 159]). But this calm pose is itself obviously "overstrained," and later, after the Ossian reading, he continues: "Wie kann ich vergehen? wie kannst du vergehen? Wir *sind* ja!—Vergehen!—Was heißt das? Das ist wieder ein Wort! ein leerer Schall ohne Gefühl für mein Herz. . . . Sterben! Grab! ich verstehe die Worte nicht!" (pp. 178–79). "How can I pass away? How can you pass away? After all, we *are*!—Pass away! What does that mean? It's just a word, an empty sound producing no feeling in my heart. Death! The grave! I don't understand these words." What this passage shows is not how far he has come, but how far he still has to go before he can claim to have "decided" to die; surely at some point, before the end, he will have to "understand" the word "death," and we have no way of judging whether his resolution will be equal to the test. The suggestion, especially in view of the actual messiness of the event, is that Werther's suicide, up to the last minute, is *not* the inevitable result of sufficient causes. To the question of how he manages to carry out the deed, we must answer: we do not know. At the last moment something happens which, as far as we can tell, is uncaused, hence beyond our systematic comprehension, something we should perhaps have to call "free."

Or we think of his last letter as a whole, which is clearly intended to torment Lotte in the very process of exalting her, and so continues what had always been his manner of treating her. He has by no means abandoned the confused habits of his life; his "decision" to die is not yet complete. His thinking is not concentrated but diffuse. Perhaps it is even significant that before killing himself he loads *both* pistols ("Sie sind geladen" [p. 189]), which does not say much for his single-minded focus on suicide. Again, Goethe takes steps, in his revision, to make these points clearer. In the first version, the letter of 8 December, in which Werther admits a definite doubt concerning his "Muth zu sterben" (p. 152), "courage to die," comes just before the change to third person. In the revision the letter is dated four days later and quoted by the editor, which denies us the opportunity of imagining (as we otherwise might) that the change in narrative approach reflects, at this point, the transformation of Werther's coming death from a mere possibility into a necessity.

Yet further, why does Werther read *Emilia Galotti* in his last moments? Merely because the play is about a passionate young person who desires death? If Werther were fully and calmly determined upon suicide as a means of relieving others' difficulties as well as his own, he could have chosen a more appropriate play without even looking beyond the works of Lessing, the play *Philotas*, where the hero kills himself to avoid forcing his father into a serious military disadvantage. Emilia does not even do her own killing; it is done for her by her father, in response to her invocation of a literary precedent from Livy. But for what aspect of his death does Werther invoke the precedent of *Emilia*? Does he imagine himself somehow a victim, and if so, whose? Or insofar as his suicide is in part an act of murderous psychological aggression against Lotte—which nearly succeeds, "Man fürchtete für Lottens Leben" (p. 191), "people feared for Lotte's life"—is he casting *her* as Emilia, and himself as the Prince or Odoardo or perhaps Appiani? The reason Emilia gives for feeling she must die is that she detects in herself a force that will undermine her resolution and principles: "I have blood, father, blood as youthful and warm as anyone's." Werther could wish to apply this to Lotte in any number of possibly contradictory ways. Or does he apply it to his own feelings? Is he struggling against his own "blood," his own still unconquered involvement in life? In any case, the very complexity of association suggested by *Emilia* is significant. The focus of achieved decision does not yet characterize Werther's thoughts; his decision, the necessity of his death, is not actually there until the last instant when he manages—somehow—to pull the trigger.

The effect of the change to third-person narration, then, is both to limit Werther, to make him an object, and also (since the narrator's explanations prove inadequate) to liberate him, to suggest his quality as a free ego. Thus freedom and limitation are again made to imply each other, to occupy the same square, as it were, in the narrative grid; and our attention, again, or our speculation, is thus focused on that "secret point" where we are the whole of what we are, our will, our character, our fate, all in one.

And yet, there is a disquieting aspect to this situation from the reader's point of view. Werther's despair is still necessary, the logical result of a valid general perception of the human condition. But his death is not necessary in the same way. Whether or not we insist on regarding his suicide as an instance of truly free activity, the very opening of the question of freedom (which we can hardly avoid) presupposes that that suicide, considered objectively, has the quality of *accident*. Werther's suicide, which, in our reading alongside Montaigne, is the crucial point at which the reader's path diverges from the character's, thus no longer distinguishes the reader's situation after all. It is possible, after all, to *be* Werther and continue living. The knowledge that Goethe himself, the first reader, in a strong sense *is* Werther, yet continues to live, belongs ineradicably to the novel's historical existence. And in Goethe's response to Nicolai's parody, the "Anekdote zu den Freuden des jungen Werthers" (WA, 38:37–43), Werther and Lotte themselves appear primarily as readers of their own situation.

## Reading Doubled

The interpretation of *Werther* suggested in chapter 1 can still be salvaged. No matter how complicatedly our identification with Werther, the analogy of our situation as readers with his fictional situation, is developed, this development can always be regarded as a sharpening of the paradox of freedom and limitation, hence as a challenge to our sense of our own freedom, as training in what Montaigne calls the "arduous" task of being free. But the amount of reflection on the process of reading that is suggested, the extent to which *Werther* is a novel about reading, is still disturbing. That there should be a specific role for the reader in generating the novel's meaning, we have seen, is historically understandable. And it does not seem out of the question to argue that the reader, in performing his role, undergoes a kind of ethical training that constitutes, precisely, the novel's meaning. But surely there is a stage in our reflecting on the reader's role where its quality as training is supplanted by the quality of teaching, where the text's meaning is reduced, after all (in the process of our thinking about it), to the form of doctrine—say, the doctrine of a "secret point" of collision at the center of human nature.

Therefore, if a positive understanding of *Werther,* by way of the role of the reader, is to be sustained, it must take a somewhat more radical form, a form like that suggested by Wolfgang Kayser, in an essay on the novel's origins, where he asks, "How can one read *Werther* and nevertheless keep the will to live?"[6] Kayser's point is that Goethe himself provides a model for the reader here, in that his awareness of artistic mastery, his enjoyment of art as a form of playing, enables him, personally, to survive the Werther experience. If we apply this type of argument to the reader, however—and so take advantage of its proximity to Schiller's later doctrine of aesthetic "play"—then it turns out that our idea of the reader's role includes not only a detailed reflection upon his relation to *Werther* itself, but also a complicated philosophical reflection upon the nature of art in general. By being a work of fiction (we must now recognize), an artistic construct contrived by man for his own enjoyment—and especially the second version's conventionally omniscient, only perfunctorily disguised narrator reminds us of this quality very strongly—the novel offers us practice in deriving pleasure from exactly that paradoxical quality of human existence which Werther takes as a reason for suicide. It trains us, here and now, to take the potentially destructive torment of conscious life as an interestingly complex game, since we are already doing this by reading. Werther's personal difficulty, especially during his diplomatic service, can be plausibly diagnosed as an absolute unwillingness to take life as a game, even though he recognizes the possibility (pp. 95–96, 8 Jan.; pp. 98–99, 8 Feb.). But as readers of a novel— as readers (let it be noted) of that extravagant sort of novel which Werther and Lotte, at their initial meeting, would probably agree to despise—we are presented at least with the opportunity of adopting the opposite attitude.

Of course, playing the game of life does not mean blinding ourselves to its difficulty or danger. Werther's point of view, the perception of our consciously divided condition as problem and anguish, is necessary that the game have shape or direction, that we play it as a constant precarious balancing on the verge of self-unity, but without ever becoming absolute, or even very earnest, about achieving self-unity—since actual achievement of the "secret point" means death. Years later, Goethe compares the quest for self-knowledge to a curious kind of target shooting in which we should not insist too strongly upon hitting the bull's-eye.[7] Or we think of the notion of poetry as a game of deliberate "Irrthum," "error," in the "Vorspiel" to *Faust*. The most general ethical statement we can make about life is that, by analogy with the reading of the novel, it must have the character of a game, in which the raw material of despair is somehow transmuted into enjoyment; and this "somehow," though indefinable, is not unattainable, for it is already achieved, or at least foreshadowed, by our reading of this particular novel *as* a novel. Wherever we lay hold of *Werther* we turn up insoluble difficulties and paradoxes, and we recognize, by understanding the hero's fate, that these difficulties are deadly; we, as it were, like Werther, are playing with a pair of loaded pistols. But we are still *playing;* and self-destruction is no more a necessity for us than it is, up to the last moment, for Werther.

This is the form that a positive, aesthetically oriented reading of *Werther* must ultimately take. And there are any number of reasons for being profoundly dissatisfied with such a reading. The co-optive tendency of the aesthetic, for example, has now not only corrupted a potentially liberating vision of the human condition; it has also smuggled into our condition as readers the comparatively desperate and easily abused or perverted proposition (which Schiller later systematizes) that a healthy, balanced human existence is achievable only by way of the practice or experience of art—a proposition Montaigne might have considered insane. And the role of the reader, which we started by understanding, reasonably enough, as a means of generating meaning, has now become: to represent, to exemplify, indeed to determine and organize life itself. The logic of the aesthetic argument on *Werther* leads us eventually to the proposition that reading, in a strong sense, *is life,* which as readers we find ourselves living with a special authenticity and completeness that we must strive to reproduce elsewhere in our existence.

This proposition, however, that life itself is a kind of adjunct to reading, is wrong—not necessarily false, but wrong, in the sense that the tail's wagging the dog is wrong. Its inherent wrongness is in fact the purport of the climactic Ossian scene in *Werther* itself. Hence the situation that I call "reading doubled." Our reflection upon the process of reading *Werther* presents us with an entirely cogent interpretation of the text. But the same process, and its reflection, have implications that are wrong, implications that must stem eventually from something that is wrong with, or wrong about, reading itself. We *are* readers, unalterably; the condition of being nonreaders of *Werther* is no longer accessible to us. But at the same time, we cannot shake off the intimation that there is something fundamentally wrong with reading, or with being readers.

## "Prometheus," *Werther,* and "Ganymed"

*Werther* is not the only work of young Goethe in relation to which we can detect a sense of the wrongness of reading. The poem "Prometheus," for example, is sometimes taken to represent an opposite extreme to *Werther. Werther* is labile, "Prometheus" energetic; *Werther* depicts helplessness, "Prometheus" defiance. *Werther* abounds in complexities, "Prometheus" is brutally simple. But are the two works really that different?

The first section of the poem can be read without much trouble as a dramatic speech, Prometheus's defiance of Zeus. But in the second section we are enabled to see through the text to a level of distinctly modern thought, Enlightenment freethinking—just as, in *Werther,* we are challenged to penetrate the text and judge the fictional world objectively. The idea that the gods require men's sacrifices as nourishment and would starve, "wären / Nicht Kinder und Bettler / Hoffnungsvolle Thoren,"[8] "if children and beggars were not hopeful fools," clearly suggests that the gods *exist* only in men's foolish belief; and this idea is then developed in the scornful words, "als wenn drüber wär' / Ein Ohr . . . Ein Herz, wie mein's," "as if there were an ear up there, a heart like mine." God is exposed as a mere idea in man's mind, and a distinctly harmful idea at that: a false hope that distracts us from the humanitarian responsibility of dealing directly with real suffering in ourselves and others ("Hast du die Schmerzen gelindert," "have you ever soothed pain"); and a false humility that distracts us from the fruitful appreciation of our own real creative power, our ability to shape our own destiny ("Hast du nicht alles selbst vollendet, / Heilig glühend Herz?" "You, my sacred burning heart, have you not accomplished everything for yourself?"). The poem's speaker is not pleading for a more modern idea of god, as opposed to the notion of brute supernatural strength embodied in a Zeus; the idea of god represented by "Zeus" in the poem *is* clearly modern, presupposing the development of European Christianity, the idea of a god of the oppressed, of "children and beggars," the idea of a god who expects his believers to turn away from the things of this world: "das Leben hassen," "to hate life."

But if the poem teaches that man must rely on himself, not on some imagined "Nobodaddy aloft," then why does the poet put on the mask of Prometheus defying Zeus, why does he suggest a dramatic situation that requires the real (or at least effective) existence of god? At the end, Prometheus boasts to Zeus of having implanted in his creatures the defiant resolve, "dein nicht zu achten, / Wie ich!" "to pay you no respect, like me!" But this attitude is itself a form of *Achten* or respect; it is not mere contempt or disregard, but active defiance, thus in part a tribute to the effectiveness of the power against which it is directed. And if the fiction of Prometheus's defying Zeus is appropriate, why is it not maintained more consistently? Why does Goethe go out of his way to garble the myth of the titanomachy, as if this had been primarily Prometheus's affair in which Zeus had claimed a share of the credit? There is perhaps no reason why Prometheus should not be taken as a symbol of man's throwing off his reliance on supernatural aid; but the mention of the Titans reminds us of Prometheus as Zeus's helper, not vice versa. In any case, the questions thus raised are similar to those we ask about the narrator in *Werther:* why the change of narrative mode in the first place if it does not substantially change our point of view; why the editorial pose if it is made so easy to see through?

To the more general question, in regard to "Prometheus," there is a relatively clear answer. Human self-reliance and self-esteem presuppose human self-definition; we must know what constitutes our humanness, and from what it must be distinguished. In the later poem "Das Göttliche" ("Edel sei der Mensch"), this purpose, definition by contrast, is served by the ideas of blind nature and blind fortune, both of which, in "Prometheus," are associated with Zeus ("übe . . . An Eichen dich und Bergeshöhn"; "Weil nicht alle / Blüthenträume reiften"), and perhaps also, paradoxically, with the Titans. In order to be fully human, that is, we must clearly distinguish our own ethical and sensitive being from the unfeeling world at large. But the purpose of this distinction is that it remain in our mind as a precaution against unworthy reliance on supposedly higher powers; even in the act of rejecting the idea of a benevolent deity who does for us what we ought to do for ourselves, we thus also perpetuate that idea in our thinking, where it remains a danger. This paradox is obvious at the end of "Prometheus," where the word "achten" reminds us that defiance is a kind of tribute; and it is also present in "Das Göttliche," in the following lines:

> Und wir verehren
> Die Unsterblichen,
> Als wären sie Menschen,
> Thäten im Großen,
> Was der Beste im Kleinen
> Thut oder möchte.

[And we honor the immortals as if they were men, and were doing on a large scale what the best man does or desires to do on a small scale.]

If we believe in gods who act humanely "on a large scale," what else is this but to attribute human feeling to the world of nature and fortune, which attribution has been denied only three stanzas earlier? The question—why a poem presupposing the existence of god?—is thus replaced by a philosophical problem: in order to realize our humanity, we must reject the idea of a divinely suffused nature as being irreconcilable with our responsibility for ourselves; but the same idea is also necessary as part of our human self-definition, our sense of who and where we are, and from what we are distinguished.

    The only way out of this problem, in "Prometheus," as far as I can see, involves the role of the reader, and has to do with the inconsistency of the speaker's mythological pose, just as the meaning of *Werther* is suggested by the transparency of the "editor." In both works we must reflect on what we are doing in reading; and in the poem the unnecessariness of the speaker's mask signals us that we are engaging voluntarily in an arbitrary verbal game, which in turn trains us to adopt a flexible, artistic, playful attitude toward our language and thought in general. In the absence of such an attitude, the philosophical dilemma with which the poem confronts us remains insurmountable. What we must learn is to use the idea of god willingly, yet also with a constant unspoken irony by which our human independence is maintained; we must learn to play with the idea, and with the problems it raises, in the same way that we must accept and affirm Werther's point of view, yet manage to enjoy doing so. God must remain a significant and functioning noun in our language, yet a noun which, as in "Das Göttliche," tends to attract verbs in the subjunctive.

Thus we again come into the vicinity of our positive reading of *Werther*. Indeed, Werther himself unwittingly expounds such a reading, unwittingly describes the ethical attitude promoted not only by his own story, but also by the poem "Prometheus," when he writes to Wilhelm: "Du wirst mir also nicht übel nehmen, wenn ich dir dein ganzes Argument einräume, und mich doch zwischen dem *Entweder Oder* durchzustehlen suche" (p. 61, 8 Aug.). "You won't take it badly, I hope, if I admit your whole argument, yet still try to slip through between the Either and the Or." We too, in our turn, must admit Werther's argument—we must adopt his point of view, not only in reading but also in life—yet in such a way as not to draw his logical conclusions, at least not in action. We must grant his sense of irreconcilable alternatives in life—*either* the extravagant "torrent of genius" *or* "the complacent gentlemen" with their "garden-houses, tulip beds and cabbage fields" (pp. 18–19, 26 May), *either* "Freiheit" *or* "Einschränkung," *either* "passions, never far from madness" (p. 67, 12 Aug.) *or* the hopeless dullness of a Philistine existence—and yet our granting of this must be a kind of play, the exercise (to use Werther against himself once more) of an enjoyable intellectual "Combinationsart" (p. 68, 12 Aug.) by which we are enabled to slip between the Either and the Or. And this "must," again, by no means represents an unattainable ideal; merely by reading the novel with a certain skeptical alertness—which is part of how we read novels anyway—we already find ourselves at least in serious training for the game of life thus understood.

But in the case of "Prometheus," as in that of *Werther*, this reading is not at all comfortable, or even acceptable. That we hear it expounded by brooding Werther himself, in fact—if perhaps in fragments, and cryptically—reminds us that, as readers, we have probably already vaulted beyond ethical practice into the domain of theory, a move that our treating life as a game was supposed to have avoided. And again, in "Prometheus" as in *Werther*, our reflection upon the text runs up against the idea that the process of reading, in a sense, is itself already an achievement of the proper conduct of life, an idea that in relation to the poem is even more obviously wrong than in relation to the novel. My manhood, or my humanness, says Prometheus, is not something that comes to me in a moment of reflective intensity (e.g., in reading), but is developed *gradually*, by long experience of the real, is "forged by all-powerful time and eternal fate": "Hat nicht mich zum Manne geschmiedet / Die allmächtige Zeit / Und das ewige Schicksal."

David E. Wellbery has done an extremely detailed reading of "Prometheus" in which the textual perception, taken instance by instance, is close to unassailable. But he summarizes as follows:

> The jury which Prometheus's prosecutory speech brings to the point of judgment, the audience before which the parody is performed, the initiand whom Prometheus conducts through the rite of passage, and the truth disclosed in the hermeneutic process are all one and the same: Prometheus as the addressee of his own act of speech. . . . At every level—pragmatic, narrative, hermeneutic, figurative—the text twists into autoreferential structures in which inside and outside, meta- and object-language, producer and product coincide.[9]

There is clearly no place for a reader in this scheme, except insofar as the reader perhaps somehow simply becomes Prometheus—which would produce an instance of the aesthetic overestimation of reading that I claim Goethe is increasingly suspicious of. In fact, Wellbery cannot make room for a reader in the mechanism of meaning production without violating his own insistence on "the internal consistency of this text" (p. 338). "The 'Prometheus' ode," he asserts, "is the paradoxical enactment of human originality, the self-fashioning of mankind in the medium of poetic language" (p. 345). But does an "enactment" not require a segment of more or less real time in which to unfold? And if so, where but in the process of reading, which would thus be inflated even beyond its aesthetic life-determining role in *Werther*? Precisely to the extent that Wellbery's argument is correct, therefore—and I think it is—it is also evidence not of "consistency" in Goethe's texts, but of their tendency to split open and ooze the wrongness of reading, the wrongness of literature.

The poem "Prometheus," moreover, in its earliest manuscript version, and in all the printed collections of his poems supervised by Goethe himself, is paired with the poem "Ganymed," with which it shares the device of appearing to be a dramatic monologue for a figure from ancient myth. "Prometheus" and "Ganymed" together, in fact, display a form of the Either/Or which both bedevils and defines the ethics of life as a game. Either we insist defiantly upon the strict self-shaping of human existence, and defiantly ignore the idea of divinity that constantly insinuates itself into our very defiance, or we accept the inevitable idea of divinity and attempt to mobilize it on a human plane by deifying our own feelings, especially in relation to nature: "Heilig Gefühl, / Unendliche Schöne!" "Sacred feeling, infinite beauty!" says the poem "Ganymed."

But once we include "Ganymed" in the body of text whose readers, in performing their role, enact the game of life, our sense of a basic wrongness in reading emerges more clearly than ever. As in "Prometheus," there is an incongruity between the title "Ganymed" and what is actually said in the poem, which makes no suggestion whatever of a boy's submission to anal intercourse

with an older lover—in this case the same Zeus who is defied in "Prometheus."
The images that characterize the personified destiny ("Allliebender Vater!")
toward which the poem's speaker feels himself borne aloft, in fact, are markedly
feminine: "In euerm [the clouds'?] Schoose," "an deinen Busen," "In your lap
(or womb)," "to your breast." This is more than just incongruity; it is positive
dishonesty. Whereas in "Prometheus" the incongruity between mythological
mask and Enlightenment content can be understood as an opening, a field,
for our arbitrary activeness, in "Ganymed" the reader is instructed simply to
disregard the obvious associations of the poem's title, to forget (or at least to shut
up) about them—or perhaps to imitate what we might imagine as the speaker's
last moments of innocence before losing his virginity, before discovering that
what his "father" loves is a good deal more specific than the word "all-loving"
suggests. Have we not crossed a line here, from the heroic enterprise of human
world-shaping to the hypocrisy of the sexual prude?[10]

It is even possible that *reading itself* is what we are told to keep quiet
about in "Ganymed," that our pretension, as readers, to a kind of arbitrary
artistic mastery of our condition actually only masks the true character of reading as a both literally and metaphorically unmentionable form of submission,
a willing complicity, perhaps, in the co-optive mechanism of the aesthetic. We
will come back to *Werther* later on, and read it yet once more, with a view to
these worries.

# 3

# Egmont as a Politician

We turn now to Goethe's dramas, but we find that we have not left behind the question of reading. For the idea of reading, in an extended sense, turns out to describe neatly the character and activity of the dramatic figures we will look at; and the wrongness of reading unfolds itself in their fate. As with *Werther,* our discussion of *Egmont* will take pains to clarify the facts of the case, the presence of a world behind the text, as a corrective to those interpretive conventions that tailor the text to a preconceived ideal of rightness, harmony, closure, classicity, satisfaction. Such ideals are here entirely out of place. Goethe's dissatisfaction with literature, his developing sense of what is fundamentally wrong with literature, I contend, is the main motive force in precisely his literary endeavors.

## Who Is Egmont?

*Egmont* is a notoriously actionless play which critics have tended generally to admire (if at all) for its portrayal of character. All Egmont *does,* apparently, is insist upon *being* Egmont. When he is warned that his attempts at conciliation between the Netherlanders and their Spanish government will be reckoned high treason by the Spaniards, his only apparent reaction is to soothe himself by a visit to his bourgeois mistress. By not taking action, he in effect simply kills himself; his character, therefore, the unfettered mode of living that he refuses to relinquish or violate, appears to be the play's main focus. My point, however, is that we do not understand Egmont's character if we do not understand what he *wants.* Since he does not do anything, it seems possible to infer that he does not especially want anything either, except to continue being his own uninhibited self. This inference is not justified. Precisely Egmont's inaction reveals that he has in mind a specific political goal for himself, and I will argue that this element of political motivation is indispensable in the play's psychological architecture.

63

The idea that Egmont is a "nonpolitical individual"[1]—in the sense that his conduct, though it has political consequences, is not politically motivated— follows from the widely accepted idea of his perfect openness of character, or, as Elizabeth Wilkinson says, his achievement of "perfect freedom . . . the fulness of spontaneous living in the moment."[2] Wilkinson does not claim that Egmont is naive; in fact, she explicitly reserves a place for self-consciousness in his inner makeup:

> He represents the Netherlanders' way of life in heightened form. What in them—and in Klärchen—is naive and instinctive, is in him fully conscious and articulate. What he is by nature, he confirms by choice, giving the assent of his mind to the way he must go. The perfect freedom he possesses, freedom from fear, freedom from care, freedom from all possessiveness—this is the whole point of his committing Klärchen to Ferdinand before he dies—this freedom he also pursues by conviction. He believes in it, both in the political sphere and in the sphere of personality. (pp. 67–68)

But this is still an oversimplification. The tension between "nature" and "choice" (or action and contemplation, or naive and sentimental), a tension which is deeply ingrained as a theme in German literature and thought of the period, is a good deal stronger and more central in *Egmont* than Wilkinson is willing to admit.

Wilkinson herself, in the same essay, offers a fine general formulation of Goethe's sense of the tragic:

> For Goethe tragedy does not lie on the periphery of existence, in the exceptional case and the resounding clash, but at its centre. It begins at the point where a cell in order to grow must divide, and resides in the fact that it is the characteristic of all life to tend away from symmetry. In the human sphere it is at the heart of every silent choice in our daily living, in every renunciation and every farewell, even in every achievement, for all achievement is at the cost of infinite potentiality. . . . [Tragedy arises from] the law of compensation, which decrees that there is no gain without a corresponding loss, that one mode of response invariably excludes another because all behaviour, natural and human, takes place in the dimension of time. (p. 73)

Can these general considerations not be applied in a fairly obvious way to *Egmont*? Is Egmont's "choice" of his "perfect freedom" not also necessarily, like every choice, a renunciation of freedom? Does Egmont's "fully conscious and articulate" attitude, considered as a "mode of response," not invariably exclude "the fulness of spontaneous living in the moment"?

Wilkinson is correct in what she says about the play's "verbal texture" (p. 71). From the very beginning, where we hear of his effortlessly perfect marksmanship,[3] to the very end, where he compares his untimely death to the destruction of a growing tree (pp. 280–81), the simple, natural freedom of Egmont's being is insisted upon. Egmont himself invents the most extreme metaphor for this naturalness when he says: "Und wenn ich ein Nachtwandler wäre, und auf dem gefährlichen Gipfel eines Hauses spazierte, ist es freund-schaftlich mich bei'm Namen zu rufen und mich zu warnen, zu wecken und zu tödten?" (p. 219). "If I were a somnambulist walking on a dangerous roof-peak, is it the part of a true friend to call me by name and thus warn me, wake me and kill me?" (Note the shift from subjunctive to indicative, as if this were Egmont's *actual* condition.) But the metaphor involves an inconsistency, since it is precisely Egmont who speaks the words; the one person who cannot know anything about the sleepwalker is the sleepwalker himself—or if he is made aware of himself, this destroys him. Thus it is suggested that Egmont's self-consciousness is not merely a heightening of his nature but also an imperfection in it, as it were the dividing of a cell, the tendency of life away from symmetry. If Egmont is conscious of the quasi-somnambulistic nature of his own existence, then his being conscious conflicts with his supposed somnambulism and calls his image of himself into question.

Or we think of the scene with Clärchen in act 3, which is very carefully prepared for. Already in act 1 we are acquainted with the engaging mixture of woman and child in Clärchen; and at the end of act 2 Egmont invokes "Gute Natur" (p. 230) when leaving for her house. We have just seen him in two very trying situations, with the unruly crowd and with his secretary and Orange; now, in act 3 with Clärchen, we expect to see the true Egmont, at his most natural, free of the trappings of his position and responsibility. But when he throws open his arms dramatically, at almost the exact center of the play, it is to reveal his Spanish uniform! We see not "Graf Egmont" but the "Prinz von Gaure" (p. 190), and there is a definite feeling of wrongness about this, especially when we recall the Netherlanders' instinctive suspicion of people who appear "in Prunk und königlichem Staate" (p. 176), "in pomp and royal finery." It is in this situation, moreover, and in this costume, that Egmont then expounds to Clärchen his theory of his two selves. Here again, as in the case of the sleepwalker metaphor, his speaking creates difficulties in what he says. For if there are really two Egmonts, then it follows that Clärchen's Egmont, the natural, untroubled, spiritually whole Egmont, no longer exists except perhaps as a memory. The cell, in Wilkinson's metaphor, has divided; its original unity is irredeemably lost. Egmont, says Egmont himself, is "geplagt, verkannt, verwickelt . . . wenn ihn die Leute für froh und fröhlich halten" (p. 243), "tormented, misunderstood, entangled, when people think him happy and cheerful," whereby he all but admits that his open Netherlandic cheerfulness has become not much more than a mask.

### Egmont and Alba

Egmont's character and thinking, then, are not nearly so simple as he himself wishes to believe. When he arrives for his interview with Alba, practically the first words out of his mouth are, "Kommt Oranien auch? Ich vermuthete ihn hier" (p. 262), "Is Orange coming too? I thought he would be here." It is important that this particular falsehood is not yet required by the situation. Egmont has come to the palace *planning* to dissemble, and his intentness upon his plan has made him hasty in his attempt to dissociate himself from Orange. Nor is it hard to understand why Egmont does this, provided we credit him with a certain amount of strategic cunning. Orange had said earlier, "Vielleicht daß der Drache [Alba] nichts zu fangen glaubt, wenn er uns nicht beide auf Einmal verschlingt" (p. 229), "Perhaps the dragon will not consider it a worthwhile catch if he does not swallow us both at once"; and Egmont is now in a hurry to remind Alba of Orange's absence, in order to improve his own bargaining position and his chances of winning concessions—or at least his chances of escaping with his skin. Not only is this a reasonably transparent ploy on Egmont's part, but as we are shown in Alba's anguished doubts when he learns earlier that Orange is not coming, it could have been a successful ploy against a less determined antagonist. In any event, Wilkinson's argument that "foresight" and "wholeness of sight" determine a scale with its extremes in Alba and Egmont, respectively (pp. 63–65), does not hold.

Moreover, when he and Alba get down to business, Egmont is obviously less than sincere in much of what he says. It is all very well to argue that he "*sees* sadly into the confused, ineffectual devotion of his beloved countrymen" (Wilkinson, p. 63) while still admiring them and defending them to Alba; but this is not sufficient to reconcile the idea (expressed earlier to Clärchen) of the populace as a "Menge, mit der nichts anzufangen ist" (p. 243), "mob with which nothing can be undertaken," with the idea of "Männer, werth Gottes Boden zu betreten; ein jeder rund für sich, ein kleiner König" (p. 267), "men worthy to set foot on God's earth, each complete in himself, a little king." There is an immense difference in attitude between the two statements; and since Egmont has come to Alba intending to dissemble, we must conclude that his true feeling is more nearly expressed in the words to Clärchen.

Perhaps Alba does not see through Egmont's dissimulation, but he scores a telling point when he answers Egmont's idea of the Netherlanders as "brothers" by saying, "Und doch hat der Adel mit diesen seinen Brüdern sehr ungleich getheilt" (p. 269), "And yet the nobility have shared very unequally with these brothers of theirs." We recall Egmont's strikingly unfraternal advice to the burghers earlier ("Ein ordentlicher Bürger, der sich ehrlich und fleißig nährt, hat überall so viel Freiheit als er braucht" [p. 211], "A respectable citizen, who supports himself honestly and industriously, has everywhere as much freedom as he needs.")". And later on, when he is alone in prison, Egmont envisions his ideal of freedom as that state

> wo wir die Menschheit ganz, und menschliche Begier in allen Adern fühlen; wo das Verlangen vorzudringen, zu besiegen, zu erhaschen, seine Faust zu brauchen, zu besitzen, zu erobern, durch die Seele des jungen Jägers glüht; wo der Soldat sein angebornes Recht auf alle Welt mit raschem Schritt sich anmaßt, und in fürchterlicher Freiheit wie ein Hagelwetter durch Wiese, Feld und Wald verderbend streicht, und keine Gränzen kennt, die Menschenhand gezogen. (pp. 281–82)

> [where we experience our humanness wholly and feel human desire pulsing throughout us; where the urge to press forward, to vanquish, to seize, to use the fist, to possess, to conquer, burns through the soul of the young hunter; where the swift-moving soldier asserts his inborn right over the whole world, and in his terrifying freedom, like a hailstorm, sweeps destroying through meadow, field and forest, and recognizes no boundaries set by man.]

Egmont's own definition of "perfect freedom," in other words, is simply *un-bridled power,* with no particular sympathy for those over whom such power happens to be exercised, and Alba is therefore perhaps not far from right when he says: "Ich fürchte, diese alten Rechte sind darum so angenehm, weil sie Schlupfwinkel bilden, in welchen der Kluge, der Mächtige, zum Schaden des Volks, zum Schaden des Ganzen, sich verbergen oder durchschleichen kann" (p. 268), "I fear that the reason these ancient rights are so attractive is that they provide secret places where the clever and powerful man, to the detriment of the people and of the community, can hide or maneuver." Egmont does not seem to act deliberately against the best interest of his countrymen, but it is clear that his occasional extravagant praise of the Netherlanders does not represent what he honestly thinks, and that he is by no means incapable of insincerity and foresighted strategy. He himself has said to Clärchen, "Wenn der Soldat auf der Lauer steht und dem Feinde etwas ablisten möchte, da nimmt er sich zusammen, faßt sich selbst in seine Arme und kaut seinen Anschlag reif" (p. 239), "When the soldier waits in ambush in order to outwit his enemy, then he grips himself tightly in his own arms and chews his plan until it is ripe."

Alba, moreover, does not deliberately act against the best interest of the Netherlanders either. There is much less difference between the two men than Egmont would have us believe, and in fact Egmont's relationship with Clärchen forms an interesting parallel to Alba's with the Netherlanders. Egmont does not mean to cause harm to Clärchen, but for all practical purposes, as Schiller points out,[4] he has ruined her existence. He is to an extent aware of this when he notices the effect upon her of his ill-considered remark about her "virginal modesty" (p. 242)—her virginity being one important social asset that she no longer possesses. Nor does it seem to me, despite Wilkinson, that Egmont's bequeathing of Clärchen to Ferdinand really indicates generosity or "freedom from all possessiveness." On the contrary, precisely his feeling free to dispose of Clärchen's future shows how completely he does regard her as a possession, a "Kleinod" (p. 302). It is significant in this connection that Ferdinand and Egmont had earlier begun negotiations concerning the sale of a horse (pp. 271–72). It does not occur to Egmont to think of Clärchen as an individual with her own say in her fate, any more than it occurs to Alba that the Netherlanders might be competent to make their own choice in matters of religion. We cannot get around this by insisting that Clärchen is too young and helpless to derive any profit from being enfranchised; for if Clärchen is compared implicitly to a horse, Egmont makes exactly the same comparison explicitly in the case of the whole people of the Netherlands (pp. 267–68), whom he claims to regard as fully worthy of freedom. I suppose it is more flattering to be compared with a well-bred horse than with sheep or oxen, but the horse is still something that is used by its owner for his own ends. Mephistopheles says,

> Wenn ich sechs Hengste zahlen kann,
> Sind ihre Kräfte nicht die meine?
> Ich renne zu und bin eine rechter Mann,
> Als hätt' ich vier und zwanzig Beine.

## Egmont's Practical Goal and the Mask of Nature

If Egmont is really being insincere and indirect, if his is really the situation of a soldier in ambush, biding his time until his plans mature, then precisely what *are* his plans? If we cannot give a specific answer to this question, then we shall have to concede that all of Egmont's apparent duplicity, all the suggestions of a disharmony in his nature, merely reflect the confusion of a simple soul in a situation it cannot cope with, which leaves us with no basis upon which to defend the work, for example, against Schiller's criticisms.

But we can give a specific answer to this question. Egmont's actions are in fact governed by a specific long-range political strategy that he never loses sight of. In the famous speech to his secretary he alludes to Phaëthon and the Horses of the Sun (p. 220), a standard symbol for excessive ambition; and his next speech after that begins, "Ich stehe hoch, und kann und muß noch höher steigen" (p. 221), "My position now is high, and I can and must climb higher still." If we ask precisely what Egmont means by "climbing higher," what his ambition is directed at, the text gives us the answer repeatedly. "Hätte man uns den statt der Margrete von Parma zum Regenten gesetzt!" (p. 178), "If only they had made him regent instead of Margarete of Parma," says Jetter; and again, "Hätten wir ihn nur zum Regenten" (p. 212), "If only we had him as regent." Margarete herself informs us, "Egmont und Oranien machten sich große Hoffnung, diesen Platz [the regentship] einzunehmen" (p. 189), "Egmont and Orange had great hopes of occupying this position." And it is clear from the text that Egmont (unlike Orange) has *not* given up this hope. He is planning to become the Spanish regent of the Netherlands. Far from being unconcerned with the political situation, he uses even his secretary's amours as the opportunity for a little spying in the palace (p. 221). Later on, when he learns that his death is unavoidable, he stamps his foot, as though this were just a serious nuisance; but when Orange tells him that Alba is coming with a commission to apply drastic measures, he cries desperately, "Nein! Nein!" (p. 226), for this is a blow not at his life (which he insists is protected by his Golden Fleece) but at his hopes of power. And to Clärchen he describes his relation with the current regent in the words, "Jedes hat seine eignen Absichten" (p. 241), "We each have our own designs," adding that he has "einen kleinen Hinterhalt," his own secret thoughts, in dealing with Margarete.

Egmont is perfectly sincere when he says of his countrymen, "könnt' ich etwas für sie thun" (p. 241), "if only I could do something for them"; but he wants to do this "something" as their regent. He wants to be the rider of that particular horse. Both Orange and Margarete stand in the way of his ambition, but he bears no ill will toward either of them; he even hopes that Alba (who he knows has been placed in a strategically difficult situation) will peaceably concede a certain amount of validity to his argument "daß der Bürger von dem regiert sein will der mit ihm geboren und erzogen ist [sc. Egmont]" (p. 269), "that the burgher wants to be governed by someone who has been born and raised with him." Clärchen asks of Margarete, "ist sie falsch?" (p. 242), "is she false?" and Egmont answers, "Nicht mehr und nicht weniger, als jeder der seine Absichten erreichen will," "Neither more nor less than anyone who wants to achieve his aims"—to which the reader might be tempted to reply with Clärchen's earlier question, "Hast du das von dir abgenommen?" (p. 241), "Are you speaking of yourself when you say that?" Egmont is careful to be no more "false" than he has to be, to operate with maximum forthrightness and minimum subterfuge, in order that when he achieves his goal, he will be able to maintain himself securely: "und steh' ich droben einst, so will ich fest, nicht ängstlich stehn" (p. 221). If he remains friends with Orange and on good terms with as many of the Spaniards as possible, he will encounter much less difficulty as regent, and his own natural friendliness makes it all the easier for him to carry out the farsighted policy dictated by these considerations. But at the same time, his secret ambitions also create an inner disharmony in his existence, as it were "an alien drop" (p. 230) in his blood, which appears most clearly when "Graf Egmont" throws open his arms to reveal the Prince of Gaure.

This is Egmont's problem: that he must wear his own natural character as a mask. This is the source of that tension in Egmont for which Wilkinson finds the excellent formulation, "Egmont here becomes rigid in his adherence to flexibility" (p. 69). This is the ridge-pole upon which Egmont is balancing: that he must be his genuine self, open and natural, while at the same time not losing sight of the advantage he hopes to gain by his genuineness; that he must take care not to let care ("Sorglichkeit" [p. 230], "Sorge" [p. 282]) take hold of him, that he must therefore deliberately remind himself to bathe "the brooding wrinkles" (p. 230) from his brow;[5] that he must surround himself with genuine friends, but friends "denen er sich nicht überlassen darf" (p. 243), "to whom he may not entrust himself"; that he must show himself a true defender of his people, especially of the Netherlander's right "to be governed by his countrymen" (p. 268), while at the same time resisting any popular movement that threatens a disruption of the political status quo. All this tension and paradox in Egmont can be traced to a single thought always present in the back of his mind, his concealed ambition to become Spanish regent of the Netherlands. Everything he says or does is colored by this thought. In the conversation with Orange, when Orange first implies that Margarete may be secretly aware of serious political developments (her suggestion "daß . . . der König sich zu andern Maßregeln entschließen müsse" [p. 222], "that the king will have to decide upon further measures"), Egmont's answer is not at all to the point. He dismisses Orange's suspicions by drawing the analogy with a woman's position between "mächtige Nebenbuhler," "mighty rivals," which word does not in any sense apply to the relation between Spanish crown and Netherlandic nobility. Egmont begins this speech by admitting that he had not listened to what Margarete had been saying ("ich dachte unterdessen an was anders"), and this admission apparently describes his state of mind *now* as well; standing opposite Orange, he is occupied in his thoughts not with what Orange is saying but rather with the rivalry between the two of them for the regentship, a situation to which the word "Nebenbuhler," "rival," *does* apply.

Or we recall the first scene of the play, where Buyck says, "Muß der Soldat Friede rufen?" (p. 183), "Must a soldier call for peace?"—words we soon have occasion to apply to Egmont, when he quells the disturbance in act 2.[6] Egmont, in fact, is a soldier not only by profession but also by conviction and passion. He believes in the soldier's "inborn right over the whole world," in his terrible freedom to rage "like a hailstorm, destroying" over civilization; and in view of this it is clear that his argument against Orange's advice, his concern for the innocent victims of an eventual war, is not entirely candid. Egmont the soldier is crying "peace" here, but he is doing so because it is the Spanish government from which he hopes to receive his advancement. A break with Spain must be avoided, primarily for Egmont's own sake, and only secondarily for the sake of the people—supposing Egmont believes he will make a good ruler. That this is the way Egmont's mind has been working becomes especially clear at the end of the play, where, with his ambition utterly defeated, he is free to affirm enthusiastically precisely the carnage he had earlier claimed to be afraid of: "Und wie das Meer durch eure Dämme bricht, so brecht, so reißt den Wall der Tyrannei zusammen, und schwemmt ersäufend sie von ihrem Grunde, den sie sich anmaßt, weg!" (p. 304). "As the sea breaks through your dikes, so smash down the wall of tyranny and sweep it overwhelmingly away from the land it has usurped." If this is supposed to be a man who is worried primarily about his people's welfare, then the metaphor is exactly the wrong one, since for a Netherlander the bursting of dikes means nothing but destruction. This is Egmont the soldier talking, the true Egmont who loves nothing better than a colossal melee and cares nothing for human life, either his own or others'.

## The Strategy of Having No Strategy

Egmont's strategy for obtaining the regentship is to have *no* strategy, to lead as entirely unrestrained an existence as possible; and this is really not a bad plan, for it accomplishes three things.

First, it maintains his popularity among the Netherlanders, who believe implicitly in his altruism and candidness; precisely Jetter, the least soldierlike of the townspeople, voices the wish that Egmont were regent. Egmont claims that he has not gone out of his way to woo the populace, and in general there is no reason to doubt this, although we do hear that he makes a point of being generous even with the man "who does not need it" (p. 176). But on the other hand, he is aware of the political advantage his popularity gives him; and in fact there is even one point where he appears to betray bad conscience about this—again by way of an inappropriate metaphor. In the conversation with Alba, in the same speech in which he remarks, "Nicht jede Absicht ist offenbar," "Not every intention is obvious," he also compares religion to a tapestry and says, "Das Volk liegt auf den Knieen, betet die heiligen gewirkten Zeichen an, und hinten lauscht der Vogelsteller der sie berücken will" (p. 266), "The people kneel to worship the sacred designs behind which the bird-limer lurks, seeking to take them in." In actual fact, the Spaniards are now increasingly blatant oppressors, not deceitful charmers; the man who has ensnared the people's emotions, and is deriving a political advantage from this, is Egmont himself. Moreover, as in the case of the horse, we again observe a comparison by Egmont of the Netherlandic people to animals.

Second, Egmont's strategy of having no strategy, his deliberate unde-liberateness, also minimizes suspicion on the part of the Spaniards. Egmont is aware that he has gained a crucial advantage over Orange in this respect— "Oranien . . . hat sich in den Credit gesetzt, daß er immer etwas Geheimes vorhabe" (p. 241), "Orange has gotten himself the reputation of always being up to something secret"—and in fact, if the clear-headed Machiavell were the king's adviser, not Margarete's, Egmont's ambition would stand a good chance of being realized. It is Machiavell who says, "Will ein Volk nicht lieber nach seiner Art von den Seinigen regieret werden, als von Fremden" (p. 189), "Does a people not prefer to be governed in its own way by those who belong to it, rather than by foreigners." In a world of reasonable men, men unwilling to be "ungerecht und thöricht" (p. 225), "unjust and foolish," Egmont's waiting game, his maintenance of good relations with the resident foreigners, would probably be a winning game.

Third, and most important, however: by living tolerantly and un-restrainedly, by not executing his office to the letter of the law, Egmont also contrives to keep some *pressure* on the Spaniards, without which there would be no reason for the king to consider a change of regent in the first place. Margarete herself, though convinced of Egmont's honesty in general, suspects him on this point: "Er hat zuerst den fremden Lehrern nachgesehn, hat's so genau nicht genommen und vielleicht sich heimlich gefreut daß wir etwas zu schaffen hatten" (p. 192). "He was the first to condone the foreign teachers; he did not take his duty too seriously and was perhaps glad to see us kept hopping." And of course Alba suspects him too. In fact, Egmont's principal aim in conversation with Alba, and the reason for his praise of his people, is to convince Alba that "Es geht nicht! Es kann nicht gehen!" (p. 267), that the vital desire of this naturally noble Netherlandic race (namely, to have Egmont as regent) cannot be suppressed by force. Thus, again, Egmont's apparently easy naturalness is revealed as in truth a delicate balancing, as it were on a ridge-pole. He must execute Spanish policy vigorously enough to retain the trust of king and government, but at the same time he must allow a certain amount of unrest to develop so that a change of regent will be contemplated. And he carries out this balancing, as Wilkinson says, by placing himself in the paradoxical position of adhering rigidly to his own natural flexibility and openness.

## Egmont and His Doubles

Of course Egmont's plan is doomed from the outset, given the king's unreason-able general policies; but he does not know this and remains boldly committed to his course even after Alba appears. Only one other character in the play does not allow Alba's arrival to interfere with his normal activities, the rabble-rouser Vansen, who says of Alba,

> Laßt ihn nur erst; er muß auch essen, trinken, schlafen wie andere Men-schen. . . . Im Anfange geht's rasch; nachher wird er auch finden, daß in der Speisekammer unter den Speckseiten besser leben ist und des Nachts zu ruhen, als auf dem Fruchtboden einzelne Mäuschen zu erlisten. (p. 248)

> [Let him be a bit; he has to eat, drink, sleep like everyone else. . . . In the beginning things will go quickly; afterwards he will discover that it is better

to live in the pantry where the bacon is hanging, and to sleep at night, than
to work at hunting mice here and there in the storage-loft.]

These words remind us strikingly of Egmont's opinion about what will happen
if a new regent is sent from Spain: "Auch ihm wird die Zeit vergehn, der Kopf
schwindeln, und die Dinge wie zuvor ihren Gang halten" (p. 223). "For him
too time will pass, his head will swim, and things will go on in their own way
as before." I do not mean that Egmont is a rabble-rouser; but the presence
of certain thematic and verbal connections between him and Vansen—not to
mention the fact that he has unwittingly done some of Vansen's unsavory friends
a considerable favor (pp. 251–52)—ought at least to make us look more closely
at Egmont's apparent simplicity. Vansen is perhaps a kind of alter ego, his
relation to Egmont being that of fate to conscious intent. Consciously, Egmont
hopes to stabilize the situation in the Netherlands by becoming regent; but
circumstances are such that the effect of his actions is likely only to plunge the
nation into chaos, which is Vansen's aim.

Egmont's strategy of no strategy, his strategy of "holding himself in his
arms," remaining inactive while his plans mature of their own accord, would be
an entirely sound strategy if it were not based on one false premise concerning
the reasonableness of his opponents. And this pattern, a play built around
a central character who bases his actions upon a hope that is utterly futile
from the outset, constitutes in its turn a parallel with *Tasso* (the genesis of
which overlaps with that of *Egmont* by seven years), which lends support to the
reading we have attempted, a reading between the lines, a seeking of hidden
intentions, the type of reading that is obviously obligatory in the later play.
Nor is it difficult, in the present reading, to account for the vision of Clärchen
as Freedom. Egmont in prison is finally stripped of all hope. Now at last the
alien element in his blood, his secret ambition, is purged utterly. Now at last he
*is* Clärchen's Egmont—as he had claimed to be earlier, when in truth he had
still been the Prince of Gaure with his "Hinterhalt"—and that Clärchen should
appear in this scene therefore becomes almost a necessity. That she should appear
as "Freiheit," moreover, is appropriate, for Egmont now at last *is* free, free of
his inner tension and disharmony, free to be wholly himself, the affectionate
(and ruthlessly possessive) lover, the true patriot with no admixture of personal
interest, and of course the soldier, no longer needing to restrain his enthusiasm
at the prospect of a bloody fight, even though he himself will unfortunately not
be there to participate.

Perhaps more obvious than the parallel with *Tasso*, however, is the
parallel between *Egmont* and *Götz von Berlichingen,* which were after all printed
together in the "Ausgabe letzter Hand." There is a close relation here, but it is
not a simple similarity between the main characters. Egmont inherits from Götz
his nature as a soldier whose principal value is freedom; but like Weislingen's, his

nature is also corrupted by ambition within an existing political power structure. Freedom is a problem in *Götz,* but not the same kind of problem as in *Egmont;* for while Götz possesses his own little world, his family and walled castle, separate from the world of political intrigue and moral ambiguity, Egmont, like Weislingen, would be constitutionally unable to take advantage of such a retreat even if it were available to him. To the extent that Egmont does retreat from the world in his visits to Clärchen, he only succeeds in revealing and exacerbating the anguished division of his self into two Egmonts. If Goethe had simply wished to write a "gesteigerter Götz," he could easily have followed history in the matter of Egmont's family, which would also have motivated Egmont's remaining in Brussels.[7] As the play stands, however, Egmont's freedom is made problematic by being associated with a certain *rootlessness,* and with the corresponding need for a firm self-establishment (as regent) in the existing world.

But in the case of Weislingen, a similar internal problem is made clear to the spectator by soliloquies and asides. Why does Goethe not give Egmont a soliloquy in which to reveal his political aims? There are two answers to this question. The first is that such a soliloquy would be out of character. Egmont's strategy is to have no strategy, to lead an unrestrained existence and avoid all brooding on his long-range hopes, since brooding would deepen those wrinkles in his brow which his strategy dictates must be concealed. The second answer, however, is more important. A soliloquy on ambition would place the audience in a false relation to Egmont; it would clarify the situation by revealing his cheerful openness as *merely* a mask, or at best it would show him a weak character, like Weislingen. But Egmont cannot be dismissed in this manner. As Wilkinson says, "What he is by nature, he confirms by choice." It must remain possible to consider Egmont a titanic and tragic individual, a man who is attempting to bend *nature itself* (his own inborn character) to a personal and political end. This is the ultimate extent of his belief in the soldier's "inborn right over the whole world." Unlike Götz von Berlichingen, Egmont does not *follow* his freedom-loving nature, but attempts to *lead* his nature consciously; he attempts as it were to harness his daimon and make it work for him in the real world. Egmont, as he himself says, is Phaëthon, a man who wishes to hold the very reins of nature in his hands; and like Phaëthon he crashes, his mind filled with a vision of the holocaust to follow.

*Egmont* was finished as a play for Weimar and is therefore presumably part of what Goethe is talking about in "Weimarisches Hoftheater." The Weimar audience, Goethe says, is capable of rising above its German preference for "einfache Gewalt" (WA, 40:83), "simple power":

> Wir haben das Glück, von unsern Zuschauern . . . voraussetzen zu dürfen, daß sie mehr als ihr Legegeld mitbringen und daß diejenigen, denen bei der ersten sorgfältigen Aufführung bedeutender Stücke noch etwas dunkel, ja

ungenießbar bliebe, geneigt sind, sich von der zweiten besser unterrichten und in die Absicht einführen zu lassen. (WA, 40:78–79)

[We have the good fortune to be able to expect from our audience that they will contribute more than their admission money, and that if the first careful performance of an important work leaves some of them puzzled or displeased, they will be prepared to learn more about the work's true intention from a second performance.]

What we have in *Egmont* is a sophisticated, enigmatic work that must be pondered repeatedly and read between the lines. Goethe says almost exactly this in the *Italienische Reise:* "Die Aufnahme meines Egmont macht mich glücklich, und ich hoffe, es soll bei'm Wiederlesen nicht verlieren, denn ich weiß was ich hineingearbeitet habe, und daß sich das nicht auf einmal herauslesen läßt" (WA, 32:135). "The reception of my *Egmont* pleases me, and I hope the work will not lose by being reread, for I know what I have written into it, and I know that that cannot all be read out of it in a hurry."

## Egmont and Werther

In my *Modern Drama and German Classicism*, I argued that these basic ideas about *Egmont* can be developed into an entirely positive interpretation of the play.[8] The sequence of scenes forms a spiral that is defined by its repeated crossing of three structural spokes, representing the world of the Netherlandic people, the world of the Spaniards, and Clärchen's house, the place where Egmont is presumably closest to being himself. Egmont's hopeless self-conscious situation—his attempt to harness nature itself, yet without violating its un-reflecting naturalness—is the force that drives the spiral inexorably inward, until it arrives at the final scene where nothing but the interior of his being is represented, the final flaring up of his vital energy, and of his need to define himself, in a delusive vision of the achievement of Netherlandic freedom.

Thus an interesting parallel with *Werther* emerges. The meaning of the novel does not begin to unfold until the reader recognizes the validity of Werther's basic perceptions concerning the human condition and, consequently, the logical strictness of his descent into despair. In *Egmont*, a corresponding logical quality of fate is represented geometrically, in the implied image of the spiral, the vortex or maelstrom of the self that inevitably swallows the hero. Egmont's aim is a political one, but his strategy of having no strategy is not political in the usual sense; it is primarily reflective, an operation of the self upon itself, a repeated move inward that cannot help but produce the deadly spiral of his fate. The identification of the reader with Werther in the novel, moreover, is paralleled by an identification of the spectator with Egmont. For the alert spectator knows of Egmont's political ambition, yet at the same time does not know it in the way one normally knows things about a play; it is not *shown* to him, say, in a soliloquy. And this condition of both knowing and not knowing is exactly the condition Egmont attempts to impose on himself in his strategy of no strategy. In order to follow his ambition, he must try to remove that ambition even from his thoughts, lest it influence his actions or demeanor and so disturb the relations with his countrymen and the Spaniards on which he is banking.

In a sense, Egmont is Werther triumphant. Werther's station above the common run of men—if in fact his pretensions to being different from most other people are justified—is purely internal and unverifiable. Egmont is an aristocrat in both birth and acknowledged achievement. As we remarked in chapter 1, Werther imagines emptily three possibilities for a relatively fruitful existence: military service, diplomatic service, and ruling a people.[9] Egmont comes close to realizing all three; he is of course a military man of long standing, he acts as a kind of diplomat in his position between the Netherlanders and the Spaniards, and he is certainly a leader of his people, if not (in his hopes, not yet) their actual ruler. Werther suffers because he recognizes that the monotony of human life ("Es ist ein einförmiges Ding um das Menschengeschlecht") is never really broken. Egmont's strategy of no strategy turns that monotony—which implies the hopelessness of Alba's project—to his advantage. Werther must stand by while his bourgeois rival assumes sexual possession of his beloved. Egmont is himself the sexual possessor, and his bourgeois rival, Brackenburg, is swept aside so easily as hardly to be noticed. Werther's emotional bludgeoning of Lotte comes close to killing her, but in the end fails. Egmont's beloved does not need to be bludgeoned, but follows him (actually precedes him) willingly in death. Werther is obliged to do his own killing of himself, and shows a certain personal incompetence and confusion in the mess he makes of it. Egmont's death, while not the one he would have preferred, is carried out with military dignity and efficiency, and can at least be imagined as serving a worthy cause.

But the parallel and contrast between the two figures becomes clearest in the last moments before their death. Werther's fate, we have seen, is strictly logical only up to the point where he somehow actually manages to carry out the act of suicide. His death, in its quality as a botched job, gives the impression of accidentalness; and if we are charitable, we can understand this impression as a sign that somewhere in Werther's last moments a leap from necessity into freedom must be posited, that his death is after all an uncaused, unprecedented, arbitrary act, an authentically human act in the sense of the relation of his text to Montaigne's. In the case of Egmont, however, we do not need to speculate, for the leap from necessity into freedom is *shown* us in the play's last two scenes. The conversation with Ferdinand, which can be understood as a kind of conversation with himself, faces Egmont with the whole strict factualness and inevitability of his fate. And in the scene following, with a gesture of perfect arbitrariness, he brushes that fate aside in favor of a vision of triumph, a vision of freedom that *is* free precisely in its flouting of reality, fact, history, fate, of limitation in any form, and in its unmasking of Egmont the unashamed warrior, freed of conscience and consciousness, reveling once more in the anarchy of blood and battle.

This is not to say that Egmont, at the end, overcomes self-consciousness and achieves perfect self-unity. On the contrary, his persisting inner *division* is stressed. The stage direction that describes what he himself is seeing in his dream does not mention blood and suggests violence only in the symbol of a bundle of arrows (p. 303). There is thus a discrepancy between what he imagines and how he imagines it, since it is he himself, again, when he speaks, who adds the idea of Clärchen's blood-spattered feet and the blood-spattered hem of her garment (p. 304). And even here there is still an incongruity between what he says and what his words imply. He speaks only of "the blood of many nobles" (p. 304); but Clärchen's trampling in blood suggests much more strongly the idea of a slaughter of nameless masses. None of this, however, contradicts the idea of freedom. Freedom, after all, as in Werther's question about the nature of man, *is* inner division, man's ability to stand over against himself. And it is this freedom in a purified form, cleansed of Wertherian self-accusation and of the attempt to harness man's inevitable inner division to a self-serving political project, that is represented in the play's final vision of Egmont's joyfully visionary self-contradictions.

Egmont is Werther triumphant, in a sense that extends even to the situation of the audience of the two works. The audience of *Werther,* the readers, find themselves in a very difficult position. Each one, for himself—once he has understood the work in detail—must accept the uncomfortable condition of *being* Werther, must grasp in his own experience, as a reader, the possibility of handling this condition as a kind of game, and must then negotiate a transition by which the fleeting experience of readership becomes a center and model for the conduct of his existence as a whole. The situation of the audience of *Egmont* is much simpler and more encouraging. Egmont's last words before his triumphant vision are, "ungehindert fließt der Kreis innerer Harmonien, und eingehüllt in gefälligen Wahnsinn, versinken wir und hören auf zu sein" (p. 303), "unimpeded flows the circle of inner harmonies, and wrapped in agreeable insanity, we sink down and cease to be." In both knowing and not knowing what the play is about, we deal constantly with the problem of being Egmont. But is there any way for us to follow the "example" ("Beispiel" [p. 305], in the play's last words) of Egmont's leap into freedom, which he himself calls an "agreeable insanity"? In fact, we have *already* made that leap in the agreeable insanity of the theater, in that building, that institution, that ritual, where we gather together and subject ourselves to a vision that, like Egmont's, sweeps reality aside and substitutes the idea and image of mankind triumphantly free, a vision whose truth is guaranteed by precisely the arbitrary, agreeably insane freedom with which we insist on it.

In one respect, it is true, we lag behind Egmont. We, or at least most of us, do not embrace the innocent anarchic bloodlust of his last speeches. But in another respect we surpass him. The trouble with Egmont's leap into freedom is that it is, in a strong sense, *merely* insane, because it is utterly solitary, socially unfounded, unconnected with the real condition (which we are shown) of the Netherlandic people whom he invokes as his companions and followers. Our leap into freedom, by contrast, is grounded not only in its momentary quality as a shared ritual, in the particular performance we are attending, but also in *the institution of the theater,* the place where the agreeable insanity of freedom is woven into our social fabric. The highly questionable transition required by *Werther,* from our aesthetic experience to our conduct of life as a whole, is hardly even a problem in relation to *Egmont.* Even if I, personally, fail to shape my life in accordance with the Egmontian example, the theater as a social institution preserves, for me and others, the constant possibility of repairing that failure. It is thus the institution of the theater, and nothing else, that actually lends validity to Egmont's final vision. This at least, in substance, is the argument I proposed in *Modern Drama and German Classicism.*

## Egmont and the Reader

I do not retract that argument. I think it is valid, and I think it establishes, in the only way possible, the value of *Egmont* as a work of literature and of drama. But I also think it is wrong, not in the sense that its wrongness and its validity might be reconciled in an overarching interpretive argument that would be more valid than ever, but in the sense that its wrongness opens a space in which an entirely different kind of project, the actual historical abolition of literary or aesthetic meaning, becomes thinkable.

It will take us a while to come to the details of this idea, but the basic indications of wrongness in *Egmont* are not difficult to discern. In the first place, we cannot get around the frankly bloodthirsty quality of what Egmont understands as freedom. It can be argued, of course, that freedom in the strict sense implies anarchy, that the idea of freedom is contradicted by any notion that limits it. But why suggest just this radical line of thought in a vision of freedom that must be validated by the enduring existence of a social institution, the theater, an institution that involves not only the imposition of limits, but an obviously very high degree of organization and discipline in all those who have to do with it? Logical contradictoriness in the idea of freedom is not the issue here; we are, after all, accustomed to dealing with the paradox of freedom and limitation. What must worry us is the way the end of *Egmont,* with its insistence on blood, and on the strikingly upside-down metaphor of the sea's breaking through dikes, leaves us no room to develop that paradox fruitfully.

In the second place, I have said that part of Egmont's triumph is that he succeeds, where Werther fails, in encompassing the death of his beloved. There are a number of issues raised by this point, not the least of which is that of aggression against women, which we will come back to later. But for the time being, let us note only that Clärchen's death would not give so strong an impression of wrongness if it were *necessary*, or if even her presence in the play were necessary. From the point of view of a vision of freedom that is validated in the institution of the theater by way of our Egmontian condition of both knowing and not knowing, Clärchen obviously has no special function. And her use as a sounding board or mirror, as a spoke of the spiral, as a place for Egmont to be (and in the very act, not to be) "himself"—a condition reflected in her own innocent non-innocence—requires neither the specific motif of a mistress of lower social class nor, especially, the death of that mistress. But most important, Clärchen does not even die solely for Egmont's sake. She dies, as Egmont at the end insists, in the cause of Netherlandic freedom. She dies in despair at not having been able to awaken the spark of revolution in her people. And yet, a revolutionary assertion of freedom is not something Egmont himself had ever wanted from his people! His plan had been to keep the Netherlands subject to Spain and to become, himself, a Spanish functionary as regent. You have to break eggs, the saying goes, to make an omelette. But in the relation between Clärchen's death and freedom, it is a case of breaking eggs to make a ham sandwich.

This brings us to the third and most important area of wrongness in the play, which is suggested by the parallel between Egmont and Vansen. Who, after all, is Egmont? He is working not to free his people so much as to arrange for them a form of subjection that will satisfy his own personal needs. He has been a soldier, but he now aspires to be not much more than a bureaucrat, to exercise institutionalized power, but without the dread responsibility that being an actual ruler would entail. Certain remarks of Machiavell's, we have seen, indicate that Egmont's strategy of no strategy could perhaps succeed in a world of reasonable people. But in a world of reasonable people—if we consider the matter more closely—that strategy would be either unnecessary or futile, depending on whether a reasonable person would regard Egmont as actually competent to carry out a regent's duties. In a sense, therefore, Egmont's strategy (harmless as it seems) is corrupt, by its presupposing a world of corrupt and unreasonable people—a presupposition, to judge from Alba, that may not even be strictly correct. This point has important consequences for the crucial idea of freedom, for the value of the leap into freedom, at the end of *Werther* or *Egmont*, is conditioned by the character of the necessity from which the leap is taken. And whereas in *Werther* necessity is represented by the inexorable logic of truth, of the human condition, in *Egmont,* where everything depends on the hero's strategy, necessity is represented by the geometry of corruption. At the very least, a shadow thus falls on the philosophical aspect of Egmont's leap into freedom.

Who, after all, is Egmont? And what exactly is his relation to Werther? Whatever else he is, Werther is a seeker of truth. His brooding, however disastrous its consequences, is a brooding on valid perceptions of the human condition. Egmont, by contrast, is a strategist, and would never, but for his strategy, have involved himself in the brooding struggle to avoid brooding that characterizes him. Egmont, in other words, is the player of a game that is strikingly similar to the game of life as the reader of *Werther* is encouraged to experience it, the game of not knowing what we know, and of somehow harnessing this tension to the pursuit of practical aims. Egmont is related less to Werther himself than to the reader who is identified with Werther, and his play is in the end a play about reading. But the game as Egmont plays it is corrupt, having lost its relation with truth. The geometry of *Egmont,* the spiral of corruption, is thus not parallel to logical necessity for Werther, but is necessity at a step further along, a necessity that poisons reading itself. The wrongness of *Egmont,* even in the theater, is the wrongness of reading, the wrongness of our aesthetic relation to literature, even in the theater.

We can perhaps see this a bit better if we go back, yet once more, to the question of freedom. I have argued elsewhere that one cannot understand *Tasso* without knowing something about Italy in the time of Gregory XIII.[10] But historical knowledge is even more obviously useful in relation to *Egmont,* since it turns out that freedom, in a limited sense, was possible for the Netherlands after all, yet that Egmont's "example" had nothing to do with its achievement. After the execution of Egmont (and Hoorn) in 1567, Orange, whose property had been confiscated, did make an unsuccessful invasion; but the popular unrest that plagued Spanish governors in subsequent years was probably prompted more by Alba's taxation policies than by anything else. And by the time any real Netherlandic political freedom was secured in 1579, under Orange, it was freedom only for the northern provinces, whereas Belgium (and Egmont's Brussels), even at the time of Goethe's play, had still not emerged from its long history of foreign government and brutal fighting both with and among foreign armies.

Egmont, therefore—especially as he is presented in the play, with no family to keep him in Brussels—is damaged by the comparison with Orange. In practical matters he is blind and ineffectual, unable to see beyond the Spanish status quo and the prospect of becoming regent. And when his practical hopes fail, he leaps to the other extreme, into a vision of freedom that is not only barbaric, but also still ineffectual, since it has nothing to do with real possibilities. It is Orange who follows the difficult middle course, the course of a Montaigne, by which, it turns out, freedom might actually to an extent be served in human existence. Egmont, by contrast, is a man who has learned to brood, who has learned to ride the violent pendulum of consciousness between ineffectual extremes, in a kind of travesty of his girlfriend's "Himmelhoch jauchzend / Zum Tode betrübt" (p. 237), "exulting to the heavens, saddened to death"; he is a man, in effect, who has undergone the experience of identification with Werther, while at the same time retaining sufficient detachment to play this condition as a political game. He is, in short, a picture of exactly the reader *Werther* requires, and so, in his corruption, a picture of the wrongness of reading, of reading as *both* a sacrifice of the attainable reality of freedom (represented by Orange and the Netherlands) for the sake of the idea (self-consciousness as mastery) *and* a sacrifice of the idea in favor of a deluded belief in the efficacy of reflective game-playing.

In fact, if reading itself is thus radically wrong, then perhaps Egmont's final vision of freedom as mere anarchy makes sense after all, as a vision of the kind of disastrous renewal that is required *in literature*. And that the figure trampling in the blood of literature, in this vision, is a *woman,* perhaps also makes sense.

# Prometheus and Saturn:
# The Three Versions of
# *Götz von Berlichingen*

We began our discussion of wrongness in literature by talking about the role of the reader and the co-optive aesthetic move. We could easily have applied the last idea to Egmont, whose ambition, from the outset, exposes his Netherlandic patriotic energy to co-option in the Spanish cause. (Seen in this light, Egmont's death is nothing but wrong, being as pointless from the Spanish perspective as it is useless for Netherlandic freedom. Co-option of the Catholic nobility, in any case—not their beheading—was one of the principal devices used later by Alexander Farnese to preserve Spanish rule in the southern provinces.) But what exactly is at issue here: co-option *by* literature, or the co-option *of* literature? If the latter, then co-option to what end? We can open this question, in Goethe's sense, by asking after the independent critical operation of literature—of poetic vision or signification or textuality—with respect to society and politics. Can literature exist without being co-opted? The very form of drama, in which a literary text and a gross material reality are made to occupy the same space, is under certain circumstances an index of the urgency of this question.[1] In Goethe's career, the question can be traced in the development of a single literary project which, for the time being, we will call *Götz von Berlichingen*.

## The Question of Versions

In *Dichtung und Wahrheit* Goethe describes his revision of *Götz von Berlichingen* as mainly an elimination of the passionate excesses of the original version, especially with respect to the figure of Adelheid.

> Da ich mich [in writing *Götz*], ohne Plan und Entwurf, bloß der Einbil-
> dungskraft und einem innern Trieb überließ, so war ich von vorn herein
> zeimlich bei der Klinge geblieben, und die ersten Acte konnten für das, was
> sie sein sollten gar füglich gelten; in den folgenden aber, und besonders gegen
> das Ende, riß mich eine wundersame Leidenschaft unbewußt hin. Ich hatte

83

mich, indem ich Adelheid liebenswürdig zu schildern trachtete, selbst in sie verliebt, unwillkürlich war meine Feder nur ihr gewidmet, das Interesse an ihrem Schicksal nahm überhand, und wie ohnehin gegen das Ende Götz außer Thätigkeit gesetzt ist, und dann nur zu einer unglücklichen Theilnahme am Bauernkriege zurückkehrt, so war nichts natürlicher, als daß eine reizende Frau ihn bei dem Autor ausstach, der die Kunstfesseln abschüttelnd, in einem neuen Felde sich zu versuchen dachte. Diesen Mangel, oder vielmehr diesen tadelhaften Überfluß, erkannte ich gar bald, da die Natur meiner Poesie mich immer zur Einheit hindrängte. Ich hegte nun, anstatt der Lebensbeschreibung Götzens und der deutschen Alterthümer, mein eignes Werk im Sinne, und suchte ihm immer mehr historischen und nationalen Gehalt zu geben, und das, was daran fabelhaft oder bloß leidenschaftlich war, auszulöschen; wobei ich freilich manches aufopferte, indem die menschliche Neigung der künstlerischen Überzeugung weichen mußte. (WA, 28:199–200)

[Working without a plan or outline, simply following my imagination and an inner drive, I had from the outset pretty much stuck to the point, and the first acts could be seen as reasonably close to what they were meant to be. In the following acts, however, and especially toward the end, I was unconsciously overwhelmed by a strange passion. In trying to make Adelheid attractive, I had fallen in love with her myself, and had involuntarily consecrated my pen to her service. Her fate became the main interest, and since Götz is rendered inactive toward the end anyway, and returns to activity only in his unfortunate participation in the Peasants' War, nothing could be more natural than that an attractive woman should capture the fancy of the author who, shaking off the shackles of art, envisaged a new field for his work. This lack, or rather this culpable excess, quickly became plain to me, since the nature of my poetic efforts constantly pushed me toward unity. From this point on I concentrated on my own work, rather than on Götz's history of his life or on German antiquity. I sought to give my work more and more historical and national substance, and to eliminate elements that were fantastic or merely passionate, which meant sacrificing a great deal, since human inclination was being subordinated to artistic conviction.]

This description is generally accepted as a summary of the differences between the two versions, although there is some uncertainty about precisely where the increased "historical and national substance" of the second version is to be found, and about precisely why Goethe recalls having regarded that second version as a mere preliminary stage in the development of his changed conception.

Ohne also an dem ersten Manuscript irgend etwas zu verändern, welches ich wirklich noch in seiner Urgestalt besitze, nahm ich mir vor, das Ganze umzuschreiben, und leistete dieß auch mit solcher Thätigkeit, daß in wenigen Wochen ein ganz erneutes Stück vor mir lag. Ich ging damit um so rascher zu Werke, je weniger ich die Absicht hatte, diese zweite Bearbeitung jemals

drucken zu lassen, sondern sie gleichfalls nur als Vorübung ansah, die ich
künftig, bei einer mit mehrerem Fleiß und Überlegung anzustellenden neuen
Behandlung, abermals zum Grunde legen wollte. (WA, 28:200)

[Without changing anything in the first manuscript, which I still actually
possess in its original form, I set about rewriting the whole thing, and did this
with such energy that in only a few weeks an entirely renewed piece lay before
me. I worked all the faster for having no intention ever to publish the second
version, which I regarded as itself only a preliminary exercise that would later
serve as the basis for a more thoroughly and deliberately reconceived treatment
of the subject.]

Must we assume that Goethe in the end never bothered with this further
development of *Götz*? Or can we, after all, say something about the third
version of the play?

These questions can perhaps be dismissed as having more to do with
Goethe's long-term memory while writing *Dichtung und Wahrheit* than with
*Götz* itself. But it is not as easy to dismiss his letter to Herder of July 1772:

genug, es [das Stück, *Götz*] muß eingeschmolzen, von Schlacken gereinigt,
mit neuem edlerem Stoff versetzt und umgegossen werden. Dann soll's wieder
vor Euch erscheinen. Es ist alles nur gedacht. Das ärgert mich genug. Emilia
Galotti ist auch nur gedacht, und nicht einmal Zufall oder Caprice spinnen
irgend drein. Mit halbweg Menschenverstand kann man das Warum von
jeder Scene, von jedem Wort, mögt' ich sagen, auffinden. Drum bin ich
dem Stück nicht gut, so ein Meisterstück es sonst ist, und meinem eben
so wenig.

[Enough, it must be melted down, freed of slag, alloyed with new nobler
material, and recast. Then it shall be presented to you again. There is nothing
in it but thought, which is what irritates me. *Emilia Galotti* is likewise merely
cerebral, and not even chance or caprice relieves this quality. With any sort
of intelligence, one can figure out the Why of every scene, indeed, I might
say, of every word. Therefore the work doesn't please me, however much a
masterpiece it might be considered, and my work doesn't please me either.]

Among the critics who have treated the first and second versions of *Götz*, Ilse
Graham makes the most cogent attempt to deal with this letter, to show how
the second version of *Götz* is less cerebral ("gedacht") than the first. But her
discussion is focused almost entirely on the verbal texture of the play, on Goethe's
replacement of patterns of rational argument by subtler patterns of imagery,
and so does not directly address the question of major structural changes in the
revision, or especially the question—if we take both the letter and *Dichtung
und Wahrheit* seriously—of how the revision can be at once both less cerebral
and less passionate.[2]

### *Götz* and Shakespeare

Let us begin with an easier question. Herder had written to Goethe, apropos *Götz*, "daß Euch Schäcksp. ganz verdorben [hat]," "that Shakespeare has ruined you entirely," and Goethe acknowledges that this criticism is just. In what sense, if any, is the second version therefore less Shakespearean? I think the answer to this question, from Goethe's point of view, has to do with the speech "Zum Schäkespears Tag," which was composed only a month or so before the first *Gottfried*. We can see the connection if we consider the figure of Weislingen.

In the original *Gottfried*, some interestingly conflicting statements about Weislingen are made by characters who are presumed to be truth-tellers. The rough-and-ready peasant in the opening scene, after the wagoner has described Weislingen as "a good-looking man of great dignity," replies, "Mir gefällt er nich er ist nit breitschultrig und robust genug für einen Ritter, ist auch nur fürn Hof,"[3] "I don't like him, he's not broad-shouldered and robust enough for a knight, only good for a courtier." But Liebetraut, the notorious teller of uncomfortable truths at the bishop's court (*JG*, 2:114), says of Weislingen, "Es ist ein fürtrefflicher Mann hat wenig seines gleich. Und wenn er nie an Hof gekommen wäre, könnte er unvergleichlich geworden seyn" (*JG*, 2:116), "He's an excellent man with few equals; and if he had never come to court, he could have been incomparable." Which truth is true? Is Weislingen *too* good for court life, or *only* good for court life? In the revised version, both of the statements in question are deleted; but in the original version they are given considerable emphasis, and I think it is evident that they are both meant to be true.

In another passage that was deleted in the revision, Weislingen is clearly paralleled with Götz's son Carl. Elisabeth says to her sister-in-law:

> Schwache, passen an keinen Plaz in der Welt, sie müssten denn Spitzbuben seyn. Deswegen bleiben die Frauen wenn sie gescheut sind zu Hause, und Weichlinge kriechen ins Kloster. Wenn mein Mann ausreit es ist mir gar nicht bang. Wenn Carl auszöge ich würde in ewigen Ängsten seyn. Er ist sicherer in der Kutte als unter dem Harnisch. (*JG*, 2:139)

> [Weak people don't fit at any place in the world, unless they are villains. If women are smart, therefore, they stay at home, and weaklings creep into a monastery. When my husband rides out, I am not worried at all. If Carl were to ride out, I would be in unending fear. He'll be safer in a monk's habit than in armor.]

And Marie answers immediately, "Mein Weislingen ist auch sanfter Natur, und doch hat er ein edles Herz," "My Weislingen also has a soft nature, but his heart is noble." The similarity between the words "Weichlinge" and "Weislingen" is too obvious to be missed. Weislingen belongs *both* at court and away from court because he is one of those weaklings who, according to Elisabeth, actually belong at no place in the world.[4] Like little Carl, Weislingen is naturally connected with Götz; he is bound to Götz by a spontaneous feeling which, in the world of this play, is as much a part of nature as the bond between father and son. But neither Carl nor Weislingen is strong enough to live up to this natural connection. "Seine Gegenwart bändigt mich fesselt mich," says Weislingen of Götz in another subsequently deleted passage, "Ich binn nicht mehr ich selbst, und doch binn ich wieder ich selbst" (*JG,* 2:107). "His presence hems me in, fetters me. I am no longer myself, yet I am myself again." Insofar as he is now, with Götz, his natural, free self again, he has no business at court. But he is still not strong enough to keep from comparing himself invidiously with Götz; instead of simply affirming his natural attachment, he is bothered about being "der zweyte," "second best" (also deleted), and this weakness marks him as belonging amid the political competition and backbiting of the court after all.

Weislingen is like those misguided "noble souls" in the Shakespeare speech who live in "the Elysium of so-called good taste, where, sleep-fuddled in tedious twilight, they halfway are, and halfway are not." He complains that he is himself, yet not himself. His weakness is not exactly the weakness of the slavish adherents of French taste in the Shakespeare speech, but it is the same type of weakness, an inability to measure up to "nature." The excellence of Shakespeare's plays, says Goethe, their capturing of the "secret point" in human existence, is due to the quality of his characters as pure "nature." But in the Shakespeare speech, and in the figure of Weislingen, "nature" does not mean merely a given property of all humans. On the contrary, human nature, or a human being's participation in nature at large (we recall Montaigne), is fully realized only as an achievement of will. A special strength and determination are needed in order to measure up to what nature requires of us. And the tragedy of Gottfried von Berlichingen, in the first version, is that he lives in a time and in a historical situation that is dominated by individuals in whom the strength and will necessary to achieve human nature are lacking. "Die *Schwachen* werden regieren" (*JG,* 2:227, my emphasis), "the *weak* will rule," he says in his last speech, which in the second version becomes "Die Nichtswürdigen werden regieren" (*JG,* 3:297), "The vile will rule." The deadly constellation of weaklings, which includes not only Weislingen and little Carl, but (in the first version) even Sickingen, when he succumbs to Adelheid's charms, is introduced by Brother Martin, who first appears to Gottfried, significantly, as a bad omen, as "Was schwar[zes] im Wald" (*JG,* 2:92),[5] "something black in the forest"— which words, as we might by now expect, are missing in the revision. Brother Martin, Weislingen, little Carl, Sickingen, and we must probably add Marie to the list: none of these people are vile, none of them *nichtswürdig.* But they are all weak to the extent of lacking the whole vital Shakespearean determinacy that is required of the world if a Götz von Berlichingen is to exist effectively in it.

The first version of the play is thus by no means an attempt to emulate Shakespeare. The special quality of Shakespeare, according to Goethe, is precisely that *all* his major characters have the achieved human nature, the "Colossal greatness" that is at least potentially present in Gottfried and a few of those who surround him—and of course in Adelheid—but is tragically absent elsewhere. The first version of *Gottfried,* rather, is a dramatized argument intended to demonstrate our *need* for Shakespearean sensibility and Shakespearean drama. The morass of weakness, of half-and-halfness, in which Gottfried vainly struggles to be his own free self is Goethe's holding up of a mirror to *us,* to our "ruined taste." Thus at least one apparent contradiction in Goethe's judgment of his own work is cleared up; for the *Geschichte Gottfriedens* is over-cerebral *by* being over-Shakespearean, in that it attempts to demonstrate what drama should be without itself actually being the kind of drama it advocates. It is too intellectually and polemically conscious of Shakespeare for its own good.

## Weislingen and the Court

Whatever Goethe says in *Dichtung und Wahrheit,* therefore, polemical-intellectual Shakespearism was the main fault he recognized in *Gottfried* at the time, and it is this fault that he concentrates on remedying in the second version. As I have suggested, he does so in large measure by changing the figure of Weislingen. In the first version, after Götz gives vent to his initial reproaches, the captive Weislingen protests, "Lasst mich reden—" (*JG,* 2:108), "Let me speak," but he never does get to speak at any length in the remainder of the scene. In the revision, at the same point, he delivers a long and reasonable defense of the princes' position, in his speech beginning, "Du siehst die Fürsten an, wie der Wolf den Hirten" (*JG,* 3:195), "You regard the princes as the wolf regards a shepherd." Götz, to be sure, answers effectively, but the result is now a standoff—Weislingen's general point about institutions remains as valid as Götz's about personalities—whereas in the first version Götz had simply dominated the exchange. Or we think of the scene that begins with Adelheid's telling Weislingen, "Die Zeit fängt mir an unerträglich lang zu werden" (*JG,* 2:140, 3:225), "I'm beginning to get intolerably bored." In the first version Weislingen becomes hysterical and ridiculous. He actually thanks Adelheid for liberating him from the evil "magic" of "friendship" and "human affection" that had attached him to Götz; he imagines himself blowing up, from his mouth, a storm that will wreck Götz's ship; "Woe to you, Gottfried!" (*JG,* 2:143), Adelbert will show his renewed courage by *talking* to the emperor about you. Adelheid could as well be mocking as praising him when she says, "Mich däucht ich sehe einen auferstandnen verklärten Heiligen in dir" (*JG,* 2:144), "I seem to see a resurrected and transfigured saint in you." But in the second version, the same scene ends in a relatively businesslike discussion of the measures Weislingen has already taken against Götz ("Auch Adelheid sind wir nicht so träg als du meynst" [*JG*, 3:227], "we are not as inactive as you imagine, Adelheid"), as well as of the ins and outs of the political situation in the empire. And accordingly, in the scene with the emperor which follows, Weislingen's bloated rhetoric of the first version is replaced by calm argument.

In the second version, then, Weislingen is no longer a mere weakling who fits "nowhere in the world," but rather a man whose proper place is in the milieu of court and politics, a competent and effective administrator. In the opening scene of the new version, he is simply referred to as "a powerful lord" (*JG*, 3:176). The truth-teller Liebetraut, when setting off to lure him back from Götz, says in the first version, "Der Händedruck eines Fürsten, und das Lächlen einer schönen Frau, halten fester als Ketten und Riegel" (*JG*, 2:127), "The handclasp of a prince and the smile of a beautiful woman hold more securely than bolts and chains." But in the second version this sentence becomes, "Der Händedruck eines Fürsten, und das Lächeln einer schönen Frau! Da reißt sich kein Weisling los" (*JG*, 3:213), "The handclasp of a prince and the smile of a beautiful woman! No Weisling can tear himself free of these." The statement is now a judgment on Weislingen's character as a courtier. In the first version, in the deleted passage mentioned above, Liebetraut had judged Weislingen to be a person with no real business at court, no place in court life; now, in the second version, he suggests confidently that *a* Weislingen, a man of Weislingen's type, can have no real existence away from court.

Yet further, in the first version, the scene of Adelheid's boredom ("Die Zeit fängt mir an unerträglich lang zu werden") is followed by the scene in which Georg reports Weislingen's open treachery, while in the second version the order of these scenes is reversed. Weislingen's abject confusion is no longer presented as an anticipatory explanation of his treachery, but rather his treachery now simply happens in the natural course of events, as Liebetraut had predicted, and we then see him trying, in a relatively businesslike way, to make the best of the situation with Adelheid. Or we note that in the second version, Marie emphasizes Weislingen's and Götz's closeness in age (*JG*, 3:189) only a few moments before Götz admits that he can no longer fit into the garment he is offering Weislingen (*JG*, 3:191). Götz, in other words, whom we might otherwise regard as the healthy, free, Shakespearean individual, has grown not only old but fat (a sign of essential *inactivity*? giving the lie to his own, and others', idea of himself), whereas his exact contemporary Weislingen, in the supposedly decadent, unhealthy atmosphere of the court, has apparently succeeded better in retaining his youth, his fitness, and of course his sexual attractiveness.

In the first version of the play, the episcopal court at Bamberg is primarily a focal point of the world's general weakness, against which Gottfried struggles in vain. Adelheid's presence, assuming we are to take her as an example of Shakespearean individuality, only underlines that quality of the court, in that she is repeatedly frustrated in her search for a personally and sexually and politically satisfactory male partner, and in that her search—by way of Weislingen, Sickingen, and Franz's shared name—repeatedly carries her in the direction of Gottfried's Shakespearean orbit. But in the second version, this distinction in value between Götz's world and that of the court is not nearly so clear. Weislingen is now the principal indicator. In the first version we recognize that court life has seduced him away from his own true natural humanity; in the second version we are shown that he has flourished at court, and would doubtless continue to flourish if he were not captured by Götz. The court at Bamberg is by no means viewed positively, even in the second version; but then, as Nägele shows, the text also undermines the validity of Götz's confidence in his own vigorous but fragmented activeness (Nägele, pp. 71, 73).

　　The important point is that in the second version, Götz's influence causes Weislingen to question the value of his life at court: "Können sie [meine Freunde am Hof] mir geben wornach ich strebe" (*JG,* 3:194), "Can the circle at court give me what I am striving for." (The same monologue in the first version [*JG,* 2:106–7] ends with a weak, vacillating Weislingen already questioning his newly reestablished relation with Götz.) And it is now this questioning attitude that saps Weislingen's strength and impairs his effectiveness when he later returns to the court. In the second version, it is not the court that seduces him away from nature, but rather it is Götz who, by the power of words, thoughts, doubts, and questions, seduces him away from a political and social life for which he is by nature well suited. Why should he question the value of life at court? In the debate with Götz, as we have seen, he now holds his own ("Du siehst die Fürsten an, wie der Wolf den Hirten"); he demonstrates the essential pointlessness of Götz's apparent activity, however justified some of Götz's complaints may be; he argues persuasively that in a reasonable political sense, Götz does not really *act* at all, that he in effect merely indulges himself, as it were grows fat. In the second version, therefore, there is no longer any putatively objective reason for preferring Götz's path. The two paths, Götz's and Weislingen's, are unalterably opposed, but the tragedy of the situation is that neither path is demonstrably wrong. Both Götz and Weislingen have the ultimate welfare of their land and people at heart. What more can be required of them than that each follow his own path as vigorously and directly and unquestioningly as possible, even though both paths probably lead nowhere? In the first version, it is Weislingen's lapse from nature into weakness that produces his constant tormented self-questioning; in the second version, it is the tormented self-questioning awakened unnecessarily in him by Götz that blunts what might otherwise be at least his effort to exercise a beneficial political influence.

And what has happened to the figure of Adelheid? In the first version, where Goethe suggests he had fallen in love with her himself, she is a fully developed Shakespearean female villain, not far from a Goneril, and her presence thus emphasizes Weislingen's weakness. Not only does Weislingen lack the natural human strength to remain loyal to Gottfried; he is not even strong enough to be a real villain, to betray Gottfried on his own. His betrayal must be the work of another focal point of vigorous human nature, which he finds in Adelheid. His is a thoroughly corrupted, parasitic humanity. Hence the base, superstitious quality of his thoughts on the balky horse, in the first version (*JG*, 2:138); and if, at the end of that speech, he recognizes that the true source of his difficulty lies in himself, this recognition does not enable him to change himself. Adelheid, in the first version, is a *pendant* to Gottfried, a vigorous human force operating in the other direction. Gottfried's motives may be nobler, but when he decides to do something, he does not trouble himself with difficult moral questions any more than Adelheid does. He and Adelheid represent the same basic Shakespearean human type; and the tragic quality of the first version arises not from Adelheid's villainy, but from a situation that enables the forces of weakness, "Die Schwachen" who will rule the future, to benefit from her natural strength. Adelheid is a tragic figure, and her tragedy mirrors Gottfried's; like him, she is mired in the historical debilitation of mankind.

In the second version, however, the case is different. Adelheid's personal development is now curtailed, and Weislingen is no longer primarily an example of anti-natural weakness. His monologue about the balky horse (*JG*, 3:223) is no longer superstitious at all, but is taken up by a relatively clear warning to himself about the actual dangers of his situation at court, since that situation has been complicated by his renewed relationship with Götz and Marie. Götz and Adelheid are no longer the two powerful poles between which his weak, impressionable personality hovers; his vacillation is now simply the anguish of an individual whose natural and comfortable sphere of activity (court and politics) has been presented to him (by Götz) as an object of doubt. But then why is Adelheid's role not curtailed even further? Why not let Weislingen experience his inner conflicts with respect to the court as a court, as a political arena, without introducing the motif of sexual temptation? Why is the court still represented for him by Adelheid?

## Weislingen's Melancholy Murderer

The answer I propose to this question implies a slight but crucial modification of Adelheid's function in the play's structure. If in the first version she is a pendant to Götz, in the second version, from Weislingen's point of view, she is a *symbolic extension* of Götz's influence, a vision of what court life becomes for even a thoroughly competent and committed courtier, like Weislingen, who has begun to have doubts about it. Adelheid is the difference between what the court had been for Weislingen earlier and what it is for him when he returns to it with his mind infected by doubt. The courtier, the soldier, the politician, the representative of *vita attiva,* like Weislingen, functions properly only as long as he is entirely absorbed in his activity. When he begins to think— especially in the complicated philosophical area suggested by Götz, involving the question of freedom of the individual in a world that can never satisfy the claims of such freedom (we recall Goethe's idea of "*prätendirte* Freyheit")—it follows necessarily that the enveloping element of his earlier active existence now stands over against him as an alienated object, an unattainable ideal, tantalizing, confusing, treacherous, ultimately destructive—in a word, Adelheid. Adelheid's seduction of Weislingen, in the second version, is merely an image, a symbolic refiguration, of Götz's seduction of him. In the first version, it is the inertia of weakness, represented mainly by Weislingen, that wears down and destroys Götz. In the second version, it is *speculative self-consciousness*—represented mainly by Götz's grand but ineffectual and philosophically untenable vision of freedom—that operates via the symbolic agency of Adelheid to disorient and destroy Weislingen.

In the second version, a simple structural device is introduced that makes clear Götz's ultimate responsibility for Weislingen's destruction. The *heimliches Gericht* is retained, but the scene of Adelheid's death is removed; in fact, Adelheid's death is not even mentioned. The ringing, portentous guilty verdict is now followed immediately by the death not of the symbolic agency, but of the mind, the real person, behind it, by the death of Weislingen's real murderer, Götz von Berlichingen. In the first version, the court scene and the scene of Adelheid's death go together as a pair; the first requires the second for its completion. If it was necessary, therefore, to eliminate the death scene, as part of the reduction of Adelheid's prominence, then surely the court scene should also have been removed. That Adelheid's end is not even mentioned in the scenes that follow leaves the court scene hanging, waiting for a concrete application; our attention is thus drawn to the relation between the court's verdict and the only significant event of the play that follows it, Götz's death. Again, it is Götz, as the sower of doubt, the initiator of a hopelessly complex melancholy self-consciousness, who has caused Weislingen's degeneration and destruction.

This cryptic emphasis on Götz's responsibility for Weislingen's death is important not so much in itself as for what it says about Götz in general. It is one of the devices that associate Götz more closely, in the second version, with the idea of *vita contemplativa,* self-consciousness, prophecy, visionary intellect. In *Dichtung und Wahrheit,* Goethe suggests that his fascination with Adelheid as a person, in the first version, had been a way of compensating for his hero's growing inactivity. The curtailment of Adelheid's role, accordingly, now emphasizes Götz's inactivity, brings it more into focus, shows more clearly the speculative character of his idea of freedom, the absence of any possible goal in the real world toward which his thought and effort might tend. Or we think of the figures of Carl, Marie, and Brother Martin. Simply by removing the image of Martin as a bad omen, and by removing the strong association of Carl with Weislingen, Goethe has allowed these unworldly figures to become primarily part of Götz's own aura, a revelation of the underlying truth about him. We are reminded strongly of Brother Martin, after all, when Götz, like St. Martin, offers to share his clothes with Weislingen; and little Carl's story of the generous child is to an extent the story of his own father's over-generous character, even down to the detail of Götz's belief in his ability to "cure" Weislingen by human contact. Götz is not by any means a worldly individual. What he actually does— his robberies, his feuds, his Robin Hood exploits—serves only to express an impotent dissatisfaction with the way the world is going, the way he himself prophetically recognizes the world must go. His only action of direct political consequence is his misguided agreement with the peasant rebels. The idea of constructive political action is beyond him. He is, in the second version, a melancholy speculative philosopher, a visionary; his violent actions and words are the attempt to maintain contact with a reality from which his own thought alienates him. His broken body has become a symbol of broken consciousness; his need for humane effectiveness arises precisely from a knowledge of human futility, of the impossibility of human-to-human contact (hence his iron hand) in any form that might actually reshape the world. Nägele's reading concludes by focusing on the "aporia" disclosed in the image of Götz's writing, on the unmasking of the "Fiktion der Unmittelbarkeit" (p. 76); my contention is that this quality of the text is the main point of the second version.

Given the work's imaginative environment, it should not surprise us to discover in the new Götz an intellectual or visionary or prophet. During the same period, Goethe was working or planning to work with Socrates and Mohammed as dramatic figures, and his Prometheus is as much a visionary philosopher as a fighter or artificer. But Götz surpasses Prometheus in experiencing the irreconcilability of philosophical speculation with concrete achievement, and so approaches more closely—for all his superficial simplicity—the figure of the melancholy Saturnian visionary. Götz destroys not only Weislingen, but also himself, in that his humane sensibilities do not permit him to renounce the contradictory, therefore unspecific and futile project of realizing the idea of freedom in historical actuality, in the "necessary course of the whole." In Goethe's letter to Herder, the opposite of the term "gedacht," "cerebral," is not "felt" or "lived" or even "imaged"; if it were, then the second version of the play would not be less passionate than the first. The implied opposite of "gedacht" is "geschaut," in the sense almost of "beheld." The first version had been based too exclusively in literary polemic; the second is focused more upon melancholy prophetic *vision* and its problems in the real world.

The second version is thus both less cerebral and less passionate than the first, for the work has now been reconceived as visionary drama, drama of the mind. But this reconception is not fully carried out in the work as published. To say that the second *Götz* "is" a visionary drama would be wrong. Götz is never actually shown indulging in melancholy self-consciousness; his thorough pessimism toward the end of the play is the same in both versions, and nothing he himself says compels us to interpret the pessimism of the second version as different from that of the first, as prophetic melancholy rather than thwarted Shakespearean downrightness. In order to perceive the visionary tendency at all—in order to recognize that when Götz insists he is "ein Feind von Explicationen" (*JG*, 3:197), "an enemy of explanations," he is actually resisting a deep truth in his own nature—we must be attentive to a web of subtle structural relations; that tendency might escape us altogether if we did not possess the first version for comparison. What I claim, therefore, is only that Goethe, in revising, *wished* to develop the play in the direction of visionary drama, of drama focused upon the tragic attempt to combine prophetic vision with direct activity in the world.

## The Third Version

Goethe admits in *Dichtung und Wahrheit* that he did not manage to carry out his wishes in revising *Götz,* that he succeeded in producing only a "Vorübung" for something yet to come. But a "preliminary exercise" for what? Perhaps an even deeper reconception of the plan was needed. Perhaps the story of Götz von Berlichingen—even though it does combine a prophetic idea of freedom with a striving to remain active in the real world—is simply not as amenable to visionary-dramatic treatment as Goethe had thought. Perhaps the third version will make use of a different story and a different hero, a more obviously Saturnian hero, a figure more obviously resembling the Renaissance magus, a figure who, in the very course of his visionary or magical speculations, will arrive ineluctably at the impossible but irresistible imperative of direct contact with, and direct influence upon, the real world, a figure who will yearn for simplicity, for unsullied intensity of experience, and will inevitably achieve disaster. Perhaps, in other words, the third version of *Götz von Berlichingen* is *Faust.* Perhaps it is significant in this regard that Götz's agreement with the rebels, his pact with the devil, as it were, is actually seen by the audience in the second version, whereas in the first version it had been excluded as a kind of ineffable mystery, as the "secret point" (necessarily offstage in a world that does not meet Shakespearean standards) at which a Shakespearean Götz experiences his inevitable collision with the "necessary course of the whole."

Goethe had certainly made sketches for *Faust* some considerable time before the second version of *Götz;* and so we should perhaps say that the intellectual material of *Götz,* after the second version, is absorbed into the stream of the *Faust* project. In any case, Goethe was by no means averse to revising his youthful works after long periods of time, as witness *Werther.* That he does not revise further the second version of *Götz* (except for the theater adaptation of 1804, which he refused to have printed [WA, 13/1:185–360]), even though he admits its imperfection in *Dichtung und Wahrheit,* therefore suggests that the creative impulse behind the work had found another outlet. Moreover, *Götz* and *Faust* are related as the two specifically German endeavors among Goethe's major early dramatic projects. And once we understand that the revision of *Götz* represents a move toward tragedy focused on the futility of striving to combine speculative vision with human effectiveness in the world, then (given Goethe's idea of the German "national" character by the time of *Dichtung und Wahrheit*) we find that the assertion about "historical and national substance" has become relatively intelligible. For in the second version, Götz, as a visionary, is not far from what Goethe now increasingly identifies as the typical, intellectually isolated German individual, with no real aptitude for politics on a large scale, but clinging doggedly to a doomed faith in the ability of his own private illumination to master and, if need be, reform the world.[6] We will return to the "historical and national" aspect of the *Götz/Faust* project later, from quite a different angle.

There is also a piece of physical evidence that supports my point, the well-preserved manuscript of the first version of *Götz,* which is mentioned in *Dichtung und Wahrheit* and in fact still exists. Goethe did not as a rule take such good care of the manuscripts of works he later revised; otherwise we should probably possess, for example, a prose *Tasso* and a more reliable version of *Wilhelm Meisters theatralische Sendung.* But the manuscript of the *Geschichte Gottfriedens von Berlichingen* was very carefully preserved, and how else can we explain this care on Goethe's part, if not as he himself explains it in *Dichtung und Wahrheit*? The *Geschichte Gottfriedens* is not really a "first version" at all, but is a completely different work from the published *Götz.* The latter, in fact, is more provisional than the former; it shows definite signs of beginning to tumble into the great imaginative vortex that eventually resulted in *Faust.*

In *Dichtung und Wahrheit,* Goethe says that he quickly recognized the faults of the *Geschichte Gottfriedens,* "since the nature of my poetic efforts constantly pushed me toward unity," and continues, "From this point on I concentrated on my own work, rather than on Götz's history of his life or on German antiquity." By his own "work," does he mean here *Götz* alone? Is he claiming to have achieved "unity" in a text which, a few lines later, he characterizes as a provisional sketch for future development? On the contrary, I think we can now confidently read this passage to refer to a unity of focus in Goethe's "work" as a whole, a focus in various poetic projects upon the problem of the "secret point," the problem of practical activity in relation to a speculative or prophetic vision that at once inspires and torments the ego, the vision of a Prometheus, Mohammed, Socrates, of the developed, brooding Götz, later of Werther, Egmont, Tasso, Faust.

## *Götz, Faust,* and Reading

The "secret point" of the Shakespeare speech does not disappear, as a central shaping idea, with Goethe's abandonment of polemical Shakespearism in the revision of *Götz,* but the manner of its literary presence and operation changes considerably. In the first *Gottfried,* it is primarily an aspect of character and marks the difference between strong and weak individuals, between those in whom the collision of freedom with necessity is fully realized and those in whom it is obscured, confused, blunted by an over-civilized fear of human nature. In the second *Götz,* where the boundaries of individuality have begun to blur, where Götz and Adelheid are no longer strictly distinct from one another, let alone the mighty Shakespearean antagonists they had been earlier, and where Weislingen's otherwise perfectly viable mode of individual existence is compromised by contact with the aura of self-questioning that now surrounds Götz, the question of freedom and necessity has become more a problem in the structure of the play's meaning with respect to history. In *Werther,* correspondingly, the structural aspect of the question is developed by its association with the shift from epistolary form to third-person narrative. In *Egmont,* the quality not only of problem, but of collision, is strongly marked in the relation between the final vision of freedom and our knowledge of historical reality, and in our sense of the theater as an "agreeable insanity" with respect to the reality beyond its doors. And I have argued elsewhere that the use of structures of theatricality to actualize the idea of the "secret point" in human nature is already experimented with in the play *Stella.*[7] The focus of meaning thus shifts from a relatively objective location in the fictional world to the realm of structure, in a sense that involves the relation between the work and its audience. In the case of *Götz,* this relation is what Goethe stresses when he speaks of the revision's increased "historical and national substance."

What we have, then, is a development in the direction of an aesthetic conception of literature—in the sense that the unfolding of meaning depends on a reader's or spectator's recognition of his particular role in relation to the work. The original *Gottfried* expresses a strong anti-aesthetic tendency. The task of drama is to be Shakespearean, to put individuals on the stage who are entirely self-sufficient in their quality as "nature." The play is a "Raritäten Kasten," a showcase of natural rarities that are what they are with or without our responding to them in any particular way. But the very force of this polemic in *Gottfried,* and the very need for it, are proof that in its own historical time, it is futile. Literature does not even begin to operate except within a web of public expectations, preconceptions, pre-understandings that form precisely the idiom in which it proclaims itself as literature. And if these expectations imply an aesthetic conception of meaning, then no text, however aggressively polemical, can escape meaning what it means in that spirit. "Nature" itself is now divided between object and response. It is the very nature of "posterity" to "misrecognize" or "misapprehend" literature in this manner. Woe to such a posterity ("Wehe der Nachkommenschaft die dich verkennt" [*JG*, 2:227, 3:297]), say the play's last words.

Goethe's move in the direction of the aesthetic is therefore the only possible avenue for *continuing* the campaign opened in *Gottfried*. The aesthetic cannot be avoided. It must be met head-on, in structures that expose the wrongness of reading *in* reading, especially by permitting the work's mode of reception to stare back at itself out of the fiction. And while the second Götz is not yet a reader in quite the sense that Egmont is, let alone the characters in *Tasso*, the third Götz, who is Faust, is at last the reader par excellence, perhaps the very archetype of the reader in Western literary imagining.

Faustus, from his beginnings, is marked principally as the solitary midnight reader of forbidden books. And his adventures, in practically all accounts, tend strongly to be a transparent allegory of the adventures of a reader—whether or not the particular author of something like the *Historia von D. Johann Fausten* (1587) is aware of it. Faustus makes impossible trips through time and space. He visits papal and imperial courts and Turkish castles; he conjures up Alexander the Great and the heroes of the Homeric epics, including of course Helen of Troy; he sticks his nose in everywhere, from the heavens above to the meanest taproom. But he never participates significantly in the types of life he observes, and never accomplishes anything; he only amuses himself, sometimes sexually, sometimes with pointless cruelty, often under the protection of magical invisibility, and even the knowledge he acquires is of no special use either to him or to others. He is a caricature of the idle, passive reader, to whom every conceivable human experience is available in a kind of purified form, requiring neither ability nor courage nor effort on his part, and stripped of whatever discomfort or responsibility normally attends it.

He is, moreover, a creature of the sixteenth century, in which the spread of literacy and the ever increasing supply of books for sale at modest prices bring about a change in the very idea of reading. Prior to the development of printing and mass bibliopoly, the reader, even *as* reader, was strongly oriented toward his community, defined in his person and bound in his activity by the web of social and organizational ties along which reading material, in manuscript form, was disseminated and exchanged. But once the money in my pocket enables me to be a reader, whenever I wish, of practically whatever I wish, I have become, as a reader, anonymous. I have become a radically solitary reader, a reader as daydreamer, for whom the magic of reading offers *escape* from the bonds of the

community. I have become Faustus, in the sense that Faustus is an image of the
aesthetic reader, the reader without social responsibility, reflectively attentive to
the pleasurable movements of his own soul as the source of value and meaning
in what he reads.[8]

Of course Goethe's Faust is not Faustus in exactly this sense. He is more
an anti-Faustus or anti-reader, whose first major magical project, involving the
girl Gretchen, is an attempt to put books behind him and to regain the possibility
of responsible action. It is as if Faustus, the original aesthetic reader, appalled
by two centuries' further development of the aesthetic view, were now trying
to undo the damage by reversing his own role, in the same way that the first
*Gottfried* resists being what it after all is, drama in and of an aesthetically
disposed age. And Faust's project, within the fiction, is as necessarily doomed
to futility as Goethe's first version (*Gottfried*) of the eventual *Faust* project
had been.

But *Faust* itself, the completed project, is perhaps a different matter.
In my *Goethe's Theory of Poetry*, I argue that that huge work is conceived and
constructed with a view to defeating utterly the process of reading it;[9] and I will
refer to that argument from time to time in the following. Here, however, we
will approach the same structure of problems from a different point of view.

## Prometheus, Saturn, Shakespeare, and Olympian Zeus

The wrongness of reading, under the sign of the aesthetic, has to do with
the exposure of the reader to co-option; and Goethe's sense of this relation is
developed very clearly in the revision of *Götz*. We have mentioned the difference
between Gottfried's original prophecy, "the weak will rule," and the revised
prophecy, "the vile (or worthless, or valueless) will rule." Let us look at more of
those two passages.

> Verschliesst eure Herzen sorgfältiger als eure Truhen.[10] Es kommen die Zeiten
> des Betrugs, es ist ihm Freyheit gegeben. Die Schwachen werden regieren,
> mit List, und der Tapfre wird in die Netze fallen womit die Feigheit die Pfade
> verwebt. (*JG*, 2:227)

> Schließt eure Herzen sorgfältiger als eure Thore. Es kommen die Zeiten des
> Betrugs, es ist ihm Freyheit gegeben. Die Nichtswürdigen werden regieren
> mit List, und der Edle wird in ihre Netze fallen. (*JG*, 3:297)

> [Close up your hearts more carefully than your treasure-chests (rev.: more
> carefully than your gates). The time of deceit is coming, free rein is given to
> deceit. The weak will rule (rev.: the vile will rule) with cunning, and the brave
> man will fall into the nets which cowardice has woven over the paths (rev.:
> and the noble man will fall into their nets).]

In the first version, the brave man (recognizable by deeds) is bogged down in a world covered with traps set by cowards. In the second version, the noble man (recognizable presumably by his quality of mind) falls into a trap that is apparently set just for him by his worthless adversaries. In the first version we are warned to treat our hearts like a treasure-chest that is kept in secret and sought by the sneak-thief (cf. Matt. 6:19–21; Luke 12:33–34). In the second version our heart is compared to our courtyard (protected by gates), a place to which even strangers might normally have access, but which we are now advised to be more careful of. The danger envisaged in the second version, then, is that by maintaining our normal openness to the world, we may admit the unprincipled individual who will use precisely our nobility of mind to entrap us and turn our energy to his ends—which is almost a definition of co-option.

But in the second *Götz,* co-option is not only suggested; it is shown, in the scene where Götz makes his commitment to the peasant rebels, a scene that is no longer characterized by whatever sort of incomprehensibility or mystery had kept it offstage in the original *Gottfried.* In that scene, Kohl threatens Götz, "Götz sey unser Hauptmann, oder sieh zu deinem Schloß, und deiner Haut," "Götz, be our captain, or watch out for your castle, and your skin," and gives him two hours to decide. But Götz responds, "Was brauchts das. Ich bin so gut entschlossen—jetzt als darnach" (*JG,* 3:278), "There's no need of that. My decision already stands—now or later." Götz is *already* inclined, in his basic nobility, to accept the leader's role for the peasants, in order, he hopes, to control them and help them to their violated rights without further atrocities. Precisely the best side of his nature, in other words, is co-opted by a group whose majority is bent on anarchy and violent revenge against the upper classes.

And if we ask what this has to do with co-option in the realm of literature, an indication is given us in the relation of Götz and Weislingen, which is also an instance of co-option. Weislingen, again, in the second version, is understood to have been, before his capture, an entirely competent and effective leader in political and military affairs. But unlike many of his fellow nobles— whose acts of injustice and arbitrary cruelty we hear about often enough in the play—he is also a man of principle, sensitive to questions of right and wrong. This is the side of his nature by which Götz seduces him.

The debate between them, as I have said, is more or less a standoff. Weislingen advances an argument based on the idea of the necessary political stability of the empire as a whole (*JG,* 3:195–96). Götz counters by pointing out that what happens locally has little to do with principles established at the imperial level; but he turns out to be most concerned, now, with the fate of a boy whom he had sent to spy on the Bishop of Bamberg, and who had been caught and handled roughly (*JG,* 3:196–97). And even though this concern tells *against* Götz—since we have already heard, from Sievers in the first scene (*JG,* 3:176), about how Götz had sent spies to prepare for taking the bishop captive, and since Götz himself emphasizes that his boy had been captured in a time of declared truce with the bishop—still his insistence on the disorder of local politics, hence on the constant danger of having one's principles violated by the local effects of one's activity, is enough to awaken the fatal element of doubt in Weislingen's mind. Weislingen's first thoughts, before their debate, when Götz leaves him alone for a moment, concern his sense of alienation from the episcopal court (*JG,* 3:194), an alienation that marks him as a man of vision and principle ("Können sie mir geben wornach ich strebe"), the sort of man whose actions, on balance, might have a beneficial effect even in the corrupt political situation that surrounds him, provided he can continue to use his talents even while struggling self-critically to avoid being compromised. But then the principled side of his nature is co-opted into Götz's world of doubts and dreams. And when he does return to the court after all, he has simply despaired of preserving his principles; the potentially fruitful tension between his inner sense of striving and the world in which he must work is gone. He has now truly become what Götz had called him, a "tool" of the princes (*JG,* 3:197), who, in his conversation with the emperor, defends uncritically, not to say shamelessly, the proposition that eliminating three petty nobles—Sickingen, Selbitz, and (he hesitates here) Berlichingen—will restore order in all Germany (*JG,* 3:232–33).

There are thus two clear co-optive moves in the play, and it is significant that in neither case does the ostensible agency of co-option actually benefit. Neither the interest of those who have real vision (Götz and his allies) nor the interest of those who have real grievances (the peasants) is ultimately served. Nor, for that matter, does the ultimate bearer of responsibility, the emperor, gain anything. The winners in this game, as Götz says, are "die Nichtswürdigen," the venal princes, who have no vision, no principles, no significant grievances, and no sense for the responsibility entailed by their position. Of course, our idea of Götz as a prophet in these matters must now include the recognition that his own activity contributes to the coming of what he foresees.

This brings us to the question of a literature at once both co-optive and co-opted, for which the structure of *Götz* is a fairly clear allegory. In the age of aesthetics, where meaning depends on the performance of the reader's role, the reader of literature is always in some sense co-opted. His own thought (employed in generating the work's meaning) is given back to him in a form that is developed in ways that are beyond his control. Like Weislingen at Götz's castle, he finds himself buying into thoughts and attitudes that are undeniably his own, yet have also somehow received the power to change or disorient him. This process is strictly private, presupposing the institution of the solitary reader; and from the individual's point of view—considered as a process of developing new self-perspective—it is not even necessarily injurious.[11] But it also has a public aspect, insofar as literature remains a social institution. And on the public level, it is literature that is co-opted by its readers; literature, dependent as it is on the reader's performance, *is* nothing in society but what its readers make of it.

This public phase of literature's existence is suggested in *Götz* with strong ominous overtones. Götz concludes the little scene in which we see him as a *literary* man, writing his memoirs, with the words, "Und Gott sey dank worum ich warb ist mir worden" (*JG,* 3:273), "And thank God, what I courted (or wooed, or asked for) has been given to me." The choice of words is interesting, because it suggests both the courting (or seduction) of Weislingen and literature's aesthetic courting of the reader. But no sooner does Götz pronounce these words than Lerse and Georg appear, and we hear, for the first time, of the peasants' rebellion. "What I asked for has been given to me," says Götz. What literature in the aesthetic sense asks for, without knowing it, is the development of unfocused, uncontrolled social forces by which it is co-opted.

The rebellious peasants are, so to speak, the public version of what Weislingen is in private. Motivated originally by the sound principles of justice and freedom, to which many of them, as individuals, still express allegiance, they are unable to sustain those principles as a collective in public life. They are thus an image of the literary public, to whom the very identity of literature in society is entrusted. For the literary public (and by consequence literature, which they represent) cannot possibly operate in a cohesive and socially productive manner, since what they share, what makes them a group, is precisely a turning away from the social toward the individual, the reader's aesthetic co-option into a realm of ideas, especially the idea of freedom, that—far from controlling or regulating his activity—are made to depend for their very meaning on his strictly private performance as a reader. Literature therefore, in its public aspect, cannot help but manifest itself in a form that is easily discredited, like the peasants and their captain Götz. And the winners, again, are "die Nichtswürdigen," those who do not bother with idea or principle, but are content to wield whatever political advantage they possess as unscrupulously as they think they might need to. The whole literary process is thus always available to be co-opted by whoever benefits most from the practice of power politics.

The allegory is perhaps not as direct and persuasive as it would have been if it had been part of the original plan for *Gottfried.* But we can satisfy ourselves about its existence by looking at the related figure of Prometheus, who has two distinct aspects for Goethe. In that he "forms men," first of all, Prometheus is the same figure as Shakespeare, the creator of artificial human beings who turn out to be nothing but "nature" itself. At the same time, however, Prometheus's forming of men is also an image of the aesthetic operation of literature upon its reader, the co-option of the reader into a role in the production of meaning. This aspect of Prometheus is especially clear in the poem, where, as we have noted, the eighteenth-century reader is obliged to see himself as a kind of game-player with respect to the contradictory tendencies in his notion of a higher power. And it is in this light, I think, that we must read the co-optive move carried out by Jupiter in the second act of the dramatic fragment *Prometheus*. Aided by Minerva, Prometheus has given life to his statues; and Mercury now suggests that Jupiter use his lightning bolts to destroy them. But Jupiter responds:

> Sie sind! und werden sein!
> Und sollen sein!
> Über alles was ist
> Unter dem weiten Himmel,
> Auf der unendlichen Erde
> Ist mein die Herrschaft.
> Das Wurmgeschlecht vermehrt
> Die Anzahl meiner Knechte. (WA, 39:204)

> [They are! and will be! and it is right that they be! Over all that exists under broad heaven and on endless earth, dominion is mine. *That* race of worms increases the number of my servants.]

Mercury then asks permission to declare Jupiter's authority to the new human race, but again Jupiter is a step ahead of him:

> Noch nicht! In neugeborner Jugendwonne
> Wähnt ihre Seele sich göttergleich.
> Sie werden dich nicht hören, bis sie dein
> Bedürfen. Überlaß sie ihrem Leben!

> [Not yet! In the newborn rapture of youth, their soul imagines itself godlike. They will not hear you till they need you. Leave them to their life.]

There is no need to impose divine authority on humans, because they will eventually impose it on themselves. Or in terms of the allegory of literature, the reader, in the feeling of godlikeness induced by his aesthetic involvement in the very generation of the idea of freedom, will soon prove himself politically inept to the extent that he will positively require the imposition of an unscrupulous but correspondingly efficient higher power. This aspect of the fragmentary work becomes clearer still if the poem "Prometheus" was really meant to open the third act.[12]

And once we understand the role of Prometheus in the development of the idea of the wrongness of literature, we can also understand fully the painful personal resonance of this thinking for Goethe. For it now turns out that not even Shakespeare himself (in the guise of Prometheus, the former of natural men)—let alone the advocacy of Shakespeare in *Gottfried*—is spared co-option in the age of aesthetics. The poet, who had imagined himself a revived Prometheus, now finds that he has assumed the role of a brooding, subterranean Saturn, oppressed by the knowledge of how his work must inevitably be misused in the public light of day. The two-sided idea of "forming man" is the trap in which he is caught; and perhaps therefore Montaigne, who says, "Les autres forment l'homme; je le recite," is at least a "friend" in this darkness. Which brings us back to chapter 1 and *Werther.*

# Part II

# The Undoing of Literature

$$\widehat{\phantom{xx}} 5 \widehat{\phantom{xx}}$$

# Lotte's Name and Lotte's Body

In the discussion of *Werther* in chapters 1 and 2, one thing we showed is that it is possible to carry out an interpretation of the novel without saying much about Lotte. We do have to mention her from time to time, as the object of some action or inner movement or phrase of Werther's; and we did talk about the typical side of her culturally unfulfilled existence, in connection with the idea of seeing through Werther's discourse to something like a reality behind it. But perhaps it is time we asked whether Lotte, in her own right, is any sort of force, has any independent effect, whether, in short, she *is* anyone, in the novel.

## The Woman and the Text

We have already discussed the letter of 30 May, the one immediately preceding Lotte's first appearance in the book's final version, the letter that ends with Werther's resolve to avoid actually seeing the widow who is the object of her young servant's devotion. The parallel with our situation vis-à-vis the object of Werther's devotion is clear; and in chapter 2, taking this parallel as a challenge, we found we could make certain objective judgments about Lotte after all. But the effect of these judgments is to uncover what is typical about her, not what is unique or characteristic. Even after the introduction of the third-person narrator, who perhaps could tell us more about Lotte than Werther is willing to, and could even plausibly document her character and condition—why should Werther be the only one who writes letters?—we find we are still in the dark about her. Another passage that was added in the revision calls our attention to this state of affairs:

> Was in dieser Zeit in Lottens Seele vorging, wie ihre Gesinnungen gegen ihren Mann, gegen ihren unglücklichen Freund gewesen, getrauen wir uns kaum mit Worten auszudrücken, ob wir uns gleich davon, nach der Kenntniß

107

ihres Charakters, wohl einen stillen Begriff machen können und eine schöne
weibliche Seele sich in die ihrige denken und mit ihr empfinden kann.
(p. 155)[1]

[What passed in Lotte's soul during this period, how her attitudes were set
toward her husband and toward her unhappy friend, is something we hardly
dare express in words, even though our knowledge of her character enables
us to form an unspoken conception and would enable a fine feminine soul to
think its way into hers and to feel with her.]

In the very act of speaking of "our" knowledge of Lotte's "character," the narrator
also intimates that such knowledge can be perfected only in a "feminine" soul,
which implies, again, that knowledge about Lotte is knowledge about what
women share, about what is *typically* good or noble or sensitive in women.

The narrator, that is, or "editor," as he calls himself, does not bring with
him a new perspective on the story, but merely picks up where Werther leaves
off. In the only letter he writes to Lotte before receiving the news of her marriage
to Albert, Werther works around to the subject of his relations with women,
and especially with Fräulein von B.., the one "weibliches Geschöpf" (20 Jan.,
p. 97), the "female creature" (!) to whom he is drawn. Lotte, he suggests, should
be honored to represent the standard by which Frl. von B.. is judged, and Frl.
von B.., he insists, freely accepts the honor of being compared to Lotte (pp. 97–
98). Again, the categories of character and understanding are subordinated to
those of type and judgment; and we recognize that this had also been the case
throughout Book 1, in Werther's writing *about* Lotte, which is concerned not
to know her, or even to describe her very closely—we think of his making a
silhouette in lieu of a portrait (24 July, p. 57; 20 Feb., p. 100)—so much as to
*stage* her in a series of quasi-dramatic scenes, beginning with her distribution
of the children's bread (16 June, pp. 26–27) and ending with her moonlight
speech on death and the afterlife and her mother (10 Sept., pp. 81–86).

This last scene is especially significant because of the length at which
Lotte herself actually speaks—or gets her speech transmitted by Werther. For
what she says here, despite its passion, says much less about her than, for
example, Albert's arguments on suicide say about him (12 Aug., pp. 64–72).
Albert's character is focused by Werther's opposition, whereas Lotte's speech,
with Werther's full approval (if not Albert's [p. 84]), becomes not much more
than a kind of aria. When it happens that Werther does not approve of what
Lotte has to say, later, in the conversation where she asks him to stay away until
Christmas Eve (pp. 155–58), he quickly dismisses her pleas and arguments as
belonging to her married state, or to trite social prejudices, rather than to her
character, and so tries to sever the connection between what she says and what
she is. Indeed, even in her aria on immortality he upstages her by insisting
repeatedly on the greater complexity of his own feelings, since he alone knows

that (in his intention) he and Lotte and Albert are now actually together for the last time in this life.

But is it only Werther, or Werther and the "editor," who thus suppress Lotte's personal being? Or does her suppression have to do with the relation between the woman and the *text,* this text that establishes a kind of hierarchy of characters by giving Werther a family name but no first name, while denying family names to Albert and Lotte, and denying Lotte even the dignity of her whole Christian name, Charlotte, which is reduced to its feminizing and (in effect and in origin) diminutive suffix? The second alternative is supported by parallels elsewhere in Goethe. In *Faust,* it is Margarete's speaking in verse that abstracts her into the world of the text, out of the sheer accidental reality for which Faust desires her.[2] And Faust's possession of Helena is marked by her learning to speak in rhyme. We might recall *Egmont* here as well, where Clärchen, as an allegory of freedom, is assimilated to an ideal level of the text that has little to do with her own or her lover's real existence.

But the strongest reason for thinking of *Werther* in these terms is that in real life, Goethe used the book to assert his possession of a real woman, Charlotte Kestner, to translate her frustrating reality into a form that would be irrevocably his property, under his authorial control. Of course we are in the habit of saying that the relation of a text to a particular real person does not engage its quality *as* text, which in aesthetic terms means its relation to the anonymous or generic reader, the reader as role. But this theoretical position, in the present case, is itself a move of appropriation, and one that Goethe actually makes: when he writes to the Kestners, in October 1774, that his book is an "innocent mixture of truth and falsehood" which they must learn to experience "more purely" (i.e., more aesthetically, more as a pure text by which to have one's feelings co-opted); and when he writes to Johann Christian Kestner, on 21 November 1774, "Werther must—must be!—You don't feel *him,* you feel only me and yourselves and what you speak of as being pasted into the book." Goethe, who never tires of calling attention to the silhouette of Lotte hanging in his room, has now devised, in the form of text, a more complete way of possessing her. In the November letter he promises cryptically that "within a year" he will "extinguish" whatever his book has given the Kestners cause to complain of, all the "suspicion, misinterpretation, gossiping." "Remember my promise," he resumes later in the same letter. "I alone can produce what will free you from everyone's talk, from even the breath of suspicion. I have it in my power, but it is still too early!" These words sound less like a promise than like a proprietary claim, almost a threat. Exactly what is Goethe promising? To make some sort of public (or published) declaration?—which would only defeat its purpose by drawing attention to the issue, and to the Kestners. The idea of power suggests the converse of the statement he actually makes. "I have it in my power to free you" means: as things stand, I have *you* in my power.

Among Goethe's early works, *Iphigenie auf Tauris* will probably be regarded as the strongest counterexample to the idea of the textual suppression or appropriation of women. But the situation looks less unambiguous when we recognize that *Iphigenie* is very similar in structure to the poem "Prometheus." Its thought is obviously directed at the religious and humane sensibilities of an eighteenth-century audience, while its mythical background, much of its rhetorical surface, and certain specific motifs, like Orestes' dream of an unreconciled Tantalus, suggest that these sensibilities can never tear themselves free of what they might prefer to dismiss as blood-soaked superstition. Iphigenie's, in this regard, appears to be the voice of humane reason. Sigurd Burckhardt argues that the main action of the play is Iphigenie's learning to speak, her "emancipating herself through speaking," a process in which we see "language in its state of becoming," hence the achievement of "truth in human terms."[3] The other characters, all men, must still learn to speak after her model. And yet, the one supernatural event in the extended plot that is not subject to a reasonable psychological or political explanation is Iphigenie's miraculous abstraction from under the knife at Aulis, and her transportation into exile among the Tauridians. Her presence on the stage, her very body, is a constant sign of that plot-presupposition, and so is strictly irreconcilable or incommensurable with the fabric of rational discourse she herself strives to develop. We and the male characters, once we have learned the emancipated human use of language, can (so to speak) reenter our own century and leave the mythological machinery of the text behind us. But in doing so, we also leave behind Iphigenie, who (by existing) cannot escape that machinery any more than Tantalus can his punishment. The departing Greeks do in a sense leave Iphigenie behind. For they cannot set sail until her discourse-lesson has been learned, which means that her learning and teaching function is over, and she is taken aboard ship as not much more than an object. The parallel with the statue of Artemis works both ways.[4]

This is perhaps not an instance of suppression and appropriation of the woman in exactly the manner of *Werther*. Lotte's voice is constantly muffled or distorted, Iphigenie's rings out as a model. But the two works are not separated by as much as we might have supposed. And the motif of Iphigenie's *body*, as the agency that traps her in a textual (mythological) structure by which her own thought is compromised, suggests a line of argument that will carry us a good deal further in the following.

## Lotte and Literature

The idea of the operation of text *as* text upon a woman—whether fictional or real (or perhaps, somehow, both)—involves a number of inherently questionable theoretical leaps that will have to be justified retrospectively when we have established a broader context for the argument. But the narrower idea of a tension or opposition between Lotte and literature, the idea that literature is used *against* Lotte, at least by Werther—and I think I can show, not only by Werther—is easily supported. We have already discussed Werther's aggressiveness toward Lotte, his gloating about her having passed the pistols to him, his characterization of her friendly affection for him as "a poison that will destroy me *and her*" (21 Nov., p. 131, my emphasis).[5] And we have talked about his constantly staging her in his letters. But there are two instances where he goes beyond just making a staged scene out of what she happens to do, where he reveals a desire to shape their relation according to the model of a work of dramatic literature in which the principal woman dies more or less by her own hand—a desire, that is, to enlist literature in getting her to kill herself. It is clear from his first letter, in any case, that at the place he had just left he had succeeded in driving a woman, "Die arme Leonore" (4 May, p. 5), to some sort of desperate extremity.

The more obvious of these two instances of literary aggression involves Lessing's *Emilia Galotti,* the book Werther is reading on the night of his suicide. As we have noted, there are various ways of explaining his interest in just this play. But given certain assumptions about how Goethe understood Lessing, assumptions that are borne out by such works as *Clavigo* and *Stella,* the correspondences that suggest themselves most strongly are: Lotte to Emilia, Werther to the Prince Hettore Gonzaga, Albert to Appiani—especially since Werther on several occasions dreams of Albert's death (21 Aug., p. 114; 10 Oct., p. 123) and even of killing him (p. 160). If we understand, namely, that Emilia dies in despair, having been shown, by the prince, both the possibility of a life of emotional and sexual fulfillment and her own exclusion from such a life, then the parallel with Lotte's situation is clear—at least in Werther's view of her situation, his conviction that only he could offer her true fulfillment (29 July, p. 113)—and by rights she ought to despair as well.[6]

The second instance is somewhat less clear and has to do with Werther's association of himself with Hamlet, which we have mentioned. It comes to the surface in the conversation with Albert on suicide, when Werther tells the story of the girl who had drowned herself, the story of Ophelia, except that the girl had been of lower social class. The story is not one of seduction and abandonment. The girl's desires are aroused, she is ready to be taken sexually, "sie ist bis auf den höchsten Grad gespannt" (10 Aug., p. 70), and at this point her lover leaves her; Werther speaks of her failure to recognize that her loss could have been made up by another man (p. 71), which implies that her virginity is intact, that she is neither pregnant nor fallen into the sort of "ill repute" (p. 70) that she herself, in happier days, had contributed to establishing for others. Her lover (or suitor) has aroused her, torn her out of the "narrow circle" of her earlier life (p. 69), then left her utterly disoriented, in a kind of madness; he has made of her a bourgeois Ophelia. And if we assume that Werther recognizes in Lotte what we do, the limitedness of her aptitude in matters cultural and literary, then it is not hard to imagine the back of his mind occupied with the plan of drawing her out of *her* narrow circle, into a world where large knowledge, subtle allusion, difficult ideas, suspect emotions, and (eventually) unmanageable desires become entangled in a manner that she must lack the skill to deal with, in a manner that must cost her her needful bourgeois orientation in life, leaving her an Ophelia or a "poor Leonore."

Neither of these literary fantasies succeeds in actually killing Lotte. But this insight into Werther's aggressive tactics draws our attention to the relation between Lotte and the literary character of the text that does include her, the whole novel in which we are reading of her. In particular, what happens if we take seriously the fiction of the "editor"? Before the change to third-person, the novel is fully naturalized in its narrative form; the fiction of its presenting us with genuine letters is entirely plausible. The "editor," to be sure, is not as plausible. But if we resolve for a moment to believe in him, as a person living in the same world as the characters, then we must ask how he can justify publishing what he has collected, which includes a great deal of uncomfortably intimate material about Albert and especially Lotte—a question that is doubly pointed for being parallel to the question we might ask in real life about Goethe, with respect to Charlotte Kestner and her husband.

In Goethe's case, some readers might say ex post facto that the existence of *Werther* as a work of art was worth a certain amount of inconvenience to the Kestners. But the "editor" has no pretensions to being an artist. He is, as far as we can tell, an undistinguished worker in the literary industry of the time who takes the opportunity (probably for money) to tickle the feelings of the reading public with the papers (and perhaps the more or less doctored interview material) he has been lucky enough to get his hands on. He makes the obligatory gesture of saying he has changed the names in his text, at least place-names (26 May, p. 16, footnote). But even if he has changed Werther's name (from, say, "Jerusalem"), the identities of his characters will be no secret to people who read newspapers, especially the people who count most, people who actually know, or live near, Albert and Lotte.

This literary pieceworker, then, whether he would admit it or not, is carrying out an attack on Lotte. And that he is doing so, as it were, in the name of literature, is clear from the two footnotes he adds to Werther's letter of 16 June (pp. 29, 30), where he explains his omission of the names of the German authors whom Lotte finds boring and those whom she approves of. He does not take any special trouble to protect or disguise Lotte, because he has nothing to fear from her. But as a German literary man, he has a strong personal interest in staying on good terms with as many of his German colleagues as possible, and so wishes to avoid all "cause for complaint" (p. 29). If we take the editorial fiction seriously, therefore, if we judge the editor as we would any other character, by his actions, then we recognize in him a man who has callously sacrificed Lotte's personal well-being to the business of literature, without even permitting her the insignificant retaliatory gesture of expressing (with real names) her own literary opinions.

In this regard, however, the editor is himself also a sacrifice thrown *to us,* since the judgment we make about him is one we would find it much harder to make, much farther outside our literary habits, about the book's actual "author"; he thus perhaps deflects our attention and our criticism from the author. Or perhaps he is not a sacrifice so much as a baited trap. For as soon as we judge the editor to have attacked Lotte unfairly on behalf of literature, we too, the readers, as participants in the literary business, are implicated. In omitting the names that might cause controversy, the editor displays an interest in literary solidarity; he hopes, especially, that the literary community will close ranks about him in case it is suggested that his text exploits people's real suffering, especially Lotte's. And we, as readers, belong inescapably to that literary community. Again the wrongness of reading emerges, but now in relation to the oppressed condition of a woman. And again there is a parallel in *Faust,* where the placement of the prose scene, "Trüber Tag," with respect to the Walpurgis Night and its Dream sequel, establishes a connection between *our* activity, as players of the game of literature, and Faust's inability to find a way of dealing with his moral responsibility for Gretchen's fate.[7]

It may appear that we are working in two different directions here: exposing Goethe's unscrupulous use of literature to achieve the personally satisfying closure of his messy relationship with Lotte Buff-Kestner; and crediting Goethe with the exposure of an inherent wrongness in literature, in reading, in the character inevitably assumed by a text under the influence of aesthetic philosophy. But if we are correct in inferring, behind Goethe's early work, an experience of the *radical* wrongness of literature, of wrongness in that field to which the work still inescapably belongs, of a wrongness, therefore, that must infect even the perception of its wrongness, then the condition of being pulled in different directions is exactly what we shall expect. The "classical" habit of thought, which distinguishes strictly between the grand historical integrity of the opus and the deplorable messiness of daily life, has no relevance here. We are left with a conceptually compromised view of Goethe, which is at the same time the view of a Goethe himself constantly compromised by his own efforts at resolution. And this Goethe, I contend, makes a difference to us in ways that the authorized classical version, perched on its paper Olympus, never could.

## Ossian and the Aesthetics of Rape

The novel's repeated move of appropriation or suppression prompts us, *ex negativo,* to ask: who *is* Lotte? what is the *object* of this need to appropriate or suppress? Obviously we can receive no positive answer to this question from the text before us, which, *as* a literary text, is precisely what suppresses or conceals it. But at least we recognize that that presumed object has to do with gender, with Lotte as woman, because the crime against her is imagined not only as a kind of murder, but also as a kind of rape.

The long passage of Ossian-translation with which Werther clubs Lotte into submission in their final encounter is interesting because, in the context of the novel, *it means nothing whatever.* It does contain stories of thwarted love and betrayal, and it is loaded with the pathos of grieving for a world in which everything of beauty or bravery or nobility is doomed. But it produces nothing even remotely approaching the detailed psychological insights that arise from the allusions to *Hamlet* and *Emilia Galotti.* Its introduction into the novel, in fact, is placed strongly under the sign of the accidental. Lotte just happens to have the manuscript handy, in a desk drawer, at a time when she needs something to occupy Werther's attention (p. 165). And the effect of the reading upon Werther and Lotte is attributable to nothing more specific than the violent but amorphous *mood* of desperate melancholy that it calls forth in them.

We are thus reminded of Werther and Lotte's first meeting, where the single word "Klopstock" reduces them both to tears (16 June, p. 36), where, in other words, a highly crafted piece of language, which had asserted a controversial position in the religious discussion of its time, is reduced to nothing but the lachrymose mood of two of its readers. Here, therefore, as in the case of Ossian, the aesthetic view of literature is invoked—not to say travestied— the idea that the work achieves its very existence only in the reader's response. The issue of the aesthetic is also suggested by the character of the Ossian text as a translation, for translation is precisely the *reading-into-being* of a text. The translator occupies a reader's distance from his text, which is measurable by the difference between two languages, while at the same time he also *creates,* as a writer, exactly that text. He is, in this sense, an ideal positive image of the aesthetic reader, emblematizing the proposition that reading operates as a genuine co-writing or co-production of meaning. And it is this image that is at least called into question by the absence of meaning that characterizes the interpolated translation in *Werther,* by the fact that any text at all could be substituted, provided only that Werther and Lotte (and perhaps the reader) agree to feel desperately miserable in response to it.

But these considerations raise an interesting question. If the word "Klopstock" is enough to provoke sympathetic tears in Werther and Lotte at the beginning of their relationship, why should the word "Ossian" not do as well at the end? Or if Werther and Lotte have been emotionally exhausted to the point where the mere memory of a text can no longer have the required effect, still, why can *the reader* not be satisfied with the word "Ossian," or with a relatively short description, psychologically elaborated, of the reading scene?

Perhaps the reader needs to be clubbed into submission too. But if so, then the Ossian text is not really suited to its purpose, since it makes considerable demands on our detailed rational attentiveness, merely in order to keep the names straight. Moreover, once it has been decided to reproduce the text to which Werther and Lotte respond, the question of *how much* text arises. Never mind what the text is, or what it says, as long as we can plausibly imagine its evoking the requisite emotions. The question is: are three wheelbarrows of text needed to do the job, or would two and a half wheelbarrows accord better with the reader's sense of emotional time?

As soon as this question is asked, of course, it becomes clear that there is no answer. Or the answer is different for every individual reader, which means that there is no answer. At the very climax of *Werther,* then, where the presentation ought to reach a maximum of focus and exactness, we find ourselves looking at a text that does not need to be there, that could just as well be another text, or a longer or shorter fragment of itself, without suffering any change in its narrative function. And given what that function is, to ensnare the reader emotionally—I use the singular here, since Werther and Lotte obviously do not share a single position, but rather each undergoes an entirely different emotional extremity, in a solitude, for each, that is belied by their physical contact, then confirmed by the closing of the door between them (pp. 176–77)—I think we are clearly justified in reading it as a reductio ad absurdum of literature in the aesthetic sense. The text itself has become a blank space, an excuse for the reader to feel something. A text now receives value or meaning only by way of our finding it in the desk drawer at a time when, for whatever reason, we need emotional stimulation or release. And if a single text—by whatever dynamics of accident or publicity (perhaps by providing fuel for gossip)—serves what seems to be roughly the same purpose for large numbers of people, then we have a classic in the making.

As soon as this conclusion is drawn, moreover, it becomes applicable to the whole text of *Werther* in relation to the reader. We are reminded now that the "editor" does not wait until the end of the book to make his presence felt. The very first words are in fact his:

> Was ich von der Geschichte des armen Werther nur habe auffinden können, habe ich mit Fleiß gesammelt und lege es euch hier vor, und weiß, daß ihr mir's danken werdet. Ihr könnt seinem Geiste und seinem Charakter eure Bewunderung und Liebe, seinem Schicksale eure Thränen nicht versagen.
>
> Und du gute Seele, die du eben den Drang fühlst wie er, schöpfe Trost aus seinem Leiden, und laß das Büchlein deinen Freund sein, wenn du aus Geschick oder eigener Schuld keinen nähern finden kannst. (p. 3)

> [Whatever I have been able to find out of the story of poor Werther I have collected diligently and now set it here before you and know that you will

thank me for it. You cannot deny your admiration and love to his mind and character, nor your tears to his fate.

And you, good soul, who feel the same pressure as he, take solace from his suffering, and let this little book be your friend when, through fate or through your own fault, you can find none closer.]

The whole book thus stands under the sign of an appeal to the reader's emotional solitude, an invitation not so much to read the text as to fill it with one's own uncommunicated being.

But the association of the text as a whole with the Ossian episode takes us a step beyond merely the idea of the wrongness of reading. For the Ossian episode is clearly a rape, in the sense that a gesture normally signifying love is used to carry out an act of aggression, violence, hatred. It is in fact a particularly cruel form of rape, in that the victim herself unknowingly provides her attacker with the instrument, the text, that he uses against her—just as she later handles the pistols he uses in his second attack—and in that the victim, if we can believe the editor about the "look of love" with which she leaves the room (p. 176), apparently does not even know she has been raped.

The idea of the wrongness of reading, or the wrongness of literature, has thus been gendered, and given sharp contours, as a man's quasi-sexual attack on a woman. What precisely do these new components of the complex signify in the literary domain? What, after all, is literature, or the literary text?

## The Struggle for the Body

Like Hamlet, Werther gets to play a scene after he is, in effect, dead. But the scene he plays is a grotesque parody of Hamlet's. Hamlet has business to attend to, including the killing of Claudius. Werther lies in his bed, with half his brains blown out, and rattles with the fragment of his respiratory system that still works, while a procession of people, all male, weep over him and kiss him (pp. 190–91). The whole scene, in fact, including the time before he is discovered, lasts exactly twelve hours, from midnight, when he shoots himself (p. 189), till noon, when he dies. Again we think of Hamlet, who, when Horatio reminds him that the time will be short before news arrives of what has happened to Rosencrantz and Guildenstern in England, responds: "It will be short; the interim is mine, / And a man's life's no more than to say 'one' " (V.ii.73–74). Like Hamlet's life, Werther's life is but to say "one." To judge by the clock, his death happens in the same instant as his shooting. And yet somehow, between this instant and itself, the twelve hours of his messy, botched, accidental, and pointless dying are stretched.

It is not difficult to interpret these perceptions, once we recognize the tendency of *Werther,* the whole text, to mirror itself within itself, as it does in the Ossian fragment. For the extended instant of Werther's dying is clearly another such reproduction of the text as a whole. If, as we have seen, Werther's death is accidental with respect to the rigorous logic of his despair, then it follows that the machine of his despair, which is the whole story, is accidental with respect to his death. His death is given, inevitable, actual, from the very beginning; and the text is concerned with nothing but an accidental postponement of that death with respect to itself, which happens to give us the opportunity to weep over Werther and "hang on his lips" (p. 191) so to speak. "What is man, that he is permitted to complain about himself," says Werther in his first letter; and these words already mean his death, by meaning or seeking the supersedure of self-consciousness. Or we think of the words with which that first letter opens: "Wie froh bin ich, daß ich weg bin!" (p. 5), "How glad I am to be away!" Death is the whisperer here as well, since being "away" is strictly unattainable in life—as Werther himself later explains in his meditation on the words "here" and "there" (21 June, p. 39). Werther's death is present from the outset, as the foundation of the whole text, which in turn, by containing anything different, is as accidental, as replaceable, as the Ossian text, as pointless as the twelve hours of Werther's dying.[8]

This accidental or provisional quality of the text clearly belongs to Goethe's strategy for dealing with the aesthetic presupposition in literature. But if we think of it in relation to the idea of the supersedure of the physical—in Werther's suicide, in his and Lotte's speculations on the afterlife, in the young psychotic's happy time when he is "von sich" (p. 136), detached from the miserable chained creature in the madhouse—then the question of the *body* arises, the component of our being that constitutes our exposure to the accidental, the impediment between ourselves and our perfected being in death. In this regard, the text—the whole text, including the third-person section—assumes the character not of meaning or signification or description or feeling, but of *symptom,* the symptom of a sickness that is a disorder *of* the body while at the same time a disorder constituted *by* the body. I say "the" body advisedly, for the mechanism of aesthetic identification, which we have discussed in detail, ensures that the text cannot be a symptom of Werther's condition without also being, perhaps even more directly, a symptom of the reader's.

That the condition we mean pertains to the body is indicated by more than just the idea of the accidental and the involvement of the text in the actions of suicide and rape. "Werther, you are very sick," says Lotte (4 Dec., p. 139), when his composure collapses under (he says) the emotional weight of her music-making; and we are reminded of the association of emotional difficulties with physical sickness, which Werther denies when it is suggested by the pastor's wife (1 July, p. 45) but then embraces when arguing with Albert about suicide (12 Aug., pp. 68–69). Or we think of the uncertainty of the boundary between mental and physical illness in the case of the mad boy who had loved Lotte, or of the list of physical symptoms that drive the young servant to attack his mistress (4 Sept., pp. 116–17), as Werther later attacks Lotte.

But it is at the end of the book, as an aspect of the climax, that the body is most clearly identified as the site of the condition symptomatized by the text. During the twelve hours of Werther's dying, which are a model of the text as a whole, only his body, with no mental or verbal component, occupies the center of the action. And when he finally dies, in the text's last words, we read:

> Um Zwölfe Mittags starb er. Die Gegenwart des Amtmannes und seine Anstalten tuschten einen Auflauf. Nachts gegen Eilfe ließ er ihn an die Stätte begraben, die er sich erwählt hatte. Der Alte folgte der Leiche und die Söhne, Albert vermocht's nicht. Man fürchtete für Lottens Leben. Handwerker trugen ihn. Kein Geistlicher hat ihn begleitet. (p. 191)

> [At twelve noon he died. The presence of the magistrate (Lotte's father) and his handling of matters prevented a crowd scene. Toward eleven that evening he had him buried at the spot he himself had chosen. The old man followed the body, and his sons, Albert was unable to. People feared for Lotte's life. Manual workers carried him. No clergyman accompanied him.]

There is nothing unusual about the idea that it is "he" (Werther) who dies, or that the old man buries "him," especially since "he" had been the living agent who had requested the grave site (p. 188). Then, however, we hear that the old man and his sons followed "the body," "die Leiche," which means unambiguously the *dead* body, and at this point we might permit ourselves a sigh of relief. For this word, "die Leiche," marks the *end* of the text. "Werther" ("he") is now complete, achieved, done with, separated from the dead lump of flesh. But unfortunately, the sentence continues: "Albert was unable to." At least one important absence mars the text's solemn closing ceremony. Then another sentence, probably explaining where Albert is: "People feared for Lotte's life." Suddenly Werther is not done with after all, but still operative, still on the attack against Lotte, whereupon, in the last two sentences, the word "him" is resurrected. In strict grammatical terms, given the naming of two other men in the paragraph, the reference of this pronoun ought to be unclear. That we know it means "Werther" therefore lends it a certain ominous weight. The thing, the body, that is being carried away, as deep as we might wish to bury it, is still "him," still "Werther," still the site of the disorder that produces the text, just as the text itself, even when finished, is not done with, not strictly past, but remains (it would not be a text if it did not) as the symptom of a bodily disorder that we must still get used to recognizing as our own.

The intimate association of the body (especially Werther's) with the text, in its turn, enables us to say something more about the rape scene. For it now appears that what Werther is aiming at in the attack—especially since his instrument is a piece of text—is in effect the *textualization* of Lotte's body, which would combine the quasi-sexual violation of her privacy as a person with the achievement of her death—in the same sense that Werther himself is always already dead in his fusion with the text of the novel. Lotte, again, had innocently provided the weapon, in her aria on the theme "Wir werden sein!" (10 Sept., p. 83). And Werther (in effect) means now to force her to make good on her words, in an aesthetic understanding of them, by abducting her body into the domain of text, of literature, of reading, of aesthetics, of fundamental disorder, of death.

What does it mean, therefore, that the rape scene itself, and Lotte's apparent survival of the text, suggest the possibility of dismissing Werther's attack as a *failed* attempt at rape? What is the exact relation of *Lotte's* body to the text? We can develop this question by asking a simpler one, about the exact meaning of the short cryptic letter of 10 October:

> Wenn ich nur ihre schwarzen Augen sehe, ist mir es schon wohl! Sieh, und was mich verdrießt, ist, daß Albert nicht so beglückt zu sein scheinet, als er— hoffte—als ich—zu sein glaubte—wenn—Ich mache nicht gern Gedanken- striche, aber hier kann ich mich nicht anders ausdrücken—und mich dünkt deutlich genug. (p. 123)

> [When I but see her dark eyes, it makes me feel good! But look, what annoys me is that Albert does not seem to be as happy as he—had hoped—as I— would believe myself to be—if—I don't like all these dashes, but I cannot express myself otherwise here—and, I think, clearly enough.]

One of the things Werther is dreaming of here, with his "if," is clearly Albert's death. But is there any possible objective basis for his perception that Albert is less happy than he ought to be? In fact, there is. Albert and Lotte have been married for about eight months, and Lotte *is not yet pregnant*—unlike Lotte Buff, who bore her first son a little more than a year after marrying Kestner. This may even be part of what Werther is actually thinking, comparing his own love for Lotte, supposedly for herself alone, with Albert's more conventional idea of a wife's function.

The possibility of Lotte's pregnancy is never mentioned in the novel; but there are plenty of signs pointing at it, especially her oath, at her own mother's deathbed, to "be the mother" of her siblings (10 Sept., pp. 83, 85). And why does Goethe, in the fiction, push Lotte's marriage up to February (20 Feb., p. 100), from April (1773) when the Kestners were married, if not to give Lotte plenty of time to get pregnant, and indeed time to bear a child, by the story's end at Christmas? In any event, it is extremely important that Lotte is not pregnant. If she were an expecting mother, the center of her existence would be shifted toward the domain of family and generations, away from the domain of culture and intellect and society, which is from the outset the scene of her relationship with Werther. Pregnancy and motherhood offer a woman substantial protection, as is shown by the negative example of the widow who is amorously attacked by her servant, and who is exposed to the appropriative designs of several men, including her estate-hungry brother, in large part because she is childless (4 Sept., p. 118). It might be maintained, in fact, that if Lotte had gotten pregnant in time, the whole text of *Werther* would not exist. Would Werther think of returning to her, in June or July, if Albert's proprietary right had been sealed by her pregnancy? Would he even be attracted to her in the same way? Would she have either the time or the inclination for the many attempts she evidently makes to stabilize their relationship, to shape and regulate his ever more difficult and unpredictable feelings? Perhaps she would not even need to show him the door. She would be otherwise occupied, both externally and internally, and the relationship would wither.

The body of the man, Werther, is continuous with the text, which is the symptom of its disorder. The potentially fruitful body of the woman is a kind of explosive that bears within itself the possibility of the text's simple nonrealization, its reduction to nothing. The very existence of the text, therefore, in which the aesthetic reader is implicated (implicated by his body, his physical senses, if we take the term "aesthetic" seriously), is a struggle for Lotte's body, an attempted rape and murder. And the survival of that female body, conversely, is an instance of *resistance* to the text, or to the aesthetic in general.

## The Limits of the Aesthetic

The project of resistance or opposition to the aesthetic is bedeviled especially by the problem of leverage. How does one get outside the aesthetic view, or aesthetic practice? Where are its limits? The anti-aesthetic polemic of Goethe's original *Gottfried* proves futile, for in order to operate at all, that polemic must engage its reader in precisely the aesthetic manner, by calling forth in us a reflection upon reading that turns out to be an integral element of the work's very existence. The plays of Shakespeare themselves, in our time, are undermined by this dilemma. Shakespeare's characters perhaps *are* in truth pure "nature." But they are so *for us* only by way of our reflection upon their difference from our own readerly condition, a condition we could leave behind (if that were possible) only at the cost of losing precisely the idea of nature that we would require in its place. Hence the feeling of wrongness in reading that nags us constantly in Goethe's early work. But this feeling, however carefully we attend to it and articulate it, no more alters our condition than Werther's excruciatingly meticulous self-reproaches do his. For our knowledge of the wrongness of reading still itself belongs to the aesthetic machinery of literature, as a co-option of what ought to be our private being into the sphere of text and meaning.

The main vehicle in which Goethe attempts to deal with this dilemma is the *Faust* project. In saying this, I refer especially to the argument of my book *Goethe's Theory of Poetry,* which supplements the discussion here. With respect to the question of genre, for example, I think it can be shown that the theatrical aspect and the quasi-narrative aspect of *Faust* are played against one another in such a way that the work as a whole defeats any possible idea we might form of our relation to it as recipients, which means that the aesthetic mechanism can never get started. And even if a way can be found to incorporate this or other similar features of the text into an aesthetic conception of its meaning, still, I contend, the text is set up so as to anticipate, to thematize or structuralize in advance, any such critical or readerly move. *Faust* out-aestheticizes the aesthetic; it engages the reader so completely that it is no longer the reader—considered as a subject capable of irony, a possible target for co-option—who is engaged. In the terminology of *Goethe's Theory of Poetry,* "the meaning of *Faust* is realized only by our turning away from it";[9] one is a reader only by not being a reader in the aesthetic sense. And this quality of the work, in turn, is developed and confirmed by its not being strictly a text in the first place, but rather an open-ended public project, parallel, in this, to its companion piece, *Wilhelm Meisters Wanderjahre,* which is not strictly a novel, but rather the staging of its ostensible genre, "modern ironic novel," as a huge European religious project.[10]

Our present concern, however, is the relatively simple anti-aesthetic move devised by Goethe in *Werther,* where the limit of the aesthetic, the limit of the text's co-optive power, is marked by a woman's body. And in this regard, again, it is important—however unfortunate the consequences for Mr. and Mrs. Kestner—that the body in question is not strictly a textual or fictional construct, but is at least associable with a *real* body, a real female body, in fact, that does carry out its resistance to the textual by producing children, a body whose reality marks the point where text is thwarted, where text stops and the possibility of leverage against the aesthetic is established.

But nothing useful is implied about how this possibility is to be exploited, how this leverage may be brought to bear. And it is certainly not implied that the female body *in general* provides us with a means of resisting or overcoming the aesthetic predisposition of our literary culture. The conclusions we draw from *Werther,* in the sense of the argument of this chapter, are valid exclusively in relation to *Werther;* Lotte's body operates as it does here only because the text is set up so as to profile its operation. The case may perhaps be an extreme and therefore instructive one. *Werther,* from the editor's opening words on, may perhaps be regarded as the aesthetic text par excellence, a quality that is confirmed by the elaborate mechanism of identification between Werther and the reader. Thus the encounter, even in *this* text, with limits to the aesthetic—as represented, incidentally, not only by Lotte's body, but also by the presence of the strictly pre- or anti-aesthetic texts of Montaigne ("Les autres forment l'homme; je le recite")—perhaps gains a certain exemplary value. But no sense of a possible anti-aesthetic program is developed. If *Werther* accomplishes anything at all, it only succeeds in placing every other poetic text under the obligation to construct its own self-resisting aesthetic mechanism.

And yet, the idea of *gender difference* does hold a special sort of promise, the idea that the difference between men and women might be construed as a fundamental difference in *the relation of individual and text*. As soon as we are compelled or persuaded to acknowledge a difference of this type—even if it is not exactly the difference built into the structure of *Werther*—the aesthetic view of the text, or of literature, collapses. The question here is not an objective one: whether or not there are significant differences between the ways different individuals manage their relation to the same text. If we look at this question dispassionately, the answer is probably yes; but this is not the issue. What matters is whether we are convinced, in the process of carrying out our role as readers, that the result of this process is the meaning of the text itself, the realization of the "work," whether, in other words, we are comfortable with the *expectation* that other readers will enact a role substantially similar to ours. When this expectation is thwarted—the expectation itself, not any particular avenue for confirming it—the very idea of the aesthetic is called into question.

I am not using the term "aesthetic" in its Kantian meaning, but there is a clear parallel, at this stage in the argument, with Kant's discussion of judgments of taste. We cannot judge an object to be beautiful, says Kant, without attributing the same judgment, the same feeling of entirely disinterested pleasure ("Wohlgefallen ohne alles Interesse"), to *every* other observer; we must "believe we have reason to ascribe a similar pleasure to everyone."[11] Similarly, one cannot read a text in the aesthetic sense without assuming that the role one plays, as reader, is precisely the role of *the* reader, the anonymous individual, who could be anyone at all, faced with the particular text in question. If I recognize that the role I am performing as reader is more or less exclusively mine, then the performance of that role is no longer integrated with the meaning or realization of the text, and the aesthetic structure of literature collapses.

Hence the suggestiveness of Goethe's manipulation of gender difference in *Werther*. If I am compelled to recognize that a large number of individuals (differently gendered) will necessarily find themselves in a relation to the text that is fundamentally different from mine, if I recognize, therefore, that *the* reader—who I used to think I was—does not exist, then I must confront a radical challenge to my whole idea of literature. I do not claim that Goethe actually achieves such a dismantling of the aesthetic in *Werther*. The fact that the reader of this text is in a strong sense gendered male does not prevent a perceptive woman from adopting that role for the time being. And even if I am a woman, the fact that Lotte's body constitutes a move of resistance to the text does not necessarily imply anything about my body, let alone my thoughts as a reader. What, after all, would "resistance" to the text, especially bodily resistance, mean in a reader, if not simply our putting the text aside, our not being a reader in the first place? But the suggestiveness of Goethe's procedure remains, and points us in at least a promising direction.

## Lotte's Name and the Shame of Reading

There is one indication in *Werther* that Goethe is trying to do more than just be suggestive. It involves only a very small piece of text; and in order to understand it, we must begin by recognizing that Goethe, like most of us, had a thing about names. Especially the name "Charlotte" is important to him, which Lotte Buff shares with the other major love of his relatively early life, Charlotte von Stein, and which is then prominently resurrected in *Die Wahlverwandtschaften*. In fact, it is possible to understand Goethe's relationship with Frau von Stein, which he calls "a persisting resignation" (his letter to her of 2 May 1776), as a rewriting of his own life in the form of the story *Werther* might have become if Lotte had been a mother, or at least pregnant, before Werther's return. Frau von Stein had three surviving sons, one of whom Goethe later practically adopted for a period of three years.

Not only the name "Charlotte," however, but also its components and anagrams are important to Goethe—the initial C, for instance, which is shared by his mother, his beloved sister, and later his wife. And the name "Ottilie," practically an anagram of "Lotte," belongs both to real life and to *Die Wahlverwandtschaften*, where it is played, in its turn, against the name "Otto." But the variation of "Lotte" that concerns us now, in *Werther*, is the one that occurs in the sentence "Emilia Galotti lag auf dem Pulte aufgeschlagen" (p. 191), "Emilia Galotti lay opened on the desk." At this point in this novel, in the naming of the one external object that we now know had occupied Werther's attention in his last moments, I think it is impossible not to hear the name "Lotte" in "Galotti." And it is also important that there is no typographical indication whatever, in any manuscript or significant printed version, that the words "Emilia Galotti" are the title of a play. The sentence almost says that the *person* Emilia Galotti "lay opened on the desk." Moreover, given that the German "aufgeschlagen"—although it is the normal expression for a book's being open—is definitely more graphic than English "opened," suggesting something closer to "thrown open"; and given the even stronger sexual component in Emilia Galotti's story than in Lotte's, the image of her death as a kind of deflowering (the breaking of a rose) at the hands of her father: we are tempted to hear, as it were from behind the text, the sentence, "Emilia Galotti (or, cryptically, Lotte) lay on the desk with her legs spread."

If we are willing to follow this trail of suggestions, the results turn out not to be as outlandish as we might have expected. Werther's suicide, namely, is now understood as the climax of a masturbatory fantasy; and the idea of a *textual* attack on Lotte's body is given a graphic dimension in the suggested use of that body as a presumably printable pornographic image. To the combination of rape and murder (sexual violence and mortal violence), which is the text's relation to Lotte, now corresponds, neatly, the combination of masturbation and suicide, two forms of self-induced climax connected by the well-established metaphorical association of orgasm with death. The idea of masturbation, in any event, operates prominently in the *Faust* project, and is the transparently masked main theme of Goethe's chaotic little farce-opera *Der Triumph der Empfindsamkeit,* which in character and imagery obviously parodies *Werther,* and where the pornographically employed body of the beloved woman is actually detached from her person in the form of a life-sized doll.[12]

But the results from the point of view of the reader are more far-reaching. The implied scene in which Werther, preparing to die, stares down at a book that, in being thrown open, itself *is* the pornographic image it contains, is an uncomfortable mirroring of our actual situation as readers, staring down at the open book *Werther.* Reading in the aesthetic sense, we must recognize, is nothing but a form of masturbation, the autoerotic stimulation in ourselves of feelings that have no real human or social function at all, feelings that in truth have nothing to do with the constitution of beauty or the constitution in the text of a critically illuminated fictional "world." Aesthetics, as the doctrine of literary world-creation in this sense, is but a theoretical papering-over of the radical solitude, the furtive and ashamed self-gratification, that is really our activity, our role, as readers.

This much, in the abstract, could be derived from considerations developed earlier in this chapter. But the specific image of masturbation, as I say, is an indication of Goethe's seriousness here, because it magnifies the effect of the invocation of gender difference with respect to the quality of text as text. For *both* the masculine *and* the feminine reader—and what is more important, for diametrically opposed reasons in the two cases—the difficulty of accepting the role of the reader now comes as close as possible to being insurmountable, however much we insist on the reader's duty to suppress his or her personal situation for the sake of the text or the fiction or literary meaning. The difficulty is still not absolutely insurmountable. Literature can still be rescued, even in the form of its humiliating exposure in *Werther.* There is no necessary limit to the shamelessness of the reading public. Literature's death is here no more strictly necessary than Werther's is within the fiction. But the extremely offensive device of the masturbatory image, again, reflects a seriousness of purpose in Goethe that will lead us along different paths later on.

# Heroes and Fleabags and Women: Gender and Representation in *Penthesilea*

To complete the main interpretive argument on Goethe, we turn to a work Goethe did not write. Later we will discuss the point at which Goethe definitively abandons the specific form of the anti-aesthetic project represented by *Götz, Werther,* and *Egmont;* and I have already indicated that the anti-aesthetic aspect of *Faust* and the *Wanderjahre* resides as much in their contrived public situation as in their structure as texts. But Heinrich von Kleist's *Penthesilea* permits us to view the whole range of possibilities opened by Goethe's early work. Its focus on gender, especially, complements the procedure in *Werther,* with regard both to technique, in its use of the theater, and to conceptual development, in that the quandary of the age of aesthetics is approached by way of the problem of representation.

## Representation and Its Failure

"So viel ich weiß, giebt es in der Natur / Kraft blos und ihren Widerstand, nichts Drittes,"[1] "As far as I know, there is in nature only force and its opposition, no third," says Odysseus in the course of his exposition of past events in the first scene of *Penthesilea.* This statement involves both a truism and a contradiction. A truism insofar as it is a kind of paraphrase of Newton's third law of motion, the law of equal and opposite actions, which states basically that a force cannot be observed (or even imagined) except in relation to a resisting force. If we agree that whatever happens in nature is a Newtonian "action," or the operation of forces, then Odysseus turns out to have said merely: the only thing that happens in nature is that things happen in nature. But at the same time—Odysseus begins with the words, "As far as I *know*"—the notions of force and resistance make up an *analysis* of happenings in nature, a tailoring of nature to systematic knowledge (especially with the allusion to Newton), a *representation* of nature, whence the statement becomes a contradiction. For the analytic or articulating process of representation *is* precisely that "third thing" Odysseus denies, that third element without which "nature" in effect would not exist, since we could not say or know or think anything about it.

And like the third element in the play's main action—Penthesilea and her Amazons, considered as a third in relation to the two opposed armies of Greeks and Trojans—representation as process always *interferes* with the structure or operation of its ostensible object, always brings with it an element of confusion or uncertainty that must be denied by people, like Odysseus, who are interested in clear categories of thought and want the represented object, say "nature," simply to be there, in and of itself. Thus, if we are willing for a moment to regard the Amazon attack as an allegory of the interference of representation as process with representation as object, the whole play allegorizes a familiar Kleistian obsession: the disruptive effect of the representational operation of consciousness in an otherwise somehow simple or natural or "graceful" state of affairs.

Nor is this association of Penthesilea with the process of representation at all far-fetched. She is attracted to the Greeks in general and Achilles in particular because she has heard of their exploits in song (*P,* 2110–40). When she arrives, therefore, it is as if a reader of the *Iliad* had intruded into the midst of the poem's action, a person for whom that action is not bitter immediate reality, as it is presumably for the Greeks and Trojans, but rather a delightful fabric of representation. This ironic structure—in the sense of the older notion of "Romantic irony"—this direct meeting between fictional characters and the fiction's reader, culminates at the point where Penthesilea reveals to Achilles her knowledge not only of his large public exploits, but also of the intimate scene of his sympathy and lamentation with Priam, as recounted in Book 24 of the *Iliad* (*P,* 2199–2202).

The process of representation is never strictly separable from its object or product. The problem of representation—or in Kleist's puppet-theater terminology, the problem of consciousness—arises precisely from the uncontrollable involvement of representational moves in every human action and situation. But there are distinctions to be observed here. In scene 4 of *Penthesilea,* for example, both Odysseus (*P,* 486–92) and Diomedes (*P,* 511–19) take the role of what we might call spin doctors, representing Achilles' desperate flight from the Amazons as a deed of positive martial achievement, thus as it were producing the laudatory poetic version of the event only moments after the fact. This is representation in the service of reality, of concrete military goals, by way of its production of such qualities as morale, fighting spirit, self-confidence. But the level of representation that is folded back into the Trojan War action by Penthesilea's appearance is a level at which precisely the governing realities of that action are called into question. What had been matters of life and death to the Greeks now turn out to be representable as objects of a superior aesthetic attentiveness that takes no sides (or both sides) in the battle; the question of the historical existence and mission of the Achaean alliance turns out now to be replaceable by the question of its usefulness as a gene pool. To the extent that these representational moves infiltrate the Greeks' own consciousness, they must cause confusion or vertigo, in the form of that loss of the sense of belonging to one's own real communal situation which characterizes especially Achilles in the play's early scenes.

In any case, the idea of representation as interference, or as problem, is insisted upon constantly *for a theater audience* (we shall see that this is crucial) by the relation of what "actually" happens offstage to the strenuous and elaborate, but in the end evidently inadequate attempts of characters onstage to represent those events in language. The stage of *Penthesilea* is thus not only a site of representation in the obvious sense. It is a site, specifically, of the *failure* of representation, of representation as an obscuring filter, a barrier, a form of especially verbal interference in our relation to the presumably real.

A certain discomfort with this line of thought is caused by Kleist's letter to Goethe of 24 January 1808, in which he says that *Penthesilea* is "ebenso wenig für die Bühne geschrieben, als jenes frühere Drama: der Zerbrochene Krug,"[2] "every bit as untheatrically written as that earlier drama *Der zerbrochene Krug.*" And did Kleist really believe that an author of his relatively minor stature could expect a performance elaborate and expensive enough to include scenes with large animals, with horses and even elephants? Perhaps Goethe himself answers this question when, in response to the letter just quoted, he relegates Kleist to that class of foolish young men, "die auf ein Theater warten, welches da kommen soll" (*SWB,* 2:806), dramatists who write for a theater that does not exist. But whether or not an uncut performance of *Penthesilea* is, or was, possible, I will argue that the actuality of the theater, a theater in which even the most outrageous stage directions are carried out fully, is indispensable to the very being of the text, that the text is in effect not there except in such a theater.

Kleist's focus on representation, finally, has the effect of turning inside out, so to speak, the problem of the aesthetic as it appears in Goethe. The reader's role in constituting the meaning or fiction of a text is now observed (via Penthesilea as reader) from *within* the fiction. Now, therefore, it is not the reader's involvement with the text, not the co-optive tendency of literature, not the presumed existence of a role for *the* reader, that causes difficulties, but rather the reader's detachment, like Penthesilea's at Troy, the Kantian idea of the aesthetic as including no personal interest, no commitment, no taking of sides, on the reader's part. In the end, however, this change of perspective on the problem does not alter the problem itself.

## The Dissolution of Reality

How can we speak of representation as "interference"? How can we know of such interference or measure it without direct access to the "real," to the "object," which we start by admitting is impossible? The notion of representational interference, it seems, inevitably presupposes that "dogma of a dualism of scheme and reality" which Donald Davidson argues we can easily do without.[3] And if what we are talking about is really a "dogma," then our ability to dispense with it amounts more or less to an obligation.

I will argue that there is nothing dogmatic at all about the view of problems of representation that is opened by *Penthesilea*. Not only *can* we think in terms of representation as interference—and without the aid of any strict dualism involving "reality"—but we are in fact positioned with respect to Kleist's play in such a way as to undergo the *unavoidability* of our thinking in those terms, an unavoidability that has to do with the operation of gender in our experience. The question of translatability between what I will call different "representational frames" ("conceptual schemes" in Davidson, more or less) turns out not to be crucial. Even an absolute demonstration of translatability, if it were possible, would not affect the fabric of problems that is activated in Kleist's theater.

For the time being, however, let us remain with the idea of Penthesilea and her Amazons as an allegory of the excluded "third" in nature, the process of representation that governs any particular sense we have of reality, but cannot directly appear in the reality it governs without raising disruptive questions about its realness. This allegory, even if we agree about its content and its operation in the play, is not enough to convince us that representation is an issue or problem in *our* existence. But it does make enough sense psychologically to serve as an opening of the play's structure, and of the structure of what we are actually doing as spectators.

Why are the characters of the *Iliad*, especially Odysseus, so deeply outraged when, so to speak, a reader of the *Iliad*, Penthesilea, mixes into their battle? The point is that the presence of a reader has the effect, for the Greeks, of unmasking reality itself, the reality of "Kraft" and "Widerstand" by which they must orient themselves in existence, as a fabric of representation. In more general terms, the mere recognition of representation as a common and arbitrarily applicable human artistic activity (in the guise, say, of writing or reading), hence the recognition of the representability of all facts in our existence, inevitably raises the question of whether those facts are not *already*—always already—constituted as a form of fanciful representation, and so threatens to disorient us by dissolving the quality of objective realness in our world. This is the problem of aesthetic wrongness. Especially the practice of reading in the aesthetic sense accustoms us to the experience of something that is very like a "reality," yet is constituted mainly by our acceptance of a particular role (our *free* acceptance, as we cannot help but insist) with respect to it. And to the extent that this habit infects our relation to reality itself—by way, for example, of the analogy between freedom of the imagination and freedom of the will, which Kant, and then Schiller, fondly suppose can be restricted to the domain of "symbol"[4]—our commitment and effectiveness in dealing with reality are undermined.

The problem, then, for Odysseus and the Greeks, is not that they cannot understand what the Amazons are up to. Achilles has no trouble understanding when the matter is explained to him; and the other Greeks, we have noted, are by no means without skill in tailoring fact as representation. What the Greeks fear (on both the literal and the allegorical level) is that merely by permitting themselves to be occupied by the *question* of the Amazons, or by permitting themselves to be drawn too far into the complexities of the idea of representation, merely by engaging the idea of aesthetic experience, they might lose the sharp sense of immediate task and purpose that stabilizes their existence.

This way of looking at *Penthesilea* is useful, especially, because it reveals a crucial structural symmetry in the play and provides a structural (not psychological) answer to the question of why Achilles' challenge provokes Penthesilea's bestial fury. For Achilles intrudes into Penthesilea's world in almost exactly the same way she has intruded into the Greeks' world, and must be eradicated for the same reason. The symmetry here is not mechanically strict. Whereas Penthesilea occupies from the outset (as a virtual reader of the *Iliad*) a position of comprehensive aesthetic or representational mastery with respect to the Greeks' daily business, Achilles, in the course of the play, must grope laboriously toward a similar position with respect to the Amazons. His first long speech, in scene 4 (*P,* 587–615), is built on the metaphorical relation between love and war; and for most of the speech, it is not at all clear which is the tenor, which the vehicle, in this relation. At the end, when he speaks of dragging Penthesilea after his chariot, he seems to show that war is what he is really talking about; but an element of uncertainty evidently remains, a sense of the need to find his way into a still obscure representational frame, in effect a different reality. Then, after he unhorses Penthesilea, tries to revive her, and discovers that the Amazons are unwilling to use their deadly weapons against him (*P,* 1121–64), he apparently decides that love, after all, is the key to their behavior. And even though this view is based on a mistake—since the Amazons would have killed him without hesitation, but for Penthesilea's having specifically forbidden it (*P,* 852–55)—still it turns out to be accurate enough in practice to enable him to use his own unarmed body as a decoy in recapturing the queen.

Now, however, in scene 15, thanks to Penthesilea's mistaken belief that he is a captive, no longer an enemy, Achilles learns from her the whole history of the Amazons; he becomes in effect a reader of the poem that the Amazons live, just as Penthesilea is in effect a reader of the *Iliad*. At only one point in her account does he seem seriously disturbed by what he hears, when she confirms "the monstrous tale" (*P,* 2006) according to which all the Amazons, including herself, have undergone a "barbaric" (*P,* 2014) amputation of the right breast. But even here, he is neither mystified nor irreversibly alienated. He follows the rest of her story attentively, appears to understand exactly how her world, her representational field, operates, and appears to acknowledge the possibility of living in such a world, for all its dreamlike (*P,* 2018) or, as it were, lunar differentness (*P,* 2032) from his own.

Precisely this ability to make an intellectual and imaginative leap into the world of the Amazons, in fact, is what gets Achilles destroyed. For when he later issues the challenge to single combat, after Penthesilea has been rescued yet again, the one interpretation of his challenge that she cannot possibly accept is the correct one. To understand, or even to imagine as a possibility, that Achilles intends to submit himself to the Amazon scheme of things, that he intends to play along deliberately with the rules of that Amazon poem he has been made a reader of, would be inevitably to unmask the whole existentially fundamental structure of Amazon life and history as a manipulable game, a fabric of representation. Achilles, like Penthesilea in the reversed situation, is an allegory of the inadmissible "third" element in existence, which must always be effaced in order that existence retain the character of reality. Men who have been taken captive, like the Greeks we glimpse at the end of scene 6, may know as much as they like about the "dream" (*P,* 986), the Amazon representational field, in which they now operate. But the same knowledge in a man, like Achilles, who still occupies a position of aesthetic distance and mastery, undermines any sense of reality in that world.

## Penthesilea's Rage against Representation

In the crucial moments after Achilles sends his challenge to single combat, the text leaves open the possibility that, however unacceptable the correct interpretation of his action might be, still Penthesilea, on some level, does understand what is going on. Her first words, after the challenge is read, are:

> Laß dir vom Wetterstrahl die Zunge lösen,
> Verwünschter Redner, eh' du wieder sprichst!
> Hört' ich doch einen Sandblock just so gern,
> Endlosen Falls, bald hier, bald dort anschmetternd,
> Dem klafternhohen Felsenriff entpoltern. (*P,* 2370–74)

[Let your tongue be loosened by a lightning bolt, accursed speaker, before you speak again! I would just as soon hear the endless fall of a sandblock, banging now here now there as it crashes down from a sheer lofty cliff.]

The image she uses, of the collapsing precipice, recalls an experience she had herself actually undergone while first pursuing Achilles (*P,* 316–30)—including specifically the word "schmetternd" (*P,* 327)—whence the idea of the ground's disappearing under her feet is suggested, the idea of an undermining of any feeling of realness in her representationally conditioned existence. The experience of the precipice is one she shares with Achilles (*P,* 256–72); both of them have stretched the limits of their accustomed representational frames—she by violating the prohibition against allowing a prior love-choice to influence the martial phase of her activity (*P,* 2145–49)—to the point where they are threatened by the abyss of the no-longer-real. Indeed, the word "Sandblock" itself (which is not, as far as I know, an accepted geological term), by connoting both the solidity of stone and the instability of sand, suggests the idea of the representational frame, which *is* reality, yet can be undermined by mere thought.

In any case, the image of the collapsing precipice is awakened in Penthesilea by the *words* of the herald. That Achilles knows the world of the Amazons without being a captured part of it is disturbing, but perhaps still not disastrous. What is disastrous is that now, by way of the herald, he is attempting to fold his detached knowledge back into the actual operation of that Amazon reality, which is impossible if realness is to be sustained. Penthesilea is shaken by this prospect and, after her initial response, uses the space of a few lines of contentless dialogue with Prothoe to come to grips with it in her mind. Then she makes the speech that comes closest to explaining why she must destroy Achilles:

> Der mich zu schwach weiß, sich mit ihm zu messen,
> Der ruft zum Kampf mich, Prothoe, ins Feld?
> Hier diese treue Brust, sie rührt ihn erst,
> Wenn sie sein scharfer Speer zerschmetterte?
> Was ich ihm zugeflüstert, hat sein Ohr
> Mit der Musik der Rede bloß getroffen?
> Des Tempels unter Wipfeln denkt er nicht,
> Ein steinern Bild hat meine Hand bekränzt? (*P,* 2384–91)

[Even knowing that I am too weak to match him, Prothoe, he summons me to battle with him? This faithful breast of mine will touch him only when broken by his sharp spear? What I whispered to him was only a kind of rhetorical music in his ears? He does not think of the temple surrounded by trees? Did my hand garland a head made of stone?]

Can we read these words literally? Has the outcome of their previous encounters been so decisive that Penthesilea must now consider herself "weak" before Achilles? Does she really believe he has somehow suddenly conceived the desire to destroy her physically?

The metaphorical quality of combat in the text as a whole, and especially in the early speech of Achilles we have referred to, suggests a much more reasonable reading. For on the metaphorical level, it is strictly true that Penthesilea is too "weak," that Achilles cannot lose the contest he has proposed. Even if he loses the fight (deliberately or not), he has still won the contest by co-option; he has taken control of reality itself (in Penthesilea's frame) by mastering it aesthetically as a structure of representation and turning it to his own ends, and by maneuvering Penthesilea into a position where she must accept her own complicity in this process. Had he not been listening, she asks, when she had opened her mind to him completely in scene 15? Had he heard merely the "music" of her words, and not understood that their content, for her, is reality itself, not merely a story, not merely a representation that might be employed arbitrarily in the service of ideas and desires external to it? The very idea of a real world has now crumbled underfoot, and Penthesilea's literally insane attempt to rescue it—by not fighting with Achilles, but simply obliterating him—can in the end, as yet a further manipulating of representational frames, only make matters worse.

Why does Penthesilea speak exactly as she does here? The question of preserving the reality of the real, of course, cannot be directly stated without violating precisely what is meant to be preserved; it is a question that must be heard, by the sensitive mind, as a kind of whisper behind the "music" of speech. Therefore Penthesilea returns to ideas she had *already* spoken, in scene 9, after the first time she is rescued from Achilles, including the idea of attacking him with dogs, elephants, and "Sichelwagen" (*P,* 1170–73). In that earlier scene, the Amazons had concealed from her the fact that Achilles is pursuing her unarmed; she had therefore apparently had reason to believe in his intention to smash her body ("Mir diesen Busen zu zerschmettern" [*P,* 1177]), to feed it to the dogs and vultures (*P,* 1248–52), which must appear to her not merely brutal, but ungrateful, since she had at one point, still earlier, actually saved his life (*P,* 171–92). Now, however, after their conversation in scene 15, she has no reason at all to believe that he means to kill her, or that he fails to recognize her love for him. She makes the same complaint, about his insensitivity to her true purposes, that she had made in scene 9 (*P,* 1178–83, 1187–92); but the issues that operate behind her speaking are now of an entirely different order. Her words are gentle; but they already mean her rage.

## The Paradox of Representation and the Theater

Achilles, then, is to Penthesilea's world what she is to his, the folding back into reality of the excluded "third" of representation that dissolves the realness of reality and makes nonsense out of nature. This symmetry gives structure to the text, and holds together reasonably well in psychological terms. But it is still, from our point of view, only an allegory, and in fact raises questions that are much more difficult than those it answers.

What, after all, *is* a representational frame? If we retain, for the moment, the assumption that the world as organized by the Greeks and the world as organized by the Amazons are different representational frames—which is a difficult assumption to do without in reading the text—then it is clear that translatability between frames is not a serious problem. Neither Achilles nor Penthesilea is prevented from understanding the world of the other, from understanding it, in fact, in a manner that apparently includes the ability to accept it as a possible governing shape in reality. When she is rescued the second time from Achilles, Penthesilea passionately defends the "knightly custom" and the law of battle by which she ought to have remained his prisoner (*P,* 2298–2307). And he in turn, in scene 21, despite his earlier resistance, is now perfectly willing to participate in the ceremonies at Themiscyra.

But at the same time, representational frames are a matter of life and death. The two characters in the play who operate closest to the precipice, who put the most strain on the cohesion and separateness of their representational frames, Achilles and Penthesilea, are the two who must die. And the manner of their death—Achilles' as the victim in an insane, hallucinatory parody of the hunt, Penthesilea's by suicide, with a weapon whose effective materiality she concocts out of the metaphorical relations among words—suggests an overstepping of reality's bounds, hence the compensatory or retributive effect of representational frames whose reality-claim is drawn into question. How are we to understand this? Representational frames are intertranslatable, alterable, manipulable; yet they are also reality itself—in the sense that violating or ignoring or toying with the reality of, say, a sheer hundred-foot drop can get a person killed.

At the end of scene 19, Penthesilea seems already to have decided she must die: "Ich will in ew'ge Finsterniß mich bergen!" (*P,* 2351), "I will bury myself in eternal darkness." And the determining factor in her decision is not the loss of Achilles, but her personal responsibility for the failure of the whole Amazon campaign, which the high priestess has just made scathingly clear to her (*P,* 2312–41). How, then, a few seconds later, when the herald arrives, is her wish to die transformed into an insane rage against Achilles? If representational frames were not open to true translation, if Achilles, in wishing to continue his complicated interaction with Penthesilea, were simply missing the point of Amazon reality, if he had not actually penetrated and disrupted that reality, and so assumed a share of Penthesilea's responsibility, then we should expect her simply to disregard the challenge and continue in her resolve to do the right (Amazon) thing, to remove herself from the throne, and from life, as the author of an inexcusable crime against her community. Does she really believe that the literally inhuman slaughter of Achilles will create a basis on which the Amazons can resume the battle and recapture their Greeks in relatively civilized combat (*P,* 2397)? Heaven itself, in its thunder, refutes this possibility in advance.

But on the other hand, if the violated representational frame of the Amazons were not, for them, reality itself, if it were merely a policy, or a system of law set up to deal with reality, then, again, while we could account for Penthesilea's need to die, we could not account for her absolute need to kill Achilles as well. He, after all, is not a subscriber to that law, and could bear no share of responsibility for the Amazon disaster. He becomes responsible, and subject to retribution, only to the extent that that law is reality itself, requiring no subscription, no specific community membership, of those it governs.

We do not, I think, expect a theoretical untangling of this situation, a logical or psychological or otherwise systematic resolution of the paradox. What we want to know about is its *range,* the manner, if any, in which the problem of representational frames is a problem *for us.* Is Kleist merely a "hypochondriac" (apparently Goethe's view) who creates problems for himself, and for us, that we do not really have?[5] This question draws our attention to our condition as spectators in the theater, where we find ourselves acting out a paradox exactly analogous to the paradox developed by the text. For the dramatic stage is the clearest possible manifestation, in our experience, of the idea of a representational frame, a strictly shaped, limited, and edited reality that receives its quality *as* reality, as the reality of a fiction proposed by the text, only from the shaping, limiting, editing to which it is subjected. The world of the stage, moreover, is obviously manipulable and alterable, since it is sustained by mere convention, and its very purpose is to be translatable, to be held up against other versions of reality as a comment upon them. To be sure, the integrity of the stage-world is not ordinarily a matter of life and death. But in every dramatic proceeding there are limits—always located differently, depending on the particular literary and theatrical conventions that have been invoked—beyond which the whole exercise becomes pointless, as it were nonexistent, as if it had never been.

And in the case of *Penthesilea,* this inherent paradox of the theater is brought into focus by the quality of the stage as a site not only of representation, but also of the *failure* of representation. Or to put it another way, *Penthesilea* as a theatrical proceeding involves the idea of the *unrepresentable,* which is suggested by the question of the "third" element in observed nature, the process of representation; for this process, which cannot be contained within the order it creates, is arguably the general form of the unrepresentable. Again we find ourselves in the presence of a much-discussed feature of Kleist's writing, which in older criticism is treated under such rubrics as "the supernatural" and "feeling," the idea of that which is inexpressible or unaccountable in what confronts us as reality. But in *Penthesilea,* where the stage is erected as a site of the failure of representation, the idea of the unrepresentable offers itself more directly as a critical lever.

In the first instance, the unrepresentable is located in most of what happens offstage during the play, not merely because the violence and scope of that action is *difficult* to enact onstage, but because the premise on which the action is founded, the fighting of the Amazons, is *impossible* to represent, at least in relation to the conventions of representation that (by implication from the text) constitute the stage space. In this regard, the metaphorical relation of love and war, including Penthesilea's famous rhyme of "Küsse" and "Bisse" (*P,* 2981), "kisses" and "bites," names the problem of representation with which the Amazons face us. Earlier, with reference to Achilles, Penthesilea says:

> Hier dieses Eisen soll, Gefährtinnen,
> Soll mit der sanftesten Umarmung ihn,
> (Weil ich mit Eisen ihn umarmen muß!)
> An meinen Busen schmerzlos niederziehn. (*P,* 857–60)

[This steel I hold here, my comrades (because I must embrace him with steel), shall, in the softest embrace, draw him down painlessly to my breast.]

Grammatically these words are understandable; but as representation they in a strong sense fail, since the imagination cannot combine their contradictions into a single possible reality to which they might refer. Indeed, if Penthesilea is actually brandishing her sword as she speaks ("*Hier* dieses Eisen . . ."), the effect will be almost comically incongruous. Or even if we could imagine how one might overcome a man with "Eisen"—with sword, spear, or arrow—yet still manage to keep him in good condition for the gentle business of love, what should we say of the even more serious armament of the Amazons, which is mentioned more than once: the elephants, dogs, and "Sichelwagen," which I take to be chariots equipped with projecting blades at their sides, positioned so as to slice off the legs of the enemy's men and horses? What possible purpose, in relation to the Amazons' stated military goals, can be served by this stereotypically Oriental machinery of slaughter? We know, in any case, that the Amazons do kill many of the Greeks (*P,* 148–52).

As we sit in the theater, then, it is clear to us that we are receiving only a severely curtailed view of what might otherwise be the whole of the play's fiction. The stage, in fact, at times appears to act as a kind of ontological force field, changing the very nature of those who appear on it. When the Amazons actually step up before us as fighters, for example, in scene 11, it is as if the space of representation, the stage, had stripped them of all conceivable martial effectiveness. They simply fall down when the spears hit them; and the princess, who has strung her bow at line 1427, takes until line 1443 before she is ready to shoot. Penthesilea herself, at least in her language, does not escape this infection in the verbal-representational atmosphere of the stage. Offstage she fights like a tiger, but onstage she sometimes whines like the most utterly subjugated of lovelorn women. Her despair at being defeated by Achilles, for instance, culminates in the words "Staub lieber, als ein Weib sein, das nicht reizt" (*P,* 1253), "better to be mere dust than a woman who does not attract [men]," even though she herself later denies (to Achilles!) that her fighting has anything in common with the "softer" female tactic of being attractive (*P,* 1888).

On the one hand, we are enabled, as spectators of *Penthesilea,* to survey the operation and collision of what appear to be radically different representational frames. On the other hand, we have the impression of being confined within a single representational frame that excludes from our view the larger part of the fiction. Thus the structural paradox of the theater and the representational paradox developed in the fiction are combined and replicated in our sense of the spectatorial task, in such a way, for example, that the practically literal idea of a "frame" in the theater (referring to the lighted rectangle before us) is made available as a metaphor for structures in the fiction, and so in turn yet further perfects what now appears to be the work's fabric of meaning. This line of thought, moreover, along with the recollection of Achilles' love/war metaphor and of Penthesilea's description of his murder as merely a literalized metaphor (*P,* 2991–99), might prompt us to locate yet another version of the play's governing paradox in the nature of language. The idea that a particular language sets limits to its users' particular idea of reality is current in late-eighteenth-century Germany; but the manner in which a language carries out this world-shaping function, the practice of metaphor, is also always an overstepping of representational limits, hence an unmasking of the manipulability of its own world-vision. And finally, if we turn again to the theater, it might occur to us that in one strictly real sense, the figures before us, when they enter the stage space, do in fact leave behind a reality that is markedly out of harmony with their present actions, namely, the everyday reality of the actors when they are not in costume before an audience. Thus, again, our attention is drawn to a coincidence, in our experience, of the idea of the strictly real and the possibility of an overstepping of limits.

### Animals

The trouble with this pattern of allegorical references to the paradox of representation is that it is still only speculative. If we begin by acknowledging that representation (as process, as interference) is an actual and immediate problem for us, then the play's machinery of meaning, including its quality as theater, affords us the opportunity to reflect very broadly on that problem, to wallow in it intellectually. But this reflection, in turn, creates a kind of distance from the problem itself, a shield against what precisely in this play ought to be its life-and-death urgency. And precisely the operation of the theater in our reflection, which ought to bring the problem closest to what we are actually doing, here and now, as spectators, can be seen as tending in exactly the opposite direction. For our sense of the theater as a force field, a closed-off representational frame, must (it seems) imply a sense of detachment; we and the actors are cooperating to create a kind of separate and privileged intellectual space, in which, while we may perhaps not solve the problem of representation, we at least achieve a degree of ritual collective mastery over it that is denied, for example, to the characters in the fiction.

At least these considerations would be applicable *if* the theater space were anything approaching a closed representational frame. And the strongest indication that our sense of closure in the theater space, or our wish for closure, cannot be sustained, is the appearance of *animals* on the stage, Achilles' horses in scene 4, and the dogs and elephants in scene 20. In the costumed humans who perform for us, the closure of the theater space, relative to a representationally incommensurate externality, is *doubled*. Those humans are (we know) actors who merely represent their fictional characters; and the characters themselves, in turn, who are engaged elsewhere (offstage) in a strictly unrepresentable action, undergo (since they obviously become representable when we see them) a change in nature when they are subjected to the representational ritual of the stage. But the animals do not pretend; and they do not change. They *are* still, on the stage, exactly what they would be in the offstage action, or in any other imaginable part of their canine or equine or elephantine existences. This fact, along with Penthesilea's actually joining herself to the dogs, is important as a signal of the presence of the supposedly unrepresentable on the stage, and of the association of this presence with Penthesilea. The unrepresentable is not banished from the theater after all. In some sense it is actually *there* on the stage.

In what sense? The association of Penthesilea with the animals, hence with the unrepresentable, reminds us of her operation as a reader of the *Iliad,* thus, for the Greeks, as a folding back into reality of the inadmissible "third," the process of representation. Does the actual Penthesilea on the stage—somehow combining the sheer bodily presence of the actress with other attributes of the fictional character—operate in the same way *for us*? Does Penthesilea disrupt, undermine, render problematic, *our* sense of the integrity and realness of the real?

Kleist himself, in any case, is at pains to keep his readers from dismissing the appearance of animals in *Penthesilea* as non-essential. In an epigram that puts words into the mouth of "Der Theater-Bearbeiter der Penthesilea," he mocks at what would probably happen to the dogs in a performance at Weimar:

Nur die Meute, fürcht ich, die wird in W . . . mit Glück nicht
Heulen, Lieber; den Lärm setz ich, vergönn, in Musik. (*SWB*, 1:21)

[My dear sir, I fear that the howling dog pack will not be well received in
W(eimar); with your permission, I will set the noise to music.]

And in another epigram, entitled "Komödienzettel," he says:

Heute zum ersten Mal mit Vergunst: die Penthesilea,
Hundekomödie; Akteurs: Helden und Köter und Fraun. (*SWB*, 1:20)

[Today, by permission, the premiere of Penthesilea, a canine comedy; the cast:
heroes and fleabags and women.]

"Heroes and fleabags ['curs' has too many moralistic overtones] and women."
What exactly are the relations among these three categories of performer?

## The Radical Gendering of the "Human"

Our sense of the theater as a closed representational space, again, includes the
understanding that we and the actors are cooperating to define that space. We
agree tacitly on a number of artificial conventions—including a strict division
between the stage-image (object of representation) and the audience-space
(subject of representation)—and we all participate willingly in the pretense
necessary to uphold them. But the animals do not participate in the same
way. What they think, what they see, and how they interpret or pretend to
interpret what they see does not matter. All that matters is that they are there
on the stage in the form of *bodies,* different from the other material props
only in being alive. Therefore, if the "heroes" and "women" of the play are
really subject to the categorical differentiation that the epigram suggests, and
if the mode of their differentiation has to do with the animals, the "fleabags,"
that are named between them, then it follows—especially since "heroes" refers
only to the fictional images presented by the male actors, whereas "women"
refers equally to the images and to the actresses themselves—that the actual
female bodies on the stage are important, *as* bodies, in our understanding of
the work.

This brings us to the question Achilles insists upon with Penthesilea,
the question of women's breasts, and to the motif of the radical automastectomy
by which Amazons mark their tribal membership. The women on the stage
before us are all fully clothed. Even if the conventions of theatrical performance,
especially in Kleist's time, did not require this, Achilles' ignorance of Penthesilea's
bodily condition would make it necessary in this play. And some of the women
are even clothed in armor, which is doubly interesting: first, because their

clothing prevents us from ascertaining how many breasts they actually have; second, because their clothing, especially armor, makes nonsense of the very idea of the single-breasted female archer. The right breast does not interefere with a woman's using a bow unless the woman is bare-breasted; given suitably tight clothing, especially armor, the woman is at no disadvantage. Our attention is thus attracted not only by the Amazons' failure to act onstage as we are told they act offstage, but also by their simple physical ceasing to *be* Amazons (the "breastless") when they step into the representational field of the theater. Their bodies are the problem. The clothes that conceal them—and so presumably enable us to imagine that they do all lack the right breast—also shape the fiction, offstage as well as onstage (since no one claims to have seen their breasts in the offstage action), in such a way that the absence of the right breast would become pointless anyway. The women on the stage are thus, so to speak, *representationally mutilated*. Their bodies, however we look at the matter, are something other than simple, whole, discloseable female bodies.

From this point it is only a short step to the conclusion that the inability to be an Amazon in this theater is equivalent to the inability to be, wholly and completely, *a woman*. The radical womanhood of the women on the stage is what is suppressed or effaced by the process of representation; it is womanhood, in some sense, that is unrepresentable. But at the same time, of course, those women on the stage *are* still women, under their clothes. The unrepresentable, in other words, is actually present in the theater *as women,* or as the concealed and problematic bodies of women. Now we can understand the full range of the symmetry we discussed earlier: that Penthesilea allegorizes the process of representation and so unmasks as representation the male reality of the Trojan War, while Achilles as allegory performs the same type of unmasking in the world of the Amazons. Gender, namely, for Kleist, is here understood as a mode or universe of representation. The difference between men and women is not the biological difference between male and female of a single basic species, and not the difference between cultural determinations in the history of a species. It is the difference between irreconcilable modes or universes of representation, a difference that cannot be resolved within any single overarching concept of "humanity."

If humanity "is" anything at all, then it is simply the unmasking of representation, exposure to the problem of representation, an exposure that arises from the biologically and historically inevitable collison of men and women. But the stage of *Penthesilea* does not by any means pretend to embrace or display the whole of this situation. (Such a pretense would imply the existence of a single comprehensive "human" representational frame that includes both genders, which is exactly what the symmetrical structure of the tragedy denies.) This theater remains confined, as it must, within the masculine mode of representation that happens to characterize it generically in the Europe of its time. Exposure to the problem of representation, for the audience, arises solely from the actual disruptive presence of women's bodies in this theater's (for those bodies) radically alien representational field. Hence the form of Penthesilea's death scene, her *speaking* herself to death (*P,* 3025–34). For in speaking the words set down for her in this theater of representation-as-masculine, the actual woman (the actress) *does actually die,* and has been in the process of dying throughout the play, dying as that here unimaginable entity, that woman, that Amazon, which she might actually be in an unimaginably different representational context. And hence the curious metaphor of the dead oak and the living oak with which Prothoe closes the play. Only that woman who is already "abgestorben" (*P,* 3041), "died back," stripped of her here unrepresentable positive womanhood, can survive in the representational field of this theater, or this culture. To *be* a woman, conversely, is to be in collision, to be exposed to the deadly storm, in the very act of being the locus of our particular form of exposure, here and now in the theater, to the problem of representation.

Penthesilea, then, is a victim of the representational process to which our theater subjects her. But even in being destroyed, she is also, for us, exactly what she is for the Greeks in the fiction, a fundamental disruption in the representational frame to which we are committed as spectators. ("She" now means the actual woman on the stage, in her mutually mutilating relation to the fiction developed by the text.) And insofar as this disruption is attributable to gender difference alone, insofar as it therefore invalidates any overarching conception or vision or feeling of the "human," we are tempted to credit Kleist with something approaching success in the project undertaken by Goethe with *Werther,* the use of gender difference as a lever against the aesthetic. Now it is not merely the idea of our relation to a woman's body, Lotte's, that worries us; we find ourselves, rather, actually in the presence of a brute physical object—Penthesilea's body, which cannot be argued away—that defeats any conceivable idea of the "human," and so denies us the possibility of an aesthetic relation to any form of text, by making nonsense of the presumption that the constitutive readerly role I adopt will (or could) be adopted by anyone.

The trouble is that this representational disruption requires *the theater* to happen in, whereas aesthetic experience unfolds primarily for the modern solitary reader. It could be argued, perhaps, that Kleist is seeking to exploit the institution of the theater as a lever against the large social effects of the aesthetic, the debilitation of our sense for the reality of the real, the co-option of our intellectual energies in a political situation that automatically favors "die Nichtswürdigen," that worthless or valueless segment of humanity Götz warns us about. But still, if the aesthetic is to be attacked at its root, the battlefield probably has to be chosen, as in *Werther,* somewhere among the narrative genres.

## The Gender of the Theater

The idea of the problem of representation has consequences and complications that we have not yet looked into. Given the apparent male/female or Greek/Amazon symmetry in the play, for instance, the question arises: can we imagine a theater gendered feminine, in which the presence of male bodies on the stage would be the disruptive element? If such a theater could exist, if the symmetry of male and female suggested in the fiction were thus in a sense perfectible, the result, curiously enough, would be damaging to the argument as we have conducted it so far. For if each sex disrupted the representational frame of the other in exactly the same way, then the mechanism of disruption would serve as a kind of bridge, a knowable or inhabitable representational structure that would encompass the whole of humanity, or at least the whole of any human group knitted together reasonably well by communicative practices.

But the symmetry suggested by the fiction is not after all perfectible in this manner. The representational processes that characterize the genders are not parallel, not simply different ways of carrying out the same type of operation; for they involve different conceptions not only of reality, but of the whole representational dynamics of reality-constitution.

The very idea of a "frame"—and hence the possibility of the theater as a focus of self-knowledge—appears in fact to belong on the masculine side of the division. It is the Greeks who, in order to maintain a sense of reality, must exclude the "third" of representation, whereas the Amazons' method of tribal self-preservation requires that the differences between different modes of reality-formation (on the level of the "third") be kept clearly in view as objects of purposeful manipulation. As long as the battle lasts, the race of intended husbands must be led to believe that they are fighting on their own terms, for conquest or defense. Then, when the battle is over, the Amazons artfully replace that reality, for their captives, with the "dream" of the rose festival. It is the Greeks for whom coping with reality means the achievement of goals like the destruction of Troy, the establishment of irrefutable factual monuments to their activity; it is they, therefore, who embrace the principle later enunciated by Nietzsche, that action requires forgetfulness, illusion, a quasi-theatrical narrowing of horizons. But for the Amazons, achievement is never more than temporary. They do not keep their husbands; they enjoy them, use them, and release them. And we never hear anything at all about the goals or purposes of their culture when it is not engaged in the business of reproduction. Whatever the Amazons do between campaigns, we must infer, is not anything that would make sense in the theater. When they launch one of their attacks on men—or in effect, on the theater as representational frame—what they do can be spoken of, though not fully represented. But the rest of their existence lies beyond even the reach of our metaphors.

Does this mean that we must abandon the idea of Achilles as a disruption in the Amazons' sense of reality, corresponding to Penthesilea's disruption of Greek reality? At least we must refine the argument. The danger posed by Achilles to Amazon reality lies not merely in his knowing about the Amazons while still in a position to manipulate the relation between their world and his own, but in the recognition (especially Penthesilea's) that he will inevitably operate as if Amazon reality were of the same *type* as his own—focused, established, factual, consistent, quasi-theatrical—and so in effect transform it into that type of reality. That Penthesilea loves Achilles is an indisputable fact; therefore, in Greek reality, she cannot possibly intend to kill him (*P,* 2470–74). If she is bringing dogs and elephants along to the duel, then it must be because "custom" requires this (*P,* 2540); and no Greek has any trouble understanding the role of custom in forming a workable and self-consistent structure of existence. Indeed, Achilles' imposing of this type of order on Amazon reality is already figured in the fact that he receives his "knowledge" of it (scene 15) *in the theater,* where no other type of knowledge is available.

In the world of the Amazons, however, to the extent that we can make inferences about it, neither consistency nor plausible factuality has much value as a criterion of the real. A distinction as simple as that between love and mortal combat gets lost track of. An army whose only purpose is to collect captives comes equipped for mass slaughter. Penthesilea's mother, Otrere, of course knows that an Amazon is not permitted to seek out a single enemy as her lover; yet she does not balk at naming Achilles the man for her daughter (*P,* 2138), and Penthesilea is willing, for Achilles' sake, to sacrifice not only law and custom, but the very welfare of her state. What does the concept of "law" mean for an Amazon? In scene 15, Penthesilea uses the word "Gesetz" only once, in speaking of the founding of the "Frauenstaat . . . Der das Gesetz sich würdig selber gebe" (*P,* 1958–60), "women's state, worthy to give itself its own law"; and she uses the related word "Satzung" (*P,* 1970), "constitutional rule," to refer to the exclusion of men from that state. But when it comes to specific "laws" by which she herself might be limited in her actions, it is only Achilles who uses the actual word "Gesetz" (*P,* 1902, 2144), which thus assumes the character of *his* interpretive attempt to pin her down. Achilles, that is, threatens reality for the Amazons by threatening to impose law, to make their reality consistent and predictable—or, given the very existence of scene 15, by threatening to make it accessible to the theater. (In the scenes following, where Penthesilea is rescued, the word "Gesetz," "law," is neatly opposed to "Sitte," "custom." Penthesilea invokes "Sitte," in the form of "Rittersitte" [*P,* 2301], as the name of her obligation to remain a prisoner, and asks scornfully whether any "Gesetz" [*P,* 2305] has the power to free her. The high priestess responds by reminding her that it is "Sitte" [*P,* 2315], the *Amazon* version of obligation, that she had violated by seeking out Achilles in the first place, whereas an alien

"Kriegsgesetz" [*P,* 2334] is what she is following in her willingness to sacrifice the Amazon victory.)

There is, then, no possibility of a feminine counter-theater in which men's bodies would be the disruptive element. By its very nature as "frame," implying conventions of consistency, implying law, the theater is gendered masculine. But it does not follow that women are excluded as spectators, or for that matter as playwrights, from Kleist's theater, any more than they are excluded as performers. After all, the punctual disruption of representation (by women's bodies on the stage) does not exclude men from the theater, and there is no more reason why the circumferential disruption of an inferred feminine version of representation (by the quality of the theater as frame) should exclude women. Given the basic idea of gender difference suggested by the text, Kleist has created a theater in which representation is disrupted no matter how one looks at it, a theater, therefore, in which something like direct collision between the sexes is possible, with no privilege for either of the representational processes involved, a theater that perhaps thus *is,* in its entirety, that "actual" battleground of *Penthesilea* which cannot fit onto its stage.

## The Problem of the Problem of Representation

Of course the specific idea of gender difference that Kleist works with in *Penthesilea* is inherently questionable. But with respect to the issue of the aesthetic this may not matter, since it is the problem of representation as such, as an *open* problem, that is incompatible with aesthetic culture. As long as we are comfortable with the idea that the reader's role is an integral factor in constituting the meaning of a literary text, representation is not a problem. The text either engages us or fails to; meaning is either present or absent, never radically obscured. As an aesthetic reader, I am never in the condition of understanding a text, yet also suspecting my understanding of wrongness. Once the problem of representation has been opened, however, even our questioning of the means by which it is opened—the idea, say, of gender difference in *Penthesilea*—becomes *part* of the problem, itself an effect, as far as we know, of the obscuring quality of representational boundaries.

The problem of representation is defined by two propositions: that a necessary condition of our ability even to begin thinking about representational differences—however we imagine their arguments, as "frames," as "modes," as "worlds"—is that those differences be in a significant degree bridgeable by translation; but that the very concept of representation, on the other hand, is nontrivial only to the extent that it names the constitution of reality itself, whose integrity, in every particular case, is a matter of life and death. Fictional literature, literature that makes no secret of the representational processes that structure it, is therefore radically problematized by the problem of representation, as long as the latter is kept open. The reader of literature is put in the position of making appropriate and valid moves of translation, across representational boundaries, while also knowing that these moves are infected with a fundamental wrongness, the general form of the wrongness of reading that we have discussed in Goethe.

But the problem of representation has to be *kept* open, against its own logical tendency to disappear from view. For as soon as we identify the problem, we find ourselves in the position of considering representation as a primary concept, a single systematically usable name for the totality of the presumably "human" processes by which experience or history or nature is made to happen, as distinct from what we admit we cannot even imagine on the level of the thing in itself. And once we embark on this line of thought, either we arrive at what Davidson insists is a pointless "dualism of scheme and reality" or else we attempt to dispense with reality altogether, in the manner of Fichte's *Die Bestimmung des Menschen,* a book that is especially interesting here in light of Cassirer's suggestion that it might be the "Kantian" reading that precipitated Kleist's philosophical crisis of 1801.

> Es giebt überall kein Dauerndes, weder außer mir, noch in mir, sondern nur einen unaufhörlichen Wechsel. Ich weiß überall von keinem Seyn, und auch nicht von meinem eignen. Es ist kein Seyn.—*Ich selbst* weiß überhaupt nicht, und bin nicht. *Bilder* sind: sie sind das Einzige, was da ist, und sie wissen von sich, nach Weise der Bilder:—Bilder die vorüberschweben, ohne daß etwas sey, dem sie vorüberschweben; die durch Bilder von den Bildern zusammenhängen, Bilder, ohne etwas in ihnen Abgebildetes, ohne Bedeutung und Zweck. Ich selbst bin eins dieser Bilder; ja, ich bin selbst dies nicht, sondern nur ein verworrenes Bild von den Bildern.[6]

> [Nowhere is there anything permanent, neither in me nor outside me, but only ceaseless change. Nowhere do I know of being, not even of my own. There is no being.—*I myself* know not at all, and am not. *Images* are: they are the only entity that is there, and they know of themselves in the manner of images:—images that float past, without there being anything past which they float; images that are connected by images of the images, images without anything whose images they are, without meaning and purpose. I myself am one of these images; indeed, I am not even this, but only a confused image of the images.]

If we read "images" as "representations," then Fichte carries the idea of representational frames down to the level of the individual, where he discovers that the individual itself must be dispensed with—since its relation to its representations would otherwise be precisely the permanent form that is denied—so that the frame also disintegrates into image fragments, and philosophical formulation dances on the edge of nonsense.

The arguments of both Davidson and Fichte, however, arrive at positive results, in which the problem of representation is circumvented. Davidson proposes a domain of relatively fruitful thinking that simply does not include the complications of the idea of representation. Fichte follows those complications and consequences to the very end, where the collapse of reality, he claims, forms a chaotic background against which one central human truth is at last thrown into sharp relief:

> Nicht bloßes Wissen, sondern nach deinem Wissen *Thun* ist deine Bestimmung: so ertönt es laut im Innersten meiner Seele, so bald ich nur einen Augenblick mich sammle und auf mich selbst merke. (Fichte, p. 253)

> [Not mere knowledge, but *action* in accordance with your knowledge, is your destiny: these words resound loudly in the deepest part of my soul as soon as I collect myself, even for a moment, and attend to myself.]

This truth, the drive to *act,* when recognized in its true contours, against a background of "knowledge" that knows nothing, leads necessarily to a form of "faith" ("Glaube"), whereupon the illusory existential stability suggested by a supposed order of the real is replaced with a genuine stability of social and metaphysical resolve. But despite the diametrical opposition between Davidson's view and Fichte's, the positive result, in both cases, depends on the same assumption: that being human, especially in the sense of using language, is strictly prior to such particular attributes of the human as gender or culture.

And *Penthesilea,* I contend, by proposing a radically gendered humanity, is an experiment in dispensing with this assumption. I have said that the difference between men and women is the difference between "irreconcilable modes or universes of representation"; and I think this formulation is still the best we can do. But it has limitations at the deepest level. For if the idea of the representational "frame" (or quasi-theater) is gendered masculine, then we should have to speak of the feminine side of the division as "frameless" or "unframed" representation, whereupon it becomes unclear whether we are still talking about "representation" in any reasonable sense. And yet, in the theater, or in talking about the theater, where we are committed from the outset to the metaphor of the frame, what other word shall we use? In *Penthesilea,* even the idea of language does not unambiguously locate the human as such. We recall Penthesilea's last speech, where language is thematized in at least three different ways: as an ostensibly referential communication among the Amazons (since Penthesilea does then die), but with respect to an event that defies the laws of reference by not being susceptible to a linguistic triangulation of the form "in other words"; as a sign, or a symbolization via the theater, of the anti-referential theorem that even material things, a dagger or arrows, have their original and proper existence in language; and as the enactment of a violent cleft (a confinement, as it were, within different realities) between language and speaker, by which speaking becomes the death of the speaker's very body. Can we understand these ideas as aspects of a single notion of "language"? If not, what notion could we conceivably substitute for it?

Kleist thus neither dismisses the problem of representation nor makes it a springboard into "faith." He confronts it, and does so in such a way that the confrontation is not blunted by the paradox inherent in the very idea of representation. For representation is no longer a primary notion; and the paradox (the indispensable closure of representational frames, and their undeniable intertranslatability) now becomes merely a representationally (or theatrically) relativized reflection, an inevitable trace, of the event in which our sense of representation originates, the collision between the sexes—or as we have said, for want of better terms, the collision between framed and unframed representation—which in turn is "represented" in our theater only by way of the *disruption* of representation caused by the presence of actual women's bodies.

This is not to say that the element of paradox is eliminated. It reappears, inevitably, with every attempt we make to formulate the situation in which Kleist's theater places us. Suppose, for example, we decide to understand gender as the difference between exclusive representation (focused on our need for the uniquely real) and inclusive representation (exploiting the manipulability of all processes of reality-constitution). It follows that the first, the masculine mode of representation, cannot deal with the second except by a boundary-transgressing *in*clusion, in that women are assigned a natural "place" in the order of the real; and the second can deal with the first only by a strict *ex*clusion, by (we recall) the uncharacteristically named "law" that excludes men from any but a temporary sexual role in Amazon society. These paradoxes do not invalidate the formulations in which they arise. But they relativize radically the concepts involved, by tracing them (in both content and form) to an originary collision that they cannot possibly encompass, since the needful referent, a single "humanity" anterior to gender, is simply not available.

This argument can be developed, in length and complexity, as far as one wishes. Paradox breeds paradox, and the whole structure becomes more giddily speculative with every step, since it repeatedly entangles itself in the need to talk about what it insists, from the outset, must escape any orderly mechanism of representation, verbal or otherwise. But the argument itself is not what concerns us here. What deserves our attention is the manner in which this argument is brought into play in *Penthesilea,* the manner in which it is preserved against its own self-obfuscating metaphysical tendency, and against the lure of the positive result, by being attached, all but physically attached, to the women's bodies present on the stage.

## The Status of the Question of Gender

Once we have decided on this approach to *Penthesilea,* connections with the rest of Kleist's dramatic work immediately suggest themselves. The idea of the dismembered female body is developed in both *Das Käthchen von Heilbronn* and *Die Hermannsschlacht,* where it is associated ever more clearly with a masculine mode of representation, with the view of that female body as a collection of fetish objects, discrete foci of desire or pleasure. And if we recognize in *Käthchen,* therefore, not only the extreme male fantasy that it obviously is, but also a theatrical unmasking and disruption of that fantasy—which would help explain why the play's last words are not an expression of triumph, but a scratching of the persistent itch that is Kunigunde—then the shape of a similar questioning of patriotic fantasy in *Die Hermannsschlacht* and *Prinz Friedrich von Homburg* lies open before us.

But what about the question of gender in Kleist's work as a whole? Do we arrive here at a kind of bedrock in his thought? It would, I think, be more than just difficult to find in Kleist's narratives, for example, anything corresponding to the intensity of focus on gender that we find in *Penthesilea, Käthchen,* and perhaps *Die Hermannsschlacht.* Indeed, this focus in *Penthesilea* is tied to features of the work that simply are not available outside the genre of drama. Or let us reconsider the point that in *Penthesilea,* the question of gender relativizes the notion of representation, strips it of its status as a primary notion, and so enables the problem of representation to operate without logical strain as a determining element of our experience in the theater. Does the same argument not also work the other way round? Is the question of gender not also relativized by the recognition that our access to it depends here precisely on an already discredited idea of representational frames? Would those women's bodies on the stage actually *be there,* in the sense required by the question of gender, without the structure of representation they disrupt?

The conclusion we are drawn toward, I think, is that the search for bedrock questions or issues in Kleist is misguided, that there is in the end no such bedrock. But not in the sense that this conclusion might be taken as license to concoct a metaphysical scheme by which to explain and organize the various questions that occur. If Kleist in fact did read Fichte's *Die Bestimmung des Menschen,* then it is precisely this book's metaphysical move that he rejects in *Penthesilea.* What is interesting in *Penthesilea*—and perhaps everywhere in Kleist—is the sense of literature implied by a procedure that resolves relativized or desubstantialized philosophical questions into palpable actualities, into undeniable and undeniably disturbing events, on something close to a strictly material plane.

A sense of literature, that is, as something radically different from what it is viewed as under the spell of aesthetics. Not a literature of latency, waiting for the magic of the reader's imaginative participation that it might come into being, but a literature whose practically material reality precedes and resists all reading, a literature of the sort I think Goethe perceived in Montaigne—and perhaps also in texts like *Rameau's Nephew* and Cellini's autobiography—literature with an insatiable appetite for the real, at whatever cost to consistency and co-optive seductiveness. And if literature in this sense is really the unacknowledged common aim of Goethe and Kleist, then it follows that the idea of gender difference, again, is relativized, relegated to the status of a device, an accident. In the broad sweep of anti-aesthetic writing in Goethe and Kleist, the question of gender is never the main point. And yet most of the time, somehow, it still manages to make itself felt—even as early as the strange androgynous combination of Götz and Adelheid.

## ≈ 7 ≈

# Guerrilla Warfare: Goethe and the Future of Literature

We have discussed various attempts to revolutionize literature from within, by means of texts that are supposed to be insurmountably resistant to an aesthetic literary attitude. I think the following points have been established:

1. that the project of dismantling an aesthetic conception of literature is central in Goethe's work from at least as early as *Götz;*
2. that this project is not Goethe's alone, but is shared at least by Kleist and, in fact, I think, by a large number of major German authors of the period around 1800;[1]
3. that the question of gender and gender difference is related to this project, if perhaps not conceptually or logically related;
4. and finally, that the project, as long as it is approached by the methods we have discussed so far, is hopeless. As I have said, there is no necessary limit to the shamelessness of the reading public. There is therefore no text that cannot be crammed into the grinder of aesthetic presuppositions. Aesthetic pleasure, in the strict sense, can arise even in the experience of finding oneself inevitably in the wrong with respect to a text. Goethe's definitive confrontation with this truth, I contend, occurs in the mid-1790s and leads him to an entirely new view of the old project, a view in which the very idea of "literature" is exploded. Perhaps he did understand, after all, exactly what Kleist was up to in *Penthesilea,* and dismissed it as a version of what he had already, in his own work, found to be futile.

## The Question of Classical German Literature

In order to give a comprehensive, judicious, and plausible account of Goethe's idea of the future of literature, one would have to include in one's evidence at least fifty or sixty different essays and essay-sketches from various periods in the author's life, not to mention a great deal of material from letters and conversations and the autobiographical writings. The account I intend to give is neither comprehensive nor judicious, and in a sense, I admit, not even plausible. It is based on just one essay of Goethe's, which appeared in *Die Horen* in 1795 under the title "Literarischer Sansculottismus," and on an ambitious interpretation of the motif of the disappearing poem in *Die natürliche Tochter.*

It does, however, also raise the question of what we actually mean by "plausible" in the first place. Plausibility in a literary argument is generally considered a function of the amount of textual material one can attach to it; and in the case of a "classical" author, whose work is assumed to have educative value for a large community of readers, it helps if the various texts can be arranged to suggest a story of learning, growth, progress, enlightenment, "Bildung." But one consequence of arguments advanced above, and arguments yet to come, is that the "classical" Goethe, in this sense, never really existed. What we have, rather, is a man who, from very early in his career, found himself engaged in a discipline (literature) that he recognized was irreversibly infected by the structure of aesthetic thinking, hence fundamentally wrong or corrupt. Learning, or "Bildung," would be difficult to measure in a situation of this type. One either capitulates or else endures years of groping, experimentation, misdirectedness, and occasional near-insanity for the sake of the few moments of illumination when it appears that something useful might be achieved after all, moments, however, that are also part of the basic problem, since the nature of the case prevents them from being set down in a public, "classical" form, in any form that might support or justify the struggle behind them.

I claim that one such moment of intrinsically obscured illumination is detectable in the essay "Literarischer Sansculottismus." Even on the surface, this essay is an important one, for several reasons. First, it is written at exactly that point in history where for Goethe, as for many other Europeans, "the future" actually begins, that phase of the French Revolution where the sansculottes, by way of their own and others' uncertainty about who they really are and what they really want, provoke the question of whether accepted notions of government, politics, and society any longer make sense. Second, it contains a very condensed but lucid description of the pervasive character of eighteenth-century German literature, as Goethe saw it. Third, it carries out an energetic critique of the concept of "the classical," by which Goethe's own work was later to be positioned with respect to the future of German—and indeed European—literature. And beneath the surface, finally, it engages yet again the issue of the aesthetic—but in a manner much more directly related to practical political life than heretofore—and even suggests obliquely the question of gender. With reference to the role of "the writer" in "Literarischer Sansculottismus," I will say "he," not "he or she," because Goethe is obviously thinking of a community of male writers. But when he works out the same thought in *Die natürliche Tochter,* he embodies the literary impulse in a female figure, and the literary task in a plot that suggests gender issues very strongly. It is at this point that we can start talking of "Goethe as woman."

Goethe opens his attack on the article "Ueber Prose und Beredsamkeit der Deutschen," which had appeared in March and April 1795 in the *Berlinisches Archiv der Zeit und ihres Gechmacks,* with a caution about conceptual precision:

> Wer mit den Worten, deren er sich im Sprechen oder Schreiben bedient, bestimmte Begriffe zu verbinden für eine unerläßliche Pflicht hält, wird die Ausdrücke: *classischer Autor, classisches Werk* höchst selten gebrauchen.[2]

> [Whoever considers it an unconditional duty to associate definite concepts with the words he uses in speaking or writing will very seldom use the expressions *classical author, classical work.*]

He then lists carefully the "necessary conditions under which a classical writer, especially in prose, becomes possible" (p. 198), in accordance with the recognition that not even "the greatest genius" (p. 199) can escape the conditions of the historical moment in which he writes, especially the character of his "Nation." Then follows a very difficult paragraph:

> Aber auch der deutschen Nation darf es nicht zum Vorwurfe gereichen, daß ihre geographische Lage sie eng zusammenhält, indem ihre politische sie zerstückelt. Wir wollen die Umwälzungen nicht wünschen, die in Deutschland classische Werke vorbereiten könnten. (p. 199)

> [But it may not be counted against the German nation that its geographical position holds it tightly together while its political situation fragments it. We would not wish for the upheavals that could prepare the way for classical works in Germany.]

Why should Germany not even *want* a classical literature? And if the main preconditions for the production of the classical are, as they appear to be, stability and continuity, how can Goethe speak of "upheavals" ("Umwälzungen") as a preparation of the way?

Even without Goethe's insistence on conceptual precision, our task as interpreters would be to *explain* this paragraph, not to explain it away. We can start by noting that of the "conditions" that Goethe asserts are necessary for the classical, the last two would certainly not require "upheavals" in Germany. An author may aspire to "classical" status

> wenn er seine Nation auf einem hohen Grade der Cultur findet, so daß ihm seine eigene Bildung leicht wird; wenn er viele Materialien gesammelt, vollkommene oder unvollkommene Versuche seiner Vorgänger vor sich sieht, und so viel äußere und innere Umstände zusammentreffen, daß er kein

schweres Lehrgeld zu zahlen braucht, daß er in den besten Jahren seines Lebens ein großes Werk zu übersehen, zu ordnen und in Einem Sinne auszuführen fähig ist. (p. 198)

[when he finds his nation at a high level of culture, so that his own education is easy; when he has collected much material, and has before him perfect and imperfect experiments by his predecessors, and when so many outer and inner circumstances combine that he does not have to pay for a painful apprenticeship, that in the best years of his life he is able to plan a large work, to organize it, and in *one* spirit to carry it out.]

In the last part of the essay, Goethe insists that these conditions are even now in the process of being fulfilled in Germany. Earlier in the century, German authors—"scattered by birth, very differently educated, mostly left to themselves and to the impressions produced by entirely different situations" (p. 199)—had had to struggle most of their lives in order merely to form a conception of how they might serve their elusive (or perhaps nonexistent) "Nationalcultur" (p. 200). But now the situation has changed:

Denn worauf ungeschickte Tadler am wenigsten merken, das Glück, das junge Männer von Talent jetzt genießen, indem sie sich früher ausbilden, eher zu einem reinen, dem Gegenstande angemessenen Stil gelangen können, wem sind sie es schuldig als ihren Vorgängern, die in der letzten Hälfte dieses Jahrhunderts mit einem unablässigen Bestreben, unter mancherlei Hindernissen, sich jeder auf seine eigene Weise ausgebildet haben? Dadurch ist eine Art von unsichtbarer Schule entstanden, und der junge Mann, der jetzt hineintritt, kommt in einen viel größeren und lichteren Kreis als der frühere Schriftsteller, der ihn erst selbst bei'm Dämmerschein durchirren mußte, um ihn nach und nach, gleichsam nur zufällig, erweitern zu helfen. Viel zu spät kommt der Halbkritiker, der uns mit seinem Lämpchen vorleuchten will; der Tag ist angebrochen und wir werden die Läden nicht wieder zumachen. (p. 202)

[For the good fortune (unheeded by clumsy censurers) that young men of talent now enjoy, in that they can train themselves earlier, and arrive sooner at a clear style, suited to its object: to whom are they indebted for this if not to their predecessors, who, in the last half of this century, with constant effort and despite many sorts of hindrance, trained themselves each after his own manner? In this way a kind of invisible school originated, and the young man who now enters it arrives in a much larger and brighter circle than the earlier writer, who had had to grope his own way through it, by dim light, in order gradually, as it were by accident, to help expand it. The half-baked critic who would like to light our way with his puny lamp comes much too late; day has broken, and we are not about to close our shutters again.]

There is to be sure an interpretive problem here that must not be disregarded. Why, in the midst of all his light-of-day imagery, does Goethe speak of an "invisible" school? To the extent that it *is* a "school," surely it must be visible, available to be joined and learned from. If we want to take invisibility as an attribute only of the school's earliest stages, then we should have to insist on "entstand," not "ist . . . entstanden," as the correct form of the verb. And even the earlier author, says Goethe, had at least had "Dämmerschein," "dim light," to guide him in the first clumsy shaping of what "young men of talent now enjoy."

But leaving these problems aside for the moment, the above passage seems to assert that certain important preconditions for a classical prose literature are now fulfilled in Germany, especially when we read it in relation to the article Goethe is attacking. At the end of that article's first installment—the part we are certain Goethe had read—the unnamed author (who is Daniel Jenisch), having listed a number of stylistic qualities necessary for good prose, declares that such prose cannot be written unless the writer finds these qualities *already* present in his language and its tradition. Where this is not the case,

> Der Schriftsteller . . . wird entweder abgebrochen, dunkel, unbestimmt, un-
> zusammenhängend für den geübteren Denker (wenn gleich für sein Volk
> verständlich),—d.h. eine höchst unvollkommene Prose schreiben: oder er
> wird die eben erklärten Erfordernisse einer guten Prose erst *schaffen* müssen,
> welches aber in der Sprache wohl mit einzelnen Worten und Wendungen,
> allein nie mit so wesentlichen und in ihre ganze Organisation so tiefverwebten
> Stücken derselben geschehen kann.[3]

> [Either the writer (though understandable to his own people) will write in
> a manner that the trained thinker will find halting, obscure, indeterminate,
> unconnected—i.e., an extremely imperfect prose: or else he will have to *create*
> the prerequisites for good prose described above, which can be done for a
> language in the case of individual words and expressions, but never in the case
> of qualities that are more essential and more deeply woven into the whole
> organization of the language.]

Goethe, on the other hand, suggests that the laborious *creation* of a basis for good writing is exactly what the scattered and struggling authors of eighteenth-century Germany had accomplished for future generations. And yet, what they created is not a basis for the "classical"—Germany, again, does not even *want* "classical works"—but rather an "invisible school." Goethe therefore distinguishes two possible foundations or matrices for good writing, the classical and the cryptically named "invisible school"; and between these two notions, by implication, the idea of literature is stretched—or perhaps broken.

### The Parting of the Ways

In his essay, Goethe mentions the March issue of the *Berlinisches Archiv* (p. 196), in which only the first half of Jenisch's article had appeared, but not the April issue that had contained the second half. Still, I think it is clear that he had read the whole text. It is not until the second installment that Jenisch even mentions the French (pp. 374–75) and begins to develop the French/German comparison to which Goethe apparently responds in his title. And when Goethe attacks "diesen eigentlichen Sansculottismus" (p. 197), "this *true* sansculottism," in Jenisch, he seems to be alluding to the latter's dismissive view of the Revolution as a mere episode, after which the true Frenchman, the man of "wit and taste," will reemerge unscathed (Jenisch, pp. 375–76). Goethe suggests that Jenisch, who of course scorns the actual French sansculottes, himself nevertheless advocates an insidious *leveling* tendency in literature, by insisting on the one "classical" ideal of "Feinheiten" in prose, "subtleties, nuances," to which such qualities as "burning energy" and "sublime flights of the soul" must be sacrificed (Jenisch, p. 375).

And in describing the precondition of the classical that he claims is *fulfilled* in Germany—that a young man "find his nation at a high level of culture"—Goethe also practically quotes from Jenisch, who asserts that if a people (here he means the Greeks) were to produce good prose, then "that people already had to be standing at the height of culture" (p. 373). If there is a difference between the "classical" way and the German way of developing this cultural advantage, it must therefore have to do with the *other* preconditions of the classical that Goethe mentions, preconditions, perhaps, that might really be produced by "upheavals" in Germany. Goethe enumerates as follows:

> Wann und wo entsteht ein classischer Nationalautor? Wenn er in der Geschichte seiner Nation große Begebenheiten und ihre Folgen in einer glücklichen und bedeutenden Einheit vorfindet; wenn er in den Gesinnungen seiner Landsleute Größe, in ihren Empfindungen Tiefe und in ihren Handlungen Stärke und Consequenz nicht vermißt; wenn er selbst, vom Nationalgeiste durchdrungen, durch ein einwohnendes Genie sich fähig fühlt, mit dem Vergangenen wie mit dem Gegenwärtigen zu sympathisiren. (p. 198)

> [When and where does a classical national author arise? When he finds in the history of his nation great events and their consequences in a happy unity; when he does not miss greatness in the mind of his countrymen, profundity in their feelings, and in their actions strength and consistency; when he himself, suffused with the national spirit, feels himself enabled, by a genius within him, to sympathize with past as with present things.]

Although the first two of these conditions can be regarded as objective in character, Goethe formulates them from a *subjective* point of view. The question is whether a young author can be persuaded that the conditions obtain—not whether they actually do or do not obtain—which means that particular forms of education or indoctrination might be sufficient to produce them. The historical preconditions of the classical, in other words, are conditions that can be *interpreted into history.* But Goethe insists that Germany is not now in a position to produce classical literature—and, he hopes, will not be in such a position ("Wir wollen . . . nicht wünschen") in the future. Therefore the "upheavals" he speaks of, which would make "classical works" possible, must be political and ideological upheavals that would permit Germany's actual historical situation to be reinterpreted (in Goethe's view, falsely reinterpreted) into the kind of situation that favors the classical.

It is conceivable, namely, that Germany, or large parts of it, will undergo revolutions similar to the revolution in France, or that even without revolution, German politics will be infected with the idea of the parliamentary republic. It is conceivable that a German version of sansculottes (especially the more sophisticated levelers, like Jenisch, who deny genius in the name of refinement) will thus become a political force and create an "upheaval" even without manifestations quite so egregious as the Terror in France, which by 1795 appeared to have run its course. It is conceivable that the Enlightenment thought of eighteenth-century Germany will be interpreted as the intellectual prelude to a new political age more or less on the French model, the age of the new large-scale nation-state, and that what Goethe sees as "upheavals" will consequently be made to appear, in new German education, as "große Begebenheiten"—the difference, after all, lies only in one's point of view— as "great events" that reveal a "happy unity," or "sympathetic" continuity, of past and present. It is conceivable, in other words, that conditions favoring the development of a classical literature will be established in Germany, on the basis of what Goethe would consider a simple misinterpretation of the true German state of affairs.

> Und nun betrachte man die Arbeiten deutscher Poeten und Prosaisten von entschiednem Namen! Mit welcher Sorgfalt, mit welcher Religion folgten sie auf ihrer Bahn einer aufgeklärten Überzeugung! (p. 201)

> [And now look at the work of German poets and prose writers of definite repute! With what care, with what religious intensity they pursued, on their path, an enlightened conviction!]

But precisely that commitment to "enlightenment" may now provide the lever by which these authors will be twisted, after the fact, into the service of a "culture" with which they have no true connection.

There are other indications that Goethe is thinking along these lines. Why does he follow Jenisch in restricting himself "especially" (p. 198) to prose literature? Jenisch, in effect, offers him a way out by conceding that a people can have excellent poetry without yet being ready for good prose (pp. 253–54), and that French poetry has actually lost strength because of the competing prose culture (p. 376). Why does Goethe not answer by setting forth the advantages of a *poetic* culture, presumably Germany's, over what he might have painted (using Jenisch's own arguments) as the monotonous refinement of the "classical"?

I think that the trouble with such a response, from Goethe's point of view, is that it would beg the question of literature's situation in the large modern nation-state. Within the relatively small and homogeneous readership of poetry, an author might expect to participate substantially in *creating* the conditions of his reception, whereas the prose writer has much less control vis-à-vis his large and diverse audience. Shortly after accepting the restriction to prose, Goethe continues:

> der Schriftsteller so wenig als der handelnde Mensch bildet die Umstände, unter denen er geboren wird und unter denen er wirkt. Jeder, auch das größte Genie, leidet von seinem Jahrhundert in einigen Stücken, wie er von andern Vortheil zieht, und einen vortrefflichen Nationalschriftsteller kann man nur von der Nation fordern. (p. 199)

> [The author does not shape the circumstances of his birth and effectiveness any more than the active practical man does. Everyone, even the greatest genius, suffers from his century in certain respects, as he profits from it in others, and an excellent national author can only be provided by the nation itself.]

The prose writer, especially, is at the mercy of the historical condition of his "nation." And it is significant that the paragraph immediately following is where Goethe makes an apparently gratuitous and not strictly accurate remark about "the German nation": "that its geographical position holds it tightly together." It sounds almost as if there were a constricting geographical *pressure* on Germany, as if Germany, for all its current political fragmentation, were *doomed* to become the type of large nation that dictates conditions for its authors, rather than the type of relatively unregimented social unit that might conceivably follow its authors' creative lead. The "upheavals" Goethe speaks of in the very next sentence, whether we wish them or not, may be inevitable.

The issue here is literature in the large modern nation-state, and Goethe declines the opportunity to avoid it. Only a few small cultural-political changes are needed, in education, indoctrination, publicly disseminated ideology, for German literature to achieve something like "classical" status—changes that would follow quite easily if Germany were more integrated as a nation-state, and are therefore probably inevitable. And yet, Goethe suggests that it is incumbent upon German literature to find a path different from the classical. What can he mean by this, given his own recognition of a large nation's increasing control over the conditions of literary production and reception?

## The Invisible School

The passages just mentioned are followed by a long paragraph devoted to the difficult conditions under which eighteenth-century German authors had worked. "Nirgends in Deutschland ist ein Mittelpunct gesellschaftlicher Lebensbildung, wo sich Schriftsteller zusammen fänden und nach Einer Art, in Einem Sinne, jeder in seinem Fache sich ausbilden könnten" (p. 199). "Nowhere in Germany is a center of social life-formation, where authors might come together and train themselves in *one* method, *one* spirit, each in his own specialty." Scattered by birth, upbringing, and education, and by the various sorts of literary model available to them, German authors generally take a long time to develop their talent. When a German author is finally ready to produce "the unique object with which his trained mind strives to occupy itself" (p. 200), it is often too late, since the material and family worries of middle age now occupy too much of his time and energy.

> Welcher deutsche geschätzte Schriftsteller . . . wird nicht mit bescheidener Trauer gestehen, daß er oft genug nach Gelegenheit geseufzt habe, früher die Eigenheiten seines originellen Genius einer allgemeinen Nationalcultur, die er leider nicht vorfand, zu unterwerfen? Denn die Bildung der höheren Classen durch fremde Sitten und ausländische Literatur, so viel Vortheil sie uns auch gebracht hat, hinderte doch den Deutschen als Deutschen sich früher zu entwickeln. (pp. 200–201)

> [What well regarded German author will not admit, with modest sadness, that he had often enough yearned for the opportunity to submit the peculiarities of his original genius earlier to a general national culture, which unfortunately was not there for him? For the education of the upper classes by non-native customs and foreign literature, for all the advantage it has brought us, has hindered the German from developing earlier as a German.]

The adverb "früher," "earlier," is prepared for by the idea of German authors' delayed development, and it is taken up later in the idea that young authors can now develop more quickly. But it still produces a contradiction in this passage itself. For if a German "national culture," for an author to submit himself to, simply does not exist (which is what the sentence says), what difference does it make whether he seeks it "earlier" or later? The question, it seems, ought to be whether the German author can develop "as a German" *at all,* not whether he can do so earlier in life.

As far as I can see, there is only one way to deal with this difficulty. The German author finds his "national culture"—which does not exist—only *late,* because that culture, the quality of fruitful Germanness he is aiming for, is something he himself, over years of work, must *create*—or at least, "supported by contemporaries who work and strive along with him" (p. 200), assist in creating. Hence also Goethe's proposal that "the history of the training of our most prominent authors" be compiled, for the sake of "the benefit they have established" (p. 201). The *process* by which these authors grew must be remembered, not just the results of their growth. And hence the idea of the "invisible school," the "circle" that earlier German authors have opened by an act of creation, and widened for their successors. But we have seen that this idea cannot be reconciled with the idea of a "Nationalcultur"—in the modern sense that might pave the way for "classical" prose. Such a culture is not created by writers, but requires a preexisting "Nation." Exactly what, then, have those struggling eighteenth-century German writers created?

They have created an "invisible school," named here, not by accident, in a vocabulary evocative of the secret society. They have created a literary community that is national in the sense of discharging a specifically German task, but also *anti-national* in the sense of being opposed to that modern form of nationhood toward which Germany (in abrupt or gradual "upheavals") will inevitably develop, that cultural situation in which a large populace will be able to convince itself, by manipulating its educational institutions, that it possesses a "classical" prose literature. That classical literature of Germany's national future will not be literature at all, in the true sense of literary tradition, but rather "literarischer Sansculottismus." (Why else does Goethe use these words for the title of an essay that, on the surface, is concerned with much broader issues?) And the job of literature itself, the future of literature, the task of that struggling and self-creating community of Germans, along with like-minded writers elsewhere, will be to conduct an endless covert *resistance* against this form of populist modernity. The destiny of literature is *to go undergound*—although not in the sense of simply disappearing from public view. Publication is still necessary, in order that the scattered anti-national writers come to know of one another. But the published works will be read in a completely different sense, depending on whether one is positioned *inside* the "invisible school," where it appears filled with light, or *outside,* in the world of modern "nations" that obscure the light of literature by seeking intellectual justification in a delusive notion of the "classical."

Goethe's essay is still full of various kinds of anomaly, which we can now read, however, as a sign that something is happening beneath the surface of the writing, something meant for initiates, that would not make sense to a larger public. If we adopt the "standpoint" (p. 199) my argument suggests, for instance, we are no longer dismayed by the slippery ambiguity in Goethe's use of the concepts "Gesellschaft," "society," and "Publicum," "public," which *must* coincide in the essay's last paragraph (p. 203) if the optimistic posture there is to make any sense, whereas earlier in the essay— where the idea of "ein großes Publicum ohne Geschmack" (p. 200), "a large public without taste," stands in contrast to the question of how one acts "in guter Gesellschaft" (p. 202), "in good society"—they obviously do not coincide. Or how do we deal with a sentence like "der muß sehr üble Laune haben, der in dem Augenblicke Deutschland vortreffliche Schriftsteller abspricht, da fast jedermann *gut* schreibt" (p. 202), "that person must be in a very bad humor who denies Germany excellent authors at a time when almost everyone writes *well*"—as if "vortrefflich" and "gut" (which Goethe emphasizes) meant the same thing, or as if the heroic efforts and sufferings of eighteenth-century authors were vindicated by the fact that everyone writes reasonably well nowadays? And by "that person" Goethe obviously must mean Jenisch, who, however, uses the terms "gut" and "vortrefflich" exactly the other way round. Germany, he says, has practically no "good prose writers" ("gute Prosaisten"), even though it may well have "excellent poets" ("vortrefliche Dichter" [Jenisch, p. 253]).

How genuine is Goethe's presentation of himself, here, as a person of relaxed good humor? What has happened to the question of adequate expressive vehicles for "original genius," or to the problem of either finding or creating a specifically German "culture"? What we have, in this essay, is a very tricky and very delicately balanced piece of prose, whose author maintains, for his larger public, the unexceptionable stance of "ein heitrer billiger Deutscher" (p. 203), "a cheerful, fair-minded German," who is perfectly happy with things as they are, while at the same time he leaves open those cracks in the linguistic and rhetorical facade of his thought, through which the bleak vision of a coming age of "literarischer Sansculottismus" can be glimpsed—an age perhaps already foreseen by Götz von Berlichingen when he speaks of "die Zeiten des Betrugs" (WA, 8:169), "times of treachery"—an age in which literature as resistance, as underground, will never again be able actually to shape, or contribute openly to shaping, the public context of its operation.

To put it differently, literature as a unified and unifying social activity is dead. What we used to think of as literature is henceforward two different things, a public literature and a secret literature, which occupy the same textual space yet represent entirely irreconcilable worlds, worlds as different as, say, the representational processes of Greeks and Amazons in Kleist. Public literature is the literature that makes itself available for use as the more or less "classical" summary of its nation's life and development. Secret literature is a hopeless but tireless guerrilla campaign against the very idea of the nation; it is the sign of an "invisible school" that originates, as we might expect, in the politically undeveloped country of Germany, which stands apart as a spectator (a throwback perhaps, but a prophetic one) while the large nations of Europe assume—under such euphemisms as "democratic," "republican," "parliamentary"—their modern character as publicistic organizations, machines for the establishment and control of acceptable discourse.[4] Here the idea of the aesthetic and its main consequence, the exposure of literature to political co-option, reenter the discussion. Co-option is inevitable; as Götz says, "the vile will rule." And the only responsible course now, for a writer, is to destroy literature, to tear it in two, and to set out on a path where public esteem and recognition, the hope of historical greatness, the aura of classicality—even if we actually enjoy these advantages—must be put aside and permitted no contact whatever with the dark negative task now before us.

## Hermeneutics and Aesthetic Culture

The emergence of modern hermeneutics, in the form of tension and clash among at least three different versions of the hermeneutic project, is the subject of an important recent book on the German eighteenth century, Robert S. Leventhal's *The Disciplines of Interpretation*. Leventhal's argument is valuable particularly for its range, which connects specific historical points, especially about the institution of the university, with explications of difficult texts and with a theoretical reading of theory that establishes a pattern of relationships throughout hermeneutic thought up to the present. And Goethe, in this wide-ranging book, is mentioned exactly twice—which is just as it should be. For Goethe's developing idea of resistance against literature as the future of literature does not belong to the history Leventhal is writing except negatively, in that it implies resistance against *the whole* of modern hermeneutics. Even at its most thoroughly self-critical (in Friedrich Schlegel, says Leventhal), even in its most resolute avoidance of universal claims, hermeneutic thought, for Goethe's purposes, is still entirely contained within the aesthetic culture that has made literature obsolete as a fruitful public practice. Of course this does not diminish the importance of Leventhal's work for our project.

Leventhal summarizes his argument by distinguishing "three hermeneutic paradigms of the period since 1750." The first two, "semiotic interpretation" and "so-called Romantic Hermeneutics," which hypostasize, respectively, a referent detachable from the sign and "the spirit of the author," are already superseded in the period around 1800. The third, however, "the more extreme (anti-)hermeneutical position," is of persisting importance as both a guide and a problem. This paradigm, as in Friedrich Schlegel's thought on incomprehensibility,

> does not repudiate the process of interpretation, but rather redefines it as a reading of the breaks, ruptures, and difficulties that are legible on the surface of the text itself. On this reading of interpretation, the goal is not a hermeneutic consensus in the understanding of the thing (*Verständigung*) or a meeting of senses between distinct individuals or worlds (*Einverständnis*), nor finally a fusion of horizons between disparate prejudicial structures [= structures of pre-judgment], but rather the provocation that the text actually resists the interpretive moves of the reader; that its function is to cause a heightened critical confrontation or clash between readers.[5]

It appears, from the terminology of this passage, as if Goethe's worry about the future of literature were also superseded by the new hermeneutics. Resistance is now located in the very nature of the text and requires no "invisible school" in society. The aesthetic involvement of the reader in constituting meaning is now thoroughly disrupted, since the reader has disintegrated into a clashing plurality. Meaning itself, "a deep 'meaning' or sense beneath the surface of the text" (Leventhal, p. 311), is dispensed with.

But the situation is not so simple. In the first place, when I speak of Goethe's resistance against "aesthetic" culture, I am not referring to "the Kantian project of a philosophical aesthetics" (Leventhal, p. 25), or to "aesthetics" in the sense in which "from Kant to Adorno, [it] is a philosophy of the subject through and through" (Leventhal, p. 272). Aesthetic culture, as the object of Goethe's resistance, depends on the operation of the reader not as subject, but as *role*, as *the* reader, as a function, with respect to the text, by which precisely the subject is superseded or co-opted—even if that function can be described, for example, as "one in which the subject is necessarily thrown back on itself to reflect upon its own derivation and conditions of possibility" (Leventhal, p. 21). Nothing prevents even the most radical critical reflection upon subjectivity, even a "confrontation or clash between readers," from becoming a role for the reader, in my sense of the term "aesthetic." As I said in connection with the presumed tension between male and female readers of *Werther* as pornography, there is no necessary limit to the reader's shamelessness. And where I have spoken of the aesthetic reader's playing a role in the constitution of "meaning," meaning must be understood in the broadest possible sense, as the very identity of the text, not as a detachable paraphrase or authorial spirit. Training for the game of life, in this sense, is a meaning of *Werther* that is constituted in part by the aesthetic reader's performance; but it is also indistinguishable from the (thoroughly self-reflecting) process of reading itself.

If a culture of "confrontation or clash between readers" could be established, Goethe would perhaps be satisfied. But how shall such a culture avoid the self-theorizing move by which that "clash" is embedded in "an ethics of reading" (Leventhal, p. 31), where it stands revealed as a form of communication, or indeed cooperation, as the aesthetic performance of a prescribed readerly role by which, precisely, the text as "provocation" is constituted? The trouble with hermeneutics, from Goethe's perspective, is that even in its deepest (self-)questioning, it still begs the question of aesthetic culture. Leventhal suggests that the theorizing tendency of hermeneutics is kept in check by "a constant tension" with "its Other, incomprehensibility" (p. 14), the latter being understood (with Schlegel) "as an *intrinsic characteristic of texts* or as inherent *historical density or opacity* that necessarily emerges in the process of text interpretation" (p. 300). But only a small development of our argument earlier on Werther's suicide (as belonging inherently to the text as text, yet also as a strictly incomprehensible free act) would be needed to produce an instance or performance of exactly what Leventhal is talking about—in a text, however, that precisely this characteristic entangles in the wrongness of aesthetic culture.

Then, in the second place, hermeneutics as political criticism (see Leventhal on the "critique of institutionalization and discipline" [p. 26] or on "freedom of interpretation and criticism" [p. 256]) has no efficacy whatever on the level of large-scale national discourse-organization that Goethe saw, and foresaw, as marking the end of the relatively independent public force we used to call "literature." Scale makes all the difference. What on one scale might reasonably be understood as "conversation" (Leventhal, p. 27), or as the avoidance of "any attempt to move beyond discourse and linguistic interaction" (Leventhal, p. 245), becomes, in a broader compass, the insistence on free-market principles in an intellectual economy of production and consumption. The one-theoretical-move-too-many represented by Schlegel's version of the concept of "communicability" is useful, perhaps emancipatory, on the scale of an academic subject-system debate (see Leventhal, e.g., pp. 33, 247, 272, 296), but becomes mere capitulation, or active complicity, in the presence of a large public discourse that lives by rebuilding (or counterfeiting) the subject out of a communication in concepts with all their sharp edges ground off.

The notion of "destabilization," to which we will return later, and the attachment of a positive value to it (see Leventhal, pp. 14, 183, 267, 274, etc.), expresses both a hope and a fear, on the part of radical hermeneutic self-criticism, vis-à-vis large-scale political discourse. But Goethe, as early as *Götz von Berlichingen,* understands the futility of hoping for a hermeneutic influence in politics. What is Götz, the person, if not an allegory of the emancipatory hermeneutic project, which sees its task as destabilization of the large political order for the ultimate good of that order, while also avoiding an over-specific theorization of the good it hopes to achieve? And what does Weislingen represent, if not the recognition that where such a destabilizing move actually takes hold in the political structure, it produces only a self-nullifying reactionary convulsion that quickly passes, leaving politics, and discourse, as usual? In Götz's descendant, Faust, the allegory is subtilized. The commitment to magic that Faust, at the end, longs to retract is an allegory of the destabilizing capability of interpretation—"Be careful how you interpret the world; it *is* like that," says Erich Heller[6]—which turns out, however, to be only an instance of the aesthetic reader's constitution of his object, an autoerotic destabilization of the *self,* which thence finds itself in complicity with the unregenerate political order as represented in act 4 of part II.

Even Leventhal—whose work is to date the most complete and accurate account of what Goethe saw as the futile (or worse than futile) alternatives to a literature gone underground—occasionally finds himself advocating hermeneutics in a political sense. In the course of suggesting that since interpretation is basically a matter of power, hermeneutics has political potential as an internal critical self-reflection in power structures, Leventhal (pp. 30, 315) twice quotes a late aphorism of Nietzsche:

Man darf nicht fragen: "*wer* interpretirt denn?" sondern das Interpretiren selbst, als eine Form des Willens zur Macht, hat Dasein (aber nicht als ein "Sein," sondern als ein *Prozeß*, ein *Werden*) als ein Affekt.[7]

[One may not ask: "who is interpreting?" but rather interpretation itself, as a form of the Will to Power, has being (but not as a substantial "being," rather as a *process*, a *becoming*) as an affect.]

And after the second citing, Leventhal goes on to say of the will to power itself that it "is in fact nothing other than interpretation" (p. 315)—a statement which, if it were ascribable to Nietzsche, would place him squarely in the camp of hermeneutic advocacy. Nietzsche's aphorism, however, says nothing of the kind, and actually puts him closer to Goethe's position. Interpretation, says Nietzsche, as a form of the will to power, is always an *affect,* which means that hermeneutics, as the interpretation of interpretation, is not at all a powerful dialectical force that creates new critical tension, but always merely another instance of *the same affect,* which never finds itself anywhere but exactly where it started. The pretense, or dream, of a critical destabilizing of power structures merely convicts hermeneutics of *blind* complicity with the will to power—as opposed to the relatively knowing and affirmative complicity that is performed, for instance, in no. 22 of *Beyond Good and Evil.*

Hermeneutics, then—in the third place—can never be a useful basis or refuge for the literary in Goethe's sense, but is always part of the problem literature must contend with. Self-reflexivity is its very nature, and therefore it cannot possibly resist that last bit of preening in the mirror, the final theoretical move, that puts it in complicity with whatever large-scale organization of discourse obtains in the given historical moment.[8] What makes this situation especially difficult, however, is that hermeneutics, in the developed form that Leventhal calls (anti-)hermeneutics, provides the only available description of the type of reading that must characterize precisely literary resistance as Goethe tries to imagine it: a reading that refuses resolutely to constitute its object as either meaning or spirit, but reads its way, so to speak, *through* the object and into history, through the object considered as a simple instance of incomprehensibility, offering no hook for the dialectical move or universalizing gesture (see Leventhal, p. 288) that might present history itself, in turn, as anything other than simple conflict, confrontation, force, and resistance.

Reading as practiced in Goethe's resistance against literature, therefore —which I will call "reading on the edge," and give an instance of in a later chapter—must confront hermeneutics as an integral component of what it resists, yet also somehow remain blind to the mirror that precisely hermeneutics holds up to it. For to see its image in that mirror would be to make the last crucial theoretical move and so to *become* hermeneutics. The situation—whose allegory, in this respect, is Egmont, blinding himself to himself in precarious somnambulistic balance on his roof-peak—appears practically hopeless. The "invisible school," light-flooded as it may be from within, must in a strong sense be invisible even to itself, like a network of party cells. But party cells without a party, a doctrine, a purpose: and how can such a network possibly be expected to survive? These considerations will eventually bring us, and Goethe, back to the question of gender.

## Goethe in the Nineties

The shape of the problem of literature in aesthetic culture, including an anticipatory grasp of the place of advanced self-critical hermeneutics in that problem, is already evident in *Götz von Berlichingen*. But it is probably not until the 1790s that the full scope of the problem and the necessity (for all its hopelessness) of something like a literary resistance against literature itself, in the face of the discourse-organizing power of the developing European nation-state, become entirely clear to Goethe. And when, later still, in *Dichtung und Wahrheit*, he looks back on *Götz* and speaks enigmatically of having given it more "historical and national substance" in his revision, Goethe is seeing that early play, so to speak, through the lens of the 1790s. *Götz* had been made more "national," in the sense of more focused on problems that now turn out to belong to the very idea of the modern nation, but also more national in the sense of more German, exploiting what has turned out to be the unique perspective available, in a politically undeveloped ("zerstückelt") Germany, upon more advanced nations, such as France, in which an enormously expanded participation in public debate, even in the form of bloody revolution, tends not to broaden and energize discourse, not to make room for "original genius," but rather to organize and limit discourse in ways that no tyranny, no censorship, could ever have hoped for.

In the essay "Literarischer Sansculottismus," Goethe does not actually respond to Jenisch, and in fact suggests that it may not even be worth our trouble to read him. Nor is he, at any significant depth, troubled by Jenisch's attack on German literature, which is more coy, and pretentiously fastidious, than it is cutting. What worries him is the way Jenisch, in his use of the concept of the "classical," manages hardly to notice the French Revolution. What worries him is not the ways in which Jenisch is wrong, but the way in which he may be right: the possibility that if a large national discourse sufficiently uniform to support the notion of the "classical" (as applied even to *contemporary* writing) is also inherently durable enough to survive even the French Revolution unscathed, then that discourse is probably impervious, once and for all, to the influence, the tone-setting and repeatedly tone-breaking leadership, of literary energy or genius. Hence, again, the idea of an invisible school of literary resistance, especially in Germany.

Not that Goethe ever presents a clear idea of *why* literature should be preserved in its new underground form. To develop such an idea would be to make a fateful theoretical move into the domain of advanced hermeneutics, where the critical understanding of modern national discourse as an interpretive power contest (by acceding, as interpretation, to the rules of that contest) can only increase the exposure of literature to co-option. The invisible school, again, must remain invisible even to itself. It does not, of course, escape the condition of discourse as power contest. But like any guerrilla action, it survives best (if perhaps only as a serpent's bruising of heels) when it operates with rules and methods that are not only not accepted, but not even conceivable, in the world of its established and immensely more powerful adversary. When we interrogate Goethe's writings of the 1790s and later with respect to any plausible idea of the literary calling (*why* one writes), we find little that is more specific than the recognition that literature is what Goethe himself is best at, and that he intends to continue practicing it under whatever conditions.

There is in fact a document from 1797 in which this stance, this silence, is quite clearly articulated: the short third-person prose piece (WA, 42/2:506–7) that Bernhard Suphan calls (correctly) a "Selbstschilderung," "self-portrayal," on Goethe's part, and the importance of which is persuasively argued by Hans Rudolf Vaget in connection with Goethe's and Schiller's "Dilettantismus" project.[9] Goethe begins this little confession by talking about a poetic "Bildungstrieb," "educative or formative drive," in himself, which has such a huge appetite for material to work with that it inevitably leads him in "false" or nonliterary directions. He then goes into considerable detail about his disappointing but still ultimately useful experiences in pictorial art, in the "business" of government and administration, and in science; and with respect to the last, he adopts an interestingly hermeneutic standpoint, speaking of how he had learned that "in science, the formation of the mind that does the work counts more than the objects on which it works." But when it comes to literature, he suddenly says nothing at all: "It is for other people to describe the special character of his [read 'my'] poetic formative drive; unfortunately his nature has shaped itself, with respect to matter as well as form, by way of obstacles and difficulties, and gained the ability to operate with a certain amount of conscious control only at a late stage, when the time of greatest energy is past." Obviously there are echoes of "Literarischer Sansculottismus" here, but neither here nor there is anything said about *what* "he" does or learns as a poet. And yet something does get said after all, as it were by the back door. Immediately after the above passage, Goethe goes on to speak of his "mutability," the strong effect external impressions have upon him. "It is so," he says, "with books, with people, with social gatherings." But then, in the last sentence of the whole piece, he narrows it down to books alone: "He ['I'] cannot read without being determined ['bestimmt'] by the book he reads, and he cannot thus be put into

a mood ['gestimmt'] without striving—let the direction be as foreign to him
as it will—to work actively against it and to bring forth something similar."
The thought in this (probably dictated) piece is by no means fully worked out,
and even the grammar is sporadic. But the idea of the poet as one who *responds*
to literature, and whose response is a kind of resistance that works by turning
literature against itself (producing "something similar" to what he reads), is
clearly suggested.

In any case, it is also in 1797—on 26 June or thereabouts[10]—that
Goethe decides to transform his largest project, *Faust,* from literature into anti-
literature by disrupting any conceivable sense of its genre and so rendering it
not only incomprehensible but (provided we are in on what the text is doing
to itself) strictly unreadable. And above all, the 1790s see the beginning of
Goethe's close working relationship with Schiller, a man with whose character—
for very good reasons—he had thought his own completely incompatible
(see, e.g., WA, 36:246–53). Precisely their incompatibility proves valuable to
Goethe. For the invisibility of the invisible school, even with respect to itself,
requires of Goethe not a brooding submergence in the hermeneutic theory
of literature and its future, and certainly not a retreat into mere silence, but
rather, as in "Literarischer Sansculottismus," that he sustain the condition of
the "cheerful, fair-minded German," that he continue to be seen and heard,
as a focus and medium of communication for whatever subversive forces "still
live, scattered and groping, in the world" (*Faust,* l. 24), that he remain involved
in contemporary cultural and literary life. The association with an energetic
young colleague of radically different temper, who will draw him out into a
publicistic and polemical arena offering ever new points of leverage for his else
cancerous private irony, could not have come at a better time.

The progress of the *Faust* project, for example, owes a great deal
to Schiller's nagging, as does Goethe's narrative and essayistic work of the
period. But perhaps most interesting are the collaborative endeavors initiated
by Goethe, in which Schiller is used as a kind of mouthpiece to establish the
public substance and tone behind which booby traps for literature can be set.
I mean the "Xenien"—which, curiously enough, have clear points of contact,
in both content and attitude, with Jenisch's attack on German literature—
and especially the abortive project "Über den Dilettantismus," which Vaget
(pp. 126–34) shows conclusively to have been basically Goethe's idea.

There are many interesting details in the surviving "Dilettantism"
material. Of the various tabular schemata, for example, in which the "Nutzen"
and "Schaden," the beneficial and damaging effects of various types of dilettantism, are listed, the one on "pragmatische Poesie," or literature involving a
fictional action, is most drastic in its rejection of the dilettante. "Nutzen" here
simply equals zero (WA, 47:314). But the first entry under damaging effects of
dilettantism, for literature as a "whole," reads, "Mixing of genres"—at a time

when Goethe was working on *Faust,* in which the disruption of genres and their boundaries plays a crucial part! Some tricky things are going on here (as also in the "Xenien"), and they have to do, I think, with the question of why Goethe is interested in the project to begin with.

Dilettantism, I contend, was a personal problem for Goethe in ways that go beyond just his difficulties with his own nonliterary activity, especially as a graphic artist (see Vaget, esp. pp. 23–84). One of the curious things about the project notes is how little they say about the opposite of dilettantism, the condition of the master or true artist. We hear that the true artist is "born" such (WA, 47:322), and that art invites people to "enjoyment" (WA, 47:323); but we hear nothing about any useful function of art in society or history, whereas a great deal is said in the schemata about the benefits of dilettantism, and the damage it causes, in these areas. And on a sheet that was probably dictated by Goethe, and contains Goethe's penciled notes, we read:

> Art gives itself its own laws and issues commands to its time.
> Dilettantism follows the inclination of its time.
> When masters in art follow a false taste, then the dilettante imagines all the more quickly that he has reached the level of art. (WA, 47:324)

True art, that is, *governs* its time, yet is still capable of following a "false" direction in taste, which implies that in the very act of governing, of lawgiving, true art can share with dilettantism a relaxed susceptibility to contemporary "inclination." What this apparently contradictory combination of ideas adds up to, I think, is that for Goethe, the relation between dilettantism and mastery is exactly the relation between the exoteric and esoteric components of his own writing. The whole project thus becomes a huge cryptic self-portrait—of the "cheerful, fair-minded German" (*che si diletta del tempo attuale,* so to speak [cf. WA, 47:321]) who is also, at night perhaps, a guerrilla leader, making his own rules (which we do not talk about) and seeking by devious means to assert them in history.

And the dilettantism project is itself a device for the secret imposition of new rules in its time. For on the one hand, it draws a very strong distinction between the dilettante and the true master, while on the other hand, it says nothing about how to recognize the master and is meant to have a strong polemical component (which Goethe hoped Schiller would contribute [see Vaget, pp. 202–5]) directed presumably against people who are *mistakenly* considered true artists. The result would have been a radical undermining of any standards of public judgment. Only the master is in a position to mark the division between his own work and mere dilettantism; but he can do so only by proclaiming himself a master and so exposing himself to polemics (like Goethe's and Schiller's, here and in the "Xenien") that call his mastery into question. And who is to judge then? The school of true art, and especially of literature ("Schule," "Kunst-und Künstlerwelt" [WA, 47:318]), is in the final analysis therefore always an invisible school, composed of those who do not proclaim, yet still *know,* who their fellow masters are.

## Parallel Plays and a Disappearing Poem

Is this idea of belonging to an invisible school, which is denied any secure public existence, only a fleeting specter that haunts Goethe for a time in the 1790s and then is gone? Or is it his enduring view of the future of literature? At least the prospect of an anti-national literature is opened by his later insistence on the dawning epoch of "Weltliteratur." (People who are "serious" about this idea are compared to "eine stille, fast gedrückte Kirche" [WA, 42/2:503].) At least the idea of a fundamental difference in what literature is, depending on whether one is positioned inside or outside a privileged secret space, is suggested in the later poem "Gedichte sind gemahlte Fensterscheiben." At least it is clear, from any number of examples, that Goethe was capable of treating literature as a fundamentally esoteric communicative practice. But let us turn now to another work that is involved in Goethe's response to the French Revolution, *Die natürliche Tochter.*

On what grounds does the king doubt the duke's loyalty? What is the origin of the enmity between the duke and his son? What exactly is the son's political status, what is his power base? Who, and in whose household, are the spies who discover the king's intention to legitimize Eugenie? Since the duke would apparently under no circumstances ally himself with his son's party, why does the son's representative, the secretary, employ the secular priest in an attempt to persuade the duke to return to political activity after Eugenie's supposed death? Why is it not enough, for the son, that the duke simply follow his own inclination to retire from politics, and so remove himself as a potential adversary? How has the king been maneuvered into signing the document that will exile Eugenie? Or is the document a forgery? Where does the marriage condition come from, the stipulation that the ban against Eugenie may be satisfied by her marriage? It does not appear to be spelled out in the royal document. Is it part of what the Hofmeisterin has been instructed to do, or is it her own idea, as a way of sparing Eugenie the fatal voyage to the colonies? And above all, what are the political, social, and economic conditions on the basis of which everyone senses that the state is headed toward a collapse into chaos?

These questions could form the outline for an interesting histori-cal/political drama in the manner of, say, Shakespeare or Schiller, with scenes of court ceremony, scenes of plotting and treachery, scheming soliloquies of the villains, and scenes from the milieu of servants and (so to speak) sansculottes as social background. Certainly, in the first act of *Die natürliche Tochter,* enough of this possibility is suggested to whet our appetite for a play at least as broadly political as *Götz von Berlichingen* or *Egmont.* We are very much in the position of the secular priest, who is distressed by his lack of specific knowledge concerning the secret political maneuvering in which he is employed.[11] But in the play as it stands, none of the above questions are answered, although the events to which they refer are undoubtedly taking place somewhere offstage. Thus, in effect, there are *two* plays in progress here. The one that we get to see is concerned exclusively with Eugenie and her fate. But somewhere, as if written on the other side of the same sheets of paper, a large political drama is unfolding in which Eugenie's subplot—like that of Cordelia in *King Lear*—is a relatively small factor, poetically significant but without much influence on the outcome.

The structure of two parallel plays, one actual, one virtual, is interesting for any number of reasons. But what I would like to concentrate on is the motif of the sonnet that Eugenie writes and conceals in act 2, scene 4 (*NT,* 947–60). For this sonnet is addressed to the world of the other, larger play, the virtual play; and when Eugenie pushes it through a hole in the wall, it is as if she were actually inserting it into that other world, into the domain of royal and revolutionary politics. Then, however, at the beginning of act 4, the Hofmeisterin brings from that world of plots and politics a sheet of paper by which Eugenie is now absolutely controlled. I suggest that, metaphorically speaking, this is *the same sheet of paper* that Eugenie had pushed through the barrier between worlds. In her poem, Eugenie had gloried in submitting herself to the king's power; and a piece of paper, now signed by the king (*NT,* 2595), returns as the merciless instrument of exactly the power she had celebrated. Eugenie's poem, in other words, has been *hermeneutically transformed,* interpreted by an instance of power into what it now truly is. As long as we are aware of the ghostly existence of a parallel political play, it seems to me, in any case, that the idea of an allegorical connection between the paper that disappears and the paper that later mysteriously appears does not greatly stretch the imagination.

This idea is reinforced cryptically by an ambiguity in grammar. At the very point where she is about to overcome her fears and inspect the paper carried by the Hofmeisterin, Eugenie says: "Des Lebens Glück entriß mir dieses Blatt, / Und läßt mich größern Jammer noch befürchten" (*NT,* 2591–92), "Life's happiness was torn from me by this paper, which now causes me to fear yet greater misery." Nominative and accusative are indistinguishable in the first line, which can therefore be taken to mean *either* that this paper (from the king) tore the happiness of life away from me *or* that (conceivably) the vicissitudes of life (operating hermeneutically) tore this paper (the poem) away from me and give me cause to fear still greater misery. I do not mean that the character Eugenie is actually thinking in these terms. But her language makes room for the idea behind the scene of her speaking.

What is signified by the disappearing and (in a new form) reappearing document? Given that the original text is a poem, it is not difficult to read the allegory. The work of literature that is exposed to the world of politics, in this age of revolution, when the very idea of a "nation" is being reshaped, inevitably becomes a conduit of arbitrary political power by which its author is brought under control. For the domain of poetic or literary meaning and the domain of political meaning have become strictly separate—an idea that is already suggested by the basic structure of dual parallel dramas, by the apparent inability of our theater (the domain of literary meaning) to contain the drama of political intrigue.

> Diesem Reiche droht
> Ein jäher Umsturz. Die zum großen Leben
> Gefugten Elemente wollen sich
> Nicht wechselseitig mehr mit Liebeskraft
> Zu stets erneuter Einigkeit umfangen.
> Sie fliehen sich, und einzeln tritt nun jedes
> Kalt in sich selbst zurück. Wo blieb des Ahnherrn
> Gewalt'ger Geist, der sie zu Einem Zweck
> Vereinigte, die feindlich kämpfenden,
> Der diesem großen Volk als Führer sich
> Als König und als Vater dargestellt?
> Er ist entschwunden! Was uns übrig bleibt
> Ist ein Gespenst, das mit vergebnem Streben
> Verlorenen Besitz zu greifen wähnt. (*NT,* 2825–38)

[This realm is threatened by a violent revolution. The elements that are fitted together in large public life no longer wish to embrace each other with the power of mutual love for the sake of constantly renewed unification. They spring apart, and each alone moves back coldly into itself. Where was the powerful spirit of our ancestor, which united those hostile, struggling elements behind *one* purpose, which presented itself to this great people as its leader and king? It has vanished! What is left to us is a specter, which in its futile effort imagines it can lay hold of lost property.]

The "powerful spirit" that had once repeatedly reintroduced the movement toward unity in a world of implacably hostile "elements" is a *poetic* spirit. Eugenie here recalls nostalgically an age when there was still an intersection or interaction between the divisive discourse of political power and the large, inclusive, conciliatory discourse of literature. In the present age, by contrast, whenever literature moves openly into the political realm—through some hole in the wall—the literary text is simply *appropriated* by political discourse; its comprehensively unifying literary meaning or "spirit" is simply ignored, and it now "means" only the justification of whatever agency of power is in a position to lay claim to it. The idea of the "Schriftsteller," "author"—to return to the vocabulary of "Literarischer Sansculottismus"—has been replaced by the idea of the "Nationalschriftsteller," who can arise only in the bosom of a preexisting "Nation," as the supposed author of only those meanings the nation authorizes. Again, therefore, literature itself has no choice but to go underground, to preserve its manner of meaning in the form of a covert, cryptic resistance to the new idea of the national, resistance against a once perhaps fruitful idea that is now irrevocably infected with the blundering spirit of the sansculottes.

## Prostitution and Plausibility

What exactly is "Sansculottismus" in the literary sense? The word occurs only once in the body of Goethe's essay:

> Ferne sei es von uns, den übelgedachten und übelgeschriebenen Text, den wir vor uns haben, zu commentiren; nicht ohne Unwillen werden unsre Leser jene Blätter am angezeigten Orte durchlaufen, und die ungebildete Anmaßung, womit man sich in einen Kreis von Bessern zu drängen, ja Bessere zu verdrängen und sich an ihre Stelle zu setzen denkt, diesen eigentlichen Sansculottismus zu beurtheilen und zu bestrafen wissen. (p. 197)

> [Far be it from us to comment on the ill-thought and ill-written text we have before us. Not without indignation will our readers peruse those pages in the journal we have mentioned, and not without an understanding of how to judge and condemn that uneducated presumptuousness by which one hopes to push one's way into a circle of one's betters, or indeed to push one's betters aside and assume their place, that true sansculottism.]

The opposite of such arrogant and resentful presumptuousness ("Anmaßung") would presumably be an attitude of respect that observes boundaries and domains of competence—which, in Eugenie's nostalgic vision, would refer to a condition of mutual respect between the political and the poetic spheres of meaning. Given this condition, the power struggle in society (of "feindlich kämpfende Elemente") is not stopped or resolved by literature; but at least (Eugenie suggests) its elements acknowledge the differentness and value of literature's synoptic project. And literature, in turn, does not ignore or despise the political; in fact, like Eugenie's poem, it adopts a posture of submission—a posture which, as long as mutual respect obtains, is of course not taken literally, but provides the vehicle of literature's influence in the political domain.

Literary sansculottism, however, is a literature that has prostituted itself utterly to the political and now engages in its own form of power politics (its "Anmaßung"), which is designed to entangle the rest of literature in that prostituted condition. Mutual respect is now out of the question. From a literary point of view, we cannot even "comment" on a text of the sort Goethe is talking about, since to do so would be to involve that text in a literary relation with literature as a whole, hence to afford it literary status, hence to encourage its "Anmaßung," hence to cooperate in the total subjugation or co-option of literature with relation to the political.

And if we ask exactly who those "Bessere" are who must avoid contact with the literary sansculottes—better writers? better people? the "higher classes" Goethe speaks of elsewhere?—we uncover once again the essay's pervasive ambiguity. At the very end we read:

> So sieht ein heitrer billiger Deutscher die Schriftsteller seiner Nation auf einer schönen Stufe und ist überzeugt, daß sich auch das Publicum nicht durch einen mißlaunischen Krittler werde irre machen lassen. Man entferne ihn aus der Gesellschaft, aus der man jeden ausschließen sollte, dessen vernichtende Bemühungen nur die Handelnden mißmuthig, die Theilnehmenden lässig und die Zuschauer mißtrauisch und gleichgültig machen könnten. (p. 203)

> [Thus a cheerful, fair-minded German sees his nation at a handsome stage of development and is convinced that the public will also not let itself be confused by an ill-tempered critic. Let that critic be removed from our society, from which we should exclude everyone whose destructive efforts only threaten to make those who act sullen, those who participate lax, and those who survey the situation mistrustful and indifferent.]

The association of "society" with "the public"—along with the approval earlier of how well "almost everyone" writes these days—makes it seem that the author is appealing here to a very large segment of the population, perhaps to the "Nation" as a whole, at least to a majority in the sense of republican politics. But then we recall that in that earlier passage where the word "Sansculottismus" actually occurs, it had been a question of excluding precisely the propagandist of a kind of arrogant literary republicanism from a "circle of his betters," which implies a much tighter and more exclusive idea of the "society" that must be preserved. Which way does Goethe really want to be understood? Is he writing on behalf of the German "nation" as a whole? Or does he represent a small society of those "better" people whose creative sense of literature and culture must be kept separate from what literature and culture become in the hands of the large, nationally indoctrinated public that will set the tone from now on in Europe?

It is fairly clear that Goethe wants to have it both ways. He is in fact addressing the German nation as a whole, with a warning against that seductive idea of "the classical" which actually only authorizes a redefinition of literature in terms dictated by political expediency. Even from the perspective of his own more exclusive literary society, which can no longer identify itself with a "Nation," it will not hurt if this particular instance of literary sansculottism is rejected by the larger public. But even if the present attack is successful, even if a whole wave of literary sansculottism is successfully counteracted on the level of the nation as a whole, still, from within the "circle" that really matters, from within the anti-national "invisible school," we recognize that this is just one in an endless series of guerrilla actions that will make up the future of literature.

I have conceded that this argument is in a sense not plausible. In the first place, any number of Goethe's texts and pronouncements can be quoted to dispute it—for example, his later insistence on the "Classical" as the salutary opposite of the "Romantic." And I would be obliged, in each case, to uncover the cracks, the cryptic signs, the inconspicuous inconsistencies, that might be interpreted as signs of the invisible. I think I could do this; but the task would be endless. In the second place, however, the view I am suggesting requires not only that every text be interpreted on at least two different levels, but also that the interpretation from level to level automatically contradict itself. In order to be published, in order to operate at all, the text must make sense in the context of what the "Nation" decrees shall be understood as literature. But it must also make a radically different kind of sense, a sense that undercuts the very idea of "Nation," for the "invisible school" whose scattered members it reaches out to. Thus a fundamental and cherished assumption about literature, an assumption (if we believe Eugenie) that may once have constituted the very definition of literary meaning, the assumption that the literary work tends both to exhibit and to foster some form of *unity*, goes utterly by the board. And with this assumption disappears also the only possible intrinsic criterion of interpretive plausibility, the expectation that interpretations on different levels will reinforce one another.

If my argument is implausible, therefore, then it is at least inherently and incorrigibly so. My point, in fact, is that given the view of history developed by Goethe at least as early as 1795, the requirement of plausibility in interpretation, wittingly or unwittingly, is in complicity with literary sansculottism. It reinforces the co-optive move of the literary work with respect to the aesthetic reader, which is in turn (we recall Götz and Weislingen) the hook by which literature as a whole is co-opted in a larger national communicative environment. It is thus in effect a device by which the national achieves control over the literary and so works ultimately toward a totalitarian condition, where literature's ancient visionary striving for comprehensive unity has become merely the mask in which a rigid uniformity of discourse seeks to legitimize itself.

## Gender and Literature

If, for the serious writer, the connection must be severed between writing and any of the social or political mechanisms by which "literature" is publicly defined, then how shall we maintain any conception at all of why we write? What we write must become, for most practical purposes, meaningless, since meaning, in any form substantial enough to justify its vehicle, means the result of plausible interpretation in a public forum. From time to time we will perhaps be

encouraged by a feeling of special sympathy with an individual or an audience, a
feeling that enables us for a moment to believe in the existence of our "invisible
school." And in certain enigmatic novels, like *Wilhelm Meisters Wanderjahre*
with its scattered band of "Renunciants," we shall perhaps glimpse a fictional
image of that school. But are these occasional experiences enough to sustain the
resolve of a repeatedly isolated guerrilla fighter whose cause, from the outset,
is known to be hopeless? (Even—or indeed especially—if that guerrilla gets
himself painted, and hung in a museum that bears his own name, with a star
on his chest.)[12] Swashbuckling masculinity, in any case, is of no use here. The
trouble with Egmont, again, is precisely that all his energy does not free him
from dependence on a politically authorized structure of meaning, in which
personal stature and social effectiveness are defined in Spanish terms, and in
which real freedom for the people is equated with chaos.

It is here, I think, that the question of gender becomes important again,
especially as it is developed in *Die natürliche Tochter*. This play has in common
with *Iphigenie auf Tauris* that it is concerned mainly with negotiations about
the body of a woman. In *Iphigenie* the negotiations are successfully concluded;
the Greeks' motion of habeas corpus (originally thought to refer to a statue,
a body in the strictest sense) is eventually sustained, and Iphigenie is taken
home. In *Die natürliche Tochter*, by contrast, the negotiations are much more
complicated and inconclusive. Is Eugenie's body alive or dead, is it in exile or
at home, is it in a man's possession, by marriage, or not really? That this is a
question of her *body* is established by Eugenie herself in a very powerful image:

> Schon fühl' ich mich ein abgestorbnes Glied,
> Der Körper, der gesunde, stößt mich los.
> Dem selbstbewußten Todten gleich' ich, der,
> Ein Zeuge seiner eigenen Bestattung,
> Gelähmt, in halbem Traume, grausend liegt. (*NT,* 2619–23)

> [Already I feel like a limb that has died off; the body, in its health, rejects me.
> I resemble a dead man who retains his consciousness, and, a witness to his
> own burial, lies there in terror.]

Eugenie retains the ability to think and speak; but it is as if this ability made no
difference in the disposal of its vehicle, her body, over which other characters,
in the endless discussions of the play's last two acts, assert much greater power.

Is Eugenie alive or dead? Even this question becomes, in effect, a matter
of negotiation. Of the last scene in act 3, where the secular priest describes
Eugenie's death and burial to the duke and offers him spiritual comfort, Sigurd
Burckhardt remarks: "If we forget for a moment—and does not Goethe almost
force us to forget it?—that Eugenie is not really dead and buried, the scene is

characterized by a power of conviction which is only due the truth."[13] Whether or not Eugenie's body is dead is thus made to depend on who is talking and from what point of view. In any case, it is evident, from the conversation of the governess and the secretary in act 2, scene 1 (especially lines 877–85), that the question of whether Eugenie should die or be spared has been debated in detail in the parallel political drama.

The negotiation of Eugenie's life or death, moreover, is related to the question of literature by the scene between the secular priest and the duke, which is a very epitome of the corruption or prostitution of literature, a scene perhaps belonging, as Burckhardt says, "to the most monstrous that dramatic literature can show" (p. 70). In that this scene is a true and rhetorically powerful and consistent ending to the play, and to Eugenie's life—her name, as Burckhardt points out (p. 71), is never again spoken—it is an illustration of how literature can remain true to itself yet also be utterly wrong, utterly falsified or co-opted by a governing structure of meanings (in the parallel play) that have nothing to do with it. And roughly the same combination of elements characterizes the question of Eugenie's exile. Shortly after the passage discussed above, where she fears the collapse of her country and mourns its loss of poetic spirit, she resolves to marry the magistrate after all, in order not to be absent in the fatherland's hour of need.

> Im Verborgnen
> Verwahr' er mich, als reinen Talisman.
> Denn, wenn ein Wunder auf der Welt geschieht;
> Geschieht's durch liebevolle treue Herzen.
> Die Größe der Gefahr betracht' ich nicht,
> Und meine Schwäche darf ich nicht bedenken,
> Das alles wird ein günstiges Geschick
> Zu rechter Zeit auf hohe Zwecke leiten.
> Und wenn mein Vater, mein Monarch mich einst
> Verkannt, verstoßen, mich vergessen, soll
> Erstaunt ihr Blick auf der Erhaltnen ruhn,
> Die das, was sie im Glücke zugesagt,
> Aus tiefem Elend zu erfüllen strebt. (*NT,* 2852–64)

[Let him (the magistrate) keep me hidden as a pure talisman. For if a miracle happens in the world, it is accomplished by loving loyal hearts. I count not the greatness of the danger, and I may not consider my own weakness. A favorable fate will turn all this to high purposes when the time is right. And if my father and my monarch forget me, misjudged and banished by them, their gaze shall rest astonished on the preserved woman who, out of deep misery, strives to fulfill what she had promised in her happiness.]

In other words, Eugenie will remain in the country in order to be on hand when the country and its ruler need her to help restore them after the revolution. Like the scene with the secular priest and the duke, this speech is pivotal in the plot and entirely true and consistent as poetry. But it is also empty, hollowed out from beneath by not one but two parallel plays, the second being the actual history of the French Revolution, to which everyone knows this work alludes. In the very act of refusing to accept exile, Eugenie shows herself *already* in exile, banished from a type of political balance that will never again exist.

Finally, at the very end of the play, Eugenie herself participates in negotiations concerning the possession of her body in marriage, negotiations that are again inconclusive—but now deliberately so on Eugenie's part—establishing a marriage that is not a marriage. And if we read this whole series of negotiations in the light of the allegory of the disappearing poem, we arrive again at the idea of a secret negative literature: a literature whose death (its fate never again to be literature in an accepted public sense) is precisely the defense of its life against corruption; a literature exiled in the bosom of its own publicistically transformed homeland; a literature that preserves itself by being, so to speak, nothing but body, with no meaning of its own, no exposure to co-option, a mute, nameless thing to which meaning can only be attached from without, by public negotiations whose inconclusiveness leaves room for it to survive; a literature that breaks its silence (like Eugenie in the last two acts) only to negotiate itself further into the radical anomaly that has been imposed on it, only to form yet another shimmering circle of inconclusiveness around its disappearance, as sheer body, in the alien discursive fluid of its time.[14] It is, moreover, a literature that had started out from an aesthetic conception of itself, as a secret place where pleasure is stored for future solitary consumption, like the forbidden sweets that Eugenie, in her childhood, had concealed in her hole in the wall (*NT,* 994–95). But this innocent practice, as soon as it touches a matter of conceivable public concern, is quickly unmasked as the exposure of our "secret" (*NT,* 985), our very person, to the implacable co-optive mechanism of the modern nation. Only the body remains—Eugenie's body, which in this respect is still Lotte's body—as the focus of hopeless resistance that literature has now become, in the toils of what had once been the element of its own fruitful discursive activity.

But it is specifically a woman's body. In the quality of practitioners or proponents of literature as resistance, we are called upon to compare our situation with the subjugated position of women. The manner in which this text, *Die natürliche Tochter,* approaches us is figured in the magistrate's approach to Eugenie, in one of the play's most unsettling passages. Eugenie questions whether the magistrate will really be able to protect her if she marries him, and he responds:

Reicht eine Macht denn wohl in jenes Haus,
Wo der Tyrann die holde Gattin kränkt,
Wenn er, nach eignem Sinn, verworren handelt;
Durch Launen, Worte, Thaten jede Lust,
Mit Schadenfreude, sinnreich untergräbt?
Wer trocknet ihre Thränen? Welch Gesetz,
Welch Tribunal erreicht den Schuldigen?
Er triumphirt, und schweigende Geduld
Senkt nach und nach verzweifelnd sie in's Grab. (*NT,* 2191–99)

[Does any power extend into that house where the tyrant torments his fair wife, when he, according to his own fancy, acts confusedly and by his moods, words, deeds, with malicious purposefulness, undermines her every joy? Who dries her tears? What law, what tribunal can touch the guilty man? He triumphs, and her silent patience lowers her by despairing degrees into the grave.]

The magistrate—one can hardly credit it—is here trying to persuade Eugenie to marry him by painting the bleakest conceivable picture of married life for a woman, a picture in which he twice uses the concept "Sinn," "meaning, purpose," which suggests that the absolute tyranny of the husband, if perhaps not proper, is at least somehow logical. And yet this picture is no bleaker than the picture of our literary situation suggested by the play's allegory. How, and of what, is this picture meant to persuade us?

It does at least respond to our original question by providing a *conception* of our situation as an "invisible school," as inhabitants, we now understand, of something very like a woman's body, a body without a voice, or whose voice is constantly drowned out in the public negotiations that dispose of it. If we recognize ourselves as an invisible school, an unacknowledged guerrilla force, and recognize Goethe as one of our number, then it is now "Goethe as woman" we recognize. And even if we do not yet have a clear answer to the question of why we still write, at least the question has now begun to assume contour, as the question of *the possibility of a feminist literary project.* If a way can be found to assert, and make effective, the else automatically co-opted situation of women in the discourse-machine of modern national life, then perhaps some sense of direction and purpose will emerge (at least by analogy) for the strugglers of the invisible school as well.

# Bridge, Against Nothing:
# Nietzsche as Woman

ELLES AFFIRMENT TRIOMPHANT QUE
TOUT GESTE EST RENVERSEMENT.

This chapter, mainly on Nietzsche, not only plays with the idea of "bridge," in various senses, but also itself is a bridge, from the idea of Goethe to that of "Goethe." Its aim, especially, is to illustrate the *type* of argument that will be attempted on a larger historical scale in the concluding chapters. It will also, I hope, add both substance and specificity to the crucial question of the possibility of a feminist literary project.

## The Problem of Revolution

Revolutionaries are people who go out on a limb, but in such a way as to raise the question of whether their limb is not after all a bridge, the bridge to an Elsewhere that is substantially different from what we suppose ourselves able to recognize immediately as the shape of our own social or political or economic or sensory or linguistic existence. The claim to have found such a bridge—along with the absence of any basis whatever for adjudicating it—is what makes the revolutionary in thought, and makes its daring, its untenability, its vulnerable or in fact doomed situation, out on a limb. There is no need for revolutionary thought, no impetus, except where a positive value accrues to the degree of sheer differentness of its Elsewhere, which in turn, however, is exactly the degree to which the existence of a usable bridge becomes improbable, hence the degree to which that Elsewhere, in the judgment of reasonable people, stands revealed as a Nowhere, a utopia.

That revolutionary thought—or at least a revolutionary appetite in thought—persists nonetheless, in all its unreasonableness, has to do with the belief that revolutions *have happened* in history, and so might conceivably happen again. But the trouble with revolutions that are supposed actually to have happened is that we see them the wrong way round, from the wrong end of the bridge. The arrival of the bridge at its destination is visible to us, but the moment that really matters—if we are interested in learning how to recognize or validate or promote revolutionary thought here and now—the moment of the bridge's becoming, the moment at which revolution makes the leap from untenable fantasy into the historically actual, is still obscured. Precisely to the extent that we insist on the radicality of a particular revolutionary process in past history, our attempt to reconstruct that process involves us in difficulties similar to those, for example, that bedevil any attempt to eradicate the teleological component in our description of natural processes. The undeniable *existence* of the bridge obscures the quality of thought strictly out on a limb.

This consideration, I think, goes a long way toward explaining the interest aroused among non-scientists by the discussion of "scientific revolutions." Here, at least, we expect that the record—in the form of texts written with a view to maximum exactness, plus repeatable experiments—may be clear enough to support a convincing reconstruction. But what Kuhn (for instance) gives us, though it is interesting as history, is of little use for the understanding of revolution. It is a cartography of "shifts" whose very complexity—whose *lack,* therefore, of the quality of simple bridges—leaves us with a vision of gradualness that obscures the revolutionary from another direction. Even Feyerabend's more engaged and engaging argument "against method" does not escape being infected by the inherent complacency of the retrospective view. It is symptomatic that Feyerabend concludes his book with an account of the growth of its thought, a story of excited intellectual voyaging that often reads distressingly like an alumni-reunion speech.

## Problems of Feminist Theory

I will not attempt to state more exactly what I mean by "the revolutionary," or especially "the revolutionary moment." The problems of definition here are obvious, since definition itself is in a strong sense the opposite of the revolutionary; and we have just seen that there are good reasons for doubting whether it is possible to give the notion flesh by reference to particular cases from history. Perhaps the best existing attempt to evoke a revolutionary moment from the past is Trotsky's *History of the Russian Revolution.* But if so, then only because Trotsky himself strenuously *denies* that his own thought or Lenin's was ever actually out on a limb to begin with, a denial which paradoxically complements the recognition, for all the book's enormous factual detail, that his thought is in truth still out on a limb, still as revolutionary (and unfulfilled) as ever.

Our reason for discussing the question of the revolutionary here, however, has to do with the specific case of feminism, hence with a revolution (we generally acknowledge) that still needs to happen. At least for a considerable segment of feminist thought, the feminist project is either revolutionary in the fullest sense, or pointless. This follows from a particular understanding of what feminism is up against, of the depth at which women's subjugation, their occupancy of the position of "other," their function as property or medium of exchange, or as the vessel of an either perfected or monstrous "nature," is woven into the structure of especially Western culture and language. In fact, if we accept Lacan's suggestion that the unconscious "itself" is never strictly distinguishable from the historical details of its discovery and discussion, then a grasp of the phallic or patriarchal bias in Freud, as well as in Lacan, confronts feminists with a task that can be described, without much exaggeration, as *the renewal of the human psyche*—the psyche, not merely "consciousness," and certainly not consciousness in the sense that we can imagine its being "raised."

The difficulty of setting limits to this sort of project produces in feminism a tendency toward theoretical leapfrogging, the repeated undermining of theoretical positions by a showing of their complicity with what the thought as a whole is up against. But not leapfrogging in a direct line, as if toward a goal. Even a disagreement as apparently straightforward as Kelly Oliver's response to David Farrell Krell's *Postponements* has unexpected twists. Oliver competently exposes the posturing in Krell's argument, but her attempt, in the process, to sweep aside all of Nietzsche, ends by mirroring itself in the shopworn metaphor of needing to "open a space for women to articulate themselves."[1] As if, in order to meet the problem of colonizing, the whole notion of a "space" for articulation did not require radical rethinking, a rethinking, in fact, of exactly the type that Krell's idea of "postponed" articulation, for all its difficulties, shows is integral in precisely Nietzsche's philosophical project.

Or to take another instance that has to do with the space or position of speaking, Shoshana Felman's "Women and Madness" is nothing if not revolutionary:

> If, in our culture, the woman is by definition associated with madness, her problem is how to break out of this (cultural) imposition of madness *without* taking up the critical and therapeutic positions of reason: how to avoid speaking both as *mad* and as *not mad*. The challenge facing the woman today is nothing less than to "re-invent" language, to *re-learn how to speak:* to speak not only against, but outside of the specular phallogocentric structure, to establish a discourse the status of which would no longer be defined by the phallacy of masculine meaning.[2]

But the essay is also a critical response to Luce Irigaray's *Speculum:*

> If, as Luce Irigaray suggests, the woman's silence, or the repression of her capacity to speak, are constitutive of philosophy and of theoretical discourse as such, from what theoretical locus is Luce Irigaray herself speaking in order to develop her own theoretical discourse about the woman's exclusion? Is she speaking the language of men, or the silence of women? Is she speaking *as* a woman, or *in place of* the (silent) woman, *for* the woman, *in the name of* the

woman? . . . What, in a general manner, does "speech in the name of" mean? Is it not a precise repetition of the oppressive gesture of *representation,* by means of which, throughout the history of logos, man has reduced the woman to the status of a silent and subordinate object, to something inherently *spoken for*? To "speak in the name of," to "speak *for*," could thus mean, once again, to appropriate and to silence. This important theoretical question about the status of its own discourse and its own "representation" of women, with which any feminist thought has to cope, is not thought out by Luce Irigaray. . . . [A]lthough the otherness of the woman is here fully assumed as the subject of the statement, it is not certain whether that otherness can be taken for granted as positively occupying the un-thought-out, problematical locus *from which* the statement is being *uttered.* (pp. 3–4)

What exactly is the force of this criticism?

With only a slight shift of focus, Felman's attack can be read as a simple expression of *perplexity* at Irigaray's (non-)stance. If Irigaray followed Felman's advice and "thought out" her position, would this not embed her discourse *more* firmly in the history of theory? Does Felman really want a discourse about whose position one can be "certain"? Is Irigaray's "un-thought-out" position not perhaps the adumbration of a non-position, hence precisely the avoidance of both "mad" and "not mad" that Felman herself hopes for? This situation is typical of the dynamics of revolutionary thought. Irigaray and Felman each force the other out onto a limb, and it turns out to be the same limb they are both out on.

## Rhetorical Strategies and Their Limits

But the idea of revolutionary thought in progress brings with it the question of how we can possibly *recognize* such thought. To return to my opening metaphor, if we can see the whole bridge, then it turns out not to be the kind of bridge we are interested in. Or in Felman's terms, if our task is to "establish a discourse," how shall we keep it from being co-opted, from becoming a part, precisely, of "established" discourse? Obviously this problem cannot be solved; but it becomes at least approachable if we turn it around and ask: how can the revolutionary quality of a text, its participation in a revolution in progress, be integrated into its communicative structure? How can a text *identify or present itself* as revolutionary?

Let us take two instances, as it were from opposite ends of the spectrum. Of pivotal importance in Monique Wittig's *Les Guérillères,* first, is the repeated phrase "elles disent . . . ," which establishes two incompatible perspectives upon the material being recounted. (1) A distanced perspective, "our" pre- or indeed non-revolutionary perspective: since what "they say" is after all only what "they say," in a saying that merges with the visionary saying of the text as a whole and cannot claim to determine what "we" say or know or think; and since, after all, there is no unequivocal way of distinguishing the force of the "elles disent" from that of the reactionary "ils disent" in the passage where the women claim to reject *in toto* the language that had enslaved them.[3] (2) But at the same time a perspective in the midst of the revolutionized female society: since the provisional "they say" reflects the women's own resistance to any entrapment in doctrine or ideology (p. 80); and since there is after all (in French) a difference between "elles disent" and "ils disent," which is perhaps one of those accidental "intervals" in language (p. 164) that the appropriative operation of meaning cannot fill up.

Thus—as also by other devices, like negation, statements about what the women do *not* say or do—the text manages to occupy both ends of its visionary bridge without pretending actually to have built it, without compromising its situation out on a limb. I do not mean that *Les Guérillères* is therefore somehow a successful revolutionary text, or somehow more revolutionary than others that lack its rhetorical subtlety. The question is simply: how, without losing control of the problems in the very idea of the revolutionary, can the revolutionary appetite be integrated into a text's rhetorical and communicative structure? How can a text at least sketch the claim to be revolutionary (not merely shocking or angry or radically critical or bewildering) without benefit of hindsight?

The other example I have in mind is an apparently very tame essay by Nancy K. Miller, "Changing the Subject: Authorship, Writing and the Reader."[4] Miller begins by setting forth the problematic situation of feminist thought in a theoretical atmosphere conditioned by Barthes's "Death of the Author." What status has the question of women's writing or reading if "it matters not *who* writes" or "who reads" (pp. 104–5)? Precisely the "enabling move" of "destabilization of the paternal (patriarchal, really) authority of authorship" (p. 105) contributes to a situation where, for feminists, "it is difficult to know where and how to move" (p. 115). And Miller, in the face of this difficulty, avoids high theory altogether by choosing to anchor her thought firmly on this end of any conceivable revolutionary bridge, with the question: "What does it mean to read and write as a woman within the institution that authorizes and regulates most reading and writing?" (p. 112).

But a revolutionary vista is opened after all by the answer she suggests to this question: "Irony . . . a trope that by its status as the marker of a certain distance to the truth, suits the rhetorical strategies of the feminist critic" (p. 114). What does "irony" mean here? Does it distinguish feminism from the larger practice of poststructuralism, which surely, at the very least, maintains its own "distance to the truth"? Is irony a matter of hairsplitting, of making "distinctions," like Lucy Snowe in *Villette,* a matter of accepting the "relation" to an inhospitable theoretical environment while still somehow escaping "the system of institutional authorization in which [the] relation is inscribed" (p. 113)—as if this were possible? Does irony mean simply keeping silent, immobilized by "an anxiety about claiming theoretically what we [women] know experientially" (p. 115)? Can one, above all, advocate irony without being ironic in one's advocacy? What *is* "an ironic manipulation of the semiotics of performance and production" (p. 116), if not a radical disruption of the semiotic as such, opening onto a space where nothing whatever is signified?

In this suggestion, I think the other end of the bridge, the revolutionary Elsewhere, is glimpsed. The theoretical environment—Miller says "Terry Eagleton *et al.*" (p. 115), and quotes Gayatri Spivak[5]—insists on the question of an appropriate feminist "move," a move that would sacrifice in advance its specifically feminist force by responding to the wrong type of question. For the logic of the concept of "irony," in this context, suggests the idea of making *no* move, having *no* "rhetorical strategy," an idea that may be theoretically questionable (is the making of no move not itself a move?) but is not simply dismissible, since the feminist *position* evinces a mode of existence that is categorically different from that of any strictly theoretical position. That we cannot say exactly how the feminist position is constituted—Miller concludes by worrying about the question of "becoming women" or "becoming feminists" (p. 117)—does not change matters. The difference alone (from the type of theoretical position that does not exist *as* a position except by authorizing specific moves) makes room for a revolutionary reading of the notion of irony.

Again, as with Wittig, I do not claim to explain what Miller "means" by irony, and I am not setting up her text as a model. My aim, for the moment, is only to call attention to certain typical rhetorical phenomena that appear when we look at feminist texts by way of the problematics of the revolutionary.

## Nietzsche and Free Revolutionary Thought

Is anything *accomplished,* either by these rhetorical subtleties or by the endlessly involved cross-questioning of texts like Felman's and Irigaray's? Is there any basis, outside feminist thought itself, for the assertion that that thought is revolutionary in character? Or more specifically, is there any place "within the institution that authorizes and regulates most reading and writing," any place on this end of the bridge, that provides *leverage* for feminist thought considered as revolutionary?

This is the question that brings us to Nietzsche. For in Western literary tradition, Nietzsche's writings are the locus—as far as I know, the unique locus—of *free revolutionary thought,* thought that is revolutionary in its structure and problems, but despite its fondness for the metaphors of bridge and tightrope, is tied to no revolutionary project whatever—assuming we agree, for example, that "the word 'Übermensch'"[6] names not a project but an anti-project, the absence of any project. The "Übermensch" is located Elsewhere, at the far end of a bridge; but it is a bridge that, for our purposes, has no near end, no beginning, no approach, a bridge that takes shape not in our knowledge or belief or desire, but in our mere existence, a bridge (or tightrope) that we *are* (see e.g. *KSA*, 4:16, 248). The difference between Nietzsche and other revolutionary thinkers, in this regard, is not difficult to recognize in particular cases. Artaud, for instance, whom we often situate not far from Nietzsche in the discussion of the unfolding and supersedure of modernism, is much more project-focused. No less rigorously critical a mind than Derrida comes close to thinking in terms of a conceivable realization of Artaud's vision, whereas even without the actual fascist experiments to learn from, it would be clear that the whole notion of realization, or application, misses the point in Nietzsche.

I will support this characterization of Nietzsche's writings in the next section. But if we assume for a moment that it is valid, then the importance of Nietzsche for feminist thinking follows quickly. Nietzsche's writing, in which the revolutionary moment is operative, yet also denied any form of realization, in which therefore the revolutionary moment is not even speculatively subject to being obscured by hindsight, would become a study in revolutionary method, a model for revolutions in progress, the touchstone by which to know and sustain a revolutionary focus in thought, despite the absence of reasonable criteria for distinguishing such a focus from mere eccentricity, from the condition of being out on a limb. And feminism, which *is* out on a limb, exposed to any number of reductive or co-optive moves, is eminently in need of such a method or touchstone.

The existence of a more specific relation between Nietzsche and feminist thought is strongly suggested by Derrida in *Spurs*. But there are problems in Derrida's presentation, which appear less obviously in his own text than in projects, like Krell's, that use that text for support and, in the end, tend to confuse feminist issues rather than develop them. Indeed, it is not certain that the term "phallogocentrism," in itself, is not a co-optive move with respect to feminist thought, an exhortation to the wild variety of feminist initiatives that it come in from out on its limb, or limbs, and organize itself as a form of deconstruction. (If there is a besetting fault in feminist writing, it is the facile use of the verb "deconstruct.") Even as consistent and painstaking an advocate as Gayatri Spivak, in her essay "Displacement and the Discourse of Woman," raises important questions about the ability of deconstruction to operate "as a 'feminist' practice."[7]

My own view of the specific usefulness of Nietzsche for feminism is simpler than Derrida's. I will argue that in all of Nietzsche, the question of the reader's historical situation is crucial, and the question of the reader's *use* of the text in history. In later Nietzsche, however, this question becomes unanswerable. Precisely the situation of being a qualified reader, a reader addressed by the text and in a position to understand it, *denies* one the possibility of making any reasonable historical use of one's understanding. The text therefore becomes useless, except perhaps, paradoxically, from the point of view of the *disqualified* reader, the reader who is excluded from the text's projected community of understanding, the reader whom the text never speaks *to,* but only *about,* which means the (or a) woman. Thus the relation of women to the text occurs at exactly that point where the text develops what I call its free revolutionary leverage, the point of divorce or disjunction between the text's *use* and its understanding, or between use and *meaning.*

For meaning—by whatever theoretical path we approach the idea— names the implacably conservative aspect of discourse. Meaning awakens only in the bosom of meaning, of what we are eventually reduced to speaking of as "accepted" or "established" meanings, and cannot participate in the kind of discontinuity that is required by the idea of the revolutionary moment. (Again, perspective is crucial here. From the far end of the bridge, with the revolutionary moment safely past, no discontinuity is to be seen, and the revolutionary text simply means its historical destiny after all.) But in Nietzsche, the normal contiguity of use and meaning—our sense that it is wrong to use a text except in some relation (however negative) to its meaning—is utterly disrupted. Of course it is possible to "use" any text in any wildly eccentric way we can imagine. But my point is that Nietzsche's texts are set up so as to *enforce,* without limiting, such eccentricity. Spivak suggests that the task of women as readers may be "To produce useful and scrupulous fake readings."[8] I contend that Nietzsche writes in a manner that may justify even that otherwise uncomfortable and practically contradictory adjective "scrupulous."

But if the divorce between use and meaning can be deduced from Nietzsche's texts, is it not therefore itself a type of meaning? It depends on how simplemindedly we insist on understanding "meaning." If we are willing to admit any degree of hermeneutic complexity, any form of the hermeneutic circle, then the objection collapses, since the divorce between meaning and use implies a divorce of the (text as) hermeneutic object from the (text as) historical act, whereas in all of the main tradition of hermeneutic theory—from Schleiermacher's idea of understanding an author better than he understands himself down to Gadamer's notion of "hermeneutic conversation"—the very idea of meaning depends precisely on the coincidence of that object and that act. Nor can Nietzsche, at this point, be outflanked by the hermeneutics of incomprehensibility that Leventhal associates with Friedrich Schlegel, by the idea of "a process of reading in which the text was to be *utilized,* not merely grasped or 'understood,' according to its relevance, its application, its performative power."[9] For Nietzsche's texts, by "performing" precisely their divorce from historical use, *reinstitute* meaning as an inescapable (if uncomfortable) factor in our reading.

The other question that is likely to arise at this point—whether I have not gotten into the business of defining or essentializing the feminine, of putting woman in her place, or of enlisting Nietzsche to do it for me—is also fairly easy to deal with. My point about later Nietzsche is that the text forms a kind of vortex. The qualified (male) reader, by the mere act of understanding, finds himself irrevocably in a situation offering no possibility whatever of useful historical action or vision. This vortex, this ever inwardly self-gathering structure, is the only "place" defined by the texts. And the place of women (the unlimited room for women's fake but scrupulous use of the text as leverage for being or aiming Elsewhere) is simply everywhere or anywhere "else," everywhere outside that self-centralizing readerly location. Nor do I think that the echo, here, of our discussion of *Egmont* above is gratuitous. The space outside the maelstrom of the self that structures *Egmont,* the space we enter by distancing ourselves from Egmont, is a space of disorientation or wrongness, the wrongness of reading or of literature. The question now, in relation to both Nietzsche and Goethe, is whether—and if so, how—a space of this type can provide a location for the possibility of a feminist literary project.

It follows in any case, from the quality of this space as wrongness or disqualification, that no valid *general* statements can be made about feminist uses of Nietzsche—no statements sufficiently positive to provide a useful orientation for feminist thought. The argument is vacuous except to the extent that it can adduce actual particular instances of such use. The instance I will discuss below is Irigaray's *Amante marine.*

## Nietzsche and His Reader

Nietzsche's early work, through the *Unzeitgemässe Betrachtungen, Thoughts Out of Season,* is concerned primarily with history, as an attempt not to describe or to understand, but to *make history,* by suggesting a novel and complex relation between the text and its reader. The starting point, the point from which *The Birth of Tragedy* sets out, is the idea (which Kant insists on in his Copernican posture) of the history-making operancy of philosophical *systematics.*

For *The Birth of Tragedy* is constructed upon a thoroughly organized and entirely decipherable systematic basis: the radically idealistic metaphysics of "das Ur-Eine" (*KSA,* 1:38–39), the primordial self-separating Original One, borrowed from Hermetic or emanative philosophy, in which the process of self-separating or emanation is itself both the structure of all consciousness and the reality of every possible content of consciousness. The Socratic idea of a rationally knowable world given to consciousness as its strict object is of course wrong from this metaphysical point of view, but is refutable, if at all, only from *within* the Socratic thought-method, since the possibility of an objective outside with respect to such questions is denied by precisely the metaphysics that needs to be rescued. Hence the importance of the system of Kant's *Critiques,* which is credited with turning the method of "Wissenschaft" (science, or systematic knowledge) against the very delusion that had made possible the development of that method; Nietzsche speaks of "Dionysian wisdom in the form of concepts" (*KSA,* 1:128), implying that here the highest metaphysical truth is approached by a path of systematic reasoning. And the idea of Socratism turned against itself suggests in turn the idea of a historical process driven by dialectical opposition, systematics in a Hegelian sense, while the derivation of the dialectic from a single, ever anew self-realizing dualism is borrowed from the system of Schiller's letters *On Aesthetic Education*—a book Hegel himself studied while preparing the *Phenomenology.* But Nietzsche's insistence on contradiction, on dissonance, on originary dismemberment, together with the omission of Schiller's reconciling "play-drive," adds up very nearly to the positing of *difference* as a strictly primitive notion. The Apollonian and the Dionysian, at their point of full philosophical intensity as marked by the form of tragedy, *are* nothing but their difference, which in turn is the difference *of* difference, the difference by which difference itself (the Apollonian domain) is instituted. Thus any number of semiotically based systematic possibilities are suggested, theories of human being as nothing but the vessel of difference. "If we could imagine," says Nietzsche, "musical dissonance as such in the form of a human being—and what else," he continues, "*is* a human being?" (*KSA,* 1:155).

The possibility of systematic closure is therefore repeatedly present in the discourse, a type of closure that would presumably complete the work of Kant and Schopenhauer by explaining and discrediting the whole Socratic worldview. But Nietzsche does not carry out in detail any such system; only the *possibility* of closure is insisted upon, in a number of different forms. And even this possibility is often lost sight of. "We will have gained much for aesthetic science [*die aesthetische Wissenschaft*] when we have arrived not merely at the logical insight, but at an unmediated certainty of apprehension, that the development of art . . ." (*KSA,* 1:25). This, the book's first sentence, is disturbing, to say the least. How can "aesthetic *science*" discredit Socratism? And what, for a professed admirer of Kant, does science have to do with "unmediated certainty of apprehension," "unmittelbare Sicherheit der Anschauung"? It is possible to explain why Nietzsche talks this way. Again, one of precisely the systematic consequences of his thought is that human culture *constitutes* the world in which it occurs, that the particular cultural illusion by which we deal with the otherwise insupportable knowledge of the void *is* the very fabric of our existence, whence it follows that since our age is inescapably characterized by Socratic culture, we would merely delude ourselves if we claimed to occupy the point of view implied by a system that reduces Socratic culture to a finished object. But then why even suggest the possibility of a systematic supersedure of Socratism?

Or to look at it the other way round: the actual method of *The Birth of Tragedy* is Socratic in a relatively uncomplicated way, in its implied claim to achieve knowledge concerning art by way of the critical questioning of accepted prejudices (e.g., the idea of Hellenic "serenity" or "naïveté").[10] And the Socratic quality of the text, its anchoring on *this* end of the bridge to a new cultural age that its system (once perfected) would build, is thrown strongly into relief by contrast with the idea that German music and German philosophy are evidence of an "awakening of the Dionysian spirit" in contemporary Germany (*KSA*, 1:127–28). Nietzsche in fact goes so far as to assert: "Where Dionysian forces make themselves felt as tempestuously as in our experience today, there also Apollo, wrapped in a cloud, must already have descended among us; surely the next few generations will behold his most opulently beautiful effects" (*KSA*, 1:155). But if the Apollonian is "already" ("bereits") in process of realization among us, why write a *treatise* on this historical state of affairs? Is Nietzsche not here being a Socrates in advance with respect to the impending neo-Apollonian age? Is the understanding of Apollonian illusion, even the strictly correct understanding, not also a spoiling of that illusion? Again, Nietzsche *must* write in the Socratic manner. Yet in doing so, he appears to destroy the bridge to his own envisioned Elsewhere, and so writes himself out onto a limb.

We can deal with these problems, I think, by referring to the situation of the reader. If *we* recognize the possibility of a bridge in *The Birth of Tragedy,* the possibility of a complete systematic closure that will supersede the Socratic, then it would be nonsense to suggest that "the reader" is not meant to recognize it. The actual naive-Socratic quality of the argument, therefore, only invites its readers to *pretend* to be naive Socratic believers in the innocence of understanding, in their ability to understand our historical situation without thereby altering it. But on the other hand, the systematic aspect of the work (on which the bridge, the whole vision of a new artistic age, is founded) is also unquestionably Socratic in character, is indeed the ultimate in Socratic arrogance, an assertion of the dominion of an objectively valid reason over the very idea of such dominion. (We think of the preface to *The Critique of Pure Reason,* the idea of subjecting "Vernunft" [reason] itself to the method of "Wissenschaft.") We the readers, precisely in pretending to operate within the Socratic delusion, thus also occupy a systematic perspective that *is* Socratic. It follows that the reader is literally of two minds. He (I say "he" advisedly) at once both *is* and *pretends to be* a Socratic thinker. And this combination in turn fulfils exactly the central vision of *The Birth of Tragedy,* the idea of the transformation of Socratism itself into a form of art. We cannot overcome or overthrow our Socratic cultural situation, but we can overcome our subjection to it by learning to manipulate it affirmatively, by making of it an object of pretending, thus making it into the art it in truth is. We can, in Schiller's terminology, transform our "condition" into our "act." We can pretend willingly to be what we still inescapably are. The reader is thus as it were one step ahead of the text, which he looks back on and understands only by grasping what he himself is already doing as a reader. He contributes the work's meaning as much as he receives it. The real bridge (as opposed to the delusive bridge of systematic certainty) is not *there;* but it is *there to be built* by the reader, and is so exactly to the extent that the text finds itself *actually* out on a limb.

This is the kind of case one can make for speaking of Nietzsche as a revolutionary writer—although not yet a free revolutionary writer (since the project, the Elsewhere, is still focused upon), thus, for Nietzsche, not yet revolutionary enough. *The Birth of Tragedy* still imposes a specific role on the reader, and so compromises its own revolutionary force by erecting a kind of bridge (in the reader's response) after all. In terminology we used earlier, it is still entangled in the aesthetic conception of literature, still itself carries out (vis-à-vis the reader) the co-optive move by which its own revolutionary energy is exposed to co-option. Hence the developed procedure of the *Thoughts Out of Season,* especially the essay "On the Use and Abuse of History," which pins its revolutionary hopes on a group of *non*readers, the German "youth" of its time (*KSA,* 1:324ff.). For the essay is itself inescapably a form of the "history" it rails against—perhaps a radical form of what it calls "critical history" (*KSA,* 1:269–70), directed against the very practice it exemplifies, but history nonetheless, part of what must be kept from cluttering the minds of a youthful generation of cultural pioneers.

And yet, even here the bow is not strung to its tightest. Even the young nonreading history makers are imposed upon, and so in a sense made readers after all, by being assigned a specific role in the text's vision. (How else can we possibly define a "reader," except as someone who enacts a role with respect to a text?) In fact, at the conclusion of the essay, Nietzsche suggests that those coming generations may get around to reading him after all, when a state of cultural health is achieved and it again becomes possible to use history, including "critical" history, in the service of life (*KSA,* 1:332). The limbs onto which Nietzsche's revolutionary ambition drives him are thus not yet long enough to exceed the reach of his own rhetorical and visionary ingenuity. But it is still the ambition that drives him, not the ingenuity.

## Nietzsche and the Wrongness of Reading

I will not attempt to cover Nietzsche's whole development. It is enough to recognize that his early works illuminate the tensions that lead to a divorce between meaning and use in his later work. To the extent that meaning and use overlap—or indeed practically coincide, as in *The Birth of Tragedy*—the bridge to a radically new *kind* of text-using becomes unnecessary and the text's revolutionary force is compromised. The admission of a link between meaning and usefulness is equivalent to an aesthetic acceptance of the reader's role in the constitution of meaning and exposes the text to co-option by encouraging the insinuation, into our sense of what the text means, of the (normally conservative) manner in which the text happens *actually* to be used. In fact, in the last aphorism of *Beyond Good and Evil,* Nietzsche suggests that the mere *writing* of the text is already a form of use that interferes with the text's revolutionary effectiveness (*KSA,* 5:239–40). And then, in his farewell to the aphoristic mode, he "supplements" *Beyond Good and Evil* with a "polemic" for its "clarification," *The Genealogy of Morals.*[11] For *Beyond Good and Evil,* like the other aphoristic works, is a book that is too joyful and affirmative for its own good. The reader is constantly tempted to assume that the spirited and skillful and daring leaps he must make as a reader, from mountain peak to mountain peak, are in the end getting him somewhere, or getting him Elsewhere, perhaps even eventually to a place of reward where his daring (and with it, his joy) is no longer required. And this assumption must be countered. The reader, so to speak, may jump however he pleases, only not to the conclusion that there is any place worth jumping to.

A text that is at once both perfectly joyful (treating its leaps like bridges) and perfectly useless (positively denying an Elsewhere at the other end, with "a pessimism *bonae voluntatis* that not only says no and wills no but—horrible thought!—*does* no" [*KSA,* 5:137]) would be a free revolutionary text, a model of revolutionary method. And the aim of *The Genealogy of Morals* is to show *Beyond Good and Evil* as (or make it into) such a text. Especially the last section of the *Genealogy*—"What Do Ascetic Ideals Signify?"—draws an ever tightening ring about the reader. The ascetic ideal, the insidious violence of life against life itself, characterizes not only religion but also the self-distancing of science from religion, not only the pretended objectivity of science but also the philosophical critique of that pretense, and even the resolutely atheistic critique of that critique. Can the reader imagine that his own point of view somehow escapes this deadly chain?

The ascetic ideal arises with the recognition of human existence as a *problem:* "Wozu leiden?" (*KSA,* 5:411), "Why do we suffer?" And once this problem is responded to in an ascetic manner—which means simply, once it is responded to at all, once we accept it as a problem—a vicious circle is established. For the response, the justification of suffering, being itself a form of self-injury on the part of life, increases our suffering (not to mention our perplexity at its needlessness), thus makes the problem more acute, thus provokes a subtler and more devious response, and so on, until we arrive at "our problem" (*KSA,* 5:410)—as Nietzsche says to the "*unknown* friends" among his readers—which is the recognition "that in us even the will to truth [the drive to explain or justify anything, no matter what] has become conscious of itself *as a problem.*" Nor is it insignificant that Nietzsche here refers directly, if with a cryptic wink, to his reader. For if the question "Why do we suffer?" is such that any answer to it turns out to be a wrong answer, would this not also be true of the question Wozu *lesen*? or Why do we read?

The question Why do we read?—if it asks after the conceivable use in history of a particular text—is normally answered by a kind of story. In reading *The Theater and Its Double,* my eyes are opened to the narrowness of the European dramatic tradition in which writing is the dominant element, and to the relation of this tradition to certain structures of political dominance. It is therefore conceivable that a revolution in the nontextual medium of theater (foreign conventions, after all, are available) would contribute to a further opening of eyes, perhaps eventually to a revolutionizing of society. What matters here is not whether the cultural and political argument is well founded, but whether the reader's story is plausible, whether a reasonable reader can leave the text with a sense that something is to be done. Even in the case of *Les Guérillères,* the reader is not forced into a corner. The fabulous elements in the narrative (especially the women's weapons) plus the points of contact with existing Western symbolism make it possible to read that text as the sign of a fantastic visionary state of mind buried in our actual social conditions, whereupon it becomes reasonable to inquire into the future of that state of mind and its historical effects.

But in the case of *Beyond Good and Evil* and *The Genealogy of Morals,* the only available story for the reader is the story of the ascetic ideal itself. The reader cannot reasonably ignore the connection between his own activity in reading, his role in relation to the text, and the "will to truth," however firm his grasp of the "problem" of that will. (Precisely our grasp of the problem is a measure of the strength of will that drives us to read and think.) It is true that possibilities of living outside the ascetic mechanism are suggested. The pride and good taste of "coming philosophers," we are told, will be offended by the idea that *their* truth should be "a truth for everyone" (*KSA,* 5:60). But the articulation of this possibility only throws into relief the hopeless situation of the reader; for it is a possibility which, precisely by being a reader, I have *already* left behind. How can I boast of *my* truth in the very process of insinuating myself into someone else's, adjusting my thought with respect to the text? How can I claim any relation whatever to the quality of being "vornehm" (distinguished, of high rank) when the action of reading this text actually discloses only my "need" of this quality (*KSA,* 5:233)? I can employ the text in the historical direction it itself suggests only by *not* reading it, by never having read it, having no need of it. We talk a good deal these days about reading texts "against the grain"; and this talk, I think, is an index of precisely the discomfort at being a reader that Nietzsche, more than anyone else, provokes. But it is only talk, only a way of sugaring over the knowledge that our will, intelligence, and historical conscience are already irreversibly co-opted into the discourse of which we claim to be critics.

Even the perhaps honest and courageous conclusion, on the reader's part, that there is no escape from history as shaped by the ascetic ideal accomplishes nothing; for the whole tenor of the book makes this conclusion—valid as it may be—strictly unacceptable. On the level of meaning, *Beyond Good and Evil* and *The Genealogy of Morals* do nothing but thoroughly and repeatedly demolish ascetic ideals—in a manner, for example, in which the Socratic worldview is *not* demolished in *The Birth of Tragedy*, where precisely the artistic affirmation of Socratism is offered the reader as his historical task. The reader of the later books is left not out on a limb, but at a simple historical dead end, without even the vision (as in the *Thoughts Out of Season*) of a youthful generation of nonreaders to whose historical mission he might contribute by way of a reform of educational institutions. The "coming" philosophers are perhaps really on their way; there are perhaps still individuals with "an *instinct for rank*" (*KSA*, 5:217), for whom history is not hopeless. But these groups stand *in no relation whatever* to the reader of Nietzsche's text.

The meaning of *Beyond Good and Evil* and *The Genealogy of Morals* is dense, varied, complex, inexhaustible. But the intersection of the text's meaning with its usefulness in the historical situation it itself reflects is empty. The meaning of the text with respect to the idea of its usefulness in history is entirely contained in the statement: the text is useless. But it does not follow that this is a true statement, that the text *is* useless. What follows, as I have suggested, is that *if* the text is useful, then it is so only for those people who are *not qualified as understanding readers*. The situation, to say the least, is a curious one—as if, for example, a person unqualified in music were to find in the score of a Bach fugue the secret of winning at poker. But since Nietzsche's text is revolutionary in spirit (*Beyond Good and Evil* is subtitled "Prelude to a Philosophy of the Future"), since its vision of history requires that something radical be done by somebody, then this curious situation is inevitable with respect to it—without (again) being part of its meaning.

In a sense, there is a parallel here with Goethe's procedure in *Werther* in that the aesthetic is employed against itself, the reader is drawn into a role that turns out to be a dead end. In *Werther*, however, with the masturbatory scene at its conclusion, in which our use of the text as a kind of pornography is unmasked, the reader's position perhaps becomes maximally distasteful and embarrassing, but is not as strictly impossible as in Nietzsche, who in this regard benefits from the genre of his work, and from a developing Hegelian tradition in philosophy that helps cast the reader as a more historically conscious agent. And the manner in which reading is strictly defeated in *Faust*, on the other hand, does not obviously leave room for a class of unqualified readers.[12] Nietzsche's texts, by doing things and being things that are apparently not yet within Goethe's range, thus provide us with a view of the structure of problems into which Goethe (as woman) has written himself: with *Götz* and *Werther*, with the esoteric politics of

"Literarischer Sansculottismus" and the generically impossible reconception of
*Faust,* with the allegorical unwriting of political drama in *Die natürliche Tochter.*

## Setting Nietzsche: Reading as Defense

The positively disqualified reader of late Nietzsche, again, is above all the reader
who is a woman. (Again we think of *Werther,* and the relation of women readers
to the masturbation scene.) The well-known sexist aphorisms in *Beyond Good
and Evil* (nos. 231–39 [*KSA,* 5:170–78]), more than those in other books,
concentrate precisely on the inadvisability of educating women ("as if woman
were a thinking creature" [*KSA,* 5:172]), of giving them intellectual status,
of qualifying them as readers. Not that this quality of the aphorisms justifies
my argument as an interpretation of the book. On the contrary, Kelly Oliver's
outright dismissal of any attempt to read Nietzsche from a feminist perspective,
even if her psychoanalysis is questionable, comes much closer to what might
reasonably be called the *meaning,* with respect to women, of, say, *Beyond Good
and Evil*—meaning, again, in the sense that it is available to a qualified (male)
reader. But the special historical situation of women with respect to this text
persists as a possibility nonetheless; and the range of possibility here can be
opened by the discussion of two actual readings of Nietzsche, a feminist text
written by a man and a book with no feminist component written by a woman,
Derrida's *Spurs* and Susan Sontag's *Against Interpretation.*

I have mentioned Spivak's doubts about the effectiveness and legiti-
macy of *Spurs* as a feminist initiative. But it is certain that Derrida associates
"the question of woman" with the revolutionary quality of Nietzsche's writing, with its attempt to escape from an inherently conservative tradition of
meaning, from the "hermeneutic project which postulates a true sense of the
text."[13] It is also certain that Derrida reads Nietzsche as what I have called
*free* revolutionary writing, as a text to which no project or proper (meaning-
related) use can be assigned, a text that, "in some monstrous way, might well
be of the type 'I have forgotten my umbrella'" (pp. 132/133). And it is then
at least rhetorically consistent—if not logically necessary, and certainly not
demonstrable—that Derrida now feels entitled to suggest that his own text
follows Nietzsche in this respect, that it may be a text of the same "monstrous"
type (pp. 134/135). After all, one cannot talk hermeneutic sense about the
escape from the hermeneutic.

But there is one place where Derrida cannot follow Nietzsche, although he is honest enough to quote him: where Nietzsche, in *Beyond Good and
Evil,* introduces his "truths" about women by saying, "provided one knows from
the outset how completely they are only—*my* truths" (*KSA,* 5:170). Derrida's
commentary on this passage, which touches on "ontology" (pp. 102/103) in its
relation to "biographical desire" (pp. 104/105), can never get back to the simple

*exclusionary force* (excluding precisely the reader, as I have said) of Nietzsche's "my." Derrida says: "The very fact that 'meine Wahrheiten' ['*my* truths'] is so underlined, that they are multiple, variegated, contradictory even, can only imply that these are not *truths*. Indeed there is no such thing as truth in itself. But only a surfeit of it. Even if it should be for me, about me, truth is plural" (pp. 102/103). This statement is perhaps defensible as an interpretation of Nietzsche's words; but the word "me" ("moi") as Derrida uses it—here, and also where he is talking about his own text (pp. 136/137)—belongs to a universe entirely different from Nietzsche's. It means "me, whoever I might be," or "me for instance." It means in effect "one" (French "on"), and completely lacks the *exclusionary force* of Nietzsche's "my," which, whatever it may "imply," still asserts that its "truths" are after all truths—truths (to repeat) that are not hermeneutically reducible to meanings.

  And this exclusionary force is crucial for the possibility of a feminist project. Derrida scorns any "essentializing" discourse about "woman" (pp. 54/55), and suggests that such essentializing is finally put aside by "the epochal regime of quotation marks" (pp. 106/107), which surrounds all "decidable" concepts with a sphere of critical or indeed skeptical distance. But one word, in this regime, must be free of quotation marks, must simply mean what it says, the word "I" or "me" or "my." For "I" in quotation marks—meaning "whoever I might be," referring only to a *position* with respect to some concept or truth— implies that its position is in principle available to anyone, hence that its truth can become "a truth for everyone" (*KSA*, 5:60), or an essence, an "in itself" ("en soi," "an sich") after all. And how, also, shall *free* revolutionary writing operate without a strictly exclusionary "me," a word that says: whatever my revolutionary vision might be, it is not available to "you" or "us" as a project?

  The question of the "subject," or of "subjectivity," does not arise here. Or if "you" raise that broad conceptual question anyway, then this questioning is a symptom of precisely "your" exclusion from the simple, narrow particularity of my (or Nietzsche's) "I." Here is where Sontag's *Against Interpretation* comes in. For Sontag, even in accepting Nietzsche's authority in many crucial areas of cultural history,[14] also manages to follow Nietzsche in the exclusionary use of the (expressed or implied) "I." But she achieves this only by failing utterly to be "scrupulous" (we recall Spivak's use of this word) in her reading of Nietzsche. "Against" interpretation? On the basis of the inseparability of hermeneutics from metaphysics, of the "hermeneutic project" from a "truth of being" (*Spurs*, pp. 106/107), Derrida uses Nietzsche to make nonsense of the very idea of "against" as Sontag uses it: "if the form of opposition and the oppositional structure are themselves metaphysical, then the relation of metaphysics [hence also hermeneutics] to its other can no longer be one of opposition" (*Spurs*, pp. 116–18/117–19). And Sontag herself calls attention to this objection, quoting Nietzsche: "Of course, I don't mean interpretation in the broadest sense, the sense in which Nietzsche (rightly) says, 'There are no facts, only interpretations.' By interpretation, I mean here a conscious act of the mind which illustrates a certain code, certain 'rules' of interpretation."[15] As if the whole critical force of Nietzsche's statement did not depend on its meaning "interpretation" in a sense that does *not* exclude what Sontag attacks here. The existence of some threshold in self-regulating consciousness, at which interpretation changes its character, is precisely what Nietzsche denies.

It would be reasonable to say simply that Sontag gets Nietzsche wrong. She reads him to mean, in a vague general sense, "everything is subjective," a statement he in fact derides in the same aphorism (*KSA*, 12:315). But on the other hand, it follows from the divorce between meaning and use that if Sontag's text can be considered a somehow valid use of Nietzsche, then the question of meaning, of getting Nietzsche right, does not arise. Of course, the mere fact that I get Nietzsche wrong does not qualify me as a valid or fruitful user of Nietzsche. But Sontag is also a revolutionary, in something like an early Nietzschean sense. She insists on the hopeless idea of an art strictly beyond the reach of interpretation. And in a wildly paradoxical move, she embeds her text by quotation in a far-flung *literary* culture (at one point [p. 298] she says, "the writings of Nietzsche, Wittgenstein, Antonin Artaud, C. S. Sherrington, Buckminster Fuller, Marshall McLuhan, John Cage, André Breton, Roland Barthes, Claude Lévi-Strauss, Siegfried Gidieon [*sic*], Norman O. Brown, and Gyorgy Kepes") that makes her project plausible by way of the concealed supposition that art *is* what it is interpreted as being. Assuming, therefore, that we do not simply dismiss Sontag altogether—which we can always reasonably do with a revolutionary text—might we not recognize her egregious misreading of Nietzsche (and not only Nietzsche) as the assertion of a strongly exclusionary "I," an "I" very like Nietzsche's own, but in which we are prevented from participating precisely by our understanding of Nietzsche?

Sontag's text, with respect to Nietzsche, is what Derrida's text wishes it could be, a text made of outright exclusionary lies. "Je peux mentir," "I could be lying" (*Spurs*, p. 136), says Derrida. But he is not lying, not for a minute; the conceptual structure of his writing, despite the "Distances" (pp. 36/37) covered by its metaphorical, etymological, orthographic leaps, is much too tight and scrupulous. He reads (others and himself) too well. And conversely, Derrida's text is what Sontag's wishes it could be. For how shall we move past "literature" to a grasp of "the new sensibility" (Sontag, pp. 298–99) without first getting literature right, without reading (it and ourselves) to the point where it is compelled to tie up its own nagging loose ends by whatever improbable leaps?

Not that Derrida's procedure and Sontag's could ever in any sense be combined. Rather, each plays gropingly into the other's hand, like the defenders in a game of bridge, in hopes of finding the one extra trick that will at last "set"

Nietzsche the declarer, position him, fix his shape, establish him, make him at last useful and usable.

## Nietzsche as a Woman

I use the metaphor of a game of bridge with a view especially to the role of the dummy, which in French happens to be "le mort," the dead man. A hand in contract bridge opens with "bidding," which establishes the trump suit for the hand and the number of tricks needed for either side to win. The player who first bids the eventual trump suit becomes "declarer"; the cards of the declarer's partner, whose hand is now the "dummy," are turned face up for all to see after the opening lead; and in the ensuing play, the declarer plays both his or her own concealed hand and, in turn, the cards of the dummy. The player whose hand is dummy at this point becomes a pure spectator and may as well not exist.

This structure, to my mind, suggests a preter-interpretive or methermeneutic ideal. If only we could avoid playing our part in the interpretive process, our part, our activity as interpreters, which inevitably distorts what we claim to be looking for. If only we could somehow simply lay down our cards and let the text itself play (or play with) them. This is not to desire mere passivity. The cards are still *our* cards; the object of play (the contract) is still the product of a tentative cryptic communication with the interpretand, the text that declares. If we could at that point simply stop, and think about something quite different (perhaps the umbrella we have forgotten), the result would be an unprecedented type of interpretive *act,* an act by which we might finally claim to have encountered the text in its unsullied incomprehensibility, an act perhaps at last able to come to grips even with the strictly uninterpretable, even with a text characterized by the absolute divorce between meaning and use.

I think it is possible that with respect to Nietzsche—but also, indispensably, with respect to Derrida and Sontag, or at least with respect to the positions I have assigned them—Irigaray's *Amante marine: De Friedrich Nietzsche* shadows forth such an act. At least this claim is suggested by her title, which means: "the marine lover (or betrothed), a book on (de) Friedrich Nietzsche"; or "a book about (or by, or in the person of) the marine lover of (de) Friedrich Nietzsche"; or "marine lover, a book by (de) Friedrich Nietzsche." And the complexities of the title are then sustained, in the first long section, "Dire d'eaux immémoriales" ("Speaking of Immemorial Waters"), by complexities in the use of the first person, the "je" or "I." In a context dominated by the figure of Nietzsche, namely, the "I" gains exclusionary force from the mere fact of its being spoken *by a woman*—a fact which, even without grammatical indications, as in the clause "il ne fallait pas que je sois trouée" ("I should not have been holed"),[16] we cannot deny our knowledge of. For Irigaray not only *is* a woman, but is known to us (unlike Sontag) as one who speaks *as* a woman. Derrida strives to reproduce Nietzsche's exclusionary "I," and in striving necessarily fails; the *second* "I" (Derrida's) places us inescapably "amongst ourselves"—meaning, inescapably, "among men"—"unter sich" (*KSA*, 5:171; quoted in *Spurs*, pp. 64/65). But Irigaray's "I" can claim to imitate Nietzsche's—and can actually imitate, say, the marine fantasy in no. 60 of *The Joyful Science* (*KSA*, 3:424–25)—while still retaining the force that excludes both Nietzsche *him*self and his (male) reader.

Nor does it follow that Irigaray's first person is an instance of that speaking "in the name of woman" that Felman criticizes. For in the first place, it is Nietzsche himself (his exclusionary "I") who is made to speak here, to speak as he in effect had always spoken, with the voice of the Outside or Elsewhere that had automatically arisen relative to the *Egmont*-like vortex of his late texts: "But isn't that your game: that the Outside be ceaselessly drawn back inside? And that there be no Outside that you yourself had not thrown forth? My cry would thus be [the French grammatical mood here is the conditional] only the sign of your calling back" (*Am*, p. 18). And in the second place, it is also the impossible, disallowed female reader of Nietzsche who is speaking here, and who therefore requires a new *kind* of reading, a reading that produces no "unter sich," even "among women," since any such community of understanding Nietzsche is necessarily male. "For I love Division where you [Nietzsche] wish to preserve the Whole" (*Am*, p. 17). In order to be "spoken for" by this "I," even a woman must "aimer le partage," insist on division, *decline* to be spoken for: "But woman? Is not reducible to femininity. Or to lying or appearance or beauty. Except by 'remaining among themselves' ['unter sich'] and projecting 'at a distance' that other of themselves to which truth, from the origin, is hostile" (*Am*, p. 83). And the condition of being "unter sich," which reduces women to femininity—to a community of readers, whose communal bond is a shared understanding—is precisely what is denied to female readers of Nietzsche. The "I," here, is spoken by *a* woman, not by "whichever woman I happen to be."

We must be clear, however, about the status of this argument. By its own showing, it is not an interpretation of either Nietzsche or *Amante marine*. Neither the argument itself nor the bridge it erects between Nietzsche's text and Irigaray's could occur except in relation to *the question of the "I"*; and a main point of the argument is that this question *does not arise* in late Nietzsche. Nietzsche's "I," as soon as it becomes an object of questioning, as it does in Derrida, loses precisely that radically simple exclusionary quality that makes it interesting in Nietzsche, and becomes merely an instance of "the subject." The same point, for the same reasons, applies to Irigaray, where the exclusionary force of the "I," the impossibility of a communicative network (an "unter sich"), is created by a radically simple (because simply "real") gender difference. (Derrida says that "there is no truth in itself of the sexual difference in itself, of either man or woman in itself" [*Spurs,* pp. 102/103]. And it is in the space left open by that "in itself" ["en soi"], the space of utter untheorizable particularity, that Irigaray's "I" asserts its difference.)

But on the other hand, the relation between late Nietzsche and *Amante marine,* hence the whole of the present argument, presupposes precisely a raising of the question of the "I," presupposes therefore something like the "defense" against Nietzsche that I claim emerges from the (however unwittingly) interacting initiatives of Sontag and Derrida. The subject matter of the argument, consequently, the object of interpretation, is neither Nietzsche's text nor Irigaray's, but is the whole structure of response, the game of bridge, in which those texts are involved. And this structure, in turn, which in a sense originates with Nietzsche but cannot be considered an interpretation of his meaning, opens at least the possibility of a historically significant use of Nietzsche's text.

There is still a paradox here. The exclusionary force of Irigaray's "I," like that of Nietzsche's, must be prior to any raising of the question of the "I." But at the same time, it is constituted by a gender difference that implies (and requires, so to speak, for leverage) a specific difference *from Nietzsche*— from the "unter sich" as such, which specifically in Nietzsche is revealed as a male discourse-vortex—hence presupposes the relation with Nietzsche and the question of the "I" after all. That this is a paradox, not merely a confusion, has to do with Irigaray's speaking as a *dis*qualified reader of Nietzsche—not merely as an *un*qualified reader, which is how we might characterize Sontag's position. The negative force of disqualification, from Nietzsche, operates directly in Irigaray's discourse ("But isn't that your game . . . ?") as it does not in Sontag's, and collapses the "relation" Nietzsche/Irigaray, as far as the "I" is concerned, into something more like an identity. Nietzsche "himself" in a strong sense inhabits Irigaray's discourse at the point of utter untheorizable particularity marked by her "I." One is tempted to say (in a terminology we have used often enough) that Irigaray's text, and her "I," are co-opted by Nietzsche's—except that Irigaray's "I" is still radically separated from Nietzsche's, at a distance enforced by gender difference and by her explicit disqualification as a reader. More to the point, therefore, would be to say that Irigaray *mobilizes* Nietzsche's "I," enables it to do things (feminine things) it could never have done of itself, any more than the declarer can play his hand without the cards of the dummy. ("Mobilizes," not "co-opts": it is Sontag who plays the defensive game of attempting to co-opt Nietzsche, and in doing so profiles the differentness of Irigaray's maneuver.) And this whole paradox is itself, in turn, a form or aspect of exactly the exclusionary force, the escape of Irigaray's "I" from any reasonable theoretical resolution, that it expounds—this whole paradoxical situation, with Irigaray across the table from Nietzsche, yet also in Nietzsche's "own" position, which I am trying to capture in the image of declarer and dummy.

## Nietzsche as Woman

But is Nietzsche really playing the cards in *Amante marine*? This question is meaningless except in relation to the other two texts (or text types) I have mentioned, Derrida's and Sontag's, which are each, and both, a kind of defense against Nietzsche. And in this relation, I think the answer is yes. In the second main section of Irigaray's book, "Lèvres voilées," "Veiled Lips," the "je" of the first section is largely supplanted by "la femme" and "elle," "woman" and "she," and we have what appears to be a psychoanalytic-mythological-feminist essay more or less in the manner of *Speculum*. But the constantly recurring theme of this section is no. 361 of *The Joyful Science*—which also figures centrally in *Spurs* (pp. 68/69)—on women's "giving themselves out as . . ." even when they "give themselves" (*KSA*, 3:609). And Irigaray *accepts* this formulation. She plays with it and develops it; she does not dispute it. Which has obvious consequences for our sense of the structure of her own writing. By talking about "woman," she in a sense "gives herself," exposes herself to co-option by the essentializing male discourse that puts "woman" in her place. But by surrendering herself to the one specific fragment of male discourse (Nietzsche's) that she focuses on, she also calls attention to the impossibility of distinguishing her surrender from a "giving herself out as . . . ," so that her exclusionary "I" is enabled to survive beneath the surface (she etymologizes, "sub-sister" [meaning roughly "survive," *Am*, pp. 119, 122, 126]—with a play on English "sister"?) after all.

And this structure, in "Lèvres voilées," also draws Nietzsche into itself, makes him the player of the cards. For it is exactly Nietzsche's game ("giving herself [out as]") that Irigaray is playing here, even down to the detail of herself actually being a woman. It is exclusively Nietzsche's game—as Derrida's inevitably interpretive game, or Sontag's arbitrary defiance of the rules, cannot be. Which raises the possibility of the game's doubling back on itself, the possibility that it is here Nietzsche himself who—in a sense that is difficult to specify, but also difficult to set limits to—"gives himself out as" a woman.

> Ariane—double du mâle. Ne reproduit que du masculin. Que celui-ci se veuille, aussi, du féminin, redouble peut-être la mise. Ne change pas le jeu. (*Am*, p. 125)

> [Ariadne—double of the male. Reproduces only the masculine. That the latter, also, might want itself (involved in or partaking of the) feminine, perhaps doubles the stakes. Does not change the game.]

The game is unchanged, is still Nietzsche's own game ("de Friedrich Nietzsche"), even in being played through the open, proffered, upturned hand of the *Amante marine*.

But this part of the argument must be qualified in the same way as that of the preceding section. For it is also not an interpretation. It leans too heavily on an assertion concerning reality, as opposed to meaning, on the idea of the *real* openness of Irigaray's text to co-option by an established antifeminist discourse; otherwise the idea of Nietzsche's presence in that text (a strictly antifeminist presence on the level of meaning), the idea of Nietzsche's playing the cards, would be idle.

The corresponding interpretive argument (or the present argument, considered as an interpretation of *Amante marine*) would describe an ironic textual "strategy" by which Irigaray "undermines" the inevitably essentializing or colonizing tendency of any discourse focused upon the idea (however subtly shaded in terminology) of "woman." Irigaray—the argument would run—plays with that discourse on woman by borrowing from Nietzsche's version of it the paradox of genuineness and dissimulation (the idea of woman's "giving herself out as" in the very act of "giving herself"), which now supposedly disorients the reader by making it impossible for him (or even her) to decide whether the present discourse on woman (Irigaray's, in "Lèvres voilées") is not itself a complicated dissimulation, disguising a subversive feminist intent. And this disorientation, in turn—the argument would conclude—itself already "subverts" established male discourse by introducing an element of undecidability, of uncertainty, at its core.

The trouble with this argument is that it would be an instance of precisely the co-optive move to which Irigaray's text is vulnerable. "Disorientation" and "subversion," in the sense of an argument of this type, are nothing but typical moves *in* the established discourse that is supposedly called into question, nothing but the construction of an internal tension to which the discourse may then respond, typically, with its culminating move of triumphant self-reflexive closure. In the particular case, this closure is interpretive, the successful reduction of Irigaray's text to a smoothly operating interaction of meanings. Our insistence that those meanings are "subversive" or "disruptive" changes nothing, for these ideas (precisely in the course of interpreting) have themselves been fitted into the hermeneutic order. And it follows, since the interpretation is itself a co-option, that the feminist countermove (which it itself postulates) must lie entirely beyond its scope, so that a new interpretation is required, and so on.

There is no way out of this bind except by changing the terms of the argument altogether. We must recognize that we are not, in a strict sense, talking about Irigaray's text, that we are not merely bringing Nietzsche to bear (or Sontag or Derrida) upon an *understanding* of that text. On the contrary, if we are talking about anything at all—which, in the case of an argument out on a limb, is open to question—then we are talking about a situation that is too simply and strictly *real* to be hermeneutically accessible, a situation in which terms like "co-option" and "subversion" would have to name implacable historical turnings not subject to hermeneutic reconsideration. But a situation, nevertheless, that is made up of texts and relations among texts—the four present examples being a kind of cross section—texts in which the hermeneutically impossible problem posed by Nietzsche, the divorce of use from meaning, straining against the rock of gender difference, may provide paradoxically, Somewhere in relation to those texts, a form of leverage upon the hermeneutically inconceivable task of revolution, relative to the very discourse that grounds them. In order to sustain the reading of Nietzsche as *a* woman (Irigaray), in order to prevent that reading from becoming merely an interpretation of *Amante marine* (and so losing its grasp of Nietzsche's peculiar identity-relation to this text), we are thus compelled to read simply Nietzsche as Woman, and to risk, yet again, the vacuity of the idea as such, for the sake of the possibility of bridging it, the possibility of a feminist literary project.

## Woman and Intertext

These ideas could be supported and developed by further references to *Amante marine.* By the idea of Nietzsche's still uncompleted *birth* (*Am,* pp. 40, 51, 71–72); or the idea of Nietzsche's fated "announcing what can only take place after you [Nietzsche], and without you" (*Am,* p. 47), which means the divorce between meaning and use. And we have not even begun on the last section of the book, "Quand naissent les dieux."

But detailed textual exegesis would only bring us back repeatedly to the unreasonable idea of discourse revolution, and only compel us to disavow, yet again, the entirely reasonable interpretation of our own procedure as an interpretive one. What is important, I hope, is the structure of relations among texts, the game of bridge, that I have sketched, and the recognition that this structure, considered as a response to Nietzsche, is characterized by *radical multiplicity.* There is no debate, no possibility of debate, between Sontag and Derrida; there is only a gulf, into which both texts can perhaps be imagined as groping. There is hardly even a basis for comparison between Sontag and Irigaray as readers of Nietzsche. And although Irigaray's text is constantly aware of Derrida—from the first page, with the image of the "Tympan" (*Am,* p. 9)—it is not as if she took issue with Derrida's reading of Nietzsche. She simply admits Derrida—takes him, so to speak, as read—and remains irreducibly separated from him, nonetheless, by the gender difference that disqualifies her reading.

That precisely these texts form a single structure that is coherent in Nietzschean terms—coherent in the sense of metaphorically resonant and consistent—is therefore a point of some significance, as is the location of that structure, or at least, so to speak, of all its load-bearing members, in a strictly *intertextual* space, a space perhaps characterized by the origin of meaning (the sheer separation or difference of textual units) but not itself yet involved in the destiny of meaning, not hermeneutically exposed. For as soon as we can say enough about that structure—that it resembles, for example, a game of bridge—to open the question of its use or role in history, to reopen, in fact, exactly the founding question of our own relation to it, then the possibility of use without meaning is also opened, the Nietzschean Elsewhere, the possibility of a historical project that is feminist in a revolutionary sense.

I am not suggesting that the texts we have looked at, or any others that may stand in similar relations to them, either achieve or even foreshadow a usefully organized feminist discourse. Precisely the radical multiplicity of those texts, or of their specific discursive initiatives, is crucial. The solitary reader of Nietzsche—male or female, feminist or otherwise—is inevitably confronted with a kind of historical Nothingness, with the perfect uselessness of his or her endeavor. It is as if one's reading, by failing to get anywhere at all, were somehow not really happening. Only the multiple game of readings can conceivably liberate the revolutionary energies in Nietzsche, the revolutionary moment, the step out onto the limb or the bridge, which is Nietzsche's own but can take place only (as Irigaray says) "without" him. And the more strictly without him (hence the more completely his own) for being revolutionary in a feminist sense.

$\approx 9 \approx$

# Goethe and the Possibility of a Feminist Literary Project

*Das waren Deine Worte gestern: ich solle schreiben und wenn es Folianten wären es sei Dir nicht zu viel.*

A "feminist literary project," from the point of view of works like *Werther* and *Die natürliche Tochter,* is practically a contradiction in terms, since precisely literature, in its co-opted aesthetic form, literature as the conduit of "meaning" in a sense that is increasingly adjudicated—in the development of the modern publicistic nation-state, the state as discourse-machine—by raw political power, precisely literature, as representational frame, operates implacably against any feminist initiative serious enough to have the revolutionary implications suggested in chapter 8. And yet, the *possibility* of a feminist literary project is still an idea that makes sense, or at least has to make sense for the sake of the cohesion and persistence of the "invisible school" of anti-literature envisaged by Goethe. Logically, the situation seems hopeless. How can we accept the possibility of X while denying in advance the validity of any claim that X actually exists? But a path between the Either and the Or is sketched in our discussion of Nietzsche above. The intertextual game of bridge we observed—in its suggestion of a historical use for unqualified or disqualified reading—keeps alive the possibility of a feminist literary project by not belonging to, or even affecting, the *meaning* of any of the texts involved, by simply not engaging the endless hermeneia of literary history that excludes such a project. Can a similar argument—located in a similar, strictly intertextual space—be made in relation to Goethe? If so, what is the range of such an argument? What do we gain by making it?

## Reading on the Edge

The existence of Goethe's "invisible school," and its quality as a literary resistance against literature, is probably more a matter of how we read than of how we write. What we write, after all, is still always "literature," with a history from which the force of the aesthetic preconception cannot be expunged. The difference, if any, is made by how we read, or how our writing operates when

205

it is considered as a form of reading. It follows that the effective presence of an invisible school—or at least the need for it—may be measurable by the extent to which we rid ourselves of the habit of distinguishing pedantically between writing and reading, between "literature itself" and "the study of literature," between "primary" and "secondary" literature.

The currency of what we now vaguely term "literary theory" is therefore perhaps an encouraging sign. Especially the idea of authority, in the field of literature, appears to have been subjected to a rigorous and salutary scrutiny, the authority of the literary canon and of the "greatness" of canonical writers, the authority of certain parasitically canonical types of literary study, the authority, in general, of the writer over the reader. Thus, we might be tempted to conclude, the co-option of literature, its complicity in the irresponsible exercise of certain types of political and social authority, is counteracted. But the situation is not that simple. New canons are formed, new idols are erected, authority and discipleship flourish, even in the theoretical wing of what we still call our "discipline." And the condition of finding ourselves co-opted in a nested system of ever larger and less articulate discourse-machines, the condition of having our own words turned to ashes in our mouths—the remains of our own radical thinking and reading—is by no means foreign to us. The very word "theory" mirrors our problem. It suggests, by way of questionable etymologies, a seeing of the divine, a seeing of what strictly cannot be seen, a seeing that is more like reading, which sees beyond the literal, the letters, to the level of sense, and perhaps could not reach even that level without first divining still more.[1] But popularly, "theory" also implies an unwholesome detachment from practical matters, hence a special exposure to danger in situations that would not threaten a simple man who has eyes in his head. In fact these two aspects of theory, at least for us, are inseparable; reading is a dangerous business.

The text I will use to illustrate this point, Rainer Nägele's *Reading After Freud*, is a well-crafted work that maintains a perspicuous theoretical position while also engaging itself fully in the practical business of reading. The problems it finds itself involved in, therefore, the dangers it courts, cannot be dismissed as belonging only to the particular case, but in fact characterize a large historical situation. And of course that book also brings into our discussion the name of one of the major players in the intertextual game by which the possibility of a feminist literary project is opened in relation to Goethe. Nägele introduces his work as follows:

> To say that we are reading after Freud implies a determination of our reading in a much more specific sense than a merely temporal one, although that very determination entangles us in such a way in the order of time that the "merely temporal" can no longer be described as a simple sequence of before and after. The sequence of essays in this book leads to that knotting of time that Freud

calls *Nachträglichkeit*—deferred action or belatedness. In this temporality the "after" becomes constitutive of the "before."[2]

In particular, a form of reading that pays special attention to "the surface" (p. 2) will now itself enact a form of *Nachträglichkeit:* "Such a reading of literary texts that have been read . . . as signals from the depth and interiority of a specifically modern subjectivity, can itself be read as the effect of a deferred action, a belated rereading that reads what could not be read at the time of writing" (p. 2). Or more precisely, reading must take advantage of "the possibility of redeeming those elements of the past that in their own time could not enter into the economy of signification and were therefore excluded, repressed, or marginalized" (pp. 4–5).

The danger is that only a fine line separates this idea of reading from the aesthetic idea of reading, the idea of the reader's role as a constitutive factor in the text's meaning, which sets in motion the co-optive processes we have discussed. Nägele does not mean aesthetic reading. He emphatically disavows "subjectivity" as the site or goal of reading. And when he speaks of "economy of signification," he reminds us that redemptive reading presupposes an economy fundamentally *different* from the one in which the text's very identity, as a text, arises, hence that our reading must always contend with a non-negotiable gap in itself, exactly the gap that aesthetic reading (not to mention a good deal of reader-response theory and hermeneutic theory) claims to have closed. "To the degree that we are interested in reading, we are producing ever-new allegories of our reading" (p. 6), says Nägele—appealing to a version of Paul de Man that may or may not have ever actually existed. Our reading, that is, is never fully involved in itself, but is always a reading *of* our reading, a reading as it were (the *mot* is Heine's) over our own shoulder.

Nägele does not mean reading in the aesthetic sense. But the inevitable narrowness of the difference here, within a history of reading indelibly marked by the aesthetic, forces him constantly to redefine his own position, to distinguish it, for example, from "non-reading," which is "reading as a stable process of acquiring an increasing stock of cultural goods and heritage" (p. 5)—this "stock" being, in our terminology, the phantom compensation offered the aesthetic reader in return for his making himself politically ineffectual. "Reading in an emphatic sense," by contrast, the reading Nägele advocates, "is not compatible with the acquisition of cultural capital, because every such reading radically destabilizes the fragile economy of our configurations of meaning" (pp. 5–6).

But we have already talked about destabilization, in chapter 7; and here, as there, we are compelled to ask exactly *where* it occurs. Anywhere but in the minds and texts of those of us who think we know about it? What if we are ignored, or misunderstood, or fail to understand one another? The situation is full of danger, especially the danger that our work and our thought will go for nothing, a danger that Nägele, for all his stylistic aplomb, cannot suppress an awareness of: "It might be that we are among the last readers. The demise of the book, the end of the Gutenberg era of printed communication, the threat of a new illiteracy, belong by now to the standard elements of contemporary cultural critics. I have no desire to join their ranks and rhetoric. To do so would be an act of not reading" (p. 5). The qualifications added after the first sentence—and then in the next paragraph, where we hear of how "the electronic revolution" might induce us "to change our reading habits in order to decipher the alphabets, grammars, and graphemes of . . . new kinds of 'texts' "—make it appear that "readers," in that first sentence, means readers in a narrow sense from which the work of allegory or belated redemption might rescue us. But the sentence itself remains, and always threatens to get out of hand. "It might be that we are among the last readers," even in the "emphatic" sense that Nägele affirms; it might be that even reading after Freud, or reading on the edge, as I call it, has also reached the end of the line.

Meaning must be "destabilized"; our situation in the history of discourse (as grasped, at least, in "Literarischer Sansculottismus" and *Die natürliche Tochter*) is such that stability in meaning automatically becomes both the element and the mechanics of co-option. And if we ask, again, where this destabilizing happens, Nägele will answer, for the time being: in Freud, where this means not only Freud "himself," but also the mechanism of *Nachträglichkeit* by which Freud is repeatedly redeemed as a destabilizing force, destabilizing in a sense that goes beyond the idea of simply undermining our belief in the real object of meaning, the referent: "Freud's *Nachträglichkeit* is never a simple projection into the past. Contrary to recently widely publicized legends [Nägele means Jeffrey M. Masson's *The Assault on Truth*], he insists on the *real* as a precondition for memory traces, although, as we will see, the real and reality assume a complex and evasive form" (p. 177). The choice between the real and the fantastic poses no problem for aesthetic reading, reading as complicity in the co-option of literature, which simply accepts both sides of the opposition in indulging its eventually solipsistic equation of reading with life. Freud's task, and Nägele's, is therefore to be "evasive" with respect to this and all similar oppositions, whence it follows that the destabilizing effect can never be located in a general coordinate system, but can be sought only, from time to time, in the particular reading of a particular text.

Most readers will acknowledge the practical effect of destabilization in Nägele's work. There is a kind of stark symmetrical architecture in his juxtaposition of the Wolfman and Moses, which occupies the final chapter, and in his reading of Habermas alongside Freud. But it is an architecture that is not lived or worked in so much as it is haunted, by voices from the other essays and its own, by a mixture of styles that denies it the quality of being at home in its time and fills it with its own impermanence, the impermanence, after all, of an object of reading. Or perhaps it is less like architecture than like Egmont's somnambulistic balancing, between the danger of losing control of itself in mere dreams and the danger of that one theoretical step too many that will plunge it into the co-opted wakefulness of hermeneutics.

I do not think it is necessary to go into more detail here. Suffice it to say that the instability or impermanence associated inevitably with the typical guerrilla tactic of evasion is a primary form of the danger in which reading finds itself. Reading on the edge, for Goethe as well, is the reading style of the future. But the question of whether such reading *has* a future is still open.

## Tactics

Does reading on the edge, or the precariousness of its situation, really matter? Is the idea that starts haunting Goethe in the 1790s, the idea of a literary resistance against literature, still worth the difficulty of keeping alive? Fredric Jameson, in the introduction to his *Postmodernism,* suggests that the legacy of the aesthetic view, if it is still a problem at all, has at least become an entirely different kind of problem for us.

> Indeed, what happened to culture may well be one of the more important clues for tracking the postmodern: an immense dilation of its sphere (the sphere of commodities), an immense and historically original acculturation of the Real, a quantum leap in what Benjamin still called the "aestheticiza-tion" of reality (he thought it meant fascism, but we know it's only fun: a prodigious exhilaration with the new order of things, a commodity rush, our "representations" of things tending to arouse an enthusiasm and a mood swing not necessarily inspired by the things themselves).[3]

What happens in this passage, and in similar passages, is not covered by the notion of irony, but is more like a historical self-staging of the text in the manner of Nietzsche. The text does not speak "for itself," but contrives to make room for the speaking of its historical situation (and registers the consequent distortion of itself cryptically, in a distortion of Benjamin). This latter speaking, however, is not a speaking of meaning, not oriented toward even some "residual" form of "referent" (p. ix), since the historical situation in question is characterized precisely by our recognition that the last available matrix of meaning, "the modernist aesthetic paradigm," has "unexpectedly vanished without a trace" (p. xi).

We are still reading over our own shoulder—"Postmodernism, post-modern consciousness, may then amount to not much more than theorizing its own condition of possibility" (p. ix)—but now with a more aggressive and confident gesture, for the destabilization of meaning is no longer a task, but a fact, one of the "irrevocable changes in the *representation* of things" (p. ix) to which postmodernism is especially sensitive. Even the pattern of belatedness still appears, in "the 'moment' (not exactly chronological) when they ['preconditions for the new structure'] all jell and combine into a functional system. This moment is itself less a matter of chronology than it is of a well-nigh Freudian *Nachträglichkeit,* or retroactivity: people become aware of the dynamics of some new system, in which they are themselves seized, only later on and gradually" (p. xix). "Well-nigh" (but not exactly) Freudian, however, for in a world of "just more images" (p. ix), retroactivity is only a two-stage process, lacking the level of "conviction" or the "purely factual," which is "not a given, but an effect of a labor of working through" (Nägele, pp. 187–88). When Jameson speaks of working through ("we have to work all that through"), he is referring only to the level of theory, to "the obligation to rehearse those inner contradictions [of the concept 'postmodernism'] and to stage those representational inconsistencies and dilemmas" (p. xxii).

Without doubt, Jameson is better positioned than, for example, Nägele, to take on the "post-contemporary" world, to make positive and challenging statements, to exploit, paradoxically, the antiquated form of the book, his own eminently well-organized book, as a provocation, an unmasking of the unstable in its already presumably destabilized subject matter. In fact, for all its sensitivity to history, and for all its self-awareness as a "rhetorical strategy" (Jameson, p. 418), this act of positioning not only *is* blind to its large historical situation, but actively *presupposes* its blindness (trades on it, so to speak) as a condition of making positive statements, including, paradoxically, positive statements about its large historical situation. Apropos the recognition that "for the moment, global capital seems able to follow its own nature and inclinations, without the traditional precautions," without needing to worry about "labor movements and insurgencies, mass socialist parties, even socialist states themselves," Jameson continues:

> Here, then, we have yet another "definition" of postmodernism, and a useful one indeed, which only an ostrich will wish to accuse of "pessimism." The postmodern may well in that sense be little more than a transitional period between two stages of capitalism, in which the earlier forms of the economic are in the process of being restructured on a global scale, including the older forms of labor and its traditional organizational institutions and concepts. That a new international proletariat (taking forms we cannot yet imagine) will reemerge from this convulsive upheaval it needs no prophet to predict: we ourselves are still in the trough [which comes within an inch of saying "at the trough"], however, and no one can say how long we will stay there. (p. 417)

It is precisely our inability to imagine what ultimately interests us that provides us, paradoxically, with the freedom to imagine after all. It is true that we cannot understand this freedom, this "play of figuration" (Jameson, p. 411), except by way of "an essentially allegorical concept," which must "convey some sense that these new and enormous global realities are inaccessible to any individual subject or consciousness . . . or, to use the Althusserian phrase, are something like an absent cause, one that can never emerge into the presence of perception." But still, Jameson continues, "this absent cause can find figures through which to express itself in distorted and symbolic ways: indeed, one of our basic tasks as critics of literature is to track down and make conceptually available the ultimate realities and experiences designated by those figures, which the reading mind inevitably tends to reify and to read as primary concepts in their own right" (pp. 411–12). Here, at least, something positive can be undertaken, which does not seem to be so in the case of reading on the edge, or the literary resistance against literature, or—I suppose we should say—"reading after Goethe."

But what if those "ultimate realities" are not really there? What if the "trough" we are in is not really a trough, but simply our condition from now on, a condition in which our best hope is to be co-opted favorably, to remain *at* the trough as long as possible? Does the "evasive" tactics of resistance then become the only acceptable course? Or are we, rather, faced with something like Pascal's wager? Since we cannot know about ultimate reality anyway, are we obliged, in "cultural politics" (Jameson, p. 409), to adopt a positive "strategy" merely because it is positive, either "the *homeopathic* strategy" of "undermining the image by way of the image itself," or the "more modernist strategy" that Jameson calls "cognitive mapping," or some other comparable alternative?

The problem with reading after Goethe is not that it is antiquated. It is true that what haunts Goethe is the specter of discourse-control exercised in (not necessarily by) the developing publicistic-industrial nation-state in the Europe of his time. And it may be true that with the globalizing of our achievements and problems, the time of the nation in that sense is past, or passing rapidly. But even without going into the details of global communications, or of the framing of issues in informatics, doxometrics, and media-driven democratic politics, I think we shall still find it difficult to maintain that history has somehow passed by what Goethe saw as the disastrous legacy of literature, the large-scale organization of discourse, the danger of a practically automatic top-down adjudication (whether or not deliberate) of the limits of meaning.

The problem with reading after Goethe is simply that it is in no sense positive. Its business is nothing but resistance, or destabilization. It cannot possibly produce a positive achievement, since achievement as such, in whatever form, confronts it as a type of stability. And it certainly cannot build positively on the assumption of an already destabilized condition of meaning in postmodernism, because its stance is (at least) radical enough to make "destabilized condition" a contradiction in terms. In the specifically literary field, as I once tried to show apropos the *Wanderjahre,* reading after Goethe tends to take the form of an irony that is "subversive with respect to *any* established political or quasi-political order," indeed with respect to "any possible determination of its own content."[4]

The question, as far as reading after Goethe is concerned, is therefore not one of goal or vision or usefulness, certainly not one of hope in any sense. The only question is that of *contour.* Can the literary resistance against literature assume enough in the way of definite shape to keep it from simply evaporating in its own lack of content?

## The Scandal of Gender

This is the point at which the possibility of a feminist literary project becomes important. For gender difference is a special kind of difference. The problem with reading on the edge is that everything about it is marked with impermanence. Its formulations are evasive; its textual manifestations are evanescent and, at least in the realm of plausible interpretation, unverifiable; it works to destabilize every possible conceptual or hermeneutic fabric that might provide a context for it. Gender difference, on the other hand, is nothing if not permanent. And it is an obtrusive difference, not an evasive one, a difference capable of asserting itself prominently in every corner of both our material and our intellectual existence.

But gender difference is also a scandal—a stumbling block, a trap, an outrage. For despite its insistence and permanence in our experience, we cannot say definitely what *kind* of difference it is. We have, curiously enough, a much better idea of what we mean when we say "we human beings" than when we say "we men" or "we women." If we mean "human beings, and not animals," then our conception is shaped by the fact that we are, after all, animals; if we mean "human beings, and not gods," then our conception is shaped by the secret understanding that we must in some sense be gods in order to make that distinction. But the opposition "men, and not women," or "women, and not men," is generally characterized by exclusion; it tends to imply a strict inability of the speaker to imagine the other side of the gap, which is perhaps another way of saying that the difference is "performative." Or again, if we distinguish ourselves by race or tribe or nationality, then we do so on the basis of a conception of belonging to a race or tribe or nation. But one does not "belong" to a gender. Once we start thinking about gender difference, therefore, we cannot avoid entangling ourselves in the types of complication that were discussed above in connection with *Penthesilea.* We begin with what seems a concrete fact, and in no time the whole problematics of representation engulfs us.

To look at it differently, gender difference, being a difference, is unquestionably a sign. But it is a radically *dyadic* sign and so does not participate in what C. S. Peirce shows to be the irreducibly triple structure of semiosis. There is no third position from which to unfold its semiotic potential. The various positions we might try for this purpose—positions, of necessity, all roughly equivalent to "the human"—turn out inevitably not to interpret gender difference, but simply to lose track of it. And the significance of any particular gender anomaly or variation is measured, and limited, by precisely the power it uncovers in gender difference as such. The unoccupiable third position is sometimes represented in Goethe by the dead or vanishing child—Faust's two children, or the drowned baby in *Die Wahlverwandtschaften*. But if the child survives, then at least one of the parents tends to vanish, as in *Wilhelm Meisters Lehrjahre* or *Die natürliche Tochter*.

Gender difference is a scandal. It is a sign, and so belongs in principle to the sphere of meaning. But there is always a level of inquiry at which it disrupts or destabilizes any semiotic process or structure in which it is included. Jameson has one way of characterizing the postmodern that is especially interesting in this regard: "There comes into being, then, a situation in which we can say that if individual experience is authentic, then it cannot be true; and that if a scientific or cognitive model of the same content is true, then it escapes individual experience. It is evident that this new situation poses tremendous and crippling problems for a work of art" (p. 411). At least this holds for art after the establishment of the aesthetic view, in which "the phenomenological experience of the individual subject" is "the supreme raw material." But this passage, looked at only slightly askew, describes almost exactly the situation of gender difference; for gender difference is strictly undeniable in experience—in a way that practically no other experience is, except perhaps pain, which does not have the same obtrusive semiotic quality of difference. And yet, *as* experience, it is radically detached from any "model" by which it could be related to the quality of truth.

At least potentially, therefore, gender difference is a crippling problem for the work of art, a crippling or destabilization, in particular, of the fabric of meaning that constitutes a work of literature, or literature as a whole, in the aesthetic sense. But gender difference is also both permanent and marked by its permanence. It follows that if gender difference can be established in the literary field as a site of radical semiotic destabilization, then something will definitely have been gained for the literary resistance against literature; not stability or permanence (reading on the edge cannot in any sense be *identified* with gender difference), but at least a certain contour, a certain continuity of focus will have been gained, hence a certain increase in its chances for survival.

Establishing gender difference in the literary field as a site of desta-bilization, however, is not a simple matter. Literature as we know it, since at least the eighteenth century, literature in the age of aesthetics, which feeds on its reader's sense of free personal experience (in which gender difference is undeniable), cannot possibly avoid *containing* gender difference. But the mechanism of the text, the presupposition of literary meaning, in constructing the experience of *the* reader, also always semioticizes gender difference, submits it to a "model" by which it is stabilized in a relation to truth and so stripped of the quality of scandal that must characterize it on some now only inferred level of "authentic" experience.

If the idea of gender difference as a destabilizing literary force were such that we could get to it by way of a discussion of the thematic burden *of texts,* or even by way of a discussion of the structure of textuality itself, as implied *in texts,* then we should quickly recognize in eighteenth-century Germany a hotbed of the literary resistance against literature. We have already mentioned the figures of Lotte, Iphigenie, Clärchen, Gretchen, Helen, and Eugenie in Goethe, and Penthesilea, Käthchen/Kunigunde, and Thusnelda in Kleist. We could add any number of markedly powerful or markedly helpless women from the *Sturm und Drang,* plus the feminist tendency in some early German Romanticism. Even Schiller perhaps plays a role, since both *Die natürliche Tochter* and *Penthesilea* may have been shaped in part as responses to *Die Jungfrau von Orleans.* And if we recall—in connection with Lotte, Iphigenie, and Penthesilea—the structural idea of a collision between text as such and the female body, the idea of a woman's body as the limit of text, then we perhaps even find a place for Lessing. The actual body shared by Emilia Galotti and the actress who plays her, for example, stands in a very uncomfortable relation to the professional painterly judgment of its absolute beauty with which the text opens.[5] And when Minna von Barnhelm, in the grip of what she mistakenly (!) names "joy," suggests that "girls" in general are—she hesitates—"strange things" ("sonderbare Dinger," exploiting the connotation of strict materiality in a colloquial term for young females), is she merely echoing a standard male view of women's emotional unaccountability? Or do those words—in the mouth of an actual woman (the actress) who both is and is not the person who speaks them—perhaps rather mark the boundary where text stops and the body begins? Perhaps gender difference, in some oblique way, is even a factor in cases where text collides with a male body—in the poem "Ganymed," for instance, or in the relation between Mephistopheles' cosmic negativity and the (later sexually ambiguous) positivity of his bodily presence onstage, or in Herder's practically corporeal victimization by his own writing.[6]

These ideas and references could probably be organized into the reasonably cogent demonstration of something like an appetite or aptitude for literary resistance in Germany at the time in question. But the material is still all basically textual, always already involved in the mechanism of meaning, the hermeneutic exposure, that *is* text—not yet the scandal by which reading on the edge might conceivably orient itself in existence. What we require, again, for the establishment of gender difference as a scandal in the literary field is the possibility of an impossibility, the possibility of a feminist literary project.

## Goethe and the Shaping of the Argument

For all we know, the possibility of a feminist literary project is somebody's grand design, a stroke of genius, the result of an enormously complicated and far-reaching strategy for the preservation of the literary underground—Goethe's strategy perhaps, or Nietzsche's or Freud's or Derrida's or Irigaray's. But even if this were true, in whatever sense, we would be absolutely prevented from making the connection between design and fruition, since that connection would have to be made in the realm of meaning (here equivalent to intention), where a feminist literary project is not possible after all. The most we can say—if it turns out that we can say even this much—is that the possibility of a feminist project is something that happens in literature.

We can, however, say a certain amount about structures in which that possibility arises. It may be, for example, that at some point in the process a body of text is required, in which a divorce between meaning and use is carried out and placed in a relatively clear relation to the question of gender difference—which summarizes our discussion of Nietzsche in the previous chapter. In the following, I will argue that Goethe effects a similar divorce between meaning and use by creating shadow texts, texts that strictly speaking do not exist and therefore cannot be interrogated as to their meaning, texts that do not stand in any form of hermeneutic light yet still manage to make themselves available for use in history—for use, as in Nietzsche, only by strictly unqualified users, since criteria for qualification could be derived only from a pattern of meaning that is absent. The argument on Goethe is of necessity more circuitous than that on Nietzsche, whose positive *dis*qualification of women as readers, at a stroke, both drives the wedge between meaning and use and establishes gender difference as the generating principle of the Elsewhere of unqualified users. (Which does not prevent that Elsewhere, once in existence, from being inhabited and given substance by men [e.g., Derrida], and by women [e.g., Sontag] who do not write *as* women.) But the complex of relations connecting gender difference, the revolutionary appetite (however hopeless) of the invisible school, and the making of a space for nonexistent texts can still be shown without too much difficulty.

More is required, however, than just this showing. The opening of a text—say, *Beyond Good and Evil* or *The Genealogy of Morals*—to a form of use entirely detached from its meaning, still belongs, paradoxically but inevitably, to the text's meaning, is still verifiable by interpretation. We have not reached a level of intertextuality at which we can begin talking about the possibility of a feminist literary project until we can show, in relation to particular texts, an *actual* pattern of strictly unqualified use, like the game of bridge in relation to late Nietzsche. At this point, however, we will have left interpretation behind.

It is no longer even clear that the use we are talking about is a use *of* the texts we began with; to show such a connection between the use and the text would be, precisely, to qualify the user. Exactly how such an argument can be made convincing, therefore, is not a matter that can be theorized in general terms. The argument, in each case, must develop its own unique shape.

In the case of Goethe, the argument will run roughly as follows. Starting, as I have said, from certain shadow texts that arise in a direct relation to actual poetic texts of Goethe (like the political play parallel to *Die natürliche Tochter*), and arise in a manner that involves both gender difference and the idea of a literary resistance against literature, we find that later, in the domain of use, or of the "reception" of Goethe, the production of shadow texts continues, texts that still do not exist in the sense that existence implies hermeneutic exposure, but also still bear the mark of Goethe's authorship, although this mark turns out to be something like the exact negative of the mark by which authorship is ordinarily recognized. The problem is to trace a connection between these two sets of shadow texts, a connection firm enough to bear the name "Goethe," but always within quotation marks, as a sign that we mean authorship only in the sense (as with Nietzsche and Irigaray above) of the author's detectable presence as the player of the cards. And it turns out that the tracing of this connection has to do especially with the matter of gender and the possibility of a feminist literary project, in exactly the type of shadowy intertextual area, insulated from all hermeneutic intervention, where such a possibility must be located. Our willingness to make the requisite conceptual bridges will certainly be influenced by our recognition that Goethe himself was troubled by the wrongness of reading and the problem of a literary resistance against literature. But the textual evidence that supports this recognition does not have any force as evidence in the domain of use.

And yet, on the other hand, Goethe himself does make it easier for us to connect the two sets of shadow texts by contributing to the production of a level of transitional quasi-text *between* them. The texts on this transitional level—most obviously Eckermann's *Conversations with Goethe* and Bettine von Arnim's book *Goethe's Correspondence with a Child,* plus perhaps the portions of *Dichtung und Wahrheit* that Bettine in a sense dictated—are texts that definitely exist. Their quality as what I call "quasi-text" arises from an ambiguity in the matter of authorship; they all announce Goethe as their author—"everything I say here was written in my heart by you," says Bettine, even of her own diary[7]— and yet, in various ways and degrees, Goethe is also not really their author. They thus straddle the divide between meaning and use, but without by any means eliminating or transcending that divide. On the contrary, their existence creates a space, a separation, between, on one side, expressive intentions clearly attributable to Goethe, and, on the other side, uses of Goethe that border on the illegitimate (uses by unqualified users) precisely because of their claim to be more than merely a critical or exegetic using of their original. Within this space of separation, therefore, these quasi-texts adumbrate a transition between the two types of nonexistent text that must be connected in order to support the possibility of a feminist literary project.

Moreover, this transitional space is also occupied by texts that are mirror images of the ones just mentioned in that they announce an authorship (bear a signature) other than Goethe's yet still also in some manner show the mark of Goethe's authorial activity. I mean especially works of Schiller, and not only the works on which he and Goethe actually collaborated. Who, for example, is the author of *Wallenstein?* Even if we did not know that while working on *Wallenstein,* Schiller also undertook a stage revision of *Egmont;* even if Schiller did not suggest in letters that he is writing *Wallenstein,* so to speak, against his own will and inclination; even if there were not a curiously tense relation between the play and Schiller's own aesthetic writings, not to mention the essay "Über epische und dramatische Dichtung" (whose authorship, in its later publication, Goethe insists on sharing with Schiller) and the correspondence with Goethe in late December 1797: even so, it would still be fairly clear that the text of *Wallenstein* symptomatizes a kind of authorial struggle, that it reads like a version of *Egmont* overlaid with a version of *Don Carlos,* in a manner that I think is not adequately described by the concept of "influence."[8]

But an even more striking case is represented by the essay "Über naive und sentimentalische Dichtung." I use the word "essay" advisedly, for it is clear that Schiller's other expository writings in the 1790s, from "Über Anmut und Würde" on, are not essays in the usual sense—and certainly not in the sense developed by Peter J. Burgard for dealing with Goethe's essays[9]—but rather systematic aesthetic treatises in the Kantian manner. Even the epistolary form of *Über die ästhetische Erziehung des Menschen* serves mainly to keep us in mind of the putative proximity of the text's system to historical and social praxis, and does not seriously unsettle the system as system. In "Über naive und sentimentalische Dichtung," however—which opens, uncharacteristically, with a frankly unverifiable appeal to the experience of "more refined" people[10]—a number of heretofore un-Schillerian features of Goethe's essay style become clearly recognizable, especially the ironic undermining of proposed systematic structures (see Burgard, pp. 54–77, on "Der Sammler und die Seinigen") and the opening of the text toward a "Community of Writing" (Burgard, pp. 215–26).

The systematic quality of the opposition naive/sentimental—developed at the end by the opposition realist/idealist—is maintained superficially throughout; but it is also constantly threatened by its own implications. Whereas in the letters on aesthetic education the proclaimed "aesthetic" perspective is adhered to consistently (art seen from the point of view of the recipient or user), in "Über naive und sentimentalische Dichtung" both the receptive and the productive aspect of artistic experience figure in the argument, which creates problems. For in the present age, where what we imagine as the more direct contact with nature enjoyed by the Greeks has been lost, the naive *reader* is an impossibility. Our relation to nature itself is sentimental; what matters to us about nature is not what it *is*, but what it is "considered to be" (*SA*, 12:161) in the nostalgic complex of reflection and feeling with which we invest it—as Schiller says in his first paragraph. Moreover, among contemporary writers (whom we cannot distance from ourselves as historical objects, as we can, say, Homer or Shakespeare), the naive *poet* seems an impossibility as well. Or at least it ought to be extremely difficult for us to make any credible attribution of naïveté to any of our contemporaries. (The recognition that nature, for us, is only what is "considered" to be nature comes back to haunt Schiller here.) On several occasions the text appears to corroborate this point. In our time, says Schiller, poets like Homer could not exist except by "running wild," with no firm connection to "society" (*SA*, 12:186). And can we take seriously the idea of a poetic work in the production of which "reflection plays no part" (*SA*, 12:231)?

But on the other hand, if there were not, even today, something like a naive poetic spirit, in direct contact with nature, how could there still be any such thing as poetry? Would literature not collapse into a welter of philosophical criticism, with no object by which to orient itself? Therefore naive poetry *must* exist, even today; and Schiller, far from being reticent about naming names, seems intent on pushing this point to extremes. Even Lessing, "the educated pupil of criticism" (*SA*, 12:236)—Schiller thus refers to Lessing's confession at the end of the *Hamburgische Dramaturgie*—is included among those who sometimes evince the naive spirit. And the discussions of Goethe read as if they were positively calculated to provoke controversy. "Not only in the same poet," says a footnote, "but even in the same work we often encounter both types [naive and sentimental] conjoined, as for example in *Werther*" (*SA*, 12:189)—"conjoined," "made one" ("vereinigt"), as if this possibility had even been allowed for, let alone demonstrated, in the main text. (And as if the assertion, toward the very end, that such a unification of opposites is not only possible but *necessary*, in "the poetic state of mind" [*SA*, 12:249], did not call into question the whole idea of poetry with which the text had been operating.) But then perhaps the idea of "genius" excuses all inconsistencies, including the argument, apropos Goethe, on "how the naïve poetic spirit deals with a sentimental subject matter" (*SA*, 12:213). Never mind the question of how the naive spirit, *as* naive, is supposed to *conceive* such a subject matter in the first place.

There are in fact ways in which these instances of what resembles a Goethean "spirit of contradiction" (see Burgard, pp. 57–60) might have been incorporated into the basic oppositional system after all, but Schiller does not seek them out. Rather, in yet another Goethean move, he opens his text to the "dialogic" (Burgard, pp. 133–40); he practically invites attacks on his systematic proposal, for the sake (one assumes) of what is to be gained from open discussion. (Is this perhaps in part why he closes with a condemnation of the self-caricatured idealist, the "Phantast" [*SA*, 12:263]? Is a writer's uncompromising insistence on his own terminological system a symptom of this type of "fantastic" excess?) For instance, there are moments in the text—especially the passage on Shakespeare and Homer (*SA*, 12:183–87)—that have an unusual confessional quality, where Schiller presents his judgments as personal experiences and so leaves plenty of room for the reader to differ. And above all, this essay, unlike any of the earlier aesthetic treatises, is literally packed with judgments about specific writers and works, judgments that are inherently disputable, and whose discussion will inevitably shake the systematic categories that inform them.

Of course no one denies that Goethe had an "influence" on "Über naive und sentimentalische Dichtung." But again, even in reading the standard evidence for that relation—like the outrageously obtrusive letter Schiller wrote to Goethe on 23 August 1794, in which the paragraph beginning "So ungefähr beurteile ich den Gang Ihres Geistes" is practically a summary of the essay's structure—one wonders if the concept of influence does not become a bit ridiculous here. A careful reading of the essay itself moves us at least closer to the sense that Schiller, in writing it, had managed to allow a part of himself actually to be inhabited by the imposing authorial force of his colleague.

As I have said, the texts discussed here are transitional texts, texts that create the space they occupy, separating Goethe's authorship from uses of Goethe, yet also—in their quality (with respect to Goethe) of "quasi-text"—marking a kind of transition between what I will try to show are bodies of nonexistent text in the two domains they separate. And it is reasonably clear, in the three cases I have mentioned—Schiller, Eckermann, and Bettine von Arnim—that Goethe took a definite personal interest in the production of these quasi-texts. Again, it would be wrong to infer, on this basis, the existence of a grand historical design in Goethe's thought. The integrity of our argument, after all, still depends precisely upon a strict *separation* of meaning from use. But it is difficult, nevertheless, to avoid a sense of Goethe's groping into our business here, his taking an active part in at least the rough construction of the argument from which "Goethe" will emerge.

## Haunting

The last part of the argument, the part on intertext, in the domain of use, the part corresponding to the argument on the game of bridge in chapter 8, turns out to be the easiest. For practically all of the work that needs to be done has already been done, in the literature on Goethe and Freud and psychoanalysis, and especially in two fairly recent books, Avital Ronell's *Dictations* and Sabine Prokhoris's *The Witch's Kitchen*.[11] My contention, to return to the metaphor of chapter 8, is that it is Goethe who is playing the cards (or is made or permitted, *nachträglich,* to play the cards) in psychoanalysis considered as a literary project, and above all in the writings of Freud himself—writings crowned, of all things, by a Goethe Prize.

   Psychoanalysis "considered as a literary project," however, must be understood to mean the *possibility* of such a project, where the notion of a possibility that excludes its own realization, as in the case of the feminist literary project, signifies the project's necessary avoidance of any hermeneutically exposed position. Of course psychoanalysis itself has been treated, often enough, as if it were a branch or limit of hermeneutics. Leventhal, for example, sees an instance of Schlegel's hermeneutics of incomprehensibility in Freud's well-known discussion of the dream's "navel."[12]

> There is often a passage in even the most thoroughly interpreted dream which has to be left obscure; this is because we become aware during the work of interpretation that at that point there is a tangle of dream-thoughts which cannot be unravelled and which moreover adds nothing to our knowledge of the content of the dream. This is the dream's navel, the spot where it reaches down into the unknown. [Or more literally, "rests upon the unknown."] The dream-thoughts to which we are led by interpretation cannot, from the nature of things, have any definite endings; they are bound to branch out in every direction into the intricate network of our world of thought. It is at some point where this meshwork is particularly close that the dream-wish grows up, like a mushroom out of its mycelium.[13]

Leventhal comments on this text (of which he omits the last sentence, with the metaphor of the mushroom) as follows: "This 'knot' or 'tangle' (*Knäuel*) of dream-thoughts cannot be interpreted further because, strictly speaking, there is nothing left to interpret but its ever tangling, knotting structure. The interpretive work is interminable (*ohne Abschluß*) because we never arrive at an original and deep center, but only at the 'navel' that defies and contests our interpretive efforts" (p. 318).

   We could perhaps accept this commentary, even with its one obvious mistake—interpretation is interminable, Freud says, not because of the navel, but because of the dream-thoughts' illimitable *outward* ramifying—if Leventhal did not cap it by quoting Foucault to the effect that "at bottom everything is already interpretation."[14] Freud's whole point about the "navel" is that it marks the location of something that is *not* "already interpretation," something "unknown," which is *not* the same as "incomprehensible." Incomprehensibility characterizes the mesh of dream-thoughts at that nexus; but the Unknown (*das Unerkannte*), the power by which the dream is actually driven into existence, like a mushroom, is of a different order, possessing in addition that "evasive" quality of being "real" which, for instance, Nägele speaks of.

We have already had several encounters with the "real" in something close to this form, where it operates as a resistance against hermeneutics, an unmasking of the complicity of hermeneutics in aesthetic wrongness; we recall: the unaccountable but undeniable function of the real female referent of *Werther;* the realness of Irigaray's disqualification as a reader, which persists even where we accept her reading of Nietzsche as valid; the real female bodies on the stage of *Penthesilea,* and perhaps also the body of the actress as profiled by negotiation in *Iphigenie* and *Die natürliche Tochter.* Resistance thus understood must be distinguished carefully from the type of resistance that arises *within* hermeneutics. With regard to "the irreducible moment of incomprehensibility [that] constitutes interpretive desire and makes interpretation at all possible," Leventhal says: "Without the resistance inherent within the interpretive act, and the interpretation of that resistance, we miss something fundamental about the process of interpretation itself, namely *that interpretation implicates itself as interpretive object in the very process of its unfolding*" (p. 319). The crucial point here is that the resistance that articulates and energizes hermeneutics arises "*within* the interpretive act," in its very "unfolding," whereas the instances of female-gendered resistance *against* hermeneutics that we have looked at, in Goethe, Kleist, Irigaray—while they are profiled, or brought to bear (belatedly, *nachträglich*), only in their relation to textuality, hence to hermeneutics—still (precisely in that relation of *Nachträglichkeit*) are "really" located Elsewhere, beyond the Incomprehensible, in the domain of the Unknown, the strictly inter or extratextual.

The differentness of psychoanalysis, in this regard, is even clearer. For the object of psychoanalytic interpretation (of which the dream is a special case) is the *symptom.* And as both Ronell and Prokhoris understand with exceptional clarity—being indebted, both of them, to the Lacanian unsettling, or re-unsettling, of psychoanalysis—there is never a point in the development of psychoanalytic theory where the theorizing process might be said to have ceased being itself a symptom of exactly the same type as those unambiguously preexisting symptoms from which it starts out. The internal resistance of hermeneutics, the incomprehensible, arises *in the course* of an inevitably self-reflexive hermeneutic theorizing, and is thence projected (on both the theoretical and the practical level) back into the general domain of text. But in psychoanalysis, the resistance, the shadow, the quality of an ultimately untraceable symptom, is there *from the outset,* already fully developed (as "the psychopathology of every-day life," for instance, or as an "Unbehagen" in civilization) and overshadowing even the first tentative steps of theory.

In other words, to use Ronell's guiding notion, the difference be-tween hermeneutics and psychoanalysis is the difference between uncontrollable

self-reflexivity and the condition of being *haunted.* Self-reflection at once both
clouds hermeneutics and ignites all its moments of brilliance. But psychoanalysis
never achieves a comparably free and fruitful level of self-reflection; for it is
always haunted by its origin, or mired in it—this being an image that, for
Freud, connects the ideas of origin (as sought in infantile sexual theorizing)
and Goethe.[15] In chapter 8 we observed a peculiar form of interaction between
feminist texts that I called leapfrogging, where each text undermines the other
theoretically in a manner that tends toward no clear goal. It is probably
not an accident that the instances I mentioned, Felman versus Irigaray and
Kelly Oliver versus David Farrell Krell, both (at least by implication) involve
psychoanalysis—which, so to speak, either fails to overcome, or renounces the
delusion that one can overcome, the necessity of putting one foot back into the
mud in order to get the other one out. And in the case that interests us most,
neither Ronell nor Prokhoris is concerned with the way in which Freud might
be said to interpret, or even reflect upon, Goethe. What matters, rather, is that
Goethe haunts psychoanalysis by way of Freud. Prokhoris goes so far as to risk
"assigning Goethe the opaque place of founder with respect to Freud which
Freud, founding father of psychoanalysis, himself occupied for his patients and
heirs" (p. 81). "Goethe's words," she suggests, "are so many 'navels' connecting
the theoretical edifice to the 'self-analysis' as if to the womb" (p. 107); they
are "the densest point in the 'meshwork' of Freud's theory" (p. 19), that theory
which is also symptom and dream. "Freud himself becomes a phantom," in
his practice, from "his position behind the couch" (p. 91); but the "phantom"
by whom, in turn, "the man of science [is] haunted" (p. 92), the phantom
behind Freud's couch, in position to "open up the space of a transference," the
transference that drives psychoanalytic theorization, is Goethe.

   And with regard to psychoanalysis considered as a literary project,
being haunted implies a condition of radical incompleteness, in which the text
"really" does not exist as text. Prokhoris is especially eloquent on this point:

> that a text by Freud is not a rigid, imposing (funerary) monument, but the
> site of an experience of language dominated by orality. This experience is such
> that the exact moment of the encounter between desire and words becomes
> perceptible, and, with it, the movement by which the drive is transformed
> into language—but a language that contains within itself the possibility of
> a transformation back into the drive, into unconscious desire. . . . Such a
> text teeters, precariously, on the edge of unconscious desire. One might even
> say that it is nothing other than this tension or promise, and hence that it
> emerges in the gap which endlessly defers its full realization.[16] Should the gap
> be closed or the promise fulfilled, the voice of the text would be stilled. . . .
> In other words, what seems to me to take place in Freud by way of the gesture
> of writing, the process that produces a text, is a mise-en-scène of the basic
> drama of psychoanalysis. Shattering the compact fixity of the written *work,*

> a Freudian text captures the incandescence of the spoken word in its abrupt materialization—the word as efflorescence, profusion, or limitless promise of meaning. . . . The captivating power, in this sense, of the Freudian text, which both demands and resists translation, springs, then, from its mise-en-scène of analysis, a practice whose instrument is the living word. . . . The spoken word, then, in its constitutive ambiguity; the word and nothing but the word, motor of the transference *because* it is also the place where resistance is encountered. (pp. 160–61)[17]

On this view, then, psychoanalysis offers us texts that never really exist and are haunted (so in a sense authored) by Goethe. Or perhaps better, texts that resist their own existence as texts by the move of transference that involves Goethe in them—with a resistance that I think is still the resistance of Goethe's "invisible school," a resistance that is perhaps "encountered" by hermeneutics, but is not paradoxical enough (not constituted by compound self-reflection) to be comprehended under the hermeneutic rubric of the incomprehensible.

## Belatedness (Nachträglichkeit)

I will not try to recapitulate in detail the work of Prokhoris and Ronell. Suffice it to say that the two books complement each other neatly, in that Prokhoris, using mainly *Faust* as a guide, focuses on relatively large structural qualities and resonances and nodal points in psychoanalytic discourse, and in the process of its coming to be, whereas Ronell, following an associative path through the less brightly lit corners of "Goethe"—including his names, his science, and everything you ever wanted to know about "Eckermann"—produces an unfinishing web of minutiae in which the question of "How . . . Goethe came to cosign psychoanalysis" (p. ix) becomes at once too obvious to bother about and too complicated to let go of, like the question of where babies come from. But one feature of Ronell's text requires special notice here: that it is divided into two parts, the first on Goethe and Freud, the second on Goethe and Eckermann, and so performs the structure of belatedness. It is not merely that the relation with Freud illuminates the relation with Eckermann. In a strong sense, the Eckermann situation is not *there* until the Freud situation has been unfolded, until a certain bird, for example, assumes "metapsychological" factualness (Ronell, p. 166), or until parenthood (Goethe's "parental duties" [p. 165], his condition as "not the father but the mother" of the *Farbenlehre* [p. 145]) becomes what it is both *for* Freud and *in the case* of Freud, who in turn "is reminded by Goethe"—belatedly—"of his parental duties . . . as enmothering father" with respect to psychoanalysis (p. 28).

Belatedness, in this sense, is what opens the intertextual space (the game of hyper-bridge, as it were) where psychoanalysis has room to operate as a text, "cosigned" by Goethe, that does not exist. The Freud whom Ronell and

Prokhoris read is, first of all, and irreversibly, Freud in an altered state, after receiving a massive Lacanian injection of designer semiotics, from a syrinx nowhere near sterile. And for the time being, it is only along the path of this double detour that Goethe finds his way deep enough into the grain of psychoanalysis to have his own wound, in the Eckermann situation, his mouth, his dictating orality (see Ronell, p. 118), opened to the extent that it authorizes precisely our conversation about his dictating, his playing of the cards, in psychoanalysis—where it has now stopped being clear who is sitting behind whose couch. Moreover, if we recall the case of Nietzsche, who, in order to become the revolutionary he is, has to wait for poststructuralism, for New York in the sixties and an anti-hermeneutics of "new sensibility," for psychoanalysis and Lacan and feminism; and if we agree with Ronell that the writer's desire "to complete an oeuvre . . . that would be greater than himself, in excess of him" (p. 65), the "desire to be consumed and incorporated, indeed, to be the name of incorporation" (p. 107), is marked for us primarily by the name "Goethe," which marks in general "the relationship of a text to the possibility of its own survival" (p. x): then it turns out, in the light of chapter 8 above, that the case of Nietzsche is simply a belated instance and confirmation of the case of Goethe—or, if we can carry the argument that far, the case of Goethe as woman.

All this, of course, is a manner of speaking. And in another manner of speaking, these relations of belatedness, without the binding element of a single life history like that of the Wolfman, might well be named "coincidence" (Ronell, p. 5), as might also, for instance, the relation between Freud's cancer and Goethe's intermaxillary bone (Ronell, pp. 39–44). But the trouble with this type of coincidence is that, precisely *as* coincidence, it does not go away; like Goethe himself, it proves "unassimilable" (Ronell, p. xxvii). We must either get rid of it altogether (whatever that means) or else, belatedly, "incorporate" it—which leaves us with the task of establishing "Goethe," in this particular case, as "the name of incorporation," or at least as the site of a desire for that status. The argument on the game of bridge is guided by the historical paradox of Nietzsche's late texts, their position at a dead end by which the very notion of history is compromised. The guide we require in Goethe's case must be supplied by a critically focused argument on the paradox of text and nontext—or texts that do not exist, "nondiscursive formations" (Ronell, p. x).

Perhaps we can already claim to have made part of that guiding argument in the arena of discourse politics. If we ask after the status and function of Freud's citations from Goethe, and from poetry in general, if we ask what those pieces of poetic text are doing in Freud's texts, we encounter some quite serious confusion, on Freud's own part and on the part of his commentators. Freud himself often speaks of poetry as a conduit of knowledge. We think of the lines from the harper's song in *Wilhelm Meisters Lehrjahre,* which appear early on in Freud as a dream association (SE, 5:637, 639) that figures centrally in Ronell's discussion of parenthood (pp. 25–29), and which are later quoted again toward the end of *Civilization and Its Discontents* (SE, 21:133):

> Ihr führt in's Leben uns hinein,
> Ihr laßt den Armen schuldig werden,
> Dann überlaßt ihr ihn der Pein;
> Denn alle Schuld rächt sich auf Erden. (WA, 21:218)

> [You (heavenly powers) lead us into life, you let the poor man become guilty, and then you leave him to his pain; for all guilt is avenged in life on earth.]

After the last citation, which occurs in the argument that the development of civilization inevitably includes "an increase in the sense of guilt, which will perhaps reach heights that the individual finds hard to tolerate," Freud comments as follows: "And we may well heave a sigh of relief at the thought that it is nevertheless vouchsafed to a few to salvage without effort from the whirlpool of their own feelings the deepest truths, towards which the rest of us have to find our way through tormenting uncertainty and with restless groping" (SE, 21:133). "Relief," given the context (the original uses no noun, but suggests relief in the verb "aufseufzen"), can only mean relief from that "guilt" which, we have just been told, is strictly inescapable. The simple and direct knowledge transmitted by the poets, in other words, particularly by Goethe, somehow manages to counteract its own effects by easing the burden of precisely what we know to be true. Prokhoris, who says that "poetry furnishes Freud the Ariadne's thread that guides him safely through the dark labyrinth of his investigations" (p. 21), is especially gripped by this paradox, which she explains by suggesting that the poets put themselves "in a position, not to reveal knowledge . . . but to elicit a [presumably therapeutic] transference" (p. 11). Poetic discourse, she says, at least in the particular case of *Faust,* "concentrates within itself all the secret power of dreams, even while proffering the blinding clarity of a universally accessible language that rings out from our stages" (p. 80).

This is, however, not only a paradox, but also a confusion. There is certainly a sense in which the notion of orality must figure in the discussion of Goethe and psychoanalysis—in the relation between theorization and the "incandescent" word of analytic practice (Prokhoris), in Goethe's position, for and through Eckermann, not only as a writer, but as one who dictates (Ronell). But if we carry this notion a step too far—if we ask, perhaps, "what unacknowledgeable operations are *Goethe's words* called upon to carry out *inside Freud's words?*" (Prokhoris, p. 3), where we should be speaking of "texts," not "words"—then we find ourselves suddenly committed to a hermeneutically primitive view of text as the vehicle of a substantial spirit. In Prokhoris, in fact, this slippage produces something close to an actual contradiction. For if Prokhoris is right—as I think she is—in calling Freud's Goethe citations the "navels" of his theorizing, then not only a hermeneutics of expression, but even a hermeneutics of incomprehensibility must fail, since the "navel," again, is precisely that point where the "meshwork" of dream-thoughts (or by analogy, of theorizing moves) gives way to the simple reality of the Unknown.

If, therefore, we ask once more about what those pieces of Goethe's texts, and other poets', are doing in Freud's text, Prokhoris herself provides us with a more convincing answer—albeit only by way of a concessive participial construction. For whatever Freud, for his own part, says or implies about the quasi-oral transmission of spirit, or inspired knowledge, in the poetic texts he reads, those texts (especially Goethe's) operate *in his text* as instances of the "universally accessible language" of literary classicity. He quotes them because they will be recognized, because history has raised them to the position of classics. But at the same time, as Prokhoris argues, he quotes them in such a way that their historically sanctioned meaning, their universal accessibility, becomes practically irrelevant—except as the superficial contextual hook by which they are brought to rest at a particular place in the larger theoretical text. Their quality as classics is hollowed out by the subterranean pressure of the Unknown, the untextualizable, whose omphalic mark they are. (This hollowing out is perhaps suggested, but not constituted, by the idea of their expressing a secret knowledge.) Which is to say that *as* text, they exhibit nothing but their own hollowness, hence the wrongness of their public aspect, the wrongness of the classical, the wrongness of literature, the wrongness of reading. They are, in other words—whatever hand "Freud" may have had in the process—a belated awakening and confirmation of the secret literature of Goethe's "invisible school."

There is, then, at least an excuse for speaking here of belatedness rather than "coincidence." And the structure of intertext here has also become more clearly similar to the one treated in chapter 8, since it must now involve (in a position corresponding to Sontag's and Derrida's "defense" against Nietzsche) all of the nineteenth- and twentieth-century texts in whose midst the "classical" Goethe arises. Moreover, if we agree with Ronell that it is largely Eckermann who produces "the fiction of the self-composed Olympian Goethe" (p. 88), and so "gives birth to Goethe's true Personality—the one that will survive the contingencies of his personality—" (p. 126), then the belated unraveling of this procedure in psychoanalysis, in Freud, in Ronell herself, sabotages the classical Goethe at both ends of his historical span and turns loose—into history, of all places, for the time being—precisely the *contingent* Goethe, Goethe the literary guerrilla, or, in an altered and perhaps still invisible sense, " 'Goethe,' as an instance of limitless singularity" (Ronell, p. x).

## The Feminist Turn

If Goethe's haunting of psychoanalysis operates *on the level of text* as I have suggested it does, then psychoanalysis, "considered as a literary project," includes a tendency to *undo the classical,* which means, since we are talking about Goethe, something close to the classical as such—or the phallic, as we might be tempted to say, in the sense of a literary-historical giving of laws. And this tendency, in turn, suggests a bridge between the idea of the possibility of a feminist literary project, as it arises for Goethe in the vicinity of *Die natürliche Tochter,* and what we might call the strong feminist turn in psychoanalysis over the past two or three decades.

We have already discussed Irigaray's *Amante marine* and the manner in which that text is haunted by Nietzsche to a point where its meaning (or its incomprehensibility)—its very existence as a text, in the sense of its hermeneutic exposure—evaporates in a strictly intertextual space of gamelike relations. Not even the reflection upon this state of affairs, in the last part of the book, makes a difference in it: "His [Nietzsche's] sacrifice to the Idea would be inscribed in this—in having preferred it over the openness (which is always a playing for time) toward a female other. In having refused to break the mirror of the same and, again and yet again, having demanded of the other that she be his double. To the point of wanting to become her."[18] This more or less recapitulates the argument of chapter 8 above: that Nietzsche, by insisting on his historical dead end and by disqualifying women as readers, leaves aside a limitless Elsewhere into which he himself is then driven by a secret will "to become," to become woman, like Dionysus (*Am,* p. 143), as the player of the cards in *Amante marine.* But then Irigaray continues:

> Et qu'aurait changé le "oui" d'Ariane ou Diotima ou . . . Rien à sa pensée. À moins d'une femme qui refuse de l'être selon sa perspective. Qui affirme sa différence. Donc pas Ariane, abyme de sa passion. Partenaire apollinienne? Le reconstituant indéfiniment en oeuvre d'art? Le paralysant dans son devenir dionysiaque. Destin insoluble. Pressentant l'impuissance, Nietzsche se déclare crucifié. Il l'est. Mais par lui-même. (*Am,* p. 201)

> [And what would have been changed by the "yes" of Ariadne or Diotima or . . . Nothing in his (her?) thought. Unless it came from a woman who refused to be a woman according to his (her?) perspective. Who affirms her (his?) difference. Hence not Ariadne, the abyss of his (her?) passion. An Apollonian (female) partner? Reconstituting him indefinitely as a work of art? Paralyzing him in his Dionysian becoming (his becoming a woman? hence hers?). Insoluble destiny. In a presentiment of impotence, Nietzsche declares himself crucified. He is. But by his own doing.]

In this passage, the four occurrences of the possessive "sa" and one of "son," which can all mean either "his" or "her," are not merely ambiguous. Rather,

they step out of the text altogether, into the unbridgeable space of absolute disjunction between Same ("his") and Other ("her"), between Here and Elsewhere,
that precisely Nietzsche insists on; they go where they cannot be followed, like
Nietzsche's own secret "will" to become woman. They step out, leaving holes
or gaps in the text, like the three dots following "Ariadne or Diotima or . . . ,"
which mark the spot where we perhaps expect Irigaray to name herself. But she
*cannot* name herself here—except perhaps by a cryptic negativity, by not saying
"Diotima" the second time—since her relation to this text (her disqualification
as a reader of Nietzsche) is constituted by the utterly material (unsemioticized,
unnameable) fact of her being a woman. What we have, then, is a semiotic
structure (the text) with material holes in it, a thing that has no right to be
there, a text (if it is a text) that in a strong sense does not exist. In the sense,
especially, of not belonging to the domain of hermeneutics. The moment of
self-reflection is here also the moment of recognition that nothing is changed,
that the all-moving motor of hermeneutic discourse (self-reflection) is spinning
its wheel in emptiness.

This association of psychoanalysis, feminist problematics, and the text
that does not exist—which we are learning to associate, further, with Goethe—
is by no means unique in Irigaray. Jane Gallop's *The Daughter's Seduction,* to
take just one more instance, also includes a sniffing out of the material holes in
texts[19]—holes that remind us of the hole in the text of *Werther* that is displayed
by Emilia Galotti—and itself, as a text, resists its own intactness by devices
that perhaps seem a bit heavy-handed alongside those of the marine lover: long
self-questioning parentheses (pp. 88, 100, 103), a staging of "heterotextuality"
(p. 127) in two columns of text, a postscript (pp. 148–50) that marks the text's
inability to end. But on the other hand, the relatively smooth surface of Irigaray's
writing gives an impression of closure, perhaps even is a kind of closure, whereas
precisely the quality of "openness" that Irigaray insists on is foregrounded in
Gallop's procedure, not only in her self-interruptions, but also in her adoption,
at base, of a familiar critical-exegetic stance that leaves room for other texts to
operate within her own.

And when other texts do operate there, they suggest repeatedly the
possibility of the text that does not exist. Irigaray's attack on Eugénie Lemoine-
Luccioni's *Partage des femmes,* in Gallop's tracing of it, reminds us strongly
of Felman's criticism of Irigaray, which was discussed in chapter 8. Irigaray
insists on Lemoine-Luccioni's obligation to "expose her desire, her fantasies, her
transference, in other words the effects of her unconscious" (Gallop, p. 102); and
Gallop, while conceding that Lemoine-Luccioni fails to meet that obligation on
exactly Irigaray's terms, suggests that "*perhaps* she *does more,*" that occupying
"the correct, 'feminist,' revolutionary, non-masterful position" may itself be
a form of "self-mastery, self-possession," which Lemoine-Luccioni avoids by
silently acting out her desire in a Derridian "scene of writing." Like Felman

and Irigaray, Irigaray and Lemoine-Luccioni thus drive each other out onto a limb, which turns out to be the same limb, the doubly eccentric, or internally antagonistic adumbration, in involuntary concert, of a fully adequate feminist text that does not and cannot exist. And the same drama is then carried out again, at a somewhat higher temperature, in Gallop's final chapter on Dora and the dynamics of *La jeune née*.

All of this, of course, happens in the wake of Jacques Lacan and his particular version of the scandal of gender, which is involved in practically all of the scandals he has provoked. But for our purposes, it is especially interesting that one essay of his, originally a lecture delivered in German, raises by implication the question of establishing gender difference as a site of crippling or destabilization in the literary field. (Thus leading us back to Goethe's attempted use of gender difference in *Werther* and *Die natürliche Tochter,* perhaps also in, say, *Stella* and *Iphigenie,* as a lever with which to open internally the text's own unavoidable aesthetic wrongness.) For if, as Lacan asserts in "The Signification of the Phallus," the phallus is "the signifier intended to designate as a whole the effects of the signified, in that the signifier conditions them by its presence as a signifier,"[20] then it follows—whatever the situation "in the intra-subjective economy of the analysis"—that the phallus signifies *literary signification* as such, since literature is precisely that semiotic field in which the conditioning of signified by signifier itself occupies a privileged place (in degree at least, if not a unique *kind* of place) in the domain of the signified. Or in words of one syllable, what we mean by literature includes our intent to include the signifying *processes* in our sense of a text's meaning—however ultimately futile our efforts (against Lacanian "splitting" [pp. 285, 287–88]) to conceive this meaning as non-object.

But the phallus, even in its strict Lacanian distinction from the penis, still establishes gender difference: "one may, simply by reference to the function of the phallus, indicate the structures that will govern the relations between the sexes" (Lacan, p. 289). Which means that at least in theory, gender difference occurs in literature at the level of the signifying of signification itself, a level at which it cannot yet be semioticized as part of the experience, the aesthetically imposed content, of literature, and so might conceivably survive in the form of scandal. This theoretical point of course does not solve the practical problem of finding a site of fundamental destabilization in the literary field. But when we come back to the discussion of Goethe's writing, I think we will be able to give some flesh to the idea.

In any case, given the amount we have already said about Goethe, it would not be difficult to find any number of structural or conceptual patterns in post-psychoanalytic feminism to which the name "Goethe" could be attached. Without going beyond Gallop, for example, we could follow her reference (pp. 119–20) into Julia Kristeva's short piece on "Un nouveau type d'intellectuel:

le dissident,"[21] which introduces a conscious feminist turn in *Tel Quel,* and where the idea of a "type" characterized by the "singularity" of each example, or the idea of radical "dissidence" as a form of permanent living in "exile," reminds us strongly of Goethe's "invisible school" composed of authors who have in common precisely their lack of mutual contact, their failure to form the kind of communal structure that might serve them as a home. Whence we might find our way, then, to various ideas and references in Gallop that suggest the Goethean project of resistance without a goal ("infidelity" [p. 48], "difference" as opposed to "polarization" [p. 93]), and finally to the idea of "a practice, both of psychoanalysis and of writing, that attends to the specificity of the subject's desire" (Gallop, p. 101), which is not far from a paraphrase of the pedagogical conclusion Goethe draws from, of all things, his most thoroughly public work, *Faust.*[22]

But this sort of argument does not get us as far as we need to go. It is not sufficiently tight and documentable to serve as evidence of a history in the traditional sense. And if what we are interested in is a structure of belated intellectual and textual activity that is haunted by "Goethe," then the multiplication of instances where some sort of connection *can* be made will only distract us from the nodal points, the large structural relations, on which our conviction must be based: Freud's insistent quoting of Goethe, for reasons that are often not at all clear, including the specific identification (from which Prokhoris starts out [p. 2]) of "Metapsychology" with the witch in *Faust* (SE, 23:225); the collision of text as text with the female body, or with the material fact of being a woman, in Goethe (and surrounding Goethe, in Kleist, in Lessing), Nietzsche, Irigaray, and Gallop; the scandal of gender, as a possible lever for opening the co-opted historical integrity of literature, by implication in Goethe, then actually in Lacan, and of course in Freud himself, who cannot resist saying to the women in the audience of his lecture on femininity, "you are yourselves the problem" (SE, 22:113); the opposition between psychoanalysis, as haunted writing, and hermeneutics, the writing of insatiable self-reflection, as an avenue for getting outside literature's aesthetic complicity in the large-scale organization and control of discourse, psychoanalysis as text that does not exist; the resonance between a relatively clear and self-aware pattern of *Nachträglichkeit* that emerges in relation to late Nietzsche, and the more complicated and contradictory manner—at once both "classical" and underground—of the survival of "Goethe," which suggests that we might regard the former as a symptom of the latter; Goethe's actual relations with people like Schiller, Eckermann, and Bettine von Arnim, which foreshadow his character as one who dictates at greater historical removes; and of course the infratextual symptomatology of his haunting of Freud, as discussed by Ronell.

But perhaps, apropos our main concern, "Goethe as woman," there is one more question of detail we should take up here, the question of the form, specifically the gender, in which Goethe haunts Freud. The cover illustrations on the paperback of Ronell and on the original French edition of Prokhoris are both marked by strong sexual ambiguity (attached to Mephistopheles on Ronell's book); and Ronell, we have seen, frequently raises the question of the sex of Goethe as haunt (his mothering the *Farbenlehre*, his nurturing pelican's relation to Eckermann [p. 99]). Prokhoris raises the question too, but less explicitly, in her association of Faust's witch with a number of Freud's other female guides—the old woman in a letter to Fließ (pp. 85–86),[23] the guide in the Brücke dream about self-dissection (p. 98; SE, 5:452–55), the dream of the three Fates (pp. 153–57; SE, 4:204–8)—who all more or less beg to be seen as masks of Goethe himself. But perhaps most interesting is a dream Freud cannot seem to let go of, the dream of Goethe's attack on Herr M. (SE, 5:439–41, 448–49, 662–65), which associates Goethe, by way of the fragmentary essay "Die Natur," with a young man who mutilates his own genitals (SE, 5:663). "Und die Mutter, wo ist sie?—" (WA, pt. 2, 11:6), quotes Ronell from that essay, "and the mother, where is she?—"

> Mothers, abject withdrawal symptoms of phenomenological anxiety: they are there to show what is not, producing what is not as a perceptible object (the little boy in Freud *sees* what she does not have). . . . Where is she, the feminine, what is her place, what does it want? This no doubt has become a generic question by now, to which Freud responds precisely in terms of a certain nowhere and nothing of genitals, a radical suspension of the fixity of genre—the place, in fact, from where a petrifying Goethe may have arisen. (Ronell, p. 34)

A castration dream, then, featuring Goethe as Medusa, as castrated mother (SE, 18:273–74). Goethe as woman: but also in the sense of withholding "the fixity of genre," the paternal thrust of authorship, the establishment of the classical. Goethe as woman: the irrevocably self-mutilated attack on literature as such, the vestibule or *Propyläen* (Ronell, pp. 48–52, on Irma [SE, 4:107–21]), opening into the invisible school of what is not.

# Goethe in "Goethe":
# The Primal Scene

We have, then, something that looks like a structure of belated realization of the "Goethe" we developed in chapters 1–7. What remains to be uncovered is, so to speak, the primal scene that irritates this structure into being, a scene in which the production of texts that do not exist, the scandal of gender, the self-mutilation by which literature removes itself from literary history, the specter of the political consequences of the aesthetic, and the figure of Goethe as woman are all knotted together in a single act. But above all, a *real* scene: which now means, since we are interested in the possibility of a feminist literary project, a scene that takes place in literature, and is discussible as literature. Our task, in other words, is to find the literary text that marks the place of Goethe (without quotation marks) in the political-historical-critical-psychoanalytic-feminist game of "Goethe."

## Text and Symbol

Immediately we think of *Die natürliche Tochter,* where the phantom text of a Schillerian political tragedy splits off from the actual text along a male/female, exoteric/esoteric divide. But curiously enough, it is the *actual* text whose existence is called more into doubt by this split. For the phantom text, the Schillerian play, is definitely writable; it *can* exist, in the sense that we could, if we wished, write a plot that would answer the list of questions with which the discussion of the play in chapter 7 opens. And even in its not-yet-written form, the phantom text is hermeneutically accessible, since that list of questions is already an aspect of its meaning, a reasonable attempt to interpret it. But when we try to formulate a fruitful interpretive question about the actual text, we find that our questioning always depends on questions about the phantom text, even when we start out at a relatively high level of critical abstraction: when we ask, for example, why Eugenie should be cautioned not to open the casket of finery, or

how the motif of her actual death (in the secular priest's comforting of the duke)
illuminates other plot elements. Our questioning always seems to slip through
the weave of the actual text and turn into a questioning of the phantom text.
It is as if the existence of the actual text were not sufficiently assured, as if
that text were not substantial enough, for our questions to get a grip on it. In
this respect, the allegory of Eugenie's sonnet is repeated by the text as a whole,
which, in the process of being presented to us, of entering our world (as the
sonnet enters a world of power politics), is transformed into something that it
is not, transformed so completely that our questions about it change their very
nature in our mouths, and the simplest possible statement we can make, that
it exists, becomes questionable.

The *manner* of nonexistence in *Die natürliche Tochter* (the actual text),
moreover, strongly foreshadows the condition of psychoanalysis considered as
text. For no significant interpretive questioning of psychoanalysis can avoid the
question of the unconscious, which in turn can never be arrested at the level
of interpretation, but always eventually requires a questioning of that which
is recognized primarily by its being *not there* in the text. (This formulation
traces, in the other direction, Prokhoris's argument on the psychoanalytic
text as mise-en-scène of the analytic procedure that it makes the gesture of
founding.) Interpretation does not encounter here the ultimate recalcitrant
object of hermeneutics, whence it might rebound self-illuminatingly into itself,
but rather slips through the weave of the text and tends, if anything, to lose track
of itself. The relatively real situation in Goethe, where the irresistible Beyond of
the text is still manifestly writable, thus returns, in psychoanalysis, as a kind of
fantasm.

Even this relation of the real to the fantasmatic, hence the development
of the symptom, is prefigured in Goethe's writing. For if the desubstantializing
of text in *Die natürliche Tochter* allows us to sketch the *structure* of a primal
scene in the larger unfolding of "Goethe," the symptom-producing *power* of that
scene, its link to the unconscious, is traceable in Goethe's notion of "symbol," as
distinguished from "allegory." One consequence of the rehabilitation of the idea
of allegory, mainly in the wake of Walter Benjamin, is that we tend now to regard
"symbol" (in the tradition of meaning more or less established by Goethe) as an
ideological category, suggesting a politically suspect idea of "classical" totality.
But in the process we have lost sight of the question of how Goethe actually
uses the term, in particular, the question of whether "symbol" refers to any
*identifiable* object or event, anything that exists, in the literary domain.

Goethe himself—with one exception, which we will come to—never
directly suggests a positive answer to this question. When he uses the term
"symbol," the context normally indicates not a verbal but a *visible* object—or
the visual arts, or a larger, visually triggered experience (letter to Schiller, 16
Aug. 1797)—except that in his scientific writings the "symbolic" often refers

to the general operation of language (e.g., WA, pt. 2, 1:302–6, 11:167–69). Somewhere between these two fields of meaning, between image and language, it appears that we ought to be able to locate the *poetic* symbol. But can we locate it in the sense of being able to say, "X is a symbol in text Y"? When he moves into the vicinity of literature, Goethe tends to speak not of "symbols" but of "symbolism" as a *process.*

> Allegory transforms the phenomenon into a concept, the concept into an image, but so that the concept, limited and complete, can always be contained and perpetuated in the image, and expressed by means of it.
>
> Symbolism transforms the phenomenon into an idea, the idea into an image, and in such a way that the idea always remains infinitely effective and unattainable in the image and would remain inexpressible even after being expressed in all languages. (WA, 48:205–6)[1]

It is this conception of process—which Goethe elsewhere (without using the word "symbol") calls "really the nature of poetry" (WA, 42/2:146; M&R, 279)—that David Wellbery attempts to locate historically in discussing what he claims is Lessing's view of the quasi-visual transparency of poetic language; and Heinz Schlaffer, in his discussion of allegory in *Faust,* insists on the "limits" of allegory, in order to leave room for the symbolic in this sense.[2] But it is evident that the result or product of this process, the poetic symbol, does not and cannot *exist* in any sense that might expose it in the realm of hermeneutics. Such an exposure, in fact, if it could happen, would transform the symbol (or would always already *have* transformed it) into precisely a conceptual "allegory" in Goethe's meaning; for "what we articulate are concepts, and in this sense the Idea itself [associated elsewhere with the 'symbolic'] is a concept" (WA, 48:180; M&R, 375).

And yet, on the other hand, the idea of the poetic symbol in Goethe's aphorisms, despite its lacking the attribute of interpretable existence, is too clearly implied, and itself in turn too clearly has referential implications, to be dismissed as a mere gesture at some general idea of "the nature of poetry" or of the way a poet "sees" (WA, 42/2:146; M&R, 279). In fact, there are texts of Goethe's that suggest a clear *dialectical* relation between the notions of symbol and allegory, a mechanics by which each strictly implies the other in poetic structure. In *Faust,* for example, the allegorical configurations themselves, at one self-reflexive remove—by way of the question, why allegory?—have a symbolic function. And a similar point, involving the symbolic revelation *of* language *in* language, can be made with respect to the poem, "Gedichte sind gemahlte Fensterscheiben . . ."[3] But for present purposes, it is more important to consider the symbol as an indication, within the text, of what I have called "the Beyond" of the text, the locus of an unrelievable frustration in our attempt to come to grips interpretively with certain types of discourse.

In particular, I think Julia Kristeva's distinction of the "semiotic" and the "symbolic" is illuminating, despite the terminological clash that arises when it is seen in relation to Goethe's "symbolic" (since symbol is to allegory, for Goethe, as the semiotic is to the symbolic for Kristeva). Kristeva asserts:

> The semiotic activity, which introduces wandering or fuzziness into langauge and, *a fortiori,* into poetic language is, from a synchronic point of view, a mark of the workings of drives (appropriation/rejection, orality/anality, love/hate, life/death) and, from a diachronic point of view, stems from the archaisms of the semiotic body. Before recognizing itself as identical in a mirror and, consequently, as signifying, this body is dependent vis-à-vis the mother. At the same time instinctual and maternal, semiotic processes prepare the future speaker for entrance into meaning and signification (the symbolic). But the symbolic (i.e., language as nomination, sign, and syntax) constitutes itself only by breaking with this anteriority, which is retrieved as "signifier," "primary processes," displacement and condensation, metaphor and metonymy, rhetorical figures—but which always remains subordinate—subjacent to the principal function of naming-predicating. Language as symbolic function constitutes itself at the cost of repressing instinctual drive and continuous relation to the mother. On the contrary, the unsettled and questionable subject of poetic language (for whom the word is never uniquely sign) maintains itself at the cost of reactivating this repressed instinctual, maternal element. If it is true that the prohibition of incest constitutes, at the same time, language as communicative code and women as exchange objects in order for a society to be established, *poetic language would be* for its questionable subject-in-process the *equivalent of incest:* it is within the economy of signification itself that the questionable subject-in-process appropriates to itself this archaic, instinctual, and maternal territory; thus it simultaneously prevents the word from becoming mere sign and the mother from becoming an object like any other—forbidden.[4]

I quote this passage at considerable length in order to give a sense of the range of Kristeva's "semiotic," which engages not only the psychoanalytic aspect of "Goethe," but also its discourse-political aspect—"the relationship of man to meaning," insofar as the latter has become "repressive" to the extent of co-opting "theoretical reason" as such, hence requiring of us "a *discordance* in the symbolic function" (Kristeva, p. 140)—and of course its feminist aspect as well.

An instance of the poetic "symbol" in Goethe that confirms the parallel I have suggested with Kristeva's "semiotic," if we can show one, might thus reasonably be taken to supply the final link in our argument—and perhaps in Kristeva's as well. "It is probably necessary to be a woman," she says, if one wishes not merely to "account for" poetic language, but to "use it as an indication of what is heterogeneous to meaning (to sign and predication)" (p. 146), "to deal with literature," but not merely "by miming its meanderings" (p. 145). And she is certainly right, in the sense that the disruptive force, in literature, of the scandal of gender is of an order entirely different from that of, say, "Céline's anti-semitic tracts" (p. 145). But as we saw in the case of Irigaray and Nietzsche, the collision between the operation of texts and the radically real condition of being a woman is not simply something that happens of necessity when a woman writes in a manner that is sufficiently "open to bio-physiological sociohistorical constraints" (Kristeva, p. 146). (Such a necessity would itself have the form of meaning.) That collision depends, rather, on an extensive and highly attenuated interplay of intertextual relations that we shall probably have to dismiss as "coincidence" (Ronell) unless we can complete their analysis as a structure of belatedness under the sign of "Goethe as woman."

### Marriage and Incest

This brings us to the one clear instance of Goethe's actually identifying a poetic symbol. Riemer reports that on 24 July 1809, Goethe said:

> Die sittlichen Symbole in den Naturwissenschaften (zum Beispiel das der Wahlverwandtschaft vom großen Bergmann erfunden und gebraucht) sind geistreicher und lassen sich eher mit Poesie, ja mit Sozietät verbinden, als alle übrigen, die ja auch, selbst die mathematischen, nur anthropomorphisch sind, nur daß jene dem Gemüt, diese dem Verstande angehören.[5]

> [Moral symbols in the natural sciences (for example, the symbol of elective affinity invented and employed by the great [chemist, Torbern Olaf] Bergmann) have more intellectual substance and are more easily connected with poetry, even with society, than all others, which are also, even the mathematical ones, only anthropomorphic—except that the former belong to our whole character and temper, the latter to our understanding.]

The distinction between an appeal to "temper" and an appeal to "understanding," along with the idea of "the unfathomable," in the continuation of this passage, suggests that Goethe is thinking along the same lines as in his distinction of symbol from allegory. But in what sense is it possible to think of the symbol of "elective affinity," in *Die Wahlverwandtschaften,* as nonexistent, or not exposed to interpretation? In the novel itself, that idea is subjected to detailed allegorical interpretation.

I claim that precisely this allegorizing of the concept of "Wahlverwandtschaft" has the effect of isolating, and thus profiling, the symbolic dimension of the word, which is absent from the text (it is profiled precisely *by* its absence) and has to do with the idea of *marriage.* The suggestion of marriage in "Wahlverwandtschaft," the idea of the founding of blood relations on acts of choice, is obvious on the face of it. And this suggestion is then insisted upon *ex negativo* by the operation of "Wahlverwandtschaft" as an allegory of the loosening or breaking of the marital bond. The negative quality *of* the allegory is also represented *in* the allegory, in its ambiguity, its vicissitudes.

For when Eduard, Charlotte, and the Hauptmann actually discuss the idea of "Wahlverwandtschaft," they immediately get the allegory wrong by assuming that Eduard will be drawn to the Hauptmann, Charlotte to Ottilie. And the gradual replacement, then, of this wrong understanding of the allegory by a supposedly right understanding, which however fails to be fully realized in the fiction, suggests in turn the possibility that the whole idea of allegory is wrong and must cede to a *symbolic* understanding that is "inexpressible" or absent or nonexistent—especially since Ottilie, whose final refusal of Eduard is what prevents the allegory's realization, is associated not with enlightened reason, but rather (in the pendulum episode most obviously) with precisely those hidden natural forces that the allegory is supposed to represent.[6]

In any case, it is evident that the text of *Die Wahlverwandtschaften* bears a significantly negative relation to the idea of marriage. As Walter Benjamin points out, the novel is *about* marriage only by way of its developing from the forces that are liberated by the *dissolution* of marriage.[7] The text maneuvers through a kind of obstacle course of marriages without actually touching any of them except to record their dissolution: Eduard and Charlotte's actual marriage; the marriage they might have had when they were first in love; the marriage of Eduard and Ottilie as Charlotte had planned it; the Hauptmann's aborted marriage; the actual marriage that may or may not have occurred in the Hauptmann's past, to judge from Charlotte's reaction to the "Novelle" (*Wvw,* 336);[8] the various marriages, and the theoretical dismantling of marriage, represented by the count and the baroness. In this sense Mittler is an allegory of the whole text, for he, like the text, has nothing to say except when marriages come apart. And what about the famous "red thread" in Ottilie's diary? Is it really constituted by "Neigung und Anhänglichkeit" (*Wvw,* 212), "affection and devotion," as the narrator says? Is it not, rather, that Ottilie *never writes a single word* on the subject of marriage? Except perhaps in the very last entry:

> Ein Leben ohne Liebe, ohne die Nähe des Geliebten, ist nur eine Comédie à tiroir, ein schlechtes Schubladenstück. Man schiebt eine nach der andern heraus und wieder hinein und eilt zur folgenden. Alles was auch Gutes und Bedeutendes vorkommt, hängt nur kümmerlich zusammen. Man muß überall von vorn anfangen und möchte überall enden. (*Wvw,* 311)

> [A life without love, without the nearness of the beloved, is only a *comédie à tiroir,* a bad episodic piece. You pull out one drawer after the other and close it again and hurry on to the next. Even what is good and significant suffers from the wretched organization of the whole. You have to start over again at every point, and at every point you would just as soon be finished.]

Ottilie is not really talking about marriage here, but what she says is similar to what Mittler does say about marriage as an organizing unity that transfigures the accidents of our life (*Wvw,* 107). And Ottilie's mention of comedy reminds us of the count's remark that in comedy, marriage is where the text *stops* (*Wvw,* 111). If we are willing to consider, for the sake of argument, the possibility of a fundamental relation here between marriage and the Goethean "symbolic," then it might occur to us that marriage is where the text (like Ottilie's diary) *must* stop, that *marriage and textuality are radically opposed,* that marriage, with respect to any text, represents the nonexistent as such. This argument, if it can be sustained, will provide, among other things, a clear relation to *Die natürliche Tochter,* where marriage is Eugenie's escape from the textual web in which her woman's body is entangled.

In *Die Wahlverwandtschaften* it appears that the idea of marriage as a strictly *dyadic* relation is what produces the quality of symbol. For as C. S. Peirce argues, semiosis (hence text) does not happen except as the iteration of *triadic* relations, so that the novel cannot even begin until the strict dyadic integrity of the marriage at its center (Eduard and Charlotte) has already been compromised—as it is in the opening pages, by the introduction of a "third" element, the Hauptmann (*Wvw,* 12). We think of the count's recollection of Eduard and Charlotte as a young couple: "Wenn Sie beide zusammen tanzten, aller Augen waren auf Sie gerichtet und wie umworben beide, indem Sie sich nur in einander bespiegelten" (*Wvw,* 115). "When the two of you danced, everyone's eyes were directed at you and as if courted (or wooed or enticed), both of you, in that you mirrored yourselves in each other alone." Even the fractured syntax of this sentence suggests that the perfectly dyadic relation of a "predestined" (but unrealized) marriage (*Wvw,* 117), the dyadic mirroring of the mirror in nothing but its own mirroring, exists only beyond the limits of the sayable, that it belongs to the extratextual realm of the symbolic, that our attempts to see it, to lay hold of it, are actually only an *enticing* of it ("umwerben") back into the realm of text and allegory.

I do not mean that marriage—in Goethe's opinion, or in the structure of the novel's fiction—in any sense "is" an absolutely dyadic relation. My point is that the association of the idea of marriage with that of the primordial dyad of gender difference, together with the positioning of perfected or achieved marriage always just beyond the text's boundaries (where it is "inexpressible"), belongs to the symbolic operation of "Wahlverwandtschaft," to the creation of a *rift* in the text, an opening of the text into nontext, the diversion of hermeneutic energy into a domain where its needful textual object fails to exist. But the idea of marriage is not sufficient by itself to complete this operation, or to resurrect the extra-semiotic dyadic genderedness of humanity in its scandalous (Kleistian) proportions. In order to grasp fully the working of Goethean "symbolism" here—and to understand how the novel could actually become a scandal, a generating of symptoms, even in its own time—we must also consider the other, darker aspect of "Wahlverwandtschaft," which is neither named in the text nor directly represented in the fiction, the other form in which sexual choice and blood relationship can coincide, incest.

The boundaries of family relationship that define incest are ordinarily marked by a shared *name*. And while the four main characters in the novel are never given family names, precisely this lack lends an ominous significance to their shared *Christian* name, as does the almost guilty concealment of that name, by affectation in Eduard, by the Hauptmann's rank, by its feminized form in Ottilie, and by the superposition of an entirely different name in Charlotte, from which it still manages to peek out through an accident of spelling. Moreover, if we follow the text's lead and pay attention to letters, then the quality of that name, "Otto," as a palindrome suggests incest in the form of a circling return to the origin. Indeed, the whole pattern of elective affinities is spelled there, in a name composed of mirroring pairs, with each element of each pair drawn by identity to an element of the other (or perhaps by the attraction of phallic "t" and feminine "o"). What is suggested here—given that a Christian name ordinarily refers more narrowly than a family name—is a kind of radical endogamy even beyond incest. Nor does Ottilie's resolute renunciation of Eduard lift the onomastic curse from this group; for the constant companion of her last days is named "Nanny," which not only suggests Latin "naenia" or "nenia," "funeral song" (present in German literary consciousness as the title of Schiller's poem "Nänie," which in effect paraphrases the novel by saying, "Auch das Schöne muß sterben," "Even the beautiful must die"), but also conceals the name that that child had almost certainly received at baptism, yet another version of the ominous palindrome, "Anna." And all of this, in turn, brings us back to the palindrome we have already discussed, "Ehe," the German for "marriage," which we are now tempted to spell in capitals, E-H-E, with H of course standing for the Hauptmann, the intrusive third element that breaks the unity (E for "Einheit"?) of the novel's original marriage. But the elements of this broken marriage are not driven outward into the world; the marriage, rather, collapses inward, into the sign of the concealed trespass that completes its function as symbol. We think here of Benjamin's point about how the "Novelle" sets off by contrast the inward-tending isolation of the novel's central group (p. 105).

Within the fiction, the suggestion of incest is developed, first, in what we might call the primal scene, the coupling of Eduard and Charlotte in which their child is conceived, an act that especially Eduard recognizes as a "crime" (*Wvw,* 132, 358), and in which the intertwining of real and fantasmal suggests a level of unconscious desire even beyond the "double adultery" he speaks of (*Wvw,* 358), a level of guilt that the participants assuage, and so tacitly acknowledge, by their "joking" before and after the event (*Wvw,* 131–32). This act contains all four of the possible (hetero)sexual relationships in the central group: Eduard and Charlotte are physically present; Charlotte with the Hauptmann and Eduard with Ottilie are there in fantasy; and the features of the resulting baby combine the Hauptmann with Ottilie, the only match of the four that would not be tinged with guilt if it occurred (Charlotte contemplates its possibility [*Wvw*, 312–13]), hence the only one, so to speak, that sees the light of day. The whole incestuously knotted relation of the four name-bearers is thus concealed behind the innocent exterior of that doomed baby, who of course is also named Otto.

The single relationship that smacks most strongly of incest is that of Eduard and Ottilie, who are joined by a subterranean magnetic attraction that is apparently more primitive even than blood and is manifested especially in their symmetrical migraines. Even after the novel's final catastrophe, when they avoid all physical contact, this attraction continues to work, prompting the narrator to suggest that the two are in truth "only One person, in perfect unconscious contentment, satisfied with itself and the world" (*Wvw*, 396). And if we look at the history of their relations strictly from Ottilie's point of view, we recognize, in outline, a story overshadowed by the motif of the daughter's (or the father's) seduction. Ottilie traces her feeling for Eduard to a moment in her childhood when, overpowered by the beauty of his suddenly appearing figure, she had hidden herself in the lap ("Schoos," lap or womb) of her substitute mother, Charlotte (*Wvw*, 79). Her striving now is to please Eduard in every way possible, and continues unchanged even after his withdrawal ("für Ottilien ein schrecklicher Augenblick" [*Wvw*, 174]) removes the sign of the body from their relation and substitutes the sign of the law (Gallop, p. 62 et passim, on Irigaray,[9] Eduard's law-giving letter to Charlotte [*Wvw*, 170–71]), a law of separation and prohibition which she then herself internalizes after a crisis (the baby's death) that suggests guilt-ridden sexual maturation in a number of ways: in her first frankly sexual contact with Eduard ("entschiedene freie Küsse," "firm free kisses"), her glimpse of what she takes to be Charlotte's figure in the distance, her offering the warmth of her "pure naked bosom" (*Wvw*, 359–61). The posture in which she receives the final version of her law, moreover, unable to move or speak but hearing every word spoken over her (*Wvw*, 369–71), recalls Eugenie's metaphor of the "dead man who retains his consciousness" (*NT*, 2621),[10] hence the idea of marriage, and so suggests the derivation of women's condition in general from a basic incestuous tension. And it is the force of incest, finally, inside the idea of marriage and in EHE, its name, hence the concentration of sex into nothing but a family affair, with no public or social or semiotic mediation (no third, no Mittler, not even the notoriety of the count and the baroness), that raises the specter of the strict scandalous dyad of gender difference and the undoing of literature.

Indeed, there are elements in the story of Eduard and Ottilie that seem to reach back to the very origin of gender difference. It is interesting to read Benjamin's essay on *Die Wahlverwandtschaften* alongside Lacan on "The Signification of the Phallus," especially Benjamin's perception that

> In fact the boundaries of narrative with respect to painting are overstepped in the figure of Ottilie. For the appearance of the beautiful as the essential

substance of a living being lies beyond what can become the content of narrative. And yet she stands in the center of the novel. For it is not too much to say that being convinced of Ottilie's beauty is the basic condition of taking an interest in the novel. (Benjamin, p. 114)

A figure from the strictly visual domain of painting somehow planted in the center of a novel, a signifier of a fundamentally different order somehow overshadowing the verbal signification of her surroundings: it is as if the quality of *being* the phallus— as opposed to having it, in the basic differentiating of the sexes (Lacan, pp. 289–90)[11]—were somehow perfectly there in Ottilie, as if she were a woman prior to undergoing the vicissitudes of being a woman, woman newborn from the sea, like the Aphrodite with whom Benjamin associates her (pp. 118–19). Then, however, in the cruel travesty of *Minna von Barnhelm*, the scene at the inn, in which Eduard (having lost a key) stands mercilessly exposed before her (*Wvw,* 387–89), Ottilie for a moment appears to assume a still more archaic persona, which includes the attribute of having the phallus, as well as being it, in her simple negating of the document by which Eduard had meant to be represented (*Wvw,* 386–87), a document she later replaces with one of her own (*Wvw,* 394–95). It is Benjamin, again, who points out the markedly *posthumous* quality of her character as it appears in verbal expression (p. 113)—as if, in all her insistently inoffensive words, something like the law of the dead father were concealed.

I do not know how far these associations can be developed. But I do not think it is strictly necessary to develop them any further than we have. What is important is that, on the one hand, we cannot escape the definitive interpretive *authority,* with respect to the novel, of the chemical allegory and the idea of marriage (the latter being, in its inherent extratextuality, presumably available as an object of reference), while on the other hand, both these interpretive guides quickly collapse under pressure, so that we find ourselves, as in the case of *Die natürliche Tochter,* reading our way *through* the weave of the text into its Beyond, into a domain that we now associate with the Goethean "symbolic," the domain of the text that does not quite exist. It is true that with the aid of Kristeva (on incest and poetic language) and Lacan (on the phallic determination of gender difference) we can now find *names* in that domain, but those names do not in any reasonable sense interpret the text with which we began. Rather, like the Schillerian tragedy behind *Die natürliche Tochter,* they supplant that text, relegate it to a kind of nonexistence, and themselves become the object requiring interpretation—except that "interpretation," in view of what we have said about hermeneutic and psychoanalytic discourse, no longer means what it would have to in order to shed "light" on *Die Wahlverwandtschaften.*

## The Undoing of the Aesthetic

To be sure, there is "light" in *Die Wahlverwandtschaften,* and its name is "Luciane" (Benjamin, pp. 121, 128), or very nearly "Lucian" (normally "Lukian" or "Lukianos" in German, but the Latin spelling, which permits the etymological confusion, is a transparent disguise): namely, the light of *satire.* I mean that Charlotte's vulgar daughter and her crowd of admirers are permitted to invade the much more delicate and tactful world of the main characters not for the sake of contrast—what could we possibly learn from such a contrast that we do not already know?—but for the sake of showing their *similarity* with it, because they belong there.

Eduard, Charlotte, and the Hauptmann, namely—more or less like Luciane and her crew—are people whose existence is constituted entirely, and justified, if at all, by their hobbies. Charlotte's hobby is the tasteful and secure ordering of life and death, especially death. The cemetery is her main achievement, where her "care" had been for "feeling" (*Wvw,* 21)—but not, of course, for the feelings of the people who later object to her rearrangement of the headstones (*Wvw,* 200–203). In matters that affect her directly she fears change (the coming of the Hauptmann at the beginning), but she is always ready to tinker with her physical surroundings and with the lives of other people, especially Ottilie, whose education she gives herself the credit for managing (*Wvw,* 66–68), and whom she not only thinks of marrying to the Hauptmann, but had once thought of marrying to Eduard (*Wvw,* 20). The Hauptmann, as befits his manliness, is more concerned with having a substantial *effect* in the world ("wirken" [*Wvw,* 7]), although it does not take much prompting by the count to remind him that pottering around in his rich friend's estate, no matter how competently, does not amount to much of a "destiny" (*Wvw,* 133); and even after he declares himself fully satisfied with his new post as major (*Wvw,* 344), it turns out that his important affairs do not engage him so completely as to prevent his considering the possibility of returning to manage the estate yet again, as Charlotte's husband (*Wvw,* 354, 366). Eduard, for all his shortcomings, is at least more honest about the character of his existence when he says to Mittler, apropos his passionate attachment to Ottilie: "People have reproached me, not to my face, but certainly behind my back, with being an amateur and a bungler in most things. That may be true, but I had not yet found the field of endeavor in which I could show myself a true master. Show me the man who has more talent than I for being in love" (*Wvw,* 189). "In most things," Charlotte and the Hauptmann are more competent, less bungling, than Eduard. But they are still amateurs, or as Goethe would have said some years earlier, dilettantes. Their activity is focused ultimately upon the shaping and satisfying of their own feelings, hers of security and stability, his of accomplishment and personal destiny (*Bestimmung*); and Eduard, again, is

CHAPTER 10

the most honest of the three in that he opts for a talent that requires *nothing but* feeling. All three, in other words, are strictly *aesthetic* creatures. And it is their limitedness in this regard that Luciane, the satirist without knowing it, illuminates mercilessly.

Of course this view of the main characters is not the impression that most of us, as readers, receive from most of the text, where Luciane is not available to provide the context. But this is because, as novel readers, we too are inevitably (at least for the time being) aesthetic creatures. And the novel's characters, as J. Hillis Miller points out, may in turn be regarded as readers:

> The importance of the apparently casual motif of the reading over one's shoulder, introduced three times, at widely spaced intervals, in *Die Wahlver-wandtschaften,* is that it defines the mode of existence, for Goethe here at least, both of subjectivities and of intersubjective relations. To read is to exist. I exist because I read. I come into existence when I read. The act of reading is, for Goethe, the universal originating moment of subjective life and therefore of whatever relations there may be between subjectivities.[12]

Miller is not referring here to the actual reading of texts and maps and pictures in the story, although there is plenty of that. What he means is the manner in which all attempts to anchor or locate humanity with respect to the nonhuman inevitably entangle themselves in metaphors that are originally anthropomorphic, so that we never really find ourselves, but always only read ourselves.

> Far from being fixed self or substance which can see its own image in the mirror of the world, as Narcissus saw his face in the water, man, in Goethe's definition here, is without face or figure. He is neutral, invisible, without fixed image or character, like the invisible foil behind the mirror. He puts this non-entity under the whole world, including other people, as if he were the world's substance or ground. The image of himself he sees everywhere is made of the figurative transfer to himself of all the objects he confronts. . . . If man reads the world in human terms, personifies it, in turn he reads himself in terms of inanimate objects. He has no images for himself but those generated by his reflecting of himself everywhere, and no terms for inanimate objects but those illicitly projected from the human realm. (Miller, p. 15)

The trouble is that Miller reads this aspect of the text, and the chemical allegory, as more or less straight philosophy, as a representation of the way things simply are "for Goethe here at least." But given the history of Goethe's sense of the wrongness of reading, the wrongness of the aesthetic; given the satirical intervention of Luciane (again, what other function can she have?); and given, above all, the operation of "Wahlverwandtschaft" as a poetic symbol, by which our aesthetic reading of ourselves into the text is deprived of its object, its self-orientation (just as man in general, in Miller's reading of reading, is deprived of objects for orienting himself): it is clear that what is happening in *Die Wahlverwandtschaften* is something much more active, and historically specific, than the representation or enactment of a universal condition of human life.

If the novel's story, as Miller asserts, were strictly "an allegory of the laws, powers, and limitations of language" (p. 7), then we should have no choice but to accept it as an instance of the way things simply are. But actually, if we read "the bare letter symbols" of the chemical analogy (*Wvw,* 56) as literally, as "*buchstäblich,*" as possible, then we shall recognize that those letters, those *litterae,* suggest less an allegory of language than an allegory of *literature.* The seductiveness of the chemical analogy, for the three dilettantes who construct it—despite their all distancing themselves, Eduard in his joking, Charlotte in her ethical doubts, the Hauptmann in his technical knowledge—is the seductiveness of literature in its aesthetic quality. The letter game provides them with a kind of philosophical license, in exactly the sense of Miller's argument, to follow their inclinations and live life as if it were a form of reading. The *failure* of the analogy, therefore—which has to do not only with Ottilie's resistance, but also, from the outset, with the difference between Charlotte's specific aesthetic preference in life-flavors (order) and that of the Hauptmann (self-realization in accomplishment)—is in effect a turning of literature against itself on several levels, and consequently—if, from our own point of view, we connect it to the symbolic desubstantializing of the text—an undoing of the aesthetic in general.

Miller himself is much too good a reader to overlook the hermeneutically insubstantial quality of *Die Wahlverwandtschaften,* its questionable existence as text, its lack, precisely, of the opacity that provides interpretation with a foothold—except that he reads even this quality in an aesthetic sense. At the laying of the cornerstone on Charlotte's birthday, the young mason gives "an entirely charming speech in rhymed verse, which we can only imperfectly reproduce in prose" (*Wvw,* 96); and Miller comments: "The oddness is that this is a prose translation of a poem which does not exist, as perhaps the novel as a whole may be said to be. The novel is, it seems, the literal which can give the spiritual only in 'an imperfect rendering' . . . but surely no words could be more artful than Goethe's in this text" (p. 9). Artful, we infer, in that they establish precisely the spirituality of the spiritual by leaving room for the reader to participate (aesthetically) in its constitution. Not that Miller lets the matter rest at this level:

> Nevertheless, there are aspects of *Die Wahlverwandtschaften* which do not seem to be fully accounted for in this interpretation and which seem disturbingly at variance with it, even at variance with the interpretation Goethe seems to give of his own novel. These features of the text lead to an entirely different reading of it. They make of *Die Wahlverwandtschaften* another demonstration of the self-subverting heterogeneity of each great work of Western literature.

> This heterogeneity of our great literary texts is one important manifestation
> of the equivocity of the Western tradition generally. This equivocity is present
> in the languages we have used to express ourselves in that tradition, and in
> the lives we have led in terms of those languages. (Miller, p. 11)

But the move here is still basically aesthetic. Having done our part, as readers,
in constituting the "spiritual" dimension of the text, we find ourselves still
not satisfied, and must take the further aesthetic step of translating our readerly
activity back into the equivocal experience of our life's inescapable entanglement
in the problems of language as such—equivocal, but also fundamental, an
experience that hooks us up with the "great," the classical, the "living stream"
(as in the "Novelle," *by contrast* with the novel [Benjamin, p. 106]) of an
unbroken tradition.

    The point Miller misses here is very simple, and has to do with
its being a mason who recites the poem we do not get to read. For the
corresponding level of the novel, that we do not get to read, is not accessible
by any amount of aesthetic retranslation; it is a form not of personal, but of
radically *ritual* communication—the simple belonging to an "invisible school,"
like the secret society of Masons—from which our activity as aesthetic readers
simply and finally excludes us. This type of missing the point, in fact, is itself
repeatedly allegorized in the novel—and not only in the gulf separating a vague
aesthetic sense of "Wahlverwandtschaft," as a form of emotional attraction,
from the simple but precise lexical algebra by which we arrive at the symbolic
combination of marriage and incest. The development of Ottilie's handwriting
into an exact replica of Eduard's, for example, is clearly an allegory of aesthetic
literature. The text, in that we carry out our role as readers, appears to become
continuous with our own private personality, our hand, our supposedly free
experience of ourselves. But Eduard's aesthetically self-confirming reaction, in
the novel, misses the point to a degree that is almost comic: "You love me! he
cried, Ottilie, you love me! and they held each other in their arms. Who had first
clasped the other could not have been distinguished" (*Wvw,* 136). Even within
the fiction, it is obvious that what is happening here is entirely different from
two people's loving each other, and much more dangerous. Eduard's personal
existence is not confirmed, but rather it is breached, invaded, compromised,
co-opted—like that of the aesthetic reader in an age of large-scale discourse
management—by forces (perhaps "organic" forces, or "inorganic" or "metallic,"
in the still thoroughly evasive terminology of the fiction [*Wvw,* 339]) that he
positively insists on having no conception of.

## The Voice in the Text

After five chapters' worth of scene setting, as practically all readers recognize,
Goethe's novel quickly comes to focus on the figure of Ottilie. Miller is especially

eloquent on this point, and in fact ends up making a very strong version of the anti-aesthetic argument that I have invoked in taking issue with him:

> If the drama of elective affinities among the four principal characters of *Die Wahlverwandtschaften* is taken as an allegory of the crisscross substitutions in a metaphorical ratio, Ottilie, the last added and necessary fourth, is also the one who ruins the ratio. She is the unidentifiable final term, silent or absent, neither literal nor figurative, therefore not "properly" nameable. She is the "O" which deprives the proportion of its reasonable ground in the distinction between literal and figurative and therefore takes it outside the safe confines of Occidental metaphysics. (p. 16)

> Ottilie is the odd person out in the system of substitutions. As such, she undoes that system, making the "little circle of three," Charlotte, Edward, and the Captain, into a square with a missing fourth side, thereby disintegrating the figure. Ottilie is neither the literal nor the figurative, or rather she is an impossible embodiment of both. . . . [Edward] cannot possess her pleasure as his own. That pleasure remains discrete, elsewhere, unattainable, occurring always too early or too late, somewhere and sometime else. Ottilie is the mute letter, not the aesthetic spirit. She is the *Buchstabe* which undoes Edward's projected love. (pp. 19–20)

> Ottilie is a trance-like silence, a half-sleep of death. This silence cannot love or be loved. It cannot relate itself to anything or to anyone. It cannot speak. It cannot trace a visible trajectory or line. Therefore it cannot be understood by another person or, in its representation, by the reader of the novel. It remains mute, discrete, effaced. It fulfills itself in the final impenetrable silence of her death. (p. 22)

Ottilie, Miller might have said, marks the navel of the text, as does also the chapel where she is laid to rest, the omphalos if not of the world, at least of the estate, at once (like practically everything in the novel) both a ridiculous aesthetic hobby and the focus of a symbolic operation that, by not fitting into the aesthetic fabric of literature, undoes it. "Auch das Schöne muß sterben!" The very idea of the beautiful, the whole of aesthetic culture, with literature, its privileged vehicle, has outlived itself.

The only interesting point that Miller does not touch here, or at least suggest, as far as I can see, has to do with the first passage in which Ottilie's role in the novel becomes an object of technical self-reflection, the opening paragraph of part 2:

> In ordinary life we often encounter what we are in the habit of praising as a device of the epic poet, namely that when the main figures leave the scene, or conceal themselves, or give themselves over to inactivity, immediately a second or third person, heretofore hardly noticed, takes their place, and in

unfolding his whole activity, now seems to us equally worthy of attention, sympathy, indeed praise and admiration. (*Wvw*, 199)

But "in ordinary life," more or less by definition, there are no "main figures." That we pay more attention to some of the people who surround us than to others, we recognize, has to do with our own personal situation and feelings, not with some quasi-narrative structure that we "encounter" in reality. This passage, therefore, casts us (the readers) very strongly as *aesthetic* individuals, people for whom the boundary between reading and life tends to get lost track of.

And as we might expect, the wrongness of the aesthetic also makes itself felt here. For while that opening paragraph refers ostensibly to the young architect who now assumes greater importance from the women's point of view, especially Ottilie's, it quickly becomes clear to us that what is happening *in the novel* at this point (where there are, after all, "main figures") is that Ottilie, whose diary first appears in the next chapter, moves into a position of absolute prominence; the novel, henceforward, is her story. We thus have a structure exactly parallel to that of Eduard and the handwriting. What is first presented as an aesthetically manageable event within Ottilie's field of vision is quickly unmasked as a larger process that envelopes and in a sense determines her.

This structure, moreover, is then repeated yet again with respect to her diary. For although the narrator's anecdote about the red thread in the cordage of the British navy (*Wvw*, 212) is entirely convincing in itself, it turns out that the red thread in Ottilie's diary does not really exist. Benjamin, as we have noted, remarks upon the posthumous quality of that writing, its failure to give the sense of an immediate, developing complex of inner and outer experience. And Miller expands on the same perception as follows:

> Edward's prophetic dream [*Wvw*, 188] . . . echoes similar images elsewhere in the novel, the matching hands matching the matching headaches, the motif of handwriting reminding the reader again that what is involved in this kind of interpersonal relation is not persons as such, but signs, images, forms of writing. . . . Far from having the quality of subjectivity and inwardness one might expect from a young girl's diary, [Ottilie's] entries are surprisingly impersonal. They are made up of quotations, citations, maxims, and reflections such as Goethe himself composed and published elsewhere. If the "selves" of the two lovers are images or handwriting, names, these names have the capacity to move into one another, overlap, merge, and, in an ominous figure, devour one another like particle and antiparticle, leaving nothing behind, the "O" they share and which it is their destiny to become. (p. 18)

But there is more to the matter than this. For if Ottilie's diary does not *have* a red thread, still, in part 2 (here we recall the structure of the handwriting episode), it *is* the red thread, taking the lead, so to speak, in filling the text with those general observations that now become characteristic of its overall style, observations of the type, for example, with which the narrator himself now often opens his chapters—chapters 1, 3 (with a kind word for dilettantes [*Wvw*, 216]), 4 (end of second paragraph), 8, 9 (end of second paragraph), 10 (second paragraph), 13, and 15 in part 2, as against none in part 1. And when the narrator is too busy telling the story, he usually manages to find characters who keep up the production of instructive apophthegms: the architect on any number of topics, including how to handle works of art (*Wvw*, 268); the school assistant on education (*Wvw*, 279–80); the British nobleman on traveling (*Wvw*, 317–19); the "Novelle" considered as an instructive parable.

It is the handwriting episode all over again. Two clearly separated types of writing, a diary and the third-person narration of a novel, now show an uncanny tendency to become the same, in their detached aphoristic classicality, except that here it is not clear which (if not both) is moving toward the other. Indeed, there are points in the text at which, without typographical indications, we would not know where one stops and the other begins: for example, the openings of chapters 3 and 8 (*Wvw*, 216, 294), which could be tacked onto the preceding diary sections with no sense at all of a break; the end of chapter 9 (*Wvw*, 308), which would only require transposition into the present tense to become a perfectly suitable introduction in the following diary; and immediately after the same diary section, the curious present tense of the paragraph opening chapter 10 (*Wvw*, 312), as if the narrator (or for that matter, Ottilie) were developing the diary by comparing Charlotte's good cheer with its closing complaint about "life without love." Moreover, we have noted the avoidance of references to marriage in the diary, which parallels the exclusion of achieved marriage with respect to the text as a whole.

Of course, the two areas of writing do not become strictly identical. But their difference, given the strong sense of *continuity* between them, takes on the character of internal tension or breadth within a single style, which thus in turn reads more like life, like voice, than either manner of writing by itself—and in fact includes a kind of self-deprecating humor (connected with the satirical presence of Luciane) when the narrator remarks that Ottilie appears to have copied many of her observations from "some magazine or other" (*Wvw*, 238). But *whose* voice do we hear here? What combination of the narrator and Ottilie? Or perhaps—given the importance, in this associative field, of a recognition of the wrongness of the aesthetic—we should stop talking about the narrator altogether. For "the narrator," as such, is an eminently aesthetic device, a costume for us to put on temporarily while reading our way into a self-constituting experience of the fiction. Perhaps we have no choice but to step firmly away from the text's blandishments and begin speaking simplemindedly of Goethe, or perhaps "Goethe," thus making the basic narrative, too, into a strictly posthumous writing, not the pretended presence of the aesthetic. And if we now look again at the question of what it means that the two writers of part 2 become continuous, perhaps we shall find that Bettine is even more right than Benjamin (p. 119) gives her credit for, when, in one of those transitional texts not quite written by Goethe, she accuses Goethe of having fallen in love (never mind how impossibly) with Ottilie.[13]

But not with the kind of love that adds up to zero. For the combination here of two classical, posthumous sources of writing adds up, rather, to a voice, and a voice that is not classical at all, perhaps not even posthumous, yet certainly not an aesthetic invitation to our experience: the scandalous voice, rather—what else, under the circumstances, can we call it?—of Goethe as woman.

# Conclusion: Goethe as Woman

This book is about Goethe more than it is about feminism. It does not pretend to say new or interesting things about feminism, or about gender problems, in the way it pretends with respect to Goethe. Therefore I have not aimed for comprehensiveness in my use of existing feminist thought. I simply use what is useful to me, mainly the radical revolutionary feminism that I ascribe differently to different authors in chapter 8. For there is a strong analogy between the unanswerable question of how such a feminism shall express itself effectively and the similarly unanswerable question with respect to Goethe's "invisible school" of literary resistance against literature. The structure of Goethe's quandary in his own time is echoed in the structure of feminism's quandary in our time, and we abbreviate this echo by speaking of Goethe as woman.

Moreover, if we agree that gender difference has the scandalous quality discussed in chapter 9, that its constant and powerful presence in our experience is matched only by our inability to say even what type of difference it is, then "Goethe," as well as Goethe, is brought into contact with woman. For "Goethe" is the persistence of both a problem and the underground struggle it provokes, the problem of aesthetic literature, hence of a literature grown both co-optive and co-opted, the problem of national literature in an age of nation-states which, precisely by way of the development of critical hermeneutics, find themselves in possession of an unappealable organizing and arbitrating function in public discourse.[1] But does this "problem" not in the end become simply the way things are? Does the resistance by which it is kept open as a problem not in the end become sufficiently "invisible" to be, in effect, nonexistent? Or does it still have some sort of public face, something it appears "as"? It would be possible to argue here that the scandal of gender provides public access for the feminist aspect of that problem (the public co-option of literature in the task of maintaining gender relations and "identities"), which thus persists in the form of "Goethe as woman."

But what sort of connection shall we imagine between "Goethe as woman," in either of these two meanings, and Goethe's own authorial inhabiting of female figures? We recall the tension, discussed in chapter 5, between Werther's body, which is continuous with the aesthetically operative text, and

251

Lotte's, which forms a resistance to the aesthetic. Provided we have understood correctly the direction of Goethe's thinking here, we might have to speak of "Goethe as Lotte." And the problem is yet more pointed with respect to *Die natürliche Tochter,* which can be seen as a companion piece to *Tasso* (two plays about poets, one female, one male) and thence, via the *Tasso* allusion in the poem "An Werther" (WA, 3:20), finds its way into the Werther/Lotte orbit. For if *Tasso* is the tragedy of a poet in a society where even practical politics involves the recognition that the poetic operation of language is the sole foundation and guarantee of reality,[2] then Eugenie represents something much closer to the poet who Goethe, in his own view, actually was after the illuminations of the mid-1790s, the poet who finds herself living precisely the radical separation of poetry from politics, the condition of a poetry gone underground. Thus we are also reminded of the function of Lotte's female body (and later perhaps also Ottilie's), to wedge open a structure that is all too tightly, as it were incestuously, knotted together by the knowledge of truth. Again, in Eugenie's case as well as in Ottilie's, we have reason to speak of Goethe as woman.

But what is the connection among these instances of Goethe as woman? And can we find a connection that would also account for the tendency of the presence of "Goethe" in psychoanalysis to associate itself with female figures? or for Goethe's willingness to share his authorship with women, with Bettine von Arnim, and in a different sense with Marianne von Willemer? or for the role of the feminine in the relations we have sketched with Kleist and Nietzsche? The more evidence we accumulate—if evidence it is—the more evident it becomes that a convincing historical or theoretical synthesis is out of the question. With respect to "Goethe as woman," in other words, there is a point where the argument, though manifestly unfinished, seems to find itself under an obligation simply to stop.

Or if we continue at all, we must give up the aim of accounting historically for the phenomenon of Goethe as woman, and approach the topic from another direction. Suppose, for example, we turn the argument around and let Goethe as woman have the value of a simple given, not Goethe as woman in the abstract, which would presuppose the theoretical synthesis that we cannot find, but one particularly pregnant instance. Are we now better able to knit things together by using that given to account, as it were in reverse, for the political and historical and literary-historical aspects of our material?

Suppose, namely, we begin with the maximally complete appearance of Goethe as woman that characterizes the at once both immediate and posthumous voice of *Die Wahlverwandtschaften,* especially at the end.

> So ruhen die Liebenden neben einander. Friede schwebt über ihrer Stätte, heitere verwandte Engelsbilder schauen vom Gewölbe auf sie herab, und welch ein freundlicher Augenblick wird es sein, wenn sie dereinst wieder zusammen erwachen. (*Wvw,* 416)

[Thus the lovers repose next to each other. Peace hovers over their resting place, the cheerful related images of angels gaze down at them from the vaulted ceiling, and what a friendly moment it will be when they again one day wake up together.]

These, the novel's last words, make the grammatical gesture of referring forward to an envisioned future of achieved reconciliation. But in truth, the reconciliation they speak of—a "friendly" waking together, not an inaccessible ecstatic union— *is already achieved* in the language that speaks of it, in the novel's final voice, where what had once been the narrator and what had once been the character Ottilie awaken together in the form of Goethe as woman. Even the apparently misleading gesture of anticipation is reconciled here with the actuality of achievement, in that the two together reflect the paradox of lived immediacy and posthumous distance by which the voice of Goethe as woman is constituted.

Reconciliation of opposites, balance, wholeness, a peace in which "every form of bitterness had disappeared" (*Wvw*, 398): these qualities make up ever more exclusively the mood of the writing as it approaches its end, a mood that is often detectable in even the smallest textual details, in the "images" of angels, for example, whose role is to "gaze" at the dead lovers, and who are thus presented as themselves a coincidence of opposites, as both the strict object and the eternally unfailing agency of vision. Even the novel's established markers of rupture or disharmony seem now to have lost their power. Mittler, whose business is to rescue endangered marriages, and whose coming is therefore itself always a sign of discord, now reappears on the scene; and for a moment it almost seems that his blunt elaboration on the commandment against adultery plays a part in Ottilie's death (*Wvw*, 404–5). But in fact, Mittler has simply become irrelevant. The other characters are all entirely reconciled to their condition; the questions of marriage, adultery, and divorce, to the extent that they still exist, produce no tension or conflict. At the very most, Mittler unwittingly provides Ottilie with an excuse to take the final step in a gradual cessation of life that she had long since crafted for herself.

And the precipitating event in Eduard's death stands similarly under the sign of tension or opposition nullified. Eduard's discovery of the substituted goblet is introduced as follows:

Und wie den Glücklichen jeder Nebenumstand zu begünstigen, jedes Unge-fähr mit emporzuheben scheint, so mögen sich auch gern die kleinsten Vorfälle zur Kränkung, zum Verderben des Unglücklichen vereinigen. (*Wvw*, 414)

[Just as every casual circumstance, every accident, seems to favor the happy person, to lift him up with it, so the smallest incidents tend to work together toward injury or ruin for the unhappy person.]

Is it really only the second of these two parallel but opposed clauses that applies to Eduard? The incident here referred to, which perfects his misery, is also apparently the last straw that finally enables him to die and participate in the "Seligkeit" (*Wvw,* 415), "bliss," of his beloved. Again, therefore, even the simplest of oppositions tends to dissolve in the perfected voice of Goethe as woman.

   But how can Goethe as woman, in this sense, imply or account for the implacably critical or revolutionary or subversive tendencies of the argument as conducted above? If we maintain our understanding that we are talking not about theory here, but about a particular case, and if we therefore place *Die Wahlverwandtschaften* in its proper historical environment, this question is not difficult. The principal historical problem for Goethe, once again, is the co-optive power of the aesthetic—understood as a theory of understanding and a method of meaning production—a power that is capable of confounding and emptying even the idea of freedom as we might wish to derive it from Montaigne or Shakespeare. The *anti*-aesthetic initiative that therefore seems to be called for, however, as attempted in *Werther,* in *Egmont* as theater, in the *Götz* project, in any number of poems, is futile; for it is itself subject to aesthetic co-option, it cannot undo the wrongness of literature. What is required, in order to establish a tenable subversive position, is a somehow strictly *non*-aesthetic move, a text or fiction or argument in which, as in Montaigne, there is simply no place for the reader's constitutive participation.

   And it is in this way, I contend, that we must understand the development of the voice of Goethe as woman at the end of *Die Wahlverwandtschaften.* We shall not expect to find here any direct allusions to the problem of the aesthetic, or any specific awareness of the recent literary or political history of Europe, or any speculations on a Renaissance idea of freedom, or anything at all that might make that voice into the bearer of a programmatic statement subject to being co-opted. What we find here, rather, is nothing but our strict exclusion as readers from a voice now grown perfectly balanced and self-sufficient, a voice that has forgotten how to make any statement whatever. And yet, the founding operation of this voice with respect to the embattled and militant aspect of the "invisible school" remains clear nonetheless: clear from its relation, as the simple impossibility of the aesthetic, to its actual historical situation; clear from the web of structural and lexical and symbolic allusion, as discussed in chapter 10, by which the anti-aesthetic is made to emerge as a meaning from earlier portions of the novel's text; and clear from the tendency of the novel's content, now, to produce allegories of the reader's excluded situation.

   "Every need whose satisfaction is denied in reality produces a compulsion to believe" (*Wvw,* 413). This diagnosis of the condition of the crowds of pilgrims who visit Ottilie's chapel, in hopes of experiencing her healing power, of course applies to us as well, to a public of aesthetically trained readers who expect to relieve their daily frustrations by being welcomed emotionally into the text, and in the end must simply have the door shut in their faces (*Wvw,* 414). The same diagnosis applies even to the sympathetic figure of the architect, who, at Ottilie's coffin, finds himself reduced to reexperiencing the *tableau vivant* of Belisarius (*Wvw,* 412, 252)—*not* the nativity scene! (*Wvw,* 272–73)—where his business had been to reproduce, however naturally, a conventional posture of mournful understanding. Painted figures, in fact, is what we all are in relation to this fiction and this voice, painted figures like the spectator angels on the chapel vault, "related" to each other and to the characters we view only by a painted similarity (*Wvw,* 218–19) that can never acquire the pretended third dimension of aesthetic experience.

Goethe as woman, then, however scandalous our inability to classify it as a particular type of concept, does form the center of what seems a reasonably complete system in the textual and historical material we have been looking at, a system, moreover, that is fundamentally anti-Hegelian, not coinciding structurally with any possible historical unfolding of the same material. To the extent that it nevertheless appears or operates *within* history, therefore, it does so in the character of an unrelenting revolutionary or subversive potential, thus involving "Goethe," as well as Goethe, in its web of implications. And this tendency of the argument to feed on itself, finally, has two sides. It renders the whole procedure suspect from the point of view of any critic who requires a progressively explanatory exposition. But at the same time it promises an inexhaustible supply of material and argument for the critic who is willing to occupy a position categorically beyond the reach of certainty in any publicly acceptable sense.

# Notes

## INTRODUCTION

1. Peter Widdowson, *Literature* (London and New York, 1999), p. 8.

2. Judith Butler, *Gender Trouble: Feminism and the Subversion of Identity* (New York and London, 1990), p. 25.

## CHAPTER 1

1. See *Dichtung und Wahrheit,* Book 11, in *Goethes Werke,* Weimarer Ausgabe, 143 vols. (Weimar, 1887–1918), 28:52. Almost all Goethe quotations are from this edition, henceforward abbreviated WA. References to *Werther* are located by page number in vol. 19, plus the date of the letter where applicable.

2. A great deal of my argument depends on Goethe's sense of the specific technical quality of eighteenth-century literature as "aesthetic," a quality that is profiled by its absence in earlier literary conventions. Goethe's well-documented occupation with Renaissance literature in general (not only Montaigne) is therefore important here. See, e.g., Harold Jantz, *Goethe's Faust as a Renaissance Man* (Princeton, 1951); Ronald D. Gray, *Goethe the Alchemist* (Cambridge, 1952); Stuart Atkins, "Goethe und die Renaissancelyrik," in *Goethe und die Tradition,* ed. Hans Reiss (Frankfurt am Main, 1972), pp. 102–29.

3. Michel de Montaigne, *Oeuvres complètes,* ed. Albert Thibaudet and Maurice Rat, Bibliothèque de la Pléiade (Paris, 1962), p. 790. Further references, even for passages translated into English, are to this edition, and are marked MM plus page number. Translations from the essays "Du repentir," "De la vanité," and "De l'experience" are taken from Montaigne, *Selected Essays,* trans. Donald M. Frame (Princeton, 1943). Other translations from French and Latin are my own.

4. See the poem "Nicolai auf Werthers Grab," WA, 5/1:159. Goethe later uses the idea of "hypochondria" more seriously.

5. Giovanni Pico della Mirandola, *De hominis dignitate, Heptaplus, De ente et uno, e scritti vari,* ed. Eugenio Garin (Firenze, 1942), p. 106, my translation. I use Pico to represent the Renaissance notion of freedom in something like a pure state. Montaigne does not mention him, and Goethe does not seem to have read him until quite late.

6. See the excellent argument of Donald M. Frame, *Montaigne's Discovery of Man* (New York, 1955), esp. pp. 86–89, on human ignorance and mutability as the *opportunity* for a kind of free self-creation by the "virtually omnipotent" soul.

7. Cf. Plutarch, *Life of Demosthenes,* 13.2.

8. Erich Auerbach, *Mimesis: The Representation of Reality in Western Literature,* trans. Willard Trask (New York: Anchor, 1957), p. 258, says: "To be sure, this *forme sienne* cannot be put into a few precise words; it is much too varied and too real to be contained in a definition. Yet for Montaigne the truth is *one,* however multiple its manifestations." But to "discover the form" in an object, by definition, is to pin the object down, *asseurer son object,* and the logical difficulty (which Montaigne has warned us to expect) remains.

9. Rat (MM, 1755) defines "mediocrité" as "mesure"; but surely Montaigne, who claims Latin as his native language, distinguishes between *mediocritas* and *mensura.*

10. All three of these possibilities, interestingly enough, occur to Werther: military service in the letter of 25 May 1772; diplomatic service in the job he actually takes; and "regir un peuple" in the outburst "O wenn ich Fürst wäre!" (p. 123, 15 Sept.).

11. Morse Peckham, *The Triumph of Romanticism* (Columbia, S.C., 1970), e.g., pp. 15, 21–22, 41, 73–75. René Wellek—in his response to earlier expressions of Peckham's ideas in "Romanticism Re-examined," *Concepts of Criticism* (New Haven, 1963), pp. 200–201, and in his own still earlier "The Concept of Romanticism in Literary History" (orig. 1949), in *Concepts,* pp. 128–98—tries to take the edge off this negative/positive polarity by reducing Peckham's idea to that of mere "familiar states of mind—*Weltschmerz, mal du siècle,* pessimism" (*Concepts,* p. 200). But the "negative" tendency in, say, Ossian, the *Sturm und Drang,* Byron, early Goethe, Tieck, Heine, Baudelaire, etc., is more than a state of mind; as a characteristic of literary works it is also a communicative device, and this quality is what needs to be understood.

12. The diabolical and the nihilistic are clearly connected in Mephistopheles, and the Luciferian is defined as "Concentration," a kind of Wertherian turning of the self in upon itself, in *Dichtung und Wahrheit,* Book 8 (WA, 27:219). On the definite malevolence in Werther, see Thomas P. Saine, "Passion and Aggression: The Meaning of Werther's Last Letter," *Orbis Litterarum* 35 (1980): 327–56.

13. This is a real problem in Pico, as also, for example, in Byron's *Cain.* Once we *know* the system of being, are we not forced by our knowledge (despite any supposed freedom) to aim for the very highest, for the state of being "unus cum Deo spiritus factus, in solitaria Patris caligine" (Pico, p. 106)? Or if this *solitaria caligo,* at least for our purposes, is recognized as pointless, indeed as "wretchedness" or mere "unparticipated solitude" (*Cain,* I.i.162, 150), then what choice have we but to turn away from God altogether? The problem is kept open by Pico, with no pretensions to a solution, via the image of ascending *and* descending the Jacob's ladder (pp. 112–16); or compare the more conventional considerations in *Heptaplus,* IV, 5.

14. Keats's letter to his brothers of 21 December 1817, in which Coleridge is characterized as "incapable of remaining content with half-knowledge." Montaigne says of Ficino, "Mon page faict l'amour et l'entend. Lisez luy Leon Hébreu et Ficin: on parle de luy, de ses pensées et de ses actions, et si, il n'y entend rien" (MM, 852), "My page experiences love and understands it. Read him León Hebreo [Abrabanel] and Ficino: he himself, his thoughts and actions, are the subject matter, and he understands nothing." See also the preface to the *Lyrical Ballads,* on the man of science.

15. The term "aesthetic," which relates the nature of art to the receptive (rather than productive) mental faculties, is coined in Alexander Gottlieb Baumgarten's *Meditationes philosophicae de nonnullis ad poema pertinentibus* (1735).

## CHAPTER 2

1. Eric A. Blackall, *Goethe and the Novel* (Ithaca, 1976), p. 53. The word "soliloquy," below, is borrowed from the title of Blackall's chapter 2.

2. On *Werther* as a refraction of social conditions, see e.g. Peter Müller, *Zeitkritik und Utopie in Goethes "Werther"* (Berlin, 1969), Klaus Hübner, *Alltag im literarischen Werk: Eine soziologische Studie zu Goethes Werther* (Heidelberg, 1982), and chapters 2 and 3 of Horst Flaschka, *Goethes "Werther": Werkkontextuelle Deskription und Analyse* (Munich, 1987). On the specific possibility of seeing Lotte objectively, see E. Kathleen Warrick, "Lotte's Sexuality and Her Responsibility for Werther's Death," *Essays in Literature* 5 (1978): 129–35. Deirdre Vincent, *Werther's Goethe and the Game of Literary Creativity* (Toronto, 1992), has a good deal to say about Lotte in the course of an argument that involves Charlotte von Stein very deeply in the background of the novel's revision; but the level of detail at which Vincent operates is not needed in the present discussion.

3. The text is very short, and I will not bother with further page references for quotations from it.

4. Lessing makes almost exactly this point, using the word "Plan" but without reference to Shakespeare, in no. 79 of the *Hamburgische Dramaturgie*. For Goethe's basic agreement with Lessing about Shakespeare's virtues, compare no. 73 of the *Dramaturgie*.

5. The difference between my account of reading and the highly technical argument of Anselm Haverkamp, "Illusion und Empathie: Die Struktur der 'teilnehmenden Lektüre' in den *Leiden Werthers*," in *Erzählforschung: Ein Symposion*, ed. Eberhard Lämmert (Stuttgart, 1982), pp. 243–68, is that I ascribe to Goethe a critique of the *very idea* of reading on which all the theories of reading Haverkamp alludes to are based. Precisely the interpenetration of the ideas of "text" and "reading," which Haverkamp summarizes in his last paragraph, is what constitutes for Goethe what I call the aesthetic wrongness of literature.

6. Wolfgang Kayser, *Kunst und Spiel*, 2nd ed. (Göttingen: Vandenhoeck & Ruprecht, 1967), p. 23.

7. Letter to Friedrich Rochlitz, 23 November 1829.

8. The poems discussed here are in WA, 2:76–80, 83–85.

9. David E. Wellbery, *The Specular Moment: Goethe's Early Lyric and the Beginnings of Romanticism* (Stanford, 1996), pp. 328–29. Page references in parentheses below.

10. Robert D. Tobin, "In and Against Nature: Goethe on Homosexuality and Heterotextuality," in *Outing Goethe & His Age*, ed. Alice A. Kuzniar (Stanford, 1996), pp. 94–110, asserts: "By allowing Ganymede's unnatural sexuality to become part of nature, Goethe suggests yet again that sexuality can collapse the dichotomy of natural

and unnatural" (p. 109). Like Wellbery, Tobin is attempting—in vain, I think—to rescue consistency in young Goethe.

## CHAPTER 3

1. Jeffrey L. Sammons, "On the Structure of Goethe's *Egmont,*" *Journal of English and Germanic Philology* 62 (1963): 250. W. Daniel Wilson, "Amazon, Agitator, Allegory: Political and Gender Cross(Dress-)ing in Goethe's *Egmont,*" in *Outing Goethe & His Age* (see ch. 2, n. 10), accounts for some of the complexity of his situation, his "divided loyalties" (p. 143), but still insists that "Egmont is essentially *passive*" (p. 136).

2. "The Relation of Form and Meaning in Goethe's *Egmont*" (1949), in Elizabeth M. Wilkinson and L. A. Willoughby, *Goethe, Poet and Thinker* (London, 1962), p. 71. Further references to this essay are given below by page number.

3. WA, 8:174. Further references to *Egmont* are by page number alone from this volume.

4. Schiller, "Über Egmont, Trauerspiel von Goethe," in *Schillers Sämtliche Werke: Säkular-Ausgabe,* 16 vols. (Stuttgart and Berlin, 1904–), 16:185. This edition is abbreviated *SA* below. Schiller's basic argument is that *Egmont* is not convincing because we see only the hero's "Schwachheiten" (p. 183). Goethe never answers this criticism directly, but he does indicate, in "Über das deutsche Theater," a serious disagreement with Schiller's later stage-revision of *Egmont* (WA, 40:91). See also the conversation with Eckermann of 19 February 1829.

5. Schiller, pp. 183, 185, comes back twice to this phrase, which he regards as symptomatic of a weakness in the work's conception.

6. The feeling of wrongness here, that Egmont the soldier should first appear as a peacemaker, has an interesting parallel in Shakespeare, where Othello the soldier makes his first more or less public appearance with the words, "Keep up your bright swords, for the dew will rust them" (I.ii.59).

7. Schiller makes this point (pp. 184–85).

8. See chapter 5 of my *Modern Drama and German Classicism: Renaissance from Lessing to Brecht* (Ithaca, 1979), pp. 121–50.

9. See ch. 1, n. 10.

10. See my *Goethe's Theory of Poetry: Faust and the Regeneration of Language* (Ithaca, 1986), pp. 203–9.

## CHAPTER 4

1. See my *Theater As Problem: Modern Drama and Its Place in Literature* (Ithaca, 1990), esp. chapter 4 on Ionesco, pp. 137–78. Also my *Beyond Theory: Eighteenth-Century German Literature and the Poetics of Irony* (Ithaca, 1993), esp. pp. 10–13 on co-option, and pp. 269–300 on drama.

2. Ilse Graham, *Goethe and Lessing: The Wellsprings of Creation* (London, 1973), pp. 30–76.

3. I quote here not from WA but from *Der junge Goethe,* ed. Hanna Fischer-Lamberg, 6 vols. (Berlin, 1963–1974), 2:89–90. The first version of *Götz* is quoted from vol. 2 of this edition, the second from vol. 3; *JG* plus volume and page are given in parentheses. The Shakespeare essay appears in *JG,* 2:83–86; as before, I will not bother to cite page numbers for every reference to it. *JG* is somewhat easier to use here than WA, for our purposes, and has the advantage of an approximate chronological ordering of texts.

4. See Rainer Nägele, "Götz von Berlichingen," in *Goethes Dramen: Neue Interpretationen,* ed. Walter Hinderer (Stuttgart, 1980), p. 68, on the question of Weislingen's sense of identity. Nägele's remarks actually describe the first version better than the second.

5. There is no reason to doubt the reconstruction of this passage. The "zes" got dropped in the course of going on to a new manuscript page. See WA, 39:413.

6. We think of the letters to Woltmann, 5 February 1813, to Knebel, 24 November 1813, to Sara von Grotthus, 7 February 1814, and to Buchholtz, 14 February 1814, and of conversations with Friedrich von Müller, 14 December 1808, and with Luden, 13 December 1813.

7. See my *Beyond Theory,* pp. 272–79.

8. On this general matter, see my *Theater As Problem,* pp. 63–64, 131–36, and the discussion of "romance reading" in my *Beyond Theory,* pp. 21–25, 41–46, et passim.

9. Chapters 1–4 of *Goethe's Theory of Poetry* develop the argument that the act of understanding *Faust* is the act of turning one's back on it; and chapters 5–7 develop the main consequence of this point, that *Faust* is in effect simply not there for the individual recipient (e.g., the solitary reader), but is there only for an audience as strict community. Chapter 8 then deals with the genre of *Faust,* with the impossibility of locating it in respect to the distinction between drama and narrative, hence the impossibility of an adequate receptive attitude or posture for the individual.

10. This last word is hard to read in the manuscript. *JG* does not go into the problem, but simply puts a question mark in the text. WA, 39:185 reads "Tühren," and in the apparatus (WA, 39:429) suggests that this might be a correction from "Trähnen," which seems something of a stretch.

11. The tradition of reader response theory—including such figures as Henry James, Georges Poulet, and Wolfgang Iser—tends to regard the disorientation of the aesthetic reader as a uniquely effective opportunity for, and spur toward, personal growth. See the short discussion in my *Beyond Theory,* pp. 14–17.

12. WA, 39:213–15. On the complicated manuscript situation, see WA, 39:433–35.

## CHAPTER 5

1. As in chapters 1 and 2, I will give only page numbers in WA, 19, plus the dates of letters where applicable.

2. See my argument on this point in *Goethe's Theory of Poetry,* pp. 170–71.

3. Sigurd Burckhardt, "'The voice of truth and of humanity': Goethe's *Iphigenie*" (orig. 1956), trans. Lillian Reed Atkins, in his *The Drama of Language: Essays on Goethe and Kleist* (Baltimore, 1970), pp. 50, 54.

4. See the more complete discussion of *Iphigenie,* with a focus on dramatic form, in chapter 4 of my *Modern Drama and German Classicism,* pp. 97–120.

5. See ch. 1, n. 12, and the article by Thomas P. Saine mentioned there.

6. For this reading of *Emilia* and its attribution to Goethe, see Peter J. Burgard, "*Emilia Galotti* und *Clavigo:* Werthers Pflichtlektüre und unsere," *Zeitschrift für deutsche Philologie* 104 (1985): 481–94. But Burgard parallels Emilia with Werther himself.

7. See my *Goethe's Theory of Poetry,* chapter 7, esp. pp. 173–75.

8. The argument here opens onto a widespread discussion of text and death, including Jacques Derrida's comments on how "Writing carries death," in *Of Grammatology,* trans. Gayatri Chakravorty Spivak (Baltimore, 1976), p. 292. See also Peter Brooks, *Reading for the Plot: Design and Intention in Narrative* (New York, 1984), esp. chapter 4, "Freud's Masterplot" (pp. 90–112). Brooks (pp. 92–93) invokes a well-known passage from Sartre's *La Nausée* and also mentions (p. 95) Walter Benjamin's "The Storyteller," which elsewhere connects the relation of narrative and death to the strictly solitary (aesthetic) situation of the novel reader. See Benjamin, *Illuminations,* trans. Harry Zohn (New York, 1968), pp. 100–101. On some applications of this discussion to *Werther,* see Joel Black, "Writing after Murder (and before Suicide): The Confessions of Werther and Rivière," in *Reading After Foucault: Institutions, Disciplines, and Technologies of the Self in Germany, 1750–1830,* ed. Robert S. Leventhal (Detroit, 1994), pp. 233–59.

9. *Goethe's Theory of Poetry,* p. 296.

10. On the genre of *Faust,* see *Goethe's Theory of Poetry,* chapter 8, esp. pp. 215–31. The larger point, about the "antipoetic" in *Faust,* is summarized in chapter 11, esp. pp. 291–99, and chapter 12. On the *Wanderjahre,* see chapter 1 of my *Beyond Theory.*

11. Immanuel Kant, *Kritik der Urtheilskraft,* § 6, in *Kants Werke,* Akademie Ausgabe (Berlin, 1902ff.), 5:211.

12. On masturbation in *Faust,* see chapter 4 of *Goethe's Theory of Poetry,* esp. pp. 83–87, where *Der Triumph der Empfindsamkeit* is discussed.

## Chapter 6

1. Heinrich von Kleist, *Penthesilea,* ed. Roland Reuß (Basel, Frankfurt am Main, 1992) = vol. I/5 of Kleist, *Sämtliche Werke,* Brandenburger Ausgabe, lines 125–26. Further references to this text are located by *P* plus line numbers in parentheses.

2. Heinrich von Kleist, *Sämtliche Werke und Briefe,* ed. Helmut Sembdner, 2 vols., 4th ed. (München, 1965), 2:805. This edition is abbreviated *SWB* below.

3. Donald Davidson, "On the Very Idea of a Conceptual Scheme" (orig. 1974), in his *Inquiries into Truth and Interpretation* (Oxford, 1984), p. 198.

4. Kant, *Kritik der Urtheilskraft*, § 59, esp. p. 354 (reference in ch. 5, n. 11); Schiller, *SA*, 12:53.

5. See Goethe's conversation with Johann Daniel Falk, perhaps from 1809, in Johann Wolfgang Goethe, *Sämtliche Werke, Briefe, Tagebücher und Gespräche*, 40 (planned) vols., Deutscher Klassiker Verlag, part 2, vol. 6 (Frankfurt am Main, 1993), pp. 726–27.

6. Johann Gottlieb Fichte, *Werke 1799–1800* (Stuttgart–Bad Cannstatt, 1981) = vol. I/6 of J. G. Fichte, *Gesamtausgabe der bayerischen Akademie der Wissenschaften*, ed. Reinhard Lauth and Hans Gliwitzky, p. 251. Further references by page numbers in parentheses. Kleist speaks of his Kant crisis in the letter to Wilhelmine von Zenge of 22 March 1801 (*SWB*, 2:630–36). Cassirer's essay, "Heinrich von Kleist und die Kantische Philosophie," is found in his *Idee und Gestalt* (Darmstadt, 1971; rpt. of 1924), pp. 157–202.

## CHAPTER 7

1. The whole argument of my *Beyond Theory*, on the poetics of irony in late-eighteenth-century German literature, is relevant here, but perhaps especially the section on "aesthetics" versus "poetics" in Lessing (pp. 154–58). And for evidence of an ironic tension between literature and its aesthetic background in an author where one might not expect that sort of subtlety, see Michael W. Jennings, " 'Vergessen von aller Welt': Literatur, Politik und Identität in Klingers Dramen des Sturm und Drang," *Zeitschrift für deutsche Philologie* 104 (1985): 494–506.

2. WA, 40:198. References below are simply by page numbers in parentheses.

3. I quote from the original of the *Berlinisches Archiv der Zeit und ihres Geschmacks*, here from the March number of 1795, p. 254. Jenisch's article, "Ueber Prose und Beredsamkeit der Deutschen," occupies pp. 249–54 of the March number and pp. 373–77 of the April number. References below by page.

4. I will not attempt here to work out this idea in detail. That my formulation summarizes reasonably well Goethe's apprehension about the future of literature in a changing political world emerges, I think, from (1) his resistance to the aesthetic conception of literature, as this appears in his treatment of the idea and role of the reader; (2) his awareness of the entrenched position of co-optive mechanisms in both literature and politics; (3) his ambivalent use of the concept "Nation"; (4) specific text interpretations, especially those of "Literarischer Sansculottismus" and *Die natürliche Tochter* in the present chapter; and of course, (5) Goethe's skepticism concerning the efficacy and consequences of parliamentary political forms. By "discourse control," however, I do *not* mean censorship. In Kant, Rousseau, Herder, and even Lessing we find passages that indicate a *positive* valuation of censorship, precisely where the preservation of an ironic or subversive level of discourse is at stake. (See my *Beyond Theory*, pp. 239–52.) Censorship, after all, is a sign of the *failure* of discourse control—in the same way that harsh punishments, as Nietzsche points out, mark a failure to control (or co-opt)

crime. Discourse control in the modern state (whether or not traceable to a specific agent or agency) is most perfect precisely where censorship can be dispensed with.

5. Robert S. Leventhal, *The Disciplines of Interpretation: Lessing, Herder, Schlegel and Hermeneutics in Germany, 1750–1800* (Berlin, 1994), pp. 310–11. Further references by page.

6. Erich Heller, *The Disinherited Mind* (New York, 1959), pp. 26–27.

7. Friedrich Nietzsche, *Sämtliche Werke: Kritische Studienausgabe in 15 Bänden,* ed. Giorgio Colli and Mazzino Montinari (Munich and Berlin, 1980), 12:140. The translation here is Leventhal's, from p. 315.

8. I speak here from experience. Leventhal (pp. 16–17) discusses my *Beyond Theory* in detail and takes issue especially with my formulations about Herder in their relation to the book's overall argument. I cannot say that he is completely wrong. In fact, the weak spot that he identifies in my work is of exactly the same type as the weak spot—the tendency to make one theoretical move too many—that I am now arguing is inevitably present in hermeneutics. The whole of the present work can therefore perhaps be read as an attempt to limit more carefully what can be said about literary culture as Goethe experienced it. At least one minor point, I think, is cleared up by my insistence, in chapters 1–5, on the *distinction* between what literature is for a Montaigne and what it is in the German eighteenth century (cf. Leventhal, p. 16).

9. Hans Rudolf Vaget, *Dilettantismus und Meisterschaft: Zum Problem des Dilettantismus bei Goethe: Praxis, Theorie, Zeitkritik* (Munich, 1971), pp. 196–98, 212. Further references by page number.

10. See my *Goethe's Theory of Poetry,* pp. 215–22.

11. WA, 10, lines 1234–62. Further citations are by *NT* plus line numbers.

12. I mean the painting by Gerhard von Kügelgen (1810) in the Goethe-Museum in Düsseldorf.

13. Sigurd Burckhardt, "*Die natürliche Tochter:* Goethe's *Iphigenie in Aulis?*" (orig. 1960), trans. Lillian Reed Atkins, in his *The Drama of Language: Essays on Goethe and Kleist* (Baltimore, 1970), p. 70.

14. It is, further, a literature, in the terminology of the discussion of Herder in my *Beyond Theory,* pp. 257–62, that escapes the schematic grid of language and discourse only by exposing itself as a body to the grinding of that same machine. The present argument attempts, among other things, to redeem the promise of an association of the Herderian body with the female body in *Beyond Theory,* pp. 366–67.

## Chapter 8

1. Kelly Oliver, "Nietzsche's Woman: The Poststructuralist Attempt to Do Away with Women," *Radical Philosophy* 48 (Spring 1988): 29. The sentence in which these words occur is obviously faulty; a line of print appears to be missing. But the meaning is clear. Oliver is discussing David Farrell Krell, *Postponements: Woman, Sensuality and Death in Nietzsche* (Bloomington, Ind., 1986).

2. Shoshana Felman, "Women and Madness: The Critical Phallacy," *Diacritics* 5, no. 4 (1975): 2–10, here p. 10.

3. Monique Wittig, *Les Guérillères* (Paris, 1969), pp. 162–64.

4. Nancy K. Miller, "Changing the Subject: Authorship, Writing and the Reader," in *Feminist Studies: Critical Studies,* ed. Teresa de Lauretis (Bloomington, Ind., 1986), pp. 102–20.

5. Gayatri Chakravorty Spivak, "The Politics of Interpretations," *Critical Inquiry* 9 (1982–83): 259–78. Miller quotes pp. 276–77, where Spivak is responding to Terry Eagleton, *Walter Benjamin: or, Towards a Revolutionary Criticism* (London, 1981). Needless to say, I do not accept Eagleton's notion of the "revolutionary."

6. Nietzsche (see ch. 7, n. 7 for the edition), 4:248. Further references are abbreviated *KSA,* for *Kritische Studienausgabe.*

7. Gayatri Chakravorty Spivak, "Displacement and the Discourse of Woman," in *Displacement: Derrida and After,* ed. Mark Krupnick (Bloomington, Ind., 1983), pp. 169–95. The present quote is on p. 184. In a footnote, incidentally, Spivak says: "Given the tradition of academic radicalism in France, and our experience with the old New Left, 'feminist' should not be taken as a subset of 'revolutionary' " (p. 195). But this remark and its context do not affect the use of the term "revolutionary" in our argument, where thought or action, in any particular case, is understood as "revolutionary" only by being so in (precisely) a strictly revolutionary manner, so that the comparison of different cases (hence the construction of "subsets") automatically brackets the whole idea of revolution. Again, I do not claim that this idea of revolution is conceptually complete. I claim only that it names a relatively common intuitive perception concerning the unaccountability of history.

8. "Displacement," p. 186.

9. Leventhal (see ch. 7, n. 5), p. 12.

10. See my "Nietzsche's Idea of Myth: The Birth of Tragedy from the Spirit of Eighteenth-Century Aesthetics," *PMLA* 94 (1979): 420–33, esp. p. 430, on Nietzsche's *affirmation* of the development of Socratic culture.

11. "A polemic" ("Eine Streitschrift") is the subtitle of *The Genealogy of Morals;* and in the first edition of 1887, the reverse of the title page bears the note: "Dem letztveröffentlichten 'Jenseits von Gut und Böse' zur Ergänzung und Verdeutlichung beigegeben," "appended, for completion and clarification, to the recently published 'Beyond Good and Evil.' " Colli and Montinari, however, include this note neither in the *KSA* nor even in the larger "Kritische Gesamtausgabe," 6. Abt., 2. Bd. (Berlin, 1968). There may be a reason for this omission, but as far as I can see, Colli and Montinari do not explain it.

12. See chapters 5 and 7 above, and the supporting material referred to in ch. 5, nn. 9 and 10, and ch. 7, n. 10.

13. Jacques Derrida, *Spurs: Nietzsche's Styles/Éperons: Les Styles de Nietzsche,* original French plus English of Barbara Harlow (Chicago, 1979), pp. 106/107.

14. Susan Sontag, *Against Interpretation and Other Essays* (New York, 1966). See esp. pp. 49–50, 54, 88, 98, 132–33, 249–55, 260–62, 299, not to mention the whole essay "On Style," pp. 15–36.

15. Sontag, p. 5. She is quoting Nietzsche's posthumous aphorism "against positivism" (*KSA,* 12:315). She might also have used no. 22 of *Beyond Good and Evil* (*KSA,* 5:37), if this passage had not insisted uncomfortably on anti-interpretation as itself an interpretive act.

16. Luce Irigaray, *Amante marine: De Friedrich Nietzsche* (Paris, 1980), p. 9. References in the text by *Am* plus page.

## CHAPTER 9

1. Etymological authorities vary considerably here. The abridged Liddell/Scott of 1966 gives as the root meanings of θεωρός (hence of θεωρέω and θεωρία), θεός (god) and ὥρα (care, concern). The *Hand- und Schulausgabe* of Menge-Güthling from 1913 associates θεωρός with θέα (a seeing or looking at), as do the etymological dictionary of Émile Boisacq (1950) and, curiously, the unabridged Liddell/Scott of 1961. It seems to me, as a non-expert, that the etymologies involving θέα (seeing) are more probable; but it also seems clear, from the specific meaning of θεωρός as one officially commissioned to consult an oracle, that the idea of the divine (θεός) is at some point associated with the word.

2. Rainer Nägele, *Reading After Freud: Essays on Goethe, Hölderlin, Habermas, Nietzsche, Brecht, Celan, and Freud* (New York, 1987), p. 1. Further quotations by page number.

3. Fredric Jameson, *Postmodernism, or, The Cultural Logic of Late Capitalism* (Durham, N.C., 1991), pp. ix–x. Further references by page.

4. See my *Beyond Theory,* p. 57.

5. See my *Modern Drama and German Classicism,* pp. 71–72.

6. On Mephistopheles, see my *Goethe's Theory of Poetry,* pp. 67–69, 217; on "Herder's Leap into the Body," see my *Beyond Theory,* pp. 257–62.

7. Bettine von Arnim, *Werke und Briefe in vier Bänden,* ed. Walter Schmitz and Sibylle Steinsdorff (Frankfurt am Main, 1986ff.), 2:480. The epigraph to this chapter is found on 2:536.

8. For detailed arguments on which this judgment is based, see my *Modern Drama and German Classicism,* pp. 177–85, 188–202.

9. Peter J. Burgard, *Idioms of Uncertainty: Goethe and the Essay* (University Park, Pa., 1992). References by page number below.

10. *SA,* 12:161.

11. Avital Ronell, *Dictations: On Haunted Writing* (Lincoln, Neb., 1993; orig. 1986); Sabine Prokhoris, *The Witch's Kitchen: Freud, Faust, and the Transference,* trans. G. M. Goshgarian (Ithaca, 1995; orig. French 1988). References to both books below by page.

12. Leventhal (see ch. 7, n. 5), p. 317. Further references by page.

13. *The Standard Edition of the Complete Psychological Works of Sigmund Freud,* ed. James Strachey, 24 vols. (London, 1953–74), 5:525. Further references by SE plus volume and page.

14. Leventhal, p. 318, referring to Michel Foucault, "Nietzsche, Freud, Marx," in *Transforming the Hermeneutic Context,* ed. Gayle Ormiston and Alan Schrift (Albany, 1990), p. 64.

15. It is in connection with the dream of the three Fates (SE, 4:204), in which the making of dumplings from mudlike dough is associated with the making of babies (SE, 4:205), that Freud recalls (SE, 4:207) Herder's jocular association of the

name "Goethe" with "Kot," "mud" (WA, 27:311). Prokhoris (pp. 100–106) develops the associations to include the relation of Freud and Jung.

16. In her footnote at this point, Prokhoris refers to Marco Focchi, *La langue indiscrète: Essai sur le transfert comme traduction* (Paris, 1984), and Shoshana Felman, *The Literary Speech Act: Don Juan with J. L. Austin, or Seduction in Two Languages,* trans. Catherine Porter (Ithaca, 1983).

17. With regard to "the word and nothing but the word," there is a problem here that is slurred over. For "the word" is inherently a *signifier;* it no sooner is than it signifies, in a manner that takes no account of the difference between speaking and writing. This means, apparently, that the word *cannot* stand in the relation of "nothing but," since our apprehension of it always already includes the apprehension of a signified. For a discussion of this problem, and of the manner in which the structure of *theater* deals with it, see my *Theater As Problem,* pp. 205–16. In the case of psychoanalysis, it could be argued that the word exhibits the condition of "nothing but" in relation to the unconscious, since the latter is strictly immune to signification, in fact definable as that which is disjoined from any signified whatever. But within a text, this condition is impossible; and the resulting collision, in a psychoanalytic text, of two incompatible identities of "the word" perhaps justifies precisely our speaking of a text that does not exist.

18. *Amante marine* (see ch. 8, n. 16), p. 201. Here, as above, abbreviated *Am.*

19. Jane Gallop, *The Daughter's Seduction: Feminism and Psychoanalysis* (Ithaca, 1982), pp. 31–32. Further references by page.

20. Jacques Lacan, *Écrits: A Selection,* trans. Alan Sheridan (New York, 1977), p. 285. Further references by page.

21. Julia Kristeva, "Un nouveau type d'intellectuel: le dissident," *Tel Quel* 74 (Winter 1977): 3–8.

22. See my *Goethe's Theory of Poetry,* pp. 299–301, on Goethe's advice to young poets.

23. Letters to Fließ of 3 and 4 October 1897 in *The Complete Letters of Sigmund Freud to Wilhelm Fliess: 1887–1904,* ed. Jeffrey Moussaieff Masson (Cambridge, Mass., 1985), pp. 268–69.

## CHAPTER 10

1. In Hecker's standard numbering of the "Maximen und Reflexionen," abbreviated M&R below, these are nos. 1112 and 1113.

2. David E. Wellbery, *Lessing's "Laocoon": Semiotics and Aesthetics in the Age of Reason* (Cambridge, 1984); Heinz Schlaffer, *Faust Zweiter Teil: Die Allegorie des 19. Jahrhunderts* (Stuttgart, 1981), pp. 154–65.

3. On *Faust,* see my *Goethe's Theory of Poetry,* p. 156; on the poem, my *Beyond Theory,* p. 215.

4. Julia Kristeva, "From One Identity to an Other," in her *Desire in Language: A Semiotic Approach to Literature and Art,* ed. Leon S. Roudiez (New York, 1980), p. 136. Further references by page.

5. Quoted from Goethe, *Gedenkausgabe der Werke, Briefe und Gespräche,* ed. Ernst Beutler, 24 vols. (Zürich, 1948–53), 22:565. Apparently in the same conversation,

Goethe also speaks of the peasant in Schiller's *Wallensteins Lager* as "eine symbolische Figur" (22:564), which reinforces the argument below, since the peasant stands at the border or limit of the political-tragic text, as the sign of a Beyond that the text in a sense rests on, but does not articulate.

6. The association, in general, of chemistry with a philosophical idea of marriage had long been there for Goethe in his alchemical studies, especially Joh. Valentin Andreae, *Chymische Hochzeit: Christiani Rosencreutz, Anno 1459* (1616), which he mentions reading (and speaks of the possibility of using it as material for his own work) in a letter to Charlotte von Stein of 28 June 1786.

7. Walter Benjamin, "Goethes Wahlverwandtschaften," in his *Illuminationen: Ausgewählte Schriften* (Frankfurt am Main, 1977), pp. 68–69, 77. Further references by page.

8. References to *Die Wahlverwandtschaften* are located in WA, vol. 20, and marked by *Wvw* plus page.

9. See ch. 9, n. 19

10. See ch. 7, n. 11.

11. See ch. 9, n. 20.

12. J. Hillis Miller, "A 'Buchstäbliches' Reading of *The Elective Affinities*," *Glyph* 6 (1979): 1–23, quote on p. 12. Further references by page.

13. Bettine von Arnim (see ch. 9, n. 7), 2:311, also 2:297.

## Conclusion

1. On the failure of hermeneutic theory to avoid the consequences of a co-optive tendency in nineteenth-century nation building, see not only chapter 7 above, but also my essay, "Performance and the Exposure of Hermeneutics," *Theatre Journal* 44 (1992): 431–47, esp. pp. 444–46 on "Ideology."

2. See my *Goethe's Theory of Poetry*, chapter 8, esp. pp. 200–212.

# Index

BOOKS IN THE KRITIK:
GERMAN LITERARY THEORY AND CULTURAL STUDIES SERIES

*Walter Benjamin: An Intellectual Biography,* by Bernd Witte, trans. by James Rolleston, 1991

*The Violent Eye: Ernst Jünger's Visions and Revisions on the European Right,* by Marcus Paul Bullock, 1991

*Fatherland: Novalis, Freud, and the Discipline of Romance,* by Kenneth S. Calhoon, 1992

*Metaphors of Knowledge: Language and Thought in Mauthner's Critique,* by Elizabeth Bredeck, 1992

*Laocoon's Body and the Aesthetics of Pain: Winckelmann, Lessing, Herder, Moritz, Goethe,* by Simon Richter, 1992

*The Critical Turn: Studies in Kant, Herder, Wittgenstein, and Contemporary Theory,* by Michael Morton, 1993

*Reading After Foucault: Institutions, Disciplines, and Technologies of Self in Germany, 1750–1830,* edited by Robert S. Leventhal, 1994

*Bettina Brentano-von Arnim: Gender and Politics,* edited by Elke P. Frederiksen and Katherine R. Goodman, 1995

*Absent Mothers and Orphaned Fathers: Narcissism and Abjection in Lessing's Aesthetic and Dramatic Production,* by Susan E. Gustafson, 1995

*Identity or History? Marcus Herz and the End of the Enlightenment,* by Martin L. Davies, 1995

*Languages of Visuality: Crossings between Science, Art, Politics, and Literature,* edited by Beate Allert, 1996

*Resisting Bodies: The Negotiation of Female Agency in Twentieth- Century Women's Fiction,* by Helga Druxes, 1996

*Locating the Romantic Subject: Novalis with Winnicott,* by Gail M. Newman, 1997

*Embodying Ambiguity: Androgyny and Aesthetics from Winckelmann to Keller,* by Catriona MacLeod, 1997

*The Freudian Calling: Early Viennese Psychoanalysis and the Pursuit of Cultural Science,* by Louis Rose, 1998

*By the Rivers of Babylon: Heinrich Heine's Late Songs and Reflections,* by Roger F. Cook, 1998

*Reconstituting the Body Politic: Enlightenment, Public Culture, and the Invention of Aesthetic Autonomy,* by Jonathan M. Hess, 1999

*The School of Days: Heinrich von Kleist and the Traumas of Education,* by Nancy Nobile, 1999

*Walter Benjamin and the Corpus of Autobiography,* by Gerhard Richter, 2000

*Heads or Tails: The Poetics of Money,* by Jochen Hörisch, trans. by Amy Horning Marschall, 2000

*Dialectics of the Will: Freedom, Power, and Understanding in Modern French and German Thought,* by John H. Smith, 2000

*The Bonds of Labor: German Journeys to the Working World, 1890- 1990,* by Carol Poore, 2000

*Schiller's Wound: The Theater of Trauma from Crisis to Commodity,* by Stephanie Hammer, 2001

*Goethe as Woman: The Undoing of Literature,* by Benjamin Bennett, 2001